ONE NATION MANY PEOPLE

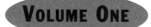
VOLUME ONE

THE UNITED STATES TO 1900

Consultants

Juan García
University of Arizona

Sharon Harley
University of Maryland

John Howard
State University of New York, Purchase College

GLOBE FEARON
Pearson Learning Group

Juan García is Associate Professor of History and the Director of the University Teaching Center at the University of Arizona. He received his Ph.D. from the University of Notre Dame. The focus of his research is Mexican and Mexican American history, U.S. history, and ethnic studies.

Sharon Harley is Associate Professor of Afro-American Studies and History at the University of Maryland. She received her Ph.D. from Howard University. She has conducted extensive research in African American women's history, focusing on the history of women workers.

John Howard is a Distinguished Service Professor at the State University of New York, Purchase College. He received his Ph.D. at Stanford University and a J.D. at Pace Law School. He is a professor in the social science department with a particular focus on law-related topics.

Executive Editor: Stephen Lewin
Senior Editor: Francie Holder
Editors: Helene Avraham, Kirsten Richert
Editorial Assistant: Mindy DePalma
Production Manager: Penny Gibson
Manufacturing Supervisor: Della Smith
Production Editor: Alan Dalgleish

Art Director: Nancy Sharkey
Senior Product Manager: Elmer Ildefonso
Book Design: Carole Anson
Electronic Page Production: Margarita Giammanco
Photo Research: Jenifer Hixson
Maps: Mapping Specialists Limited
Cover Design: Richard Puder Design

Photo Credits:
6: The Bettmann Archive; **7:** © Don West, The Picture Cube; **10:** The Bettmann Archive; **15:** The Granger Collection; **17:** Trans World Airline Photo; **18:** Library of Congress; **21:** The Granger Collection; **24:** The Granger Collection; **26:** New York Public Library; **28:** Brown Brothers; **29:** The Pierpont Morgan Library; **32:** The Bettmann Archive; **36:** The Granger Collection; **37:** The Schomberg Center for Research in Black Culture; **38:** The Bettmann Archive; **41:** The Bettmann Archive; **42:** Giraudon, Art Resource; **47:** U.T. Institute of Texan Cultures; **50:** Colonial Williamsburg; **52:** Library of Congress; **54:** The Bettmann Archive; **58:** The Bettmann Archive; **60:** New-York Historical Society; **66:** The Bettmann Archive; **68:** The Bettmann Archive; **70:** The Schomberg Center; **71:** The Granger Collection; **75:** George Catlin, Courtesy of the National Gallery of Art, Wahington DC, The Paul Melon Collection; **76:** The Bettmann Archive; **80:** Culver Pictures Inc.; **83:** The Bettmann Archive; **84:** The Granger Collection; **87:** The Granger Collection; **88:** New York Public Library; **89:** The Bettmann Archive; **92:** The Bettmann Archive; **94:** The Granger Collection; **96:** The Bettmann Archive; **100:** Library of Congress; **103:** Library of Congress; **105:** Museum of the City of New York; **108:** Zephyr Pictures; **110:** Yale University Art Gallery; **112:** Bettmann Archive; **114:** Bettmann Archive; **117:** The Granger Collection; **121:** Bettmann Archive (lent for cover); **124:** The Bettmann Archive; **126:** Library of Congress; **129:** Bettmann Archive; **131:** The Granger Collection; **134:** © Beryl Goldberg; **136:** Courtesy of the Congressional Black Caucus; **138:** AP/Wide World Photos; **140:** © Jane Feldman; **143:** The J. Clarence Davies Collection Museum of the City of New York; **146:** The Bettmann Archive; **147:** Maryland Historical Society; **103:** Library of Congress; **151:** Montana Historical Society; **154:** The Granger Collection; **156:** Bettmann Archive; **159:** The Schomberg Collection, New York Public Library; **160:** Culver Pictures; **163:** The National Archives; **165:** New York Public Library; **168:** The Granger Collection; **176:** Courtesy of the Witte Museum and the San Antonio Museum Association, San Antonio, Texas; **181:** The Bancroft Library, University of California; **185:** The Granger Collection; **186:** The Granger Collection; **190:** The Bettmann Archive; **191:** The Granger Collection; **194:** The Granger Collection; **196:** The Bettmann Archive; **198:** Library of Congress; **199:** The Granger Collection; **202:** Sophia Smith Collection; **204:** Culver Pictures Inc.; **207:** The Granger Collection; **208:** The Granger Collection; **211:** The Granger Collection; **216:** The Bettmann Archive; **219:** The Bettmann Archive; **220:** The Bettmann Archive; **224:** Library of Congress; **228:** The Granger Collection; **230:** Library of Congress; **233:** The Bettmann Archive; **236:** The Bettmann Archive; **238:** The Bettmann Archive; **240:** The Bettmann Archive; **241:** New-York Historical Society; **242:** The Rutherford B. Hayes Presidential Center; **245:** The George Eastman House; **246:** In the Collection of the Corcoran Gallery of Art, Museum Purchase; **250 (l):** The Bettmann Archive; **250 (r):** UPI/ Bettmann Archive; **251:** The Granger Collection; **254:** Kansas State Historical Society; **257:** Courtesy the Museum of New Mexico; **259:** The Granger Collection; **262:** Bettmann Archive; **264:** Culver Pictures; **266:** Library of Congress; **270:** Museum of the City of New York*; **274:** Bettmann Archive; **275:** Florida State Archives; **278:** Library of Congress; **282:** Culver Pictures; **283:** The George Eastman House; **286:** The Granger Collection; **288:** The Granger Collection; **290:** Courtesy of Cornell University; **291:** The Granger Collection; **294:** UPI/Bettmann; **296:** The Granger Collection; **302:** Culver Pictures, Inc.; **305:** The Granger Collection; **306:** The Granger Collection.

ISBN 0-8359-1534-4
Printed in the United States of America
8 9 10 11   09 08 07 06

Globe
Fearon

Pearson Learning Group

1-800-321-3106
www.pearsonlearning.com

CONTENTS

Maps

Charts, Tables, and Graphs

Unit 1
The Clash of Cultures in the Americas (Prehistory-1519)

Chapters

THE UNITED STATES IS A DIVERSE NATION.

What makes the United States so diverse?

Americans have their roots in every country of the world. The many languages and traditions they have brought with them are a source of great strength.

Looking at Key Terms

- democracy • geography • Interior plains • Coastal plains
- Pacific region • Rocky Mountain region
- Appalachian Mountain region • Intermountain region

Looking at Key Words

- **diverse:** different or varied
- **culture:** beliefs and ways of life of a people
- **immigration:** when someone moves from his or her homeland to live permanently in another country
- **adapt:** to change to fit new surroundings

- **traditions:** customs, practices, and ways of doing things that are handed down from one generation to another
- **climate:** the average weather of a place over a period of years
- **multicultural:** many cultures

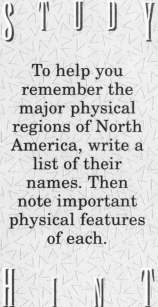

STUDY

To help you remember the major physical regions of North America, write a list of their names. Then note important physical features of each.

HINT

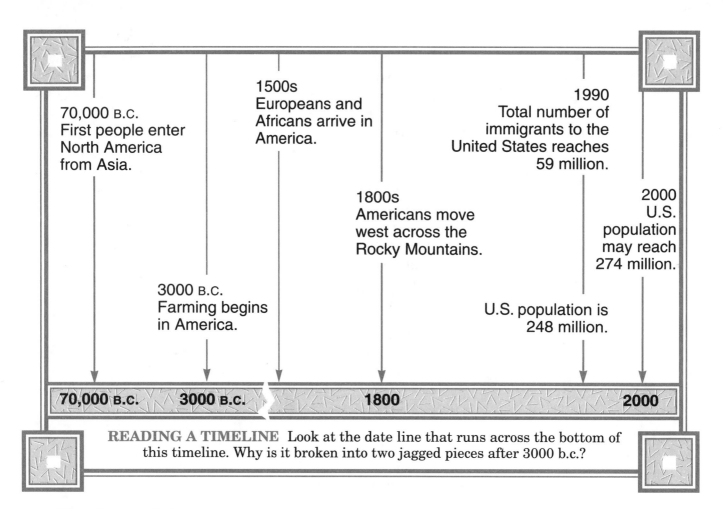

70,000 B.C.
First people enter North America from Asia.

1500s
Europeans and Africans arrive in America.

3000 B.C.
Farming begins in America.

1800s
Americans move west across the Rocky Mountains.

1990
Total number of immigrants to the United States reaches 59 million.

2000
U.S. population may reach 274 million.

U.S. population is 248 million.

| 70,000 B.C. | 3000 B.C. | 1800 | 2000 |

READING A TIMELINE Look at the date line that runs across the bottom of this timeline. Why is it broken into two jagged pieces after 3000 b.c.?

The United States is a **diverse** nation. A diverse nation is one that has a great deal of variety. Our nation is diverse in many ways. One way is in its land. The United States has every kind of climate and landform within its borders. Another way the United States is diverse is in its people.

1 The People of the United States Are Diverse.

Why is the United States called "a multicultural nation"?

Our nation, the United States, is one of the most diverse nations on earth. The people of our nation come from all over the world. They have brought different customs and traditions with them. The diversity of the American people is an important part of our history.

A multicultural nation The United States is home to many different people with different **cultures.** Culture consists of the beliefs and ways of living that a group develops. Culture also includes all the tools and objects that people make and use. It includes people's everyday activities. Culture also includes art, music, and literature. So many different cultures exist in the United States that we are known as a **multicultural** nation, or a nation of many cultures.

People of many cultures—Native American, European, African, Latin American, Asian, and Middle Eastern—have lived and worked here for hundreds of years. This great diversity has sometimes caused conflicts. However, it also has made this nation great.

A growing population The population of the United States has grown over the years. A nation's population can grow in two ways. One is through natural increase. This happens when

more people are born than die during a period. Another way is through **immigration.** Immigration is the move of someone from his or her homeland to live permanently in a new country. From 1820 to 1990 about 59 million people immigrated to the United States. These people came from all over the world. The mixing and blending of these people is a major theme in our history.

Today, the population of the United States numbers more than 248 million people. This makes it the third largest country in the world. Only China, India, and Russia have more people. By the year 2000, scientists predict that the population of the United States will be more than 274 million.

Living in the United States
Scientists believe that the first Americans came here many thousands of years ago. They walked across the land bridge that once linked Alaska with Asia. In recent times new Americans have come by ship or plane. No matter how they came, they learned to **adapt** to the life they found in America. Adapt means to change to fit new surroundings.

New immigrants sometimes gave up old beliefs and ways of doing things. At the same time, they learned new ways. Find out when your family or friends came to the United States. Did they have to learn a new language? Did they find new ways of making a living? How was life in the United States different from life in their homeland?

However, the groups that make up our nation did not give up all their **traditions.**

Reading a Map. The 48 mainland states have a great variety of climates. In which of the climate zones shown on the map below is the area in which you live? Which zone is the furthest south? Which zone is the furthest east?

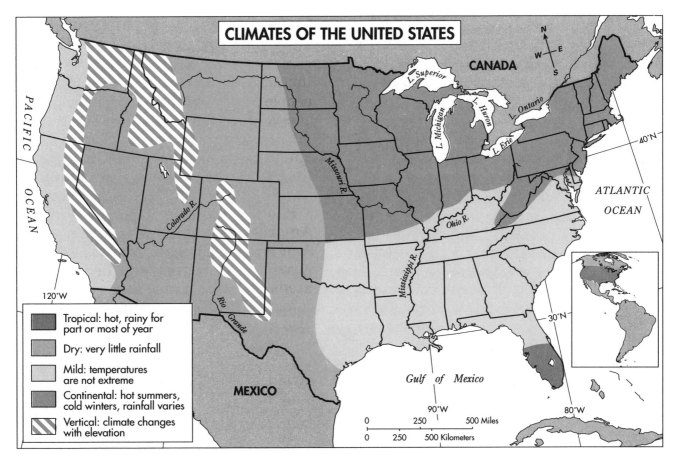

CLIMATES OF THE UNITED STATES

Tropical: hot, rainy for part or most of year

Dry: very little rainfall

Mild: temperatures are not extreme

Continental: hot summers, cold winters, rainfall varies

Vertical: climate changes with elevation

An old print from the early 1800s shows how much the first settlers from the east depended on what they could draw from their environment. Name some of the ways these settlers depended on the land around them.

Traditions are the customs, practices, and ways of doing things that are handed down from one generation to another. Today, the United States has a mix of religions, music, art, literature, foods, and holidays from all over the world.

Shared beliefs Americans differ in some ways from one another. However, we do share some beliefs and ideas. We believe in **democracy**. Democracy is a form of government in which citizens rule either directly or through elected representatives. We believe that all citizens have the right to live happy, useful, and healthy lives. We believe that citizens and the government should respect the rights of all the people. We share a common history and a common future.

1. Why is the United States called "a multicultural" country?
2. What is immigration?

2 Geography and History are Connected.

How does geography help us to understand the past?

History is the story of what happens to someone or something. Knowing about the environment where history happened is important. It makes history easier to understand. The natural environment includes all the parts of nature that affect a group. The natural environment has greatly influenced the history of the United States.

Geography and history Studying **geography** is one way to learn about the natural environment. Geography is the study of the earth and how people live on it. Geographers study the earth's physical features. Physical features include mountains, deserts, and oceans. Geographers also study natural resources, climate, land uses, and industries. Geography can show how people use the land.

Geography helps historians understand the present and the past. Geography can explain why people settled in a certain area. It can show how people used the land to make a living. Geography can sometimes explain why traditions and cultures developed the way they did.

The geography of early settlements was important. It often determined whether a settlement would succeed. When you begin to read about the history of the United States, you will notice that many early settlements were located near water. This is because people needed water to travel, to fish, and to drink. As you will read below, climate and natural resources also played a role in the success of early settlements.

Climate and land use   Climate and history are closely linked. **Climate** is the average weather of a place over a period of years. The climates of the United States are shown on the map on page 9. What is the climate in your part of the country?

Climate affects how people use the land. If a region has enough rain, the right climate, and a good growing season, people can farm there. Climate may also influence the types of animals that live in an area. Animals provide food for people. The skins of some animals can be used for clothing and shelter.

Sometimes, people can change the environment. For example, take an area where the soil is rich, the growing season is long, but water is scarce. Farmers there can bring in water to irrigate their land. Farmers in southern California have been able to produce huge crops with irrigation.

Natural resources   Natural resources are all the things that are found on the land, and in the water. These things include fish, animals, soil, forests, and minerals. Air and water are also natural resources. Natural resources influence people and history.

Rivers have long influenced life in the United States. The most important river system in the United States is made up of the Mississippi and Missouri rivers. (See the map on page 12.) These rivers flow through the Interior Plains south into the Gulf of Mexico. The Mississippi River supplies water to the people of the Interior Plains. It is also a means of travel for both goods and people.

The Great Lakes form part of the border between the United States and Canada. These five very large lakes are an important waterway for trade. Canals link the lakes. The St. Lawrence River then carries large ships out to the Atlantic Ocean. Today, crops, minerals, and goods from the center of the United States can be shipped directly to any port in the world.

Other natural resources that influence where people live and work include forests and minerals. Forests provide wood and wood products. They supply homes for animals. People use forests for recreation. Minerals such as iron ore and copper are important to industry. Almost everything we wear or use is made by iron or steel machines.

Other natural resources that come from the ground are crude oil, natural gas, and coal. These become the fuels that are our main sources of energy. The United States is fortunate to have large amounts of natural resources. These natural resources have helped make this nation very wealthy.

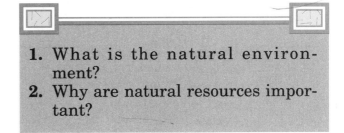

1. What is the natural environment?
2. Why are natural resources important?

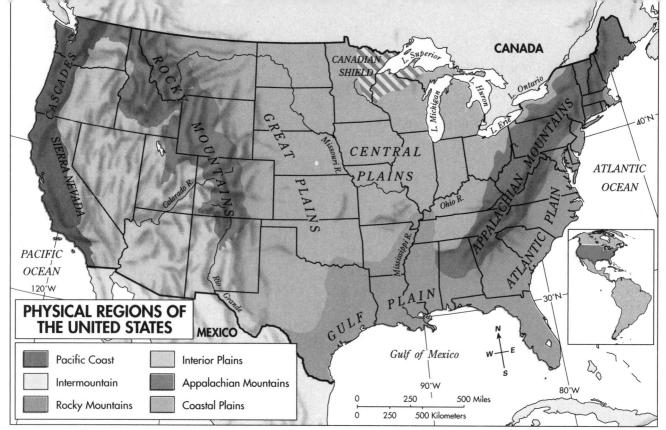

PHYSICAL REGIONS OF THE UNITED STATES

Legend:
- Pacific Coast
- Intermountain
- Rocky Mountains
- Interior Plains
- Appalachian Mountains
- Coastal Plains

Reading a Map. What region lies east of the Appalachian Mountains? Compare the map above with the map of climate zones on page 9. What region has a vertical climate? What climate zones are included in the Central Plains?

3 The United States Is Made Up of Six Regions.

How have the regions of the United States affected our history?

Geographers often use the natural environment to describe regions. The regions have some common physical features. Physical features include landforms such as mountains, hills, plains, and plateaus. Geographers divide the United States into six regions. (See the map on this page.)

Pacific region   This region is located on the western side of the United States. It borders the Pacific Ocean. The Pacific region is very rugged. Tall mountain ranges stretch across this region from Alaska to Mexico. Some of the mountain ranges come right down to the ocean.

Travel across the lands of this region is difficult. In the past, people used the Pacific Ocean to travel to other parts of the United States and the world. The largest cities in the Pacific region are located near the Pacific coast. These cities include Seattle, Portland, San Francisco, Los Angeles, and San Diego.

Intermountain region   This region lies east of the Pacific Coast. To the west are the mountains of the Pacific region. To the east are the Rocky Mountains. The Intermountain region is a harsh place. Mountains cut the region off on all sides. The wet winds from the oceans do not reach it. Therefore, the climate is very dry. Because it lacks water, the Intermountain region was among the last of the regions to be settled. However, that has changed in recent years. The Intermountain region has one of the fastest growing populations in the United States.

Rocky Mountain region   This area reaches south from Alaska through Canada into Mexico. Mountain peaks rise higher than 12,000 feet (3,658 meters). These mountains made it diffi-

cult for settlers to move west in the 1800s. The region began to grow in population when settlers found gold and other minerals in the mountains.

Interior Plains This region is a large lowland in the middle of the country. The Interior Plains stretch from Canada to the Gulf of Mexico. The Plains have some of the best grazing land and farmland in the United States. In the 1800s, cowhands handled great herds of cattle there. On the Plains, farmers grow acres of wheat.

Appalachian Mountain region This area runs along the eastern part of North America. These mountains are lower than the Rockies. In places, they are gentle and green. There are large lakes, big forests, and high waterfalls. Early settlers found this region a good place to live. Many Native Americans also lived in this region. As you will read, European settlers and Native Americans fought fierce battles over this land.

Coastal Plains This region is where Europeans first built settlements in what is now the United States. This easternmost area has two parts. The Atlantic Plain lies between the Atlantic Ocean and the Appalachian Mountains. It stretches from Miami, Florida, to Moosehead, Maine. The second part is the Gulf Plain. It lies along the Gulf of Mexico. Its most valuable resource is oil.

Plains have always been good places to live. More than 60 million Americans live on the Atlantic Coastal Plain. The Atlantic Coastal Plain has some of the nation's largest cities. Boston, New York, Charleston, and Atlanta are just a few.

A nation of regions The geography of each region in the United States has influenced its history. Geography determined how people used the land and how many people lived there. Today, geography continues to influence where and how people live. As you read this book, look for ways in which geography played a role in the history of our nation.

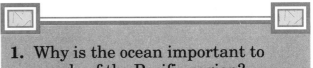

1. Why is the ocean important to people of the Pacific region?
2. Why is farming more important in the Interior Plains region than in the Atlantic Coastal plain?

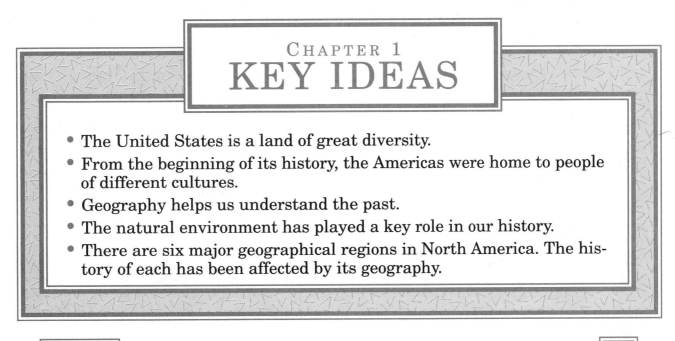

CHAPTER 1
KEY IDEAS

- The United States is a land of great diversity.
- From the beginning of its history, the Americas were home to people of different cultures.
- Geography helps us understand the past.
- The natural environment has played a key role in our history.
- There are six major geographical regions in North America. The history of each has been affected by its geography.

I. Reviewing Vocabulary

Match each word on the left with the correct definition on the right.

1. diversity
2. geography
3. culture
4. democracy
5. traditions

a. beliefs and ways of life of a people
b. customs, practices, and ways of doing things that are handed down from one generation to another
c. great variety or differences
d. the study of the earth and how people live on the earth
e. a form of government in which the citizens rule

II. Understanding the Chapter

1. How has immigration made the United States a diverse nation?
2. How do climate and natural resources affect history?
3. Compare two regions of the United States. How are they similar? How are they different?
4. Why was the Intermountain region the last to be settled? Why do you think it is growing today?
5. Give two reasons why rivers are important.

III. Building Skills: Reading a Map

Study the map on page 12. Then answer the following questions:
1. What two physical regions cover the eastern coast of the United States?
2. Which covers a greater area, the Interior Plains or the Coastal Plains?

IV. Writing About History

1. **What Would You Have Done?** Imagine that you were a settler heading westward across the United States in the 1800s. What geographical obstacles would you face, and how would you deal with each?
2. Imagine that you could live in two different climates in the United States during the year. Which two would you pick and why? Draw a picture of outdoor activities that you could enjoy in each climate.

V. Working Together

1. In small groups, choose one of the physical regions of North America that you have learned about. Your group will create a bulletin-board display that shows information about this region and how people live there. You may include drawings, written information, maps, charts, and clipped articles and pictures from magazines and newspapers in your display.
2. **Past to Present** People have always been affected by geography. With a group, discuss whether you think the environment affects people today as much as it did in the past. Then list three ideas that support your opinion.

THE FIRST AMERICANS DEVELOP GREAT CULTURES. (12,000 B.C.–A.D. 1519)

Who were the first Americans, and how did they live?

This modern-day painting shows what the market at Tenochtitlán looked like. It was painted by the famous Mexican painter, Diego Rivera.

Looking at Key Terms

- Ice Age • Pueblo • *kiva* • League of Five Nations

Looking at Key Words

- **glaciers:** giant sheets of ice
- **migration:** movement of people from one place to another
- **nomads:** people who move from place to place while searching for food
- **adobe:** bricks made of clay dried in the sun

- **drought:** a long period of dry weather
- **environment:** the surroundings of a people
- **pyramid:** a building with a square base and sloping sides shaped like triangles
- **tribute:** payments that a powerful nation forces people it conquers to make

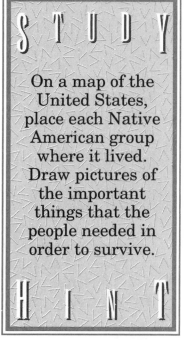

STUDY

On a map of the United States, place each Native American group where it lived. Draw pictures of the important things that the people needed in order to survive.

HINT

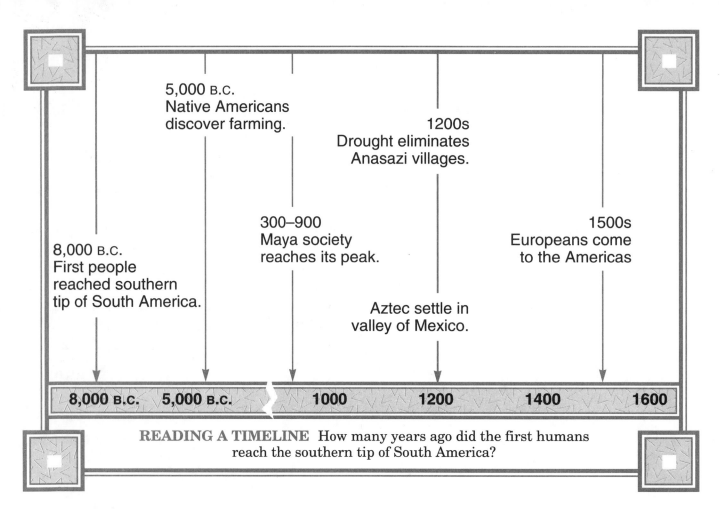

5,000 B.C.
Native Americans discover farming.

1200s
Drought eliminates Anasazi villages.

300–900
Maya society reaches its peak.

8,000 B.C.
First people reached southern tip of South America.

1500s
Europeans come to the Americas

Aztec settle in valley of Mexico.

| 8,000 B.C. | 5,000 B.C. | 1000 | 1200 | 1400 | 1600 |

READING A TIMELINE How many years ago did the first humans reach the southern tip of South America?

The hunters carefully crept across the frozen ground. A cold wind blew in icy blasts from the north. The snow pelted through their fur wraps. Still they traveled east, following the tracks of deer and giant mammoths.

The people were hungry. Hunting had been bad for many days. They pushed on, hoping to find a herd of mammoths. They needed to bring down just one of the giant animals to feed the band for many days.

1 The First Americans Arrive.

How did the first Americans come to North America?

This scene took place perhaps 30,000 years ago. The time was the **Ice Age**. It was a time when much of North America was covered by giant sheets of ice called **glaciers** (glay-shuhrz). The

hunters were following the herds across a land bridge. This was a narrow strip of land connecting the continents of North America and Asia.

The hunters did not know that they were part of a great movement of people. They knew only that they had to make a kill or starve to death. Still, these people and others like them were the beginning of a huge turning point in history.

These hunters were part of the first **migration** of people to the Americas. To migrate means to move from one place to another. Before the migration, there were no humans in the Americas. The migration took thousand of years. When it ended, the Americas were peopled from the northern end to the southern tip.

These first Americans traveled in small groups. For thousands of years, groups of hunters crossed the land bridge from Asia. Their children and grandchildren pushed farther out. They tracked animals deep into North America. Some groups wandered onto the Great Plains. Others moved east and scattered through dense woodlands. Some moved along the coast of the Atlantic Ocean. Others traveled west to the Pacific coast. Wherever they went, they were searching for new places to hunt and gather plants.

Meanwhile, over many centuries, the glaciers melted. The water level of the oceans went up. The land bridge was flooded.

Over many thousands of years, hunting bands migrated across all of North America. Later, other groups pushed into Central America. Still later, others moved into South America. About 10,000 years ago, the first people reached the southern tip of South America. These small bands of people were the first Americans. We call these people Native Americans.

Living as nomads The first Native Americans were **nomads,** or people who do not live in one place. Nomads move their homes as they search for food. Early Native Americans did not farm. They hunted, fished, and gathered wild plants. They used simple tools made of stone and wood to hunt. Other tools helped them to cut meat or to skin animals.

As the centuries passed, the groups started to change. They spoke different languages. They ate different foods. They made medicines from different wild plants. They developed different beliefs. Slowly, they began to form different cultures.

About 7,000 years ago, a group of Native Americans made a key discovery. They learned that seeds of wild plants placed in the ground will grow into new plants. This was the discovery of farming. It changed the way many Native Americans lived.

The Anasazi Native Americans lived in these Arizona cliff dwellings for about 300 years. Then they had to abandon it because of drought. Today, the only way into the dwellings is by a series of very tall ladders.

Native Americans of the north invented the game of lacrosse. Whole villages played other villages. Games could take a week to finish. Here a village of Iroquois test their skills against a neighboring Iroquois village.

With food from crops, many groups could stop being nomads. They could settle down in villages. Over many centuries, Native American farming villages grew up all over North and South America.

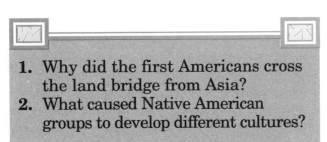

1. Why did the first Americans cross the land bridge from Asia?
2. What caused Native American groups to develop different cultures?

2 The First Americans Build Cultures.

How were the cultures of Native American groups different from each other?

On the Great Plains of North America, three scouts from the Lakota (Sioux) rode into their camp. They carried important news. They had climbed a hill and looked out to the south over the vast plains. In the distance was a small herd of buffalo. Beyond that herd was a larger herd. Far out at the hori- zon was a huge herd. "There was nothing but buffalo," said one scout.

A Lakota leader picked out the best hunters. "Today you shall feed the help- less," said the leader. "Whatever you kill shall be theirs." The young hunters cho- sen for the hunt swelled with pride. It was a great honor to be chosen to help other Lakota.

The Plains people The buffalo was the key to life for most Native Americans who lived on the Great Plains. The buffalo supplied the Plains people with most of their needs. It gave them food. It gave them skins for shel- ter and clothing. It gave them bones for tools and weapons. From spring to autumn, Plains groups were nomads. They followed the herds of buffalo and other animals. In winter, the Plains peo- ple moved to sheltered river valleys.

People of the Southwest In the hot, dry Southwest, there were different cultures. Many of the people lived in vil- lages. They farmed beans, corn, and squash. Often they had to dig canals to bring river water to their fields.

Some of the groups were great builders. The Anasazi, for example, built villages into the sides of steep cliffs. They lived in buildings made of mud brick, called **adobe** (ah-DOH-bee), that looked something like a modern-day apartment house. Some buildings had 800 rooms.

High above the river valleys, these people were safe from attack. They cut holes in the rock and used them to climb to the tops of the cliffs. There, they farmed and gathered water.

Life was hard in the villages on cliffs. Sometimes, there was a **drought** (drowt), or a period of dry weather. Often, the rain did not fall. Then the crops died. During a drought, many people would also die.

A terrible drought hit in the late 1200s. The Anasazi were forced to leave their villages. No one knows where they went or what happened to them.

Later Native Americans called the **Pueblo** (PWEB-loh) followed the ways of the Anasazi. *Pueblo* is a Spanish word for "town." It refers to the villages in which the Pueblo people lived.

Like the Anasazi, the Pueblo molded their way of life to the land around them. Pueblo buildings were made of adobe. The Pueblo grew corn, beans, and squash. These grow well in the heat and sandy soil. They made pottery from the clay that they found in the earth. Then they painted their pots and cups with dyes from plants and minerals.

The **environment**, or surroundings, shaped the beliefs of the Pueblo. In fact, the environment was an important part of their religion. They had key ceremonies to ask for successful crops. Pueblo villages had a special underground room called a *kiva*. There, Pueblo men said prayers to the spirits of rain, wind, and lightning.

People of the eastern woodlands
The woodlands of the East were home to many Native Americans. These people depended on the forests, rivers and lakes, and fertile fields. The forests gave them food and shelter. The animals of the forest provided meat and skins for clothing. Native Americans cut logs to make houses and canoes. They carved branches to make weapons and tools. The rivers and lakes were filled with fish. The fields had good soil for farming.

One of the most powerful of the woodlands groups were the Iroquois (IR-uh-kwoi). The Iroquois were powerful because they were united. In the 1600s, five groups had joined together to make up the **League of Five Nations**. Later, another group joined them. In the 1700s, the league of the Iroquois nations was used by the American colonists as a model for their new government.

All six groups within the Iroquois nation pledged to follow the rules of the league. For example, the league could not go to war unless each of the groups agreed. Thus, when the league did go to war, it was much more united than its enemies. A series of wars started in the 1600s. When it was over, the Iroquois were the most powerful group in what is now the northeastern part of the United States.

Women had a special role in Iroquois life. Women owned all property. They were in charge of planting and harvesting crops. Only men could be village leaders, but only women could elect them.

People of the Northwest The lives of the Native American people of the Pacific Northwest were closely tied to the environment. The people of the Pacific coast lived in a land where great forests grew and rivers rushed down to the sea. Giant trees grew in the forests. The rivers were alive with salmon and other fish. "You can walk across the rivers on the backs of the salmon," was a Native American saying. Whales and seals filled the nearby ocean.

EARLY NATIVE AMERICAN CIVILIZATIONS

Reading a Map. What were the three major early Native American civilizations? What were the important cities of each of the civilizations? Name some important groups located in today's United States.

The Native Americans used the local resources that they found to make life easier for themselves. They cut down the trees and floated them down rivers to their villages. They carved huge canoes. Some were as long as 60 feet! They took these canoes way out into the ocean to hunt whales and seals. Other parts of the tree were used to build houses. From the bark, the people made rope and baskets.

The people of the Northwest took what they needed to live from the land. The men fished with wooden weapons, tipped with sharpened stone points. The women wove blankets from dog hair. They made summer clothes from the bark of trees. Like other Native

American groups, the people of the Northwest found ways for the environment to support what they needed in order to live.

1. Name three Native American cultural groups
2. Why was the League of Five Nations important?

3 Native Americans Build Great Empires.

What were the great Native American empires like?

In Mexico and Central America, Native Americans developed a number of great civilizations. Among them were the Mayan and Aztec civilizations.

The Maya built one of the first empires. They were one of the earliest people to raise crops. In the dense forests of the Yucatan (YOU-kah-tan) Peninsula, the Maya built large cities. These cities were religious centers. At the heart of each city stood a stone **pyramid.** A pyramid is a huge building with a square base and sloping sides. At the top of each pyramid was a temple. Here, priests worshiped many gods and goddesses.

The Maya were great scientists. They created their own system of numbers. They developed a way of writing using picture symbols. They also invented a 365-day calendar that followed the movement of the stars and the sun. This calendar was more accurate than the one then used by people in Europe.

Mayan society reached its peak between A.D. 300 and 900. Then, for some unknown reason, this society began to decline.

More than 1,000 years ago, the Mayans built the soaring pyramids of Paplanta. These busy cities were religious centers. At the top of the pyramids were temples. The Mayans were one of the first people to raise crops.

The Aztec Another great early American civilization, north of the Maya, was the Aztec. Sometime in the 1200s, the Aztec settled in the valley of Mexico. From there, they sent out powerful armies and conquered their neighbors. They soon ruled an empire covering most of Mexico.

The Aztec built a remarkable city, called Tenochtitlan (tay-nahch-tee-TLAN) on islands in a lake. Nearly 100,000 people lived in Tenochtitlan. That made it one of the largest cities in the world at the time. One of the first Europeans to see the Aztec capital said, "It was a wonderful thing to behold."

The Aztec empire was rich. Some Aztec wealth came from trade. Aztec craftspeople wove cloth decorated with feathers. Goldsmiths made jewelry, masks, and religious objects. Merchants brought foreign goods to Aztec markets. Much of the empire's wealth came from **tribute**, or payments that the Aztec forced whomever they conquered to pay. With these riches, the Aztec built great stone temples like those of the Maya.

The Aztec government was well organized. At its head was the emperor, who was also considered a god. However, the Aztec were harsh rulers. They even made human sacrifices to please the sun god. On special days, prisoners were lined up and sent to the tops of the temples. There, their hearts were cut out by Aztec priests using sharp knives.

Because of this harshness, the Aztec were hated by the people they conquered. As you will read in the next chapter, Europeans first came to Mexico in the 1500s. They found that the people whom the Aztec had conquered were eager to join them and try to topple the mighty Aztec empire.

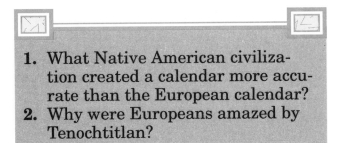

1. What Native American civilization created a calendar more accurate than the European calendar?
2. Why were Europeans amazed by Tenochtitlan?

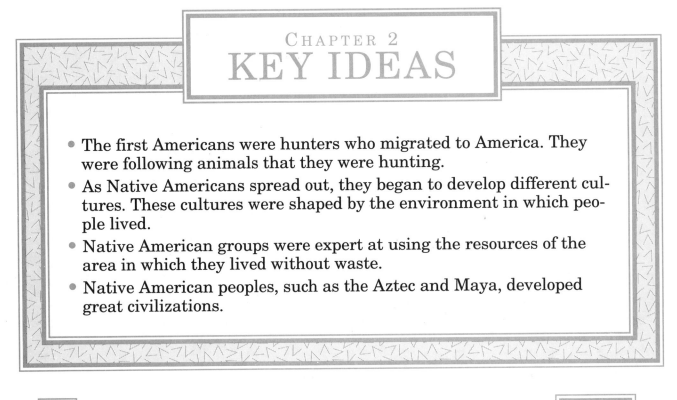

CHAPTER 2
KEY IDEAS

- The first Americans were hunters who migrated to America. They were following animals that they were hunting.
- As Native Americans spread out, they began to develop different cultures. These cultures were shaped by the environment in which people lived.
- Native American groups were expert at using the resources of the area in which they lived without waste.
- Native American peoples, such as the Aztec and Maya, developed great civilizations.

I. Reviewing Vocabulary

Match each word on the left with the correct definition on the right.

1. migrate
2. land bridge
3. adobe
4. drought
5. glacier

a. giant sheets of ice
b. Pueblo buildings made of dried bricks
c. a long period of dry weather
d. to move from one place to another
e. a narrow strip of land connecting Asia and North America

II. Understanding the Chapter

1. How did the discovery of farming affect the early Native American's life?
2. Choose two groups of Native Americans, and describe how those groups used their environment to help them survive?
3. Why were the Iroquois of the eastern woodlands so powerful?
4. What was a Pueblo *kiva*?
5. What were two inventions of Mayan civilization?

III. Building Skills: Understanding the Sequence of Events

On separate paper, copy the following terms and put them in order of time.

1. The land bridge to North America is flooded by melting glaciers.
2. Native Americans discover farming and settle down in villages.
3. Hunters cross the land bridge between Asia and North America.

IV. Writing About History

1. **What Would You Have Done?** Imagine that you are an early North American nomad. You have just discovered that planting a seed will grow food for you. Write a speech for the other members of your tribe proposing that the group should settle down and form a permanent village.
2. Imagine you are a visitor to the Aztec capital of Tenochtitlan. Write a description of the city.

V. Working Together

1. In your small groups, choose one of the Native American cultures that you have learned about. Your group will create a presentation that shows the important parts of the culture. Your group may choose to present a skit, a slide show, a video, or something else.
2. **Past to Present** With a group, talk about how the first Americans adapted to the regions where they lived. How do Americans adapt today? Report your ideas to the class.

The Spanish Reach the Americas. (1492-1550)

What happened when the first Europeans made contact with North Americans?

Columbus brought back Native Americans to present to the king and queen of Spain. After his arrival, Native Americans suffered cruelty, disease, and death.

Looking at Key Terms

- Vikings • Crusades • Muslims • Indies

Looking at Key Words

- **navigator:** a person who can steer a ship accurately across the water
- **compass:** an instrument used for showing direction
- **colony:** a permanent settlement controlled by a more powerful country
- **conquistador:** a Spanish soldier-explorer

STUDY

After you have read the chapter, write down everything you can remember from it. Then skim through the chapter, and add any ideas you left out. Use the list to study for a test.

HINT

Until the year A.D. 1000, the people of Europe knew nothing about North and South America. In that year, people from northern Europe landed on the shores of what is today Canada. These people were fierce warriors called **Vikings.** The Vikings tried to settle in the new land. They built homes, raised cattle, and farmed.

The Viking settlement did not last very long. We do not know why it did not last. Perhaps Native Americans drove the Vikings away. Perhaps the Vikings planned poorly and ran out of supplies. Whatever happened, Viking ships stopped sailing west.

Before long, the people of Europe forgot the settlement. They even forgot that a huge land lay across the Atlantic. Many people thought that the Atlantic stretched all the way to Asia. Some people began to wonder why they could not get to Asia by sailing west across the Atlantic.

1 Europeans Search for New Trade Routes.

Why did Europeans try to find new routes to Asia?

Today when we sprinkle a little pepper on our food, it is to add flavor. Five hundred years ago, spices such as pepper were far more important. There were no refrigerators to keep food from spoiling. Such seasonings as salt and cloves helped preserve food. If a piece of meat started to go bad, spices could hide the taste.

The search for spices led Europe to the Americas. Before 1095, Europeans knew little about the world beyond their borders. That year, the **Crusades** began. The Crusades were a series of wars fought over the part of the Middle East known as the Holy Land. Europeans who fought in the Crusades were known as crusaders.

At the time, **Muslims** controlled the Holy Land. The Muslims are followers of the religion of Islam. The Europeans wanted to seize Christian religious places from the Muslims.

The crusaders won a number of battles at first. However, they could not hold on to what they won. Still, the crusaders learned about many new things when they were in the Holy Land. They tasted for the first time the spices that people in Asia used to flavor their food. They saw fine silks used for expensive clothing. Europeans wanted to bring the spices and silks of Asia back home to Europe.

These spices and silks had been produced thousands of miles to the east. Europeans called this part of Asia "the **Indies.**" Muslim traders brought the silks and spices to the Holy Land.

European traders began to trade with Muslims for the spices and silks. Italian merchants bought the goods and sold them all over Europe. These traders could charge whatever they wanted for their goods.

Search for a sea route   For years, Europeans paid high prices for silks and spices. Then they realized that they could save themselves a lot of money if they could get the goods directly from the Indies. Portugal began looking for a way to sail to the Indies. In the late 1400s, Portuguese sailors tried to find a sea route to East Asia.

The person who led the search was Prince Henry of Portugal. Henry was called "the Navigator." A **navigator** is someone who can steer a ship accurately across water. Prince Henry did not actually make sea trips. However, he opened a school for sea captains and sailors from all over the world.

At this school, sailors learned about building ships and navigating. They learned how to use tools to help them navigate across the ocean. One important tool was the **compass.** It had a magnetic needle that always pointed

north. Sailors used the compass to tell the direction a ship was sailing.

Soon, Portuguese explorers were traveling south along the coast of Africa, looking for a path to Asia. In 1488, a Portuguese ship sailed around the southern tip of Africa. It was clear that Portugal had finally found a sea route to the Indies. Sailors from other countries wondered if they could find another way to the Indies.

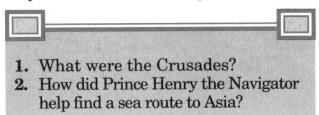

1. What were the Crusades?
2. How did Prince Henry the Navigator help find a sea route to Asia?

2 Two Cultures Meet in the Caribbean.
How did the arrival of Columbus change world history?

In May of 1492, a white-haired Italian sailor arrived at the port of Palos, in Spain. His name was Christopher Columbus. He had a plan for reaching the Indies. Instead of sailing east around Africa, why not get to Asia by sailing west across the Atlantic? Columbus believed that this would be a shorter route to the Indies. Like other Europeans, he didn't know that North and South America stood in the way.

For six years, Columbus tried to get a European ruler to listen to his plan. Finally, the king and queen of Spain agreed to help him. On August 3, 1492, Columbus sailed from Palos with three small ships. Three months later, Columbus reached an island. He was sure he had found the riches of the Indies. However, instead of rich cities of gold and spices, Columbus found Native Americans living in small villages. He still believed he had reached the Indies. So he called these people "Indians."

No one who was there could realize that they were part of a turning point in world history. The clash between Native

The invention of the compass made it possible for sailors to cross unknown seas. This drawing from the 1500s shows a sea captain using a large compass to plot out the direction of his voyage.

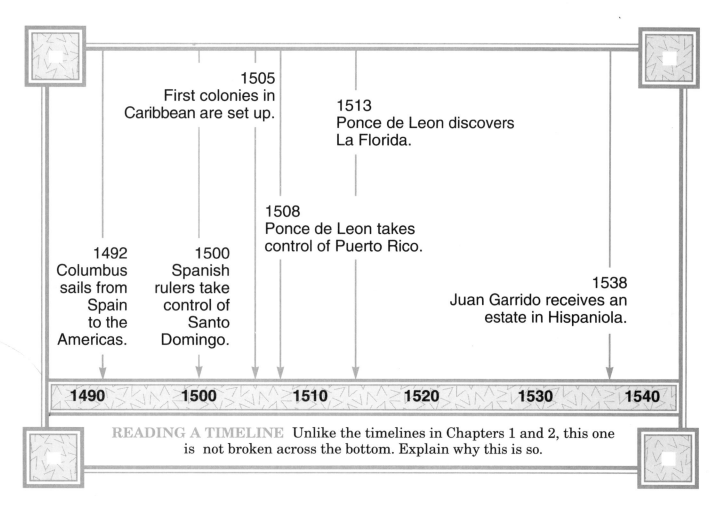

1505
First colonies in Caribbean are set up.

1513
Ponce de Leon discovers La Florida.

1508
Ponce de Leon takes control of Puerto Rico.

1492
Columbus sails from Spain to the Americas.

1500
Spanish rulers take control of Santo Domingo.

1538
Juan Garrido receives an estate in Hispaniola.

| 1490 | 1500 | 1510 | 1520 | 1530 | 1540 |

READING A TIMELINE Unlike the timelines in Chapters 1 and 2, this one is not broken across the bottom. Explain why this is so.

American and European cultures had begun. This clash would shake the Americas for the next 500 years.

The people whom Columbus had found called themselves Taino (TEYE-noh). Columbus wrote of them: "They are very well built people, with handsome bodies. If you ask for anything they have, they never say no. Rather, they invite you to share it. They show as much love as if they were giving their hearts."

Columbus continued his voyage. He landed on a larger island that he named Hispaniola, (hihs-pan-YOH-lah) or "Little Spain." There, he built a small wooden fort. Columbus picked 39 crew members to stay at the fort. The rest returned to Spain with him.

Columbus's second voyage Back in Spain, Columbus received a hero's welcome. His findings amazed the people of Europe. Many believed he had actually reached the Indies. They were sure that its wealth was just within reach.

In 1493, Spain sent Columbus back on a second trip. Columbus was supposed to set up **colonies**. Colonies are permanent settlements controlled by a more powerful country. This time, he had 17 ships and about 1,500 people. Most of these people wanted to settle in what they thought were "the Indies." Columbus also had on board five Roman Catholic priests. Their goal was to convert the "Indians" to Christianity.

This time, the Native Americans did not welcome Columbus. They were afraid that the strangers would take over their land. Native Americans on what is today called Jamaica and the Virgin Islands attacked Columbus's forces. When Columbus arrived at Hispaniola, he found his fort burned. In the ruins, he found the bodies of the men he had left behind. The men in the fort had treated the Native Americans cruelly. In return, the Native Americas had attacked and killed them.

Columbus decided to strike back. Spanish soldiers riding horses attacked the Native American villages. These animals were unknown to Native Americans. They seemed huge and fierce. The Spanish also used snarling attack dogs.

With this force, Columbus conquered the Taino. Then he forced them to build a new settlement. He ordered them to bring him gold. He also put more than 500 Taino in chains and shipped them to Spain as slaves.

In 1494, the Taino rebelled against Columbus. However, their simple weapons were no match for Spanish guns and cannon. The Spanish hunted down the Taino with attack dogs. Many Native Americans were brutally killed.

New voyages Columbus made two more voyages to North America. He explored the coast of Central and South America and claimed all this land for Spain. These places became Spanish colonies. The trade with these colonies would make Spain the richest nation in Europe.

Many Spaniards followed Columbus to North America searching for gold and glory. These Spanish soldier-explorers were called **conquistadors** (kahn-KEES-tuh-dawrz). One of the most famous conquistadors was Juan Ponce de Leon (WAHN POHN-seh deh leh-OHN).

Ponce de Leon sailed to the Americas with Columbus in 1493. He took part in the conquest of Hispaniola. In 1508, he led a force that took control of Puerto Rico. Ponce de Leon had heard stories about a "fountain of youth." By drinking the water of the fountain, a person was supposed to become young again. In

This picture of Columbus landing in the Americas was made over a hundred years ago. It shows Columbus as a hero. Native Americans are only shadows. Contrast this picture with how Columbus is viewed today.

The Spanish forced the Native Americans to work for them like slaves. Here Native Americans on the island of Hispaniola bring in gold they have dug from the ground. The gold is then weighed by the Spaniard at the table.

March 1513, he sailed from Puerto Rico and landed in a place that he named La Florida, meaning "full of flowers." He found no fountain of youth. However, he was the first European to explore the mainland of what would become the United States.

Joining Ponce de Leon were other conquistadors. One was Juan Garrido (gah-REE-doh), a free African. Garrido was known as *el conquistador negro*, or the Black Conquistador. In the 1490s, he had traveled from Africa to Spain. There, he became a Christian. In 1494, Garrido joined the Spanish army. When Garrido heard of Columbus's voyages, he decided to make his fortune in the Americas. He joined Ponce de Leon in Puerto Rico. Later, he took part in the conquest of Mexico. (see the next chapter.) Garrido

served Spain for more than 30 years. In 1538, he received an estate on Hispaniola as his reward.

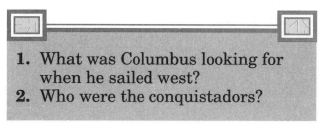

1. What was Columbus looking for when he sailed west?
2. Who were the conquistadors?

3 Hispaniola Becomes the Center of Spain's American Empire.

Why were the settlements on Hispaniola important for Spain?

The first settlers found life on Hispaniola very difficult. The hot climate was unbearable. Supplies ran out. Many colonists died from the heat and hunger. In 1496, Columbus abandoned the original settlement. He started a new one on the south coast of the island and named it Santo Domingo. This settlement was located at the mouth of a river and had a good supply of fresh water. It also had fertile soil for farming. Later, settlers discovered gold at Santo Domingo.

Columbus was a fine sailor, but he was a poor governor. In 1500, the Spanish rulers took control of Santo Domingo from Columbus. The king and queen were upset by the violence against the Native Americans. They also were angry that Columbus seemed to be always arguing with the Spanish settlers.

Native American rebellion   Under a new governor, Santo Domingo entered a period of growth. It soon became the center of Spain's empire in the Caribbean. Here, the government built the first cathedral, the first hospital, and the first university in the Americas. Enslaved Native Americans built these buildings and many

others. They also worked the farms and dug gold and silver out of mines. The gold, silver, and cotton were sent to Spain. The profits from these products did not benefit the Native Americans.

When the Native Americans rebelled against this harsh treatment, they were killed or sent to Spain as slaves. A Taino leader named Hatuey (ah-too-AY) fled Hispaniola rather than become a slave. He later fought the Spanish as they tried to settle Cuba. Hatuey was killed. However, he became a hero to later Cubans.

By 1505, the first colonies in the Caribbean were set up. Native Americans were firmly under Spanish rule. All Native American rebellions had been put down. Now, conquistadors arriving from Spain were ready to conquer new lands in the Americas.

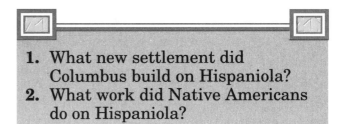

1. What new settlement did Columbus build on Hispaniola?
2. What work did Native Americans do on Hispaniola?

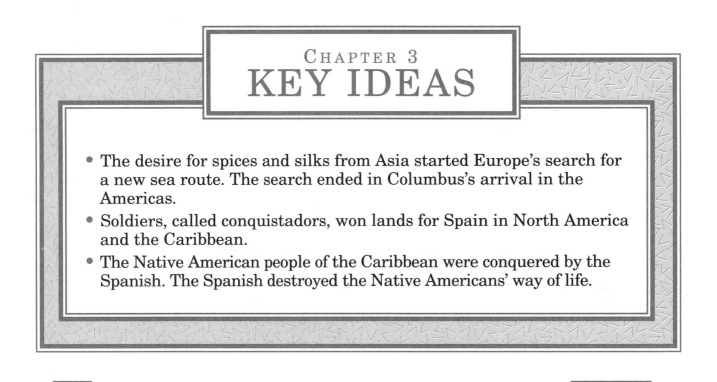

CHAPTER 3
KEY IDEAS

- The desire for spices and silks from Asia started Europe's search for a new sea route. The search ended in Columbus's arrival in the Americas.
- Soldiers, called conquistadors, won lands for Spain in North America and the Caribbean.
- The Native American people of the Caribbean were conquered by the Spanish. The Spanish destroyed the Native Americans' way of life.

I. Reviewing Vocabulary

Match each word on the left with the correct definition on the right.

1. colony   **a.** a permanent settlement
2. compass   **b.** a follower of Islam
3. conquistador   **c.** a Spanish soldier-explorer
4. Muslim   **d.** an instrument for showing direction
5. navigator   **e.** a person who steers a ship

II. Understanding the Chapter

1. In what way can the Crusades be called a success?
2. Why did Europeans seek a sea route to the Indies?
3. What happened to the Taino and other Native Americans when Columbus returned to the Americas in 1493?
4. What was Ponce de Leon looking for when he made his discoveries?
5. Who was Juan Garrido?

III. Building Skills: Making a Chart

Make a chart that shows the settlement or findings of each explorer named in this chapter. Copy the headings and grid below to get started.

EXPLORER	DATE	SETTLEMENT OR FINDING

IV. Writing About History

1. **What Would You Have Done?** Suppose you are Hatuey, the Taino leader. You have just heard that the Spaniards are marching to attack you. Do you defend yourselves or take some other action?
2. Imagine you are a member of Columbus's crew as he lands on an island in the Caribbean. Write an entry in a diary about the experience.
3. Imagine you are a Native American living in Santo Domingo. Write a speech expressing your feelings toward Christopher Columbus.

V. Working Together

1. In your small groups, think of an important event in Columbus's four voyages to North America. Create a cartoon book about the incident. Be sure to give details about what happened.
2. **Past to Present** People have always explored the unknown. With a group, discuss what you think people will explore in the future. How do you think the explorations might change the way people think?

THREE GREAT CULTURES MEET IN THE AMERICAS. (1505-1600)

How did European, Native American, and African cultures come to clash in the Caribbean?

An old woodcut shows Hernando Cortéz being greeted by worried Aztec nobles as he enters the Aztec city of Cholula. The Aztec had good reason to worry.

Looking at Key Terms

- *encomienda* • griots

Looking at Key Words

- **plantations:** large farms where one crop is grown
- **pilgrimage:** a trip to a religious shrine
- **slavery:** the system of owning people
- **vassal:** a person protected by another stronger person in exchange for service

Christopher Columbus's voyages turned world history upside down. Before 1500, people in Spain and Portugal realized that Columbus had not reached "the Indies." Rather, he had reached a vast land that they had known nothing about.

It quickly became clear that there was great wealth in these lands across the Atlantic. One Spaniard said it best: "We came here to serve God and the king, and also to get rich."

1 Spain Builds an Empire in the Caribbean.

How did Spain conquer the Caribbean islands?

To win these riches, the government of Spain had to get the Spanish to settle on the Caribbean islands of New Spain. It offered Spanish settlers a large grant of land called an ***encomienda*** (en-kom-ee-EN-dah). Anyone with this grant had the right to use the labor of Native Americans living on the land.

However, the landowner also had responsibilities. He was supposed to teach the Native Americans the Christian religion. The landowner was also expected to pay Native Americans fairly for their work.

It was easy in faraway Spain to make these rules to protect Native Americans. However, it was a lot harder to get landowners in New Spain to follow the rules. Most landowners treated Native American workers badly. Native Americans were forced to work from dawn to dusk and were whipped for almost nothing. Was there no one who would speak for the Native Americans?

The encomienda system In 1511, a young conquistador heard a sermon protesting abuses of Native Americans that was preached in Santo Domingo.

Tell me, by what right do you hold these Indians in such cruel slavery? Who gave you the right to wage such terrible wars against these people? They lived so quietly and peacefully in their land. Why do you keep them so oppressed? Should you not love them as you love fellow Spaniards? Don't you understand this?

When Bartolome de las Casas heard these words, he felt very guilty. Las Casas had come to Hispaniola in 1502. As a young man, he had helped to set up the *encomienda* system. He saw Spanish soldiers with fierce attack dogs attacking Native American villages. After hearing the sermon, Las Casas tried to repent for his actions. He became a Roman Catholic priest. He began to write to important people in Spain criticizing the way Native Americans were treated.

Conquering Puerto Rico and Cuba Las Casas moved to Cuba in 1511. He gave up his lands and became a parish priest. He watched as Native Americans were shipped in chains to Spain. Las Casas wrote the rulers of Spain: "This action will end only when there is no more land nor people to conquer. We will destroy the people in this part of the world."

Las Casas then devoted his life to ending the unjust system. However, the conquest of Cuba and Puerto Rico helped make the system even more unjust.

After the conquest, the Spanish planted sugarcane on both islands. The sugarcane was grown on large farms called **plantations.** Many workers were needed to plant the cane and cut it for the mill.

Sugar quickly became the main crop on Puerto Rico and Cuba. Native Americans were worked so hard by the

landowners that many died. Diseases such as smallpox killed many more Native Americans. Smallpox wiped out whole villages of Native Americans.

1. What was an *encomienda*?
2. What became the main crop on Cuba and Puerto Rico?

Reading a Map. To the Spanish, it was a "New World." But not for long. Which explorers traveled in what is today the state of Florida?

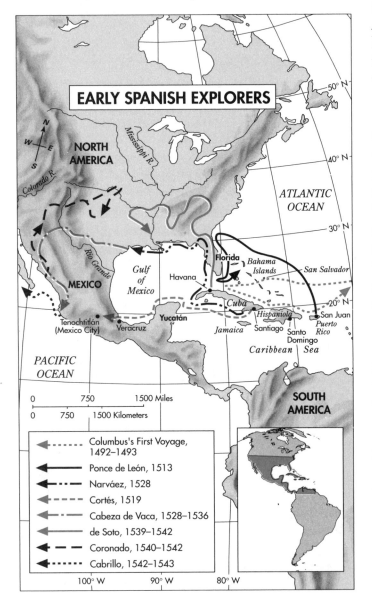

EARLY SPANISH EXPLORERS

NORTH AMERICA

Mississippi R.

Colorado R.

Rio Grande

MEXICO

Gulf of Mexico

Havana

ATLANTIC OCEAN

Florida
Bahama Islands
San Salvador

Cuba

Tenochtitlán (Mexico City)
Veracruz
Yucatán
Jamaica
Santiago
Hispaniola
Santo Domingo
San Juan
Puerto Rico

Caribbean Sea

PACIFIC OCEAN

SOUTH AMERICA

50° N
40° N
30° N
20° N

0   750   1500 Miles
0   750   1500 Kilometers

- - - - ◄ Columbus's First Voyage, 1492–1493
—— ◄ Ponce de León, 1513
—·— ◄ Narváez, 1528
- - - ◄ Cortés, 1519
- - - ◄ Cabeza de Vaca, 1528–1536
—— ◄ de Soto, 1539–1542
— — ◄ Coronado, 1540–1542
·····◄ Cabrillo, 1542–1543

100° W   90° W   80° W

2 The Heritage of Africa Arrives in the Americas.

What was the rich heritage that Africans brought to the Americas?

As the Native Americans died, the Spanish became short of labor. They began bringing enslaved Africans to take the place of the Native Americans. These Africans had been taken from their homes in chains and shipped to the Caribbean as slaves. The first few enslaved Africans came to Hispaniola in 1505. In years to come, this trickle swelled into a flood. Millions of enslaved Africans were forced to leave their homeland. They were torn from a land in which they had built up rich and valuable traditions.

Ancient Egypt   Africa was home to one of the greatest civilizations of the world. The ancient Egyptians built many fine buildings, but none were more impressive than the pyramids. These huge stone structures were built as tombs for the rulers of Egypt. They are still among the largest buildings in the world. The Egyptians also developed a system of writing and made important advances in math and medicine.

Empires of gold   Wealth of another kind developed in Africa after Egypt's decline. Far to the west, three great kingdoms arose between A.D. 500 and 1600.

The first kingdom was Ghana. The name Ghana meant gold. The ruler of Ghana was called "king of gold." When the king met his subjects, he wore a tall golden cap. At his side walked dogs with golden collars. Ghana's king was so rich that he had the largest army in the world at that time. Over 200,000 soldiers served him!

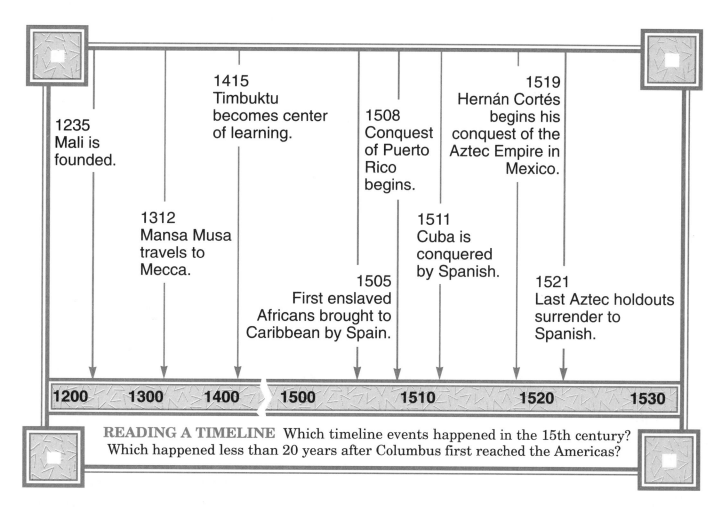

READING A TIMELINE Which timeline events happened in the 15th century? Which happened less than 20 years after Columbus first reached the Americas?

Timeline events:

1235 Mali is founded.

1312 Mansa Musa travels to Mecca.

1415 Timbuktu becomes center of learning.

1505 First enslaved Africans brought to Caribbean by Spain.

1508 Conquest of Puerto Rico begins.

1511 Cuba is conquered by Spanish.

1519 Hernán Cortés begins his conquest of the Aztec Empire in Mexico.

1521 Last Aztec holdouts surrender to Spanish.

1200 1300 1400 1500 1510 1520 1530

Around the early 1200s, the empire of Mali became powerful. Mali was as large as Western Europe. It was even wealthier than Ghana. Mali's greatest ruler was Mansa Musa (MAHN-suh MOO-suh). Mansa Musa was a Muslim. In 1324, he began a **pilgrimage** to the Muslim holy city of Mecca, in Arabia. A pilgrimage is a trip to a religious shrine.

From generation to generation, African **griots** have told the story of Mansa Musa's trip. Griots are African storytellers who memorize and pass down the history of their people.

Mansa Musa's caravan consisted of 60,000 people. He had 80 camels, each one carrying 300-pound bags of gold dust. Mansa Musa arrived in Cairo, Egypt, in the summer of 1324. The people of Cairo were stunned. They had never seen a group of people so rich. When Mansa Musa was in Mecca, he persuaded some of the finest builders

and scholars in the Arab world to return with him to Mali. They helped enlarge the city of Timbuktu (tim-buk-TOO). Workers built many handsome new buildings. Timbuktu became a major center of learning. The city had great universities and wonderful libraries. Scholars taught religion, law, and medicine at Timbuktu's universities. Students came from across Africa to study there.

Like Ghana and Mali, the empire of Songhai (sahng-HY) grew wealthy from trade. It was powerful from 1450 to about 1600. Songhai was even larger than Mali, covering most of West Africa. Its greatest ruler was Askia Muhammad (AHS-kee-uh moo-HAM-uhd). He set up a strong and fair government. He also created a system of fair taxation.

The "silent trade" The wealth of these African kingdoms depended on trade. Ghana was located on a major

A Spanish map that was drawn in 1375 shows the African kingdom of Mali and Mansa Musa's journey across Africa to the holy city of Mecca. Mansa Musa is shown wearing a crown and seated on his throne.

trade route. To the south was a region rich in gold. The salt regions of North Africa lay to the north. The people of West Africa depended on salt in their food to replace body salts lost in the heat of the region.

The rulers of Ghana held tight control over the supply of gold. They charged taxes on all gold and salt that went through their empire. The traders paid these taxes in gold. With their income, the kings had huge armies to protect the trade routes.

Because there was no common language, the trade in gold and salt took place through silent trade. Not a word was spoken between the traders. The salt traders left their blocks of salt on the ground at some distance from the gold. Then they retreated a distance. The gold traders approached to examine the amount of salt. They left what they believed was a fair amount of gold, and then they withdrew. The salt traders came back to examine the amount of gold. If they accepted it, the deal was made. If they did not, the process was repeated until an agreement was reached.

The slave trade Humans also moved along the trade routes. In Africa, there was **slavery**, or the system of owning people. It went back hundreds of years. Slavery existed in many other parts of the world, including ancient Greece and Rome.

Enslaved people in Africa had usually been captured in wars. They worked as farm laborers and servants. Slaves were often able to buy their freedom after a time. Some became members of the families to whom they were enslaved.

Slavery was about to change. In 1502, a Portuguese ship from Europe landed on the coast of West Africa. The Portuguese ship carried away Africans as slaves to another land. These Africans were the first of many millions who were taken from their homes.

Slave trading became a big business. African rulers now allowed slave raiding in their territories. Slave raiders rounded up thousands of captives for sale to the Portuguese. The slaves were brought in chains to Portuguese slave-collecting forts along the coast of West Africa.

In 1517, the Spanish king had 4,000 enslaved Africans shipped to Hispaniola. Soon enslaved Africans were working on plantations in Puerto Rico, Cuba, and Jamaica. By the middle of the 1500s, there were more Africans than Europeans on some islands.

Spanish slave owners treated enslaved Africans harshly. The Spanish were afraid that the Africans would rise up and kill them. Often, the Spanish branded and whipped slaves. Sometimes, they even hanged them. However, Africans managed to keep their traditions alive. Over time, African and Spanish ways mixed with those of Native Americans. Out of this mix came entirely new cultures. They are the cultures of Puerto Rico, Cuba, and the Dominican Republic.

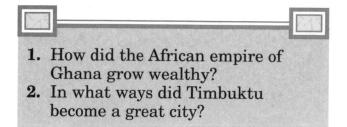

1. How did the African empire of Ghana grow wealthy?
2. In what ways did Timbuktu become a great city?

3 Spain and Native Americans Struggle for an Empire.

How did the Spanish conquer the Aztec in what is today Mexico?

The Caribbean islands brought tremendous wealth to Spain. Now many young Spanish nobles began to look to the mainland. They wanted to find adventure and gold. One of these young men was Hernán Cortés (air-NAHN kohr-TES).

Sugar cane being harvested by enslaved Africans. This print dates from the 1600s. Why was the labor of enslaved people from West Africa so important to the Spanish colonies in the Americas?

In this Aztec drawing, Cortéz is shown with Aztec messengers. At his side is Malinché, the Native American woman who spoke the Aztec language. Cortéz greeted the Aztec coldly. When they gave him gold, he said: "Is this all?"

The march to Mexico In 1511 Cortés helped conquer Cuba. Cortés was given land and gold mines, but he wanted more. He heard Native Americans tell tales about a rich nation to the west. Cortés asked the governor of Cuba to let him lead an army to conquer this land. When Cortés said he would pay for the trip himself, the governor agreed. Cortés sailed from Cuba in February 1519.

The land that Cortés found is today called Mexico. In the 1500s, it was ruled by the Aztec, a powerful warrior people. (See page 22.) The Aztec had many **vassals,** or people who had been conquered by a stronger people. The Aztec had treated their vassals cruelly. The vassals hated their conquerors and wanted to help the Spanish destroy the Aztec empire. As Cortés headed for the Aztec capital, many vassals joined him.

Cortés and Malinché. One of these vassals was a woman named Malinché (muh-LIN-chay). Malinché hated the Aztec. She spoke the Aztec language as well as that of some of the vassal people. She helped Cortés become allies with other Native American people. Without Malinché, Cortés might have failed.

From Malinché, Cortés heard stories of the wealth and power of the Aztec. Malinché also told Cortés of a god whom the Aztec believed would return one day from the east. Knowing about the god gave Cortés an advantage.

The return of a god The Aztec emperor was Montezuma (mon-teh-SOH-muh). When Montezuma heard of Cortés's arrival, he believed Cortés was the returning Aztec god. Montezuma made a decision that would cost him dearly. He sent Aztec messengers with rich gifts to the coast. He gave them these instructions: "When you see the god, say to him: 'Your servant Montezuma has sent us to you. Here are presents to welcome you home to Mexico.'"

Cortés greeted the messengers coldly. He said, "Is this all?" He made it clear what he had come for. "I and my soldiers suffer from a disease of the heart. It can be cured only by gold."

Conquest of the Aztec   In November 1519, Cortés and his army entered the Aztec capital. The Spanish were amazed by the city's large stone buildings and wide streets. "These great buildings seemed like a dream," wrote one soldier.

At first, the Aztec were friendly and treated the Spanish as gods. But the Aztec soon saw the Spanish were just men. Cortés's men took Montezuma hostage. They then killed hundreds of Aztec during a festival. Montezuma died in the fighting that followed.

The Aztec warriors fought fiercely against the Spanish. But the Spanish had guns and cannon. They also had many Native American allies. But their deadliest weapon was smallpox. This disease killed many more Aztec than did Spanish bullets.

On August 13, 1521, the Aztec surrendered to Cortés. The Spanish destroyed the Aztec city and began to build a new city on its ruins. The new city was called Mexico City. The Aztec and other Native Americans worked as slaves. They built the new Mexico City in three years. Some Aztec worked in mines digging gold and silver. These metals were shipped to Spain. The Aztec empire was gone. A new Spanish empire took its place.

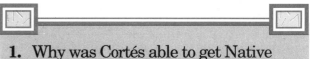

1. Why was Cortés able to get Native Americans to fight against the Aztec?
2. Why did Montezuma first welcome Cortés to Mexico?

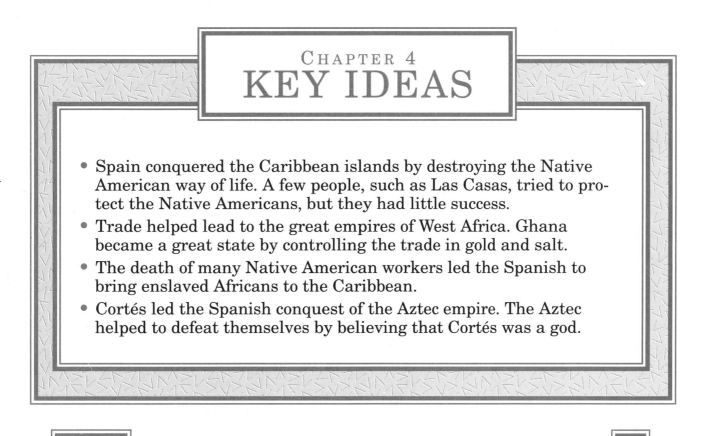

CHAPTER 4
KEY IDEAS

- Spain conquered the Caribbean islands by destroying the Native American way of life. A few people, such as Las Casas, tried to protect the Native Americans, but they had little success.
- Trade helped lead to the great empires of West Africa. Ghana became a great state by controlling the trade in gold and salt.
- The death of many Native American workers led the Spanish to bring enslaved Africans to the Caribbean.
- Cortés led the Spanish conquest of the Aztec empire. The Aztec helped to defeat themselves by believing that Cortés was a god.

REVIEWING CHAPTER 4

I. Reviewing Vocabulary

Match each word on the left with the correct definition on the right.

1. encomienda
2. Ghana
3. Mansa Musa
4. vassal
5. griots

a. a subject
b. a land grant in New Spain
c. name of an African city that means "gold"
d. African storytellers
e. African king who made a religious trip to Mecca

II. Understanding the Chapter

1. How did the encomienda system harm the Native Americans?
2. What led the Spanish to bring enslaved Africans to the Caribbean?
3. How did Mansa Musa's pilgrimage to Mecca lead to the growth of Timbuktu?
4. Why was Cortés's small army able to conquer the powerful Aztec empire.
5. What was the "silent trade"?

III. Building Skills: Making Comparisons

This chapter gives you information on three great African empires. How can you keep information on those three empires organized? Making comparison charts is one way. Use the information in this book to complete the following chart.

COMPARING WEST AFRICAN EMPIRES

Empire	Dates	Great Leader	Accomplishment
		"king of gold"	
Mali			
			set up strong and fair government and system of fair taxation

IV. Writing About History

1. **What would you have done?** Imagine that you are a Spanish landowner in Cuba in the 1500s. Would you have followed the teachings of Las Casas? Why or why not?
2. Imagine that you are with Hernán Cortés in the Aztec capital. Your comrades want to kill Montezuma. Write a speech persuading them to let Montezuma live.

V. Working Together

1. In your small groups, create a large map with art and writing showing the highlights of Ghana, Mali, and Songhai. Include dates, interesting facts about what their wealth was based on, their leaders, and their accomplishments.
2. **Past to Present** Spanish, Native American, and African influences are all a part of U.S. culture. With a group, list at least five examples of ideas or traditions that can be traced back to these three cultures.

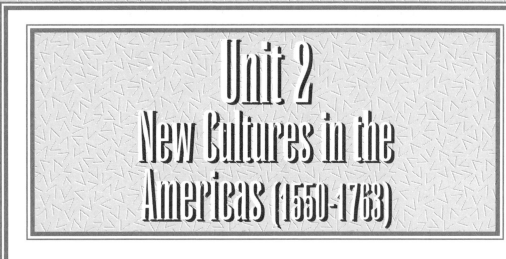

Unit 2
New Cultures in the Americas (1550-1763)

Chapters

LATINO CULTURE DEVELOPS. (1520-1700)

What was the new Latino culture that began in Spain's colonies?

A painting from 1683 shows a Mexico City festival day. Some of the city's richest and most powerful people are being driven to church.

Looking at Key Terms

- New Spain • *peninsulare* • *criollo* • *mestizo* • mulatto
- Latino

Looking at Key Words

- **export:** a resource or product sent from one country to another
- **mission:** a community run by the Catholic church
- **convert:** to persuade a person to join a religion
- **famine:** a time when there is not enough food to eat

STUDY HINT

When you study a chapter, scan the chapter first. Then read it in depth. Look at each heading and subheading. They will tell you what each section is about.

In 1520, Spain had a few tiny colonies on islands in the Caribbean. Eighty years later, Spain ruled a mighty empire in the Americas. Spain's largest colonial city, Mexico City, was impressive. It had beautiful churches, a university, and wide roads. It even had a police force.

By 1600, a new culture had developed in Spain's American colonies. The new culture would have a major influence on the history of the United States. What happened in these 80 years to create the new culture?

1 Spain Rules Its American Colonies Strictly.
What was life like in New Spain?

Silver was discovered northwest of Mexico City in 1545. Silver soon replaced gold as the greatest **export** from the Spanish colonies. An export is a product sent from one country to another. Silver made Spain a rich nation. It also made many Spanish colonists wealthy. Few people in New Spain, as the Spanish colonies were called, shared in the wealth. Most people in New Spain were very poor.

People in New Spain were expected to know their places. A very few people at the top had all the power. They told everyone else what to do. They told farmers what to plant. They told people where to build towns. Below the people at the top were members of other classes. Everyone had a place in New Spain that was understood by all.

Street scene In a typical colony in New Spain, imagine a well-dressed man on horseback riding down a busy street. He is a ***peninsulare*** (puh-neen-soo-LAH-reh). *Peninsulares* were colonists who were born in Spain. They were members of the highest class in New Spain. *Peninsulares* held all the top positions in government and the church.

Imagine that our *peninsulare* stops to talk to a woman who owns a piece of land he would like to buy. This woman is a ***criollo*** (kree-OH-yoh). While her parents came from Spain, she was born in New Spain. That made a difference then. *Criollos* owned much of the land and the mines in New Spain. Very few criollos held positions in the government. Despite their wealth, the *criollos* had little power.

Watching the *peninsulare* and the *criollo* is a darker-skinned woman in the doorway of a shop. She makes pottery for a living. She is a ***mestizo*** (mehs-TEE-soh), part Spanish and part Native American. Many *mestizos* were skilled workers then. However, they could not own land, and they could not take part in government.

Working in the *mestizo's* shop is a darker man. He is a **mulatto** (muh-LAHT-oh), part Spanish and part African. In New Spain, many mulattos were not allowed to work with *mestizos*. But this mulatto was accepted by his *mestizo* neighbors. Some mulattos were accepted by Africans.

Nearby, a church is being built. The workers are all Native Americans. They pay no attention to the other people. Along with enslaved Africans, Native Americans were the poorest class in New Spain. Enslaved Africans and Native Americans did most of the hard work. Without them, Mexico City could not have been wealthy. But none of the city's wealth went into the pockets of these workers. They were poor and would remain so.

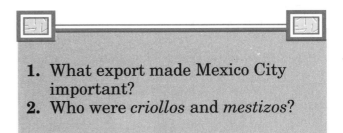

1. What export made Mexico City important?
2. Who were *criollos* and *mestizos*?

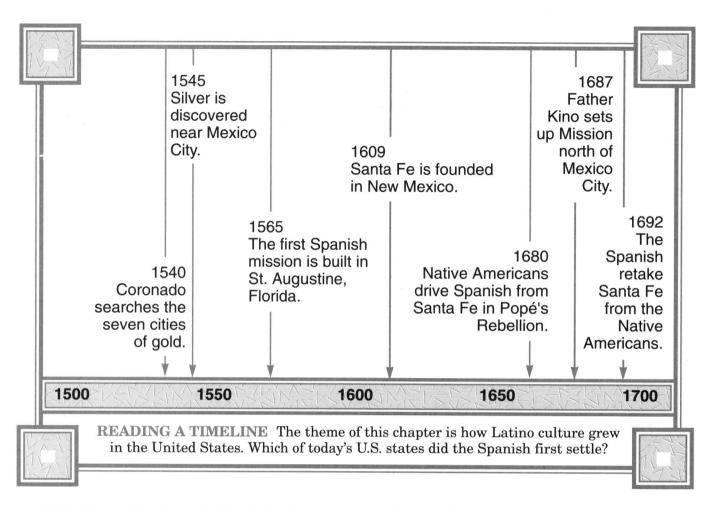

1545
Silver is discovered near Mexico City.

1687
Father Kino sets up Mission north of Mexico City.

1609
Santa Fe is founded in New Mexico.

1565
The first Spanish mission is built in St. Augustine, Florida.

1692
The Spanish retake Santa Fe from the Native Americans.

1540
Coronado searches the seven cities of gold.

1680
Native Americans drive Spanish from Santa Fe in Popé's Rebellion.

| 1500 | 1550 | 1600 | 1650 | 1700 |

READING A TIMELINE The theme of this chapter is how Latino culture grew in the United States. Which of today's U.S. states did the Spanish first settle?

2 The Spanish Explore the Borderlands.

What did Spain find in the lands north of Mexico?

In September 1539, a Spanish priest named Marcos came to Mexico City with a story that seemed unbelievable. Marcos had traveled far to the north. He said that Native Americans had led him to a city of gold. According to Marcos, the people in this city ate from gold dishes and drank water from gold cups. Marcos said that he had seen six more golden cities north of the city.

Coronado sets out Did the north have riches to match the Aztec empire? In 1540, Francisco Coronado (koh-roh-NAH-doh) set out in search of the seven cities of gold. The people of New Spain called the area to the north "the Spanish borderlands."

Coronado and his force entered what is today the southwestern United States. Coronado found no cities of gold. Instead, he found villages with buildings made of adobe mud bricks. The buildings had been built by a Native American people known as the Zuñi (ZOON-yee).

Coronado demanded that the Zuñi accept Spanish rule. His soldiers attacked villages that did not surrender. They killed many people. These attacks earned the lasting hatred of the Zuñi.

Many natural wonders For the next two years, Coronado marched through what is today the United States. He traveled in today's Arizona, New Mexico, Texas, Oklahoma, and Kansas. His soldiers came upon many natural wonders. One group traveled down the valley of the Río Grande. Another group became the first Europeans to explore the Grand Canyon.

Coronado's force crossed the Great Plains. They were amazed to see large herds of buffalo. In 1542, Coronado and his people returned to Mexico. They knew a lot about the Spanish borderlands. But they had found no gold.

Santa Fe   Spain was not particularly interested in places that had no gold or silver. It was not until 1598 that a village was built in the borderlands. That settlement did not last. In 1609, the Spanish built a village along a branch of the Río Grande. They named this village Santa Fe, or "Holy Faith." Santa Fe is the second-oldest Spanish town in the present-day United States.

Since Santa Fe had no gold or silver, officials paid little attention to it. By the 1620s, about 500 people lived in the town. But Spain hardly thought about its little outpost. Aside from a pack train of mules, the settlement was cut off from Mexico City.

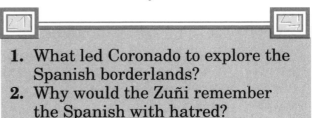

1. What led Coronado to explore the Spanish borderlands?
2. Why would the Zuñi remember the Spanish with hatred?

Reading a Map. By 1600, Spain controlled a vast empire in the Americas. What was its colony in North America called? What was the name of its colony in South America? What lands did Portugal claim?

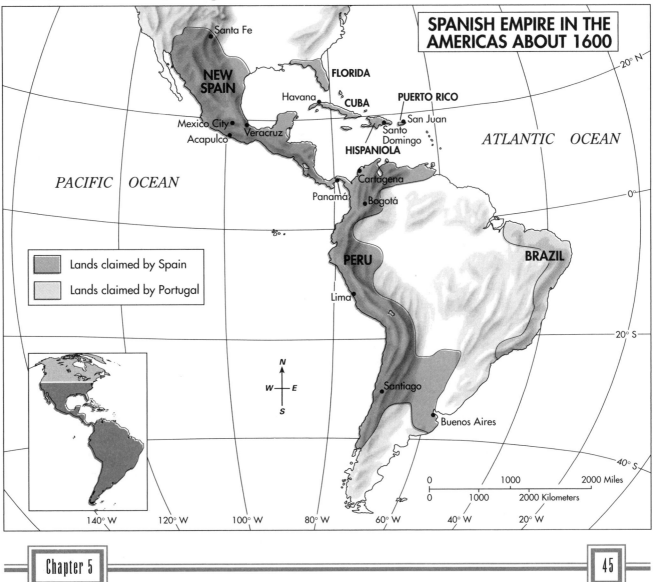

SPANISH EMPIRE IN THE AMERICAS ABOUT 1600

Santa Fe

NEW SPAIN

FLORIDA

Havana   CUBA   PUERTO RICO

Mexico City   San Juan

Acapulco   Veracruz   Santo Domingo

HISPANIOLA

ATLANTIC OCEAN

PACIFIC OCEAN

Cartagena

Panamá   Bogotá

Lands claimed by Spain

Lands claimed by Portugal

PERU   BRAZIL

Lima

Santiago

Buenos Aires

20° N

0°

20° S

40° S

140° W   120° W   100° W   80° W   60° W   40° W   20° W

0   1000   2000 Miles

0   1000   2000 Kilometers

3 Missions Convert Native Americans.

What was mission life like for Native Americans?

If Santa Fe is the second-oldest town in the United States, what is the oldest? It is St. Augustine in the Spanish colony of La Florida.

In 1513, Ponce de Leon had set out to investigate rumors of a fountain of youth. He called the land he found La Florida. (See Chapter 3.) The Spanish started some settlements in Florida, but none lasted. In 1565, they began a settlement that did survive. They built a fort at a site they named St. Augustine. Slowly, the Spanish post grew. Over the years, pirates looted it. English ships attacked it. But Spain hung on to St. Augustine. Today, St. Augustine is the oldest city in the United States started by Europeans.

Life in St. Augustine centered around the **mission.** Missions were communities run by the Catholic church. Mission priests tried to **convert** Native Americans, or persuade them to become Christian. Then, Native Americans could become "useful" members of the colonies. Missions were built from ocean to ocean across the southern part of today's United States. Many of these beautiful buildings still stand.

Mission life Each mission was made up of a school, a church, a farm, and workplaces. The missions gave Native Americans food, clothing, and a place to live. In return, Native Americans worked for the mission. Some raised crops or watched over animals. Others made goods for sale, such as cloth, candles, and furniture.

A day at the mission began with church service. Then the adults went to work, and their children went to school. At noon, everyone had lunch. Then they

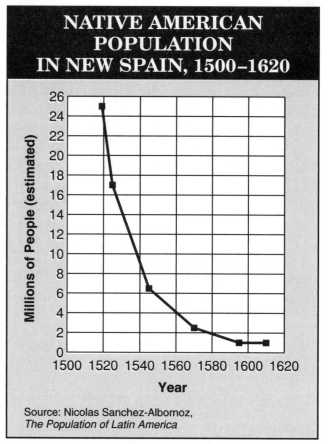

NATIVE AMERICAN POPULATION IN NEW SPAIN, 1500–1620

Source: Nicolas Sanchez-Albornoz, *The Population of Latin America*

Reading a Chart. What is the theme of this chart? What does it show about Native American population in New Spain? What is the reason for this change?

returned to school or work in the afternoon. After dinner, they were allowed to dance or sing.

Father Kino One man who did a great deal to spread the mission systems was Father Kino (KEE-noh). In 1687, Father Kino traveled on horseback into the borderlands. He converted many Native Americans. He also mapped the new lands for future use.

Kino was known as the "priest on horseback." He made over 40 trips into the borderlands and started 25 missions. He dreamed of a vast system of missions all across the borderlands. Leaders in Mexico City turned down his plan, saying it was too expensive.

However, 50 years after Kino's death, other missionaries continued his work. They built missions in today's Texas, New

The year is 1748. The Spanish mission at San Antonio struggles to survive. As armed Spanish guards watch them carefully, Native American groups are forced to build irrigation ditches for the fort at San Antonio.

Mexico, and Arizona. Later, they built missions along the coast of today's California.

The missions protected Native Americans from bad treatment by colonists. The missions gave Native Americans new skills to earn money. But the missions also took away Native American customs. To protect their cultures, many Native Americans refused to live in the missions.

Popé's Rebellion   One group of Native Americans who were unhappy with Spanish rule lived near Santa Fe. In 1675, the Spanish accused 47 Native American religious leaders of witchcraft. Four of the captives were hanged. The rest were whipped. One of these captives was named Popé (poh-PEH).

Popé swore revenge on the Spanish. Five years later, he led a rebellion. The Native Americans drove the Spanish out of Santa Fe and burned it. For the next 13 years, the Native Americans controlled the borderlands. But Native American peoples began fighting among themselves. In 1692, Spanish soldiers marched into New Mexico and retook Santa Fe.

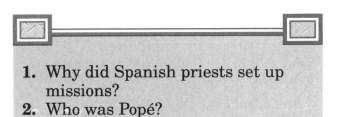

1. Why did Spanish priests set up missions?
2. Who was Popé?

4 A New Culture Develops.
How did a new Latino culture grow out of Spanish, African, and Native American roots?

The Spanish strictly controlled their colonies. However, they could not control the way of life that developed in them. For many years, there were few unmarried Spanish women in New Spain. Spanish families did not want their daughters to travel to such a faraway land. Because of this, many Spanish colonists married Native American or African American women. The culture of these children mixed European, Native American, and African traditions. Over the years, this mix became an important new culture. Today, in the United States, we call this culture **Latino**.

From three cultures Each group contributed to this culture. The Spanish contributed their language and their Roman Catholic religion. They also introduced new foods such as oranges, apples, pears, sugarcane, wheat, and rice. The Spanish brought to America useful animals such as sheep, pigs, cattle, and horses.

Native Americans made important contributions to this new culture. Europeans had never seen such foods as potatoes, tomatoes, corn, and chocolate. These quickly became important parts of their diets. Corn and potatoes were especially important. They were easier to grow and easier to store than other crops. During times of **famine,** when there is not enough food for people, these foods helped save millions of lives in Europe, Asia, and Africa.

People in the new culture started using Native American medicines to treat illness. They wore Native American loose-fitting clothes and slept under Native American blankets.

African contributions to the new culture were also great. Africans brought foods such as peanuts, yams, black-eyed peas, and bananas. Africans also brought their own music. This music had exciting rhythms that people enjoy so much today. African words became part of the Spanish language in the Americas. African religious beliefs became part of the culture.

By 1650, cities such as Mexico City and Santo Domingo were thriving centers. They had universities and bustling businesses. They had a rich trade with Europe.

Far to the north, an entirely different culture was developing. There were no large cities here. Instead, a few tiny settlements hugged the North American coast. These settlements were weak and tiny. Many of the settlers were not sure they would survive. In the next unit, we will look at these settlements and their struggle to survive.

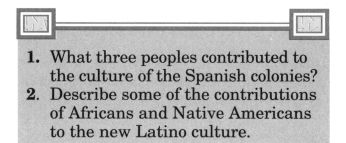

1. What three peoples contributed to the culture of the Spanish colonies?
2. Describe some of the contributions of Africans and Native Americans to the new Latino culture.

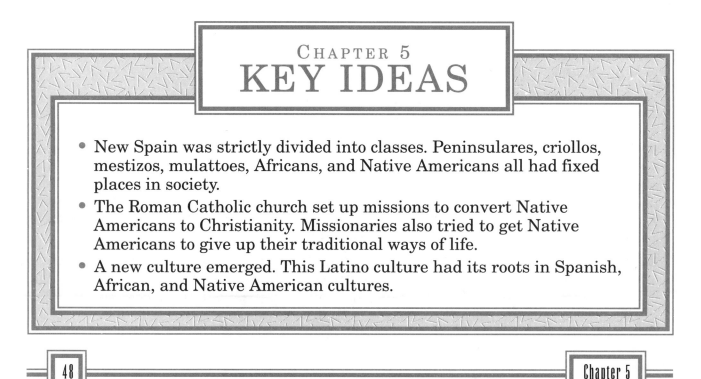

CHAPTER 5
KEY IDEAS

- New Spain was strictly divided into classes. Peninsulares, criollos, mestizos, mulattoes, Africans, and Native Americans all had fixed places in society.
- The Roman Catholic church set up missions to convert Native Americans to Christianity. Missionaries also tried to get Native Americans to give up their traditional ways of life.
- A new culture emerged. This Latino culture had its roots in Spanish, African, and Native American cultures.

REVIEWING CHAPTER 5

I. Reviewing Vocabulary

Match each word on the left with the correct definition on the right.

1. *peninsulare*   **a.** person born in America whose parents were born in Spain
2. mission   **b.** person of mixed Spanish and Native American background
3. *criollo*   **c.** person of mixed African and Spanish background
4. *mestizo*   **d.** community run by the Catholic church
5. mulatto   **e.** colonist born in Spain

II. Understanding the Chapter

1. Why do you think *criollos* and *mestizos* resented the *peninsulares* in New Spain?
2. Why did Coronado return to Mexico City disappointed?
3. How did the missions help Native Americans?
4. How did the missions harm Native Americans?
5. What did Africans contribute to Latino culture?

III. Building Skills: Summarizing

On a separate sheet of paper, write a few sentences that summarize each topic below.

1. The role of one class of people in New Spain: Africans, *criollos, mestizos,* mulattoes, Native Americans, *peninsulares.*
2. The ways that Father Kino helped expand New Spain.
3. The contributions of Spain to Latino culture.

IV. Writing About History

1. **What Would You Have Done?** Imagine you were a friend of Popé. He asks you to take part in the fight against the Spanish. Will you join him? Explain.
2. Create a drawing or painting that shows life in colonial Mexico City. Include in your artwork people from three different classes. Write a three-line caption for your picture.

V. Working Together

1. Form small groups of students. Have each group create artwork and writing (posters, short plays, other creative writing) that reflect the different experiences of people involved with Coronado's explorations.
2. **Past to Present** The mix of European, Native American, and African traditions became an important new culture in the Americas. Do you think that the culture of the United States is mixing and changing today? Discuss your opinion with a group. Give three reasons that support your position.

THE ENGLISH LAUNCH COLONIES IN NORTH AMERICA. (1497-1733)

Why did settlers from England first come to North America?

The first Africans were brought to the Virginia colony by a Dutch ship in 1619. The Africans amazed the English with their farming abilities.

Looking at Key Terms

- Virginia House of Burgesses
- Massachusetts Bay Colony
- Mayflower Compact

Looking at Key Words

- **indentured servant:** a person who agreed to work for a set time without pay in exchange for transportation to a new land
- **self-government:** the power to rule oneself
- **compact:** an agreement

STUDY

Use memory aids to remember important facts in a chapter. These may include rhymes, abbreviations, and other things that you can invent to help you remember.

HINT

Just five years after Columbus's first voyage, an English ship led by John Cabot reached North America. However, it would be another hundred years before the English began to settle in the Americas. What took so long?

England at the time was not as rich or powerful a country as Spain. However, in 1588, the English navy smashed a much larger Spanish fleet in a battle fought just off the coast of England. This battle ended Spain's control of the North Atlantic Ocean. It allowed England to begin planting colonies in North America.

1 The English Settle in Virginia.

Why was there a great conflict between democracy and slavery in the Southern colonies?

John White stood on the deck of his ship staring into the night. "Hello," he shouted toward shore. There was no answer. He shouted again into the night, but again there was no answer.

White was worried. Three years before, in 1587, he had founded a tiny settlement here at Roanoke (ROH-uh-nohk), an island just off the coast of present-day North Carolina. Soon, the settlement ran low on food. White was forced to sail back to England to get more food. Then England went to war, and he was not able to return. Now he had come back, but there was no one to greet him.

Vanished without a trace White tried not to show his concern. The next morning, he and his men rowed to shore. Something was clearly wrong. The settlement was abandoned. Houses were empty. What had happened? The only clues were carvings on two trees—"CRO" on one tree and "CROATOAN" on the other. Croatoan was the name of an island to the south.

White wanted to find the island right away, but a storm blew up. One ship was leaking badly, and the crew refused to sail. White took the other ship, but they could not find Croatoan island. They were forced to return to England. No other sign of the colony was ever found.

To this day, no one knows what became of the "lost colony" of Roanoke. Were the settlers killed? Did they starve to death? Their fate is still a mystery. It was an unlucky start for the English in North America.

Jamestown In 1606, a group of English merchants received permission from King James I to set up a colony in North America. These merchants hoped to find riches to rival the Aztec empire in Mexico.

In December 1606, three ships carrying about 100 men and boys sailed for a part of North America they called Virginia. The settlers arrived at the mouth of the Chesapeake Bay in April 1607. They traveled 60 miles (96 kilometers) upstream and began to build a village. They named it Jamestown in honor of King James I.

The settlers of Jamestown faced hard times. The village was built on swampy land that spread disease. Half the settlers were nobles who were not interested in planting crops. They only wanted to search for gold. They found no gold, and soon all their supplies were gone. Many of them died from starvation or sickness. By spring, one half of the settlers were dead.

Then Captain John Smith took over as leader. Smith was tough. He told the settlers they would have to work or go hungry. Things improved briefly. But then Smith hurt his leg badly and had to return to England.

With Smith gone, things again began to fall apart. The winter of 1609-1610 was so terrible that the settlers called it

"the starving time." Before the starving time, there were 500 people in Jamestown. When it ended, only 60 settlers were alive.

Raising tobacco   Conditions improved when a strict new governor took over. Soon, new settlers and supplies arrived from England. Then the big breakthrough came. John Rolfe discovered that tobacco could grow well in the Virginia soil. Tobacco had long been grown by Native Americans. After the Spanish conquest, it was introduced to Europe. Tobacco shipped to England made money for the settlers. Soon tobacco was Jamestown's main crop.

The beginning of slavery   As Jamestown grew, farmers needed more workers to grow tobacco. At first, these workers were **indentured servants**. Indentured servants were men and women who agreed to work for free for a set number of years. In return, they received a free trip to the colonies.

There weren't enough indentured servants to do all the work. The Native Americans refused to work for the settlers. In 1619, a Dutch ship brought 20 Africans to Virginia. These first Africans in the English colonies were indentured servants. Africans who came after them, however, were brought as slaves. Slavery would become an important part of life in the Southern colonies in the years ahead.

Self-government   Settlers held slaves, but they wanted more freedom for themselves. In 1619, the new governor of Virginia allowed the settlers to have some **self-government**. Self government is the power to rule oneself. The governor formed the **Virginia House of Burgesses.** This group was made up of English settlers elected by free white

John Smith, at the center of this picture, had a big problem. He was the leader of Jamestown. Yet many people in his colony would rather hunt for gold than make permanent houses or plant crops. How did Smith handle this problem?

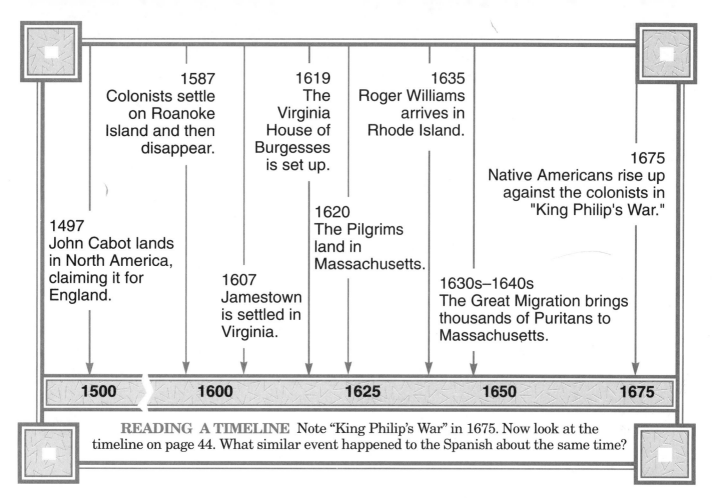

1497
John Cabot lands in North America, claiming it for England.

1587
Colonists settle on Roanoke Island and then disappear.

1607
Jamestown is settled in Virginia.

1619
The Virginia House of Burgesses is set up.

1620
The Pilgrims land in Massachusetts.

1635
Roger Williams arrives in Rhode Island.

1630s–1640s
The Great Migration brings thousands of Puritans to Massachusetts.

1675
Native Americans rise up against the colonists in "King Philip's War."

| 1500 | 1600 | 1625 | 1650 | 1675 |

READING A TIMELINE Note "King Philip's War" in 1675. Now look at the timeline on page 44. What similar event happened to the Spanish about the same time?

males in each town. This was an important first step toward self-government.

This first step toward self-government and the introduction of slavery happened in the same year, 1619. Freedom and slavery were two ideas that could not exist together. For the next 250 years, Americans would try to deal with the conflict between freedom and slavery.

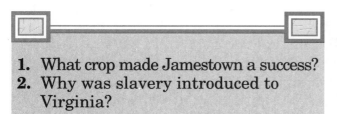

1. What crop made Jamestown a success?
2. Why was slavery introduced to Virginia?

2 English Settlers Come to New England.

Why did the Pilgrims and the Puritans come to live in New England?

Other English settlers were not like the settlers of Jamestown. The Pilgrims came to America for religious freedom. They were simple, religious people who were used to hard work. In the 1600s, England did not have religious freedom. The Pilgrims were forced to leave England because they refused to follow the Church of England. In 1620, the Pilgrims were given permission to settle in Virginia.

They sailed on a tiny ship, the *Mayflower*, on September 16, 1620. A storm blew the *Mayflower* north. Instead of landing in Virginia, they landed off the coast of present-day Massachusetts.

The Mayflower Compact Before leaving their ship, Pilgrim men signed an agreement to obey whatever laws their officers made. In the **Mayflower Compact**, Pilgrim men agreed to elect leaders and obey the laws that the leaders made. A **compact** is an agreement. Like the Virginia House of Burgesses, this compact was an important step toward democracy.

This famous painting show Puritans going to church on a snowy Sunday morning. The Puritans had a very strong faith in "pure" religion. This got them into trouble with the king of England. It led them to come to North America.

Help from Squanto   The Pilgrims built a sturdy settlement on a spot they called Plymouth (PLIHM-uhth). Still, they faced many problems. The winter was cold, and they had little food. Almost half of the people who had made the trip on the *Mayflower* died before spring. Others were too sick to do any work.

Then one March morning a tall Native American walked into the village. His name was Samoset. He surprised the colonists by speaking to them in English. He said he wanted to help the Pilgrims. A few days later, he returned with a Native American named Squanto (SKWAHN-toh). Squanto told the Pilgrims he had learned English when he was kidnapped by an English sea captain. Squanto shared his food with the starving Pilgrims. He also taught them Native American ways of growing corn, hunting for animals, and fishing.

With the help of Squanto and other Native Americans, the Pilgrims began to thrive. In the fall, they asked Squanto and about 90 other Native Americans to a feast. That first "Thanksgiving" was the start of the holiday that is held every year at the end of November.

Massachusetts Bay   Meanwhile, a second English settlement was being built near Plymouth. It was called the **Massachusetts Bay Colony.** This colony was founded by people who called themselves "Puritans." They took this name because they wanted to "purify" the Church of England. When the king punished them for criticizing the church, the Puritans decided to go to North America. There they set up a religious colony based on their beliefs. Salem, the Puritan's first town, was founded in 1628. Boston was begun in 1630. Many Puritans came to Massachusetts during the 1630s and 1640s. By 1643, there were 16,000 people living in the colony.

The Puritans believed strongly in education. In 1647, the Puritans passed one of the most important laws in American history. Towns with more than 50 families had to set up a school that was paid for by taxes. This was the beginning of the public school system in the United States.

The Puritans also believed strongly in democracy. In a democracy, people are free to govern themselves. However, the Puritans did not believe in religious freedom. All people who lived in their settlements had to follow Puritan rules. People who did not follow the rules were punished or driven out of the colony.

The founding of Rhode Island
One young minister who disagreed with the Puritans was Roger Williams. Williams felt that all people should be able to worship in their own way. He also disagreed with the Puritans' harsh treatment of Native Americans. When Williams spoke out against Puritan leaders, they drove him out of the colony.

Williams fled south with his followers in 1635. He made friends with the local Native Americans and decided to start a settlement. He called the settlement Providence. Providence was the first American town to guarantee religious freedom to all its people.

A few years later, Williams was joined by Anne Hutchinson. She had also been driven out of Massachusetts for her religious beliefs. Hutchinson and Williams founded a new colony called Rhode Island. Rhode Island welcomed colonists of every religion.

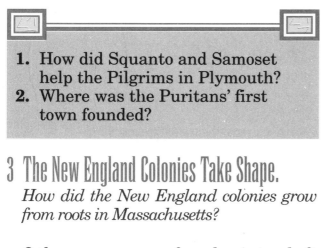

1. How did Squanto and Samoset help the Pilgrims in Plymouth?
2. Where was the Puritans' first town founded?

3 The New England Colonies Take Shape.

How did the New England colonies grow from roots in Massachusetts?

Other groups of colonists left Massachusetts to found new colonies. Some left to find religious freedom. Others left to find more or better land. A group followed Thomas Hooker south into the valley of the Connecticut River. Settlers later joined together to form the Connecticut colony. Another group headed north and settled New Hampshire. Others pushed into present-day Maine where they fished and carried on a busy trade. By 1650, settlers were pushing out all over the region they called "New England."

Wars with Native Americans
Wherever the colonists went, they found Native Americans already living there. A few of these Native Americans

Reading a Chart. When did the great growth of the African American population in the South first begin? Why did growth fall behind in the North?

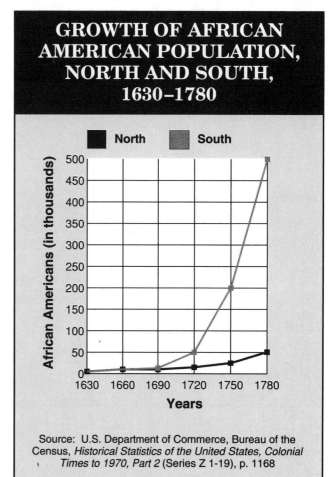

GROWTH OF AFRICAN AMERICAN POPULATION, NORTH AND SOUTH, 1630–1780

Source: U.S. Department of Commerce, Bureau of the Census, *Historical Statistics of the United States, Colonial Times to 1970*, Part 2 (Series Z 1-19), p. 1168

became Christians. However, most did not want to convert. They found themselves being pushed off their land. As New England grew, so did tensions.

In 1675, the Native American leader Metacom (MEH-tuh-kahm) launched a war to regain lost lands. Metacom, called King Philip by the settlers, united many Native American groups to fight against the settlers. The war, which they called King Philip's War, lasted three years. Both sides slaughtered their enemies. In the end, Metacom was defeated and killed. Thousands of other Native Americans were also killed. Many who survived were pushed west or north into Canada. Native Americans would no longer block the growth of the New England colonies.

By 1700, there were four British colonies in New England. They were Massachusetts, Connecticut, Rhode Island, and New Hampshire. Maine was part of Massachusetts. Vermont was part of New York.

The growth of democracy All over New England, settlers were trying to tame their environment. They set up towns, built churches, and opened shops. They grew crops in the rocky soil. By the early 1700s, New England was the center of shipbuilding and trade in the British colonies. New England boats reached ports all over the world. Foreign goods were unloaded on docks in Boston, Providence, and other towns.

Democracy took root in the New England colonies. Each New England town held regular meetings. Adult white men who held property in the towns were allowed to vote on town issues. These town meetings are still held in some New England towns today. When the time came for independence for the colonies, New England would be ready.

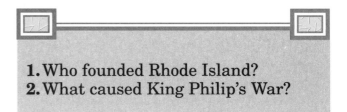

1. Who founded Rhode Island?
2. What caused King Philip's War?

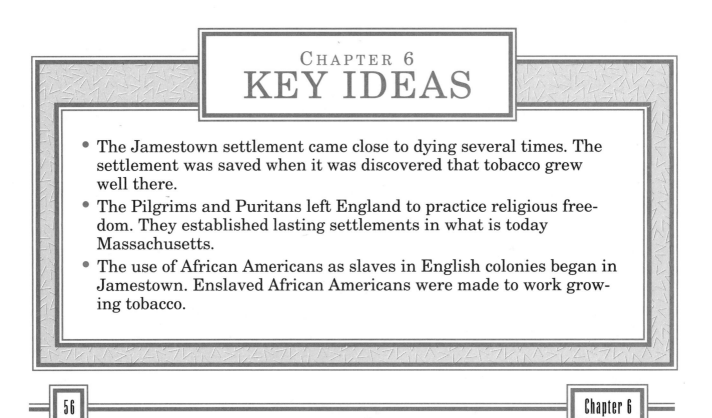

CHAPTER 6
KEY IDEAS

- The Jamestown settlement came close to dying several times. The settlement was saved when it was discovered that tobacco grew well there.
- The Pilgrims and Puritans left England to practice religious freedom. They established lasting settlements in what is today Massachusetts.
- The use of African Americans as slaves in English colonies began in Jamestown. Enslaved African Americans were made to work growing tobacco.

I. Reviewing Vocabulary

Match each word on the left with the correct definition on the right.

1. indentured servant
2. compact
3. Roanoke
4. Plymouth
5. democracy

a. the British "lost colony"
b. person who agreed to work for a number of years without pay in return for transportation
c. system where people govern themselves
d. colony settled in 1620
e. agreement between colonists to follow certain rules

II. Understanding the Chapter

1. Why did the Jamestown colony nearly fail?
2. How did a general assembly give Virginia colonists more rights?
3. Why did Roger Williams and Anne Hutchinson decide to found their own colony?
4. Why did Metacom launch a war on the English settlers?
5. How did democracy grow in New England?

III. Building Skills: Reading a Time Line

Study the time line on page 53. Then answer the following questions:

1. How long after John Cabot claimed North America for England was Roanoke colony established?
2. How long did the Great Migration last?
3. What is the first event showing the growth of democracy in England's colonies?

IV. Writing About History

1. **What Would You Have Done?** If you had been a Native American living at the time that the Pilgrims arrived, would you have helped the colonists? Why or why not?
2. Design a poster encouraging people to settle in Rhode Island. Use both pictures and words.

V. Working Together

1. Form six small groups: New Spain, Virginia, Massachusetts, Plymouth, Rhode Island, and Connecticut. Write down facts about people in your colony. Then have members from each group discuss: "How do you make a successful colony?"
2. **Past to Present** With a group, discuss how members of colonial assemblies were chosen. How are members of state legislatures chosen today? Why do you think there is a similarity?

PEOPLE FROM MANY LANDS SETTLE IN THE ENGLISH COLONIES. (1623-1752)

How were the Middle and Southern colonies different from the New England Colonies?

An old engraving shows the first women settlers landing in Jamestown. For women from London's slums, life on the American frontier was a test of courage.

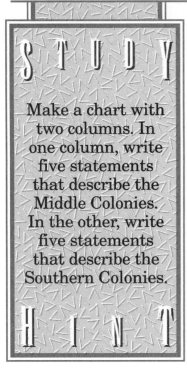

S T U D Y

Make a chart with two columns. In one column, write five statements that describe the Middle Colonies. In the other, write five statements that describe the Southern Colonies.

H I N T

Looking at Key Terms

- Middle Colonies • Southern Colonies • Quakers
- Act of Toleration

Looking at Key Words

- **synagogues:** Jewish places of worship
- **toleration:** allowing other people to practice their own beliefs and customs
- **debt:** money that people owe.
- **debtors:** people who cannot pay their bills.

- **cash crops:** crops raised for sale rather than for a farmer's personal use
- **indigo:** a plant that can be made into a blue dye
- **spirituals:** religious songs developed by enslaved African Americans

When a colonist from Maryland visited the colony of New York in 1744, he was surprised at how few people could speak English. "I heard nothing but Dutch spoken all the way," he complained. A few years later, Benjamin Franklin wrote how English-speaking and German-speaking colonists in Pennsylvania did not communicate well: "Few of the English settlers understand the German language. The two groups do not talk to each other."

The people who lived in the British colonies south of New England were very diverse. Their diversity affected the way they lived. Sometimes, it caused problems.

1 People Come to the Middle Colonies from All Over Europe.

Why did people from different countries in Europe come to the English colonies?

By 1733, there were 13 English colonies in North America. Only four of them were in New England. The rest were located south of New England in two regions, the **Middle Colonies** and the **Southern Colonies**.

The Middle Colonies were New York, Pennsylvania, Delaware, and New Jersey. The Middle Colonies had a milder climate than the New England Colonies. The soil was also more fertile.

The Dutch in New Netherlands In 1623, three years after the Pilgrims arrived, Dutch traders built a fort along the Hudson River. They called it Fort Orange. The next year, the Dutch settled New Amsterdam at the southern tip of Manhattan Island. The Dutch bought the island from the local Native Americans for a few dollars in trinkets.

The Dutch called their colony New Netherlands after their homeland.

Other people were welcome to settle in New Netherlands. In 1654, 23 Dutch Jews came to live in New Amsterdam. They were the first Jewish people to settle in North America. Other Jews would come to Rhode Island and other colonies and build places of worship called **synagogues**.

Settlers from Sweden In 1638, a small group of colonists from Sweden settled in present-day Delaware and southern New Jersey. They called their colony New Sweden. The Swedes built the first log cabins in North America. Many settlers who came after them copied these homes. The Swedes were few in number, and their colony was soon taken over by the Dutch.

The Dutch, however, would not stay in power much longer. In 1664, English warships easily seized New Amsterdam. The invasion was led by the Duke of York. After his victory, the duke renamed the colony New York. Fort Orange became Albany. Many Dutch people stayed on in New York, despite the new rulers.

The Duke of York then gave part of the land to two nobles who were his friends. The land was a reward for their loyalty and support. This land became today's state of New Jersey.

William Penn In 1681 and 1682, William Penn received grants of land from the English king. These lands now make up the states of Pennsylvania and Delaware. Penn came from a wealthy family. As a young man, he joined a religious group in England called the **Quakers** (KWAYK-uhrz). The Quakers believed in living simply and at peace with all peoples.

Penn set up the colony of Pennsylvania in 1681. Pennsylvania means "Penn's Woods" in Latin. He paid the Delaware, a Native American nation, for their land

and treated them fairly. Penn made a peace treaty with the Delaware that he kept for his lifetime. He enjoyed visiting them and joined in their sports. They said that Penn ran and jumped like a warrior.

Penn believed in **toleration** (tahl-uh-ray-shuhn). He allowed people to practice different religions in Pennsylvania. Many new settlers came to Pennsylvania from Germany and Switzerland. They became successful farmers and built their own thriving villages.

In 1688, a German Quaker group issued the first protest against slavery in North America: "Negroes are brought here against their will. Don't these poor people have as much right to fight for their freedom as you have to keep them as slaves?"

The protest did no good. Still, Africans in Pennsylvania managed gradually to win more rights than Africans in other colonies. By the middle of the 1700s, Pennsylvania had more free Africans than any other colony. These people and their descendants would lead the movement against slavery in the 1800s.

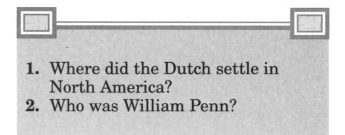

1. Where did the Dutch settle in North America?
2. Who was William Penn?

2 Other Settlers Come to the Southern Colonies.

What colonies developed in the South?

The four Southern Colonies were Maryland, Virginia, Carolina, and Georgia. They were settled mostly by people from England. You read about the founding of Virginia in Chapter 6.

William Penn signs a treaty with the Delaware in 1681. Penn paid for the land he used to start the colony of Pennsylvania. Throughout his life, he treated Native Americans fairly. After his death, things changed.

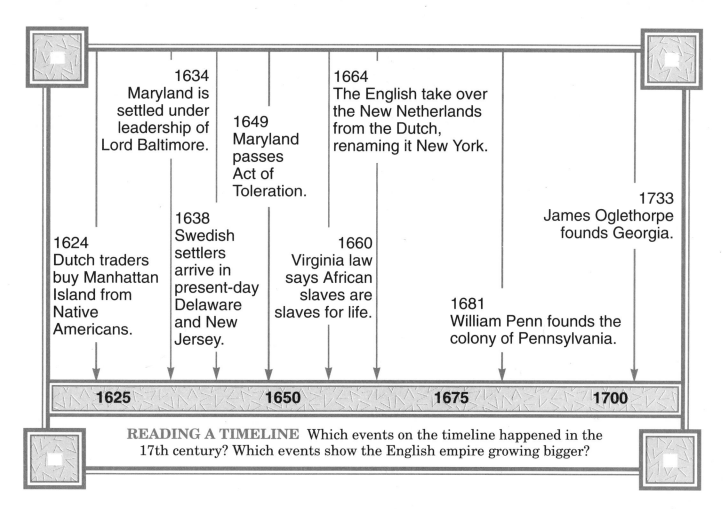

1624
Dutch traders buy Manhattan Island from Native Americans.

1634
Maryland is settled under leadership of Lord Baltimore.

1638
Swedish settlers arrive in present-day Delaware and New Jersey.

1649
Maryland passes Act of Toleration.

1660
Virginia law says African slaves are slaves for life.

1664
The English take over the New Netherlands from the Dutch, renaming it New York.

1681
William Penn founds the colony of Pennsylvania.

1733
James Oglethorpe founds Georgia.

| 1625 | 1650 | 1675 | 1700 |

READING A TIMELINE Which events on the timeline happened in the 17th century? Which events show the English empire growing bigger?

Maryland was founded by Lord Baltimore, a friend of the English king. Lord Baltimore was Catholic in a country that persecuted many Catholics. He wanted to set up a colony where Catholics could practice their religion freely. In 1649, Maryland passed an **Act of Toleration**. It provided religious freedom for all Christians.

Carolina and Georgia   Eight rich friends of King Charles II founded the colony of Carolina in 1663. The land was good for growing tobacco, rice, and cotton. The settlers built large plantations.

In 1712, Carolina split into two new colonies, North and South Carolina. North Carolina had a more varied economy. It also had a larger number of small farms. South Carolina had mainly large tobacco plantations. There, slavery and huge rice farms became a way of life.

Georgia, the last of the 13 colonies, was founded in 1733. Its founder was James Oglethorpe, a respected soldier. Oglethorpe wanted to help people in England who had been jailed for **debt** (DEHT). Debt is money that people owe. England had many **debtors** (DEHT-uhrz). Debtors are people who cannot pay their bills. In those days, debtors were thrown in jail until their families paid the debts.

Oglethorpe opened his colony of Georgia to debtors and other poor people in England. He wanted to make Georgia a colony where everyone was equal. He did not allow slavery in Georgia. He also did not allow the sale of rum.

Some of the white settlers didn't like Oglethorpe's rules. They wanted to have slavery and big farms. In 1752, Oglethorpe turned the colony over to the king. Later, slavery and large farms were allowed in Georgia.

THE THIRTEEN ENGLISH COLONIES

Colony	Date of English Settlement	Type of Colony
New England Colonies		
New Hampshire	1623	Royal
Massachusetts	1629	Royal
Rhode Island	1636	Self-governing charter
Connecticut	1636	Self-governing charter
Middle Colonies		
New York	1664	Royal
New Jersey	1664	Royal
Delaware	1664	Proprietary
Pennsylvania	1682	Proprietary
Southern Colonies		
Virginia	1607	Royal
Maryland	1634	Proprietary
North Carolina	1653	Royal
South Carolina	1670	Royal
Georgia	1733	Royal

Reading a Chart. Royal colonies were ruled directly by a king's officer. In a proprietary colony, the king gave land to a wealthy person, who paid the king and ran the colonies. Were the three earliest colonies royal or proprietary?

Growing slavery By the middle of the 1600s, there were many large plantations in the Southern Colonies. The planters more and more turned to Africans to meet their needs for labor. These Africans were not free workers but enslaved people. Less than a century after the first Africans came as free people to Virginia, most African people had lost their rights. By the 1700s, most Africans in the Southern Colonies lived according to the whip of white owners.

1. Why did slavery grow strong in the Southern Colonies?
2. What kind of people first settled in Georgia?

3 The Three Regions Are Different.

How were the sections of English colonies different from one another?

Over the years, the New England, Middle, and Southern colonies developed in different ways. The differences were mainly caused by geography.

Farming and business Farming in the New England Colonies was not easy. Winters were long and the growing season was short. The rocky soil was not good for farming. Most farmers could only grow enough to feed their families.

Because few people could make a living from farming in New England, many turned to other jobs. Shipbuilding became an important business. Some New Englanders became fishers and sailors. The fish that they caught could be dried and sold to other colonies and to England. New Englanders searched the seas for a valuable catch—whales. Whale blubber, or fat, became oil for lamps. Whalebone was made into buttons and other products. Whalebone stays helped undergarments to hold their shape.

In the Middle Colonies, the soil was more fertile, and the growing season was longer. Most farms were larger than those in New England. Some farms were large enough to hire farm laborers. The largest farms were worked by enslaved Africans. Most farms, however, were too small to use enslaved Africans.

In the Middle Colonies, farmers grew large crops of wheat, corn, and rye. Farms produced extra food, or **cash crops,** that could be sold to other colonies. Trade was also important in the Middle Colonies. Over time, manufacturing also became important.

The largest farms were in the Southern Colonies. Tobacco, rice, and **indigo** (IHN-dih-goh) were the main crops. Indigo is a plant that can be made into a blue dye. Slavery became very important to farming in the South.

Religion and education   The Puritans in New England had strict religious practices. As New England developed, religion continued to be very important.

The Puritans believed strongly in education. They created North America's first public schools. They also founded Harvard College in 1636 as a school for ministers. It was the first college in the British colonies.

Unlike New England, the Middle Colonies were home to people of many faiths and beliefs. People in the Middle Colonies were much more tolerant of different religions than people in New England were. In the Middle Colonies,

there were many more Catholics and small communities of Jews. Most schools in the Middle Colonies were run by churches. The Quakers believed strongly in education. As a result, their schools were very good. So were schools run by other religious groups.

The official church of the Southern Colonies was the Church of England. Enslaved African Americans were expected to attend the same church as the slave holders. The African slaves sat in the back and listened as white ministers defended slavery. Later, African Americans had their own ministers and started their own churches. They developed their own religious songs, called **spirituals**. Spirituals told about their love of God and their hopes for freedom.

Education developed slowly in the South. Even the children of plantation owners often did not go to school. Plantation children had tutors or were

Reading a Map. Name the 13 British colonies. What land form was the border on the west? Why did it keep the colonies from growing larger?

THE THIRTEEN BRITISH COLONIES

New England Colonies
Middle Colonies
Southern Colonies
State boundaries today

sent to Europe for school. Enslaved African Americans were not allowed to read or write. However, some learned anyway.

Cities   In the 1700s, nine out of ten English colonists lived on farms. However, towns were growing. People in the towns worked at making goods and products needed by the colonists. Other people sold these goods or shipped them to England for sale.

Out of this trade, some towns grew into large cities. The most important cities were Boston, in Massachusetts, and Philadelphia, in Pennsylvania. Next were New York City and Charleston in South Carolina.

Growing Democracy   Whites in the British colonies had more freedom than people in most European nations. In the colonies, a person from a poor white family could hope to rise to the middle class. Colonists also had political freedom. They brought to North America a tradition of governing themselves. White males who owned land could vote for members of government.

For many years, the British Parliament left the colonies largely free to govern themselves. The colonists came to think of themselves as free from British control. However, in the middle of the 1700s, Britain decided to take tighter control of its American colonies. This convinced many of the colonists that it was time to drive the British out of North America.

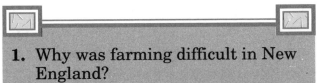

1. Why was farming difficult in New England?
2. Which section of the colonies had a strong tradition of education?

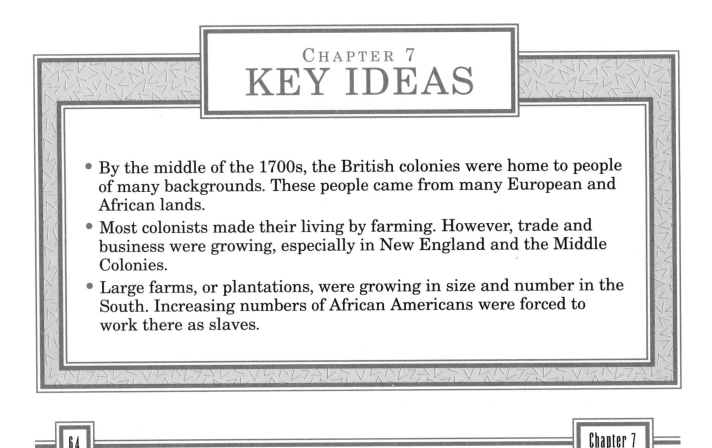

CHAPTER 7
KEY IDEAS

- By the middle of the 1700s, the British colonies were home to people of many backgrounds. These people came from many European and African lands.
- Most colonists made their living by farming. However, trade and business were growing, especially in New England and the Middle Colonies.
- Large farms, or plantations, were growing in size and number in the South. Increasing numbers of African Americans were forced to work there as slaves.

REVIEWING CHAPTER 7

I. Reviewing Vocabulary

Match each word on the left with the correct definition on the right.

1. debtors   **a.** a very large farm
2. plantation   **b.** people who cannot pay money owed
3. cash crops   **c.** Jewish place of worship
4. toleration   **d.** allowing people to practice their beliefs and customs
5. synagogue   **e.** crops raised for sale

II. Understanding the Chapter

1. Why were the Middle Colonies more tolerant than the New England Colonies?
2. Why did Lord Baltimore found Maryland?
3. Why did James Oglethorpe think that his colony of Georgia was a failure?
4. How was farming different in New England from the other colonies?
5. Which colonial region had more enslaved African Americans?

III. Building Skills: Making a Chart

On a separate piece of paper, make a chart that compares information about each group of colonies. To get started, copy the headings below.

	FARMING	**RELIGION/EDUCATION**	**GOODS TRADED AND CITIES**
New England			
Middle Colonies			
Southern Colonies			

IV. Writing About History

1. **What Would You Have Done?** You are a Dutch colonist living in New Amsterdam when the English take over. The English allow you to either return to the Netherlands or remain in New York. Explain your decision.
2. Imagine you are a Delaware Native American leader. Write a speech telling your people why they should get along with William Penn and his followers.

V. Working Together

1. Form five groups: the Dutch, the Swedes, the African Americans, the Quakers, and the Catholics. Research the way people in your group were treated in the British colonies. Then with writing, art, and maps create a mural about them.
2. **Past to Present** With a group, discuss why people came to the English colonies in the 1600s and 1700s. Why do people come to the United States today? Make a list of reasons that are similar and a list of reasons that are different.

THE PEOPLE OF THE 13 COLONIES BECOME AMERICANS. (1650-1750)

How was life in the American colonies different from life in Great Britain?

There wasn't much privacy in colonial homes. To keep their conversations private, young people used a long pole, called a "whispering rod."

Looking at Key Terms

- Middle Passage • Great Awakening • triangular trade
- freedom of the press

Looking at Key Words

- **midwife:** someone who helps with childbirth
- **assembly:** a group that makes laws
- **nationalism:** loyalty to or pride in one's country
- **racism:** separating people into different groups called races and believing some groups are superior

Eliza Lucas Pinckney was an important businesswoman in South Carolina. In 1750, she visited England where she met the king. She asked to be introduced to him as an "American." She felt different from the British. Eliza Lucas Pinckney was not alone. By 1750, many people in the 13 colonies thought of themselves as Americans.

1 Women Played an Important Role in the British Colonies.

What was life like for women in the colonies?

People began seeing themselves as Americans because colonial life was very different from life in Britain. One difference was the role of women. Colonial women had many responsibilities. They worked in a variety of jobs. They also had more legal rights than British women.

Always working   Early colonists worried about getting the basics of life – food, clothing, and shelter. Colonial women worked as hard as men to provide these. They were busy from sunup to long past sundown. About 90 percent of women lived on farms. They grew vegetable and herb gardens. Although men worked in the fields, women helped when needed. Women also helped care for farm animals.

Preparing food took a great deal of time. Women ground corn, wheat, and oats to flour and meal. They made butter and cheese. They salted meat so that it would not spoil. They pickled vegetables and dried fruit. Women cooked meals in an open fireplace. This could be dangerous. Women had to tend several fires at once to cook different dishes.

Colonial women were usually in charge of family expenses. They paid the bills and bought supplies. They made many of the things that their families needed. Women made candles for lighting their homes at night and soap for washing. They sewed the family clothing and made blankets, tablecloths, and other items.

Colonial businesswomen   Even with such heavy responsibilities, some colonial women also worked outside the home. They did almost every job done by men. Some were shopkeepers. Others ran taverns. Still others worked as blacksmiths, silversmiths, and woodworkers. Women worked as teachers, tailors, and printers. A few women even published newspapers.

Many widows took over their husbands' businesses. One such woman was Polly Spratt Provoost. Her husband died when she was only 26. Polly took over her husband's large store in New York City. She was very successful. People said almost every ship that docked in New York carried something for her store.

Another successful business woman was Eliza Lucas. When she was 17, her father put her in charge of his plantations in South Carolina. Eliza experimented with indigo seeds. Indigo is a plant that is used to make a blue dye. Eliza learned to grow plants that made an excellent dye. She shared her knowledge with other farmers. By the 1740s, indigo was a valuable crop in South Carolina.

Many skilled women earned money as **midwives.** A midwife is someone who helps with childbirth. The average colonial mother had between five and eight children. Childbirth was dangerous. The risk of a mother's dying while giving birth was as high as one chance in eight. The risk was less with a good midwife. One midwife, Mrs. Whitmore of Vermont, even traveled on snowshoes

It was unusual, but some colonial women worked as blacksmiths. Twins, Carine and Nellie Blair ran a blacksmith shop in Louisville, Kentucky.

to help her patients. She delivered over 2,000 babies by the time she was 87.

Legal rights Although they worked hard, women in colonial America had fewer rights than men. The law made men the heads of households. Men usually controlled all family property. Girls received less education than boys. As a result, most colonial women could not read or write.

Nevertheless, women in the colonies had more rights than British women. Colonial women had greater rights in their marriages. Married women had more control over their property. Laws were passed to protect widows. The laws made sure that widows got a fair share of their husbands' property.

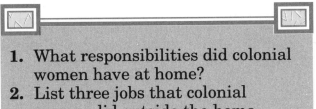

1. What responsibilities did colonial women have at home?
2. List three jobs that colonial women did outside the home.

2 African Americans Were Important in the British Colonies.

What important role did African Americans play in the life of the British colonies?

Mathias De Sousa landed at the British colony of Maryland in 1634. He was an African indentured servant. De Sousa completed his term of service. Then he built a successful trade with Native Americans. In 1641, colonists elected De Sousa to Maryland's **assembly.** An assembly is a group that makes laws. De Sousa was one of the first important free African Americans. However, most Africans in the colonies were not free. They were brought to the colonies as slaves.

Out of Africa Africans were enslaved in all the colonies. However, the Southern Colonies relied especially on the labor of enslaved Africans. Many of these people had been captured in war. Others were kidnapped in raids. Slave traders often marched captives many miles to the African coast. Many Africans died on these forced marches. When they finally arrived at the coast, captives were put in holding pens. There, they waited for shipment to the Americas.

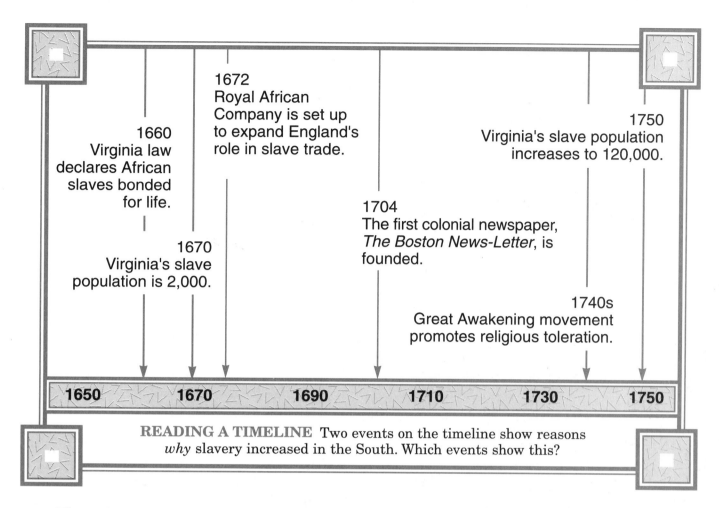

1660
Virginia law declares African slaves bonded for life.

1670
Virginia's slave population is 2,000.

1672
Royal African Company is set up to expand England's role in slave trade.

1704
The first colonial newspaper, *The Boston News-Letter*, is founded.

1740s
Great Awakening movement promotes religious toleration.

1750
Virginia's slave population increases to 120,000.

| 1650 | 1670 | 1690 | 1710 | 1730 | 1750 |

READING A TIMELINE Two events on the timeline show reasons *why* slavery increased in the South. Which events show this?

The trip across the Atlantic was even more horrifying. This journey became known as the **Middle Passage.** In order to make money, slave merchants packed as many people as they could into their ships. Hundreds were chained to the boat by the neck and legs. The ships had no sanitation. They smelled like death. Disease swept through the ships. Many ships arrived in the Americas with only half of the Africans alive.

Merchants tried to keep captives alive. They forced the Africans to exercise. Sailors brought captives on deck in shifts. Then sailors whipped them until they danced.

Africans did not submit easily to such horrors. Many preferred death. Some threw themselves overboard. Others refused food and medicine. They also fought back. There were at least 55 uprisings by Africans between 1699 and 1845. There were also hundreds of attempted uprisings.

Millions died during the Middle Passage. But approximately 10 million Africans survived the trip to the Americas. They faced a new life in chains.

Tightening the chains Colonies in the South passed laws to control slaves. Virginia passed a law in 1660 saying enslaved Africans were slaves for life. Another Virginia law said any child born to a slave mother also was a slave. This law passed slavery down from generation to generation. Other colonies followed Virginia's lead.

These laws increased the slave population in the British colonies. In 1670, Virginia had about 45,000 colonists and 2,000 enslaved Africans. By 1700, there were 16,000 enslaved Africans. By 1750, there were 120,000 people of African descent in Virginia. Almost all

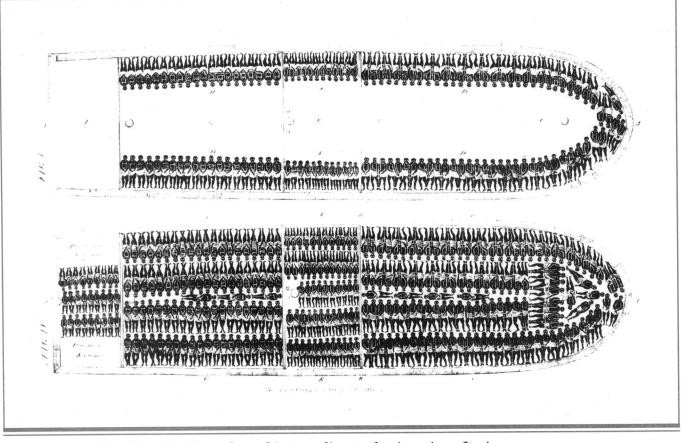

This is a real loading plan for a slave ship traveling to the Americas. It gives you an idea just how Africans were squeezed onto a slave ship so the owners could get the biggest profits from selling their human cargo.

of them were enslaved. They were about 40 percent of Virginia's population. They also made up 40 percent of all the Southern Colonies.

By the late 1600s, many English colonists began to call themselves *white* and Africans *black*. They thought of enslaved Africans as property, like cattle. They denied slaves their rights as human beings. This way of thinking is called **racism.** Racism is separating people into different groups called races and believing some groups are superior

Unjust treatment Most of the slaves in the Southern Colonies worked in the fields. Field work was backbreaking. Most Africans came from farming villages. But working as a slave was different. Owners

forced the slaves to work long hours. Many owners treated their slaves cruelly. Slaves were beaten, sometimes to death. Owners often spent as little as possible to feed, clothe, and shelter slaves.

Slaves had almost no rights. Owners could break up families by selling members off. Nothing horrified slaves more. Many remembered being torn from their mother's arms and sold.

Keeping their spirits alive Slaves fought against these terrible conditions. Some broke owners' tools. In a few cases, slaves set fire to farm buildings. Sometimes they attacked owners. Owners lived in constant fear of a slave rebellion.

Africans who were enslaved tried to keep their families together. Southern

Colonies did not consider slave marriages legal. However, men and women lived as husband and wife. They took pride in raising large families. Families often worked together. Slaves called one another "brother," "sister," "aunt," and "uncle" even when they were not relatives. This created a sense of family closeness.

Even on plantations, Africans kept alive their cultural traditions. They gave their children African names. They introduced African crops, such as yams. Food that owners gave them was made into African dishes. Craftpersons made drums and banjos similar to those used in West Africa. Africans also brought their dances to the Americas. The dances involved clapping, singing, and moving to complex rhythms.

These African traditions slipped into the culture of white colonists, too. Many enjoyed African food. African-based music was popular. In the mid-1700s, one British visitor was shocked to see white colonists in the South doing African-style dances.

In the North   There were far fewer slaves in the colonies to the North. Slaves were only 4 or 5 percent of the population. Northern farms were small. They could not be worked during the winter because of the cold climate. So it was not profitable to feed and clothe slaves all year round.

Laws also permitted slaves to win their freedom. Therefore, some African Americans in the colonies to the North were able to win their freedom. Later generations were born free. Paul Cuffe was born in 1759. Cuffe's father was a free African American. His mother was a Native American. Cuffe set up a successful shipping business. He used his money to help other people of African descent. Cuffe was one of a number of free African American business owners.

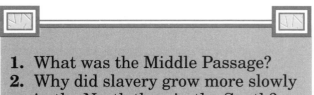

1. What was the Middle Passage?
2. Why did slavery grow more slowly in the North than in the South?

3 British Colonists Become Americans.

What led the colonists to think of themselves as Americans?

In the 1700s, a new feeling spread through the American colonies. This feeling is called **nationalism,** or loyalty to one's own country. Many colonists felt more loyalty to the

No picture of Paul Cuffe exists, just this silhouette. Cuffe was born poor, but gained great wealth. He owned many ships and warehouses.

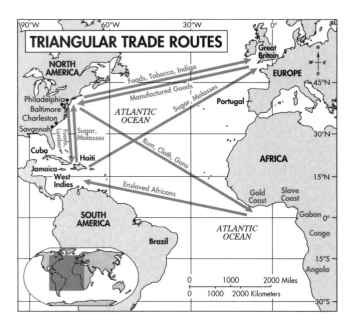

TRIANGULAR TRADE ROUTES

Reading a Map. What was the "triangular trade"? What was shipped from Africa to the Americas? What went from the British colonies to Britain?

colonies than to Britain. They felt closer to settlers of other colonies than to the British. Colonists started calling themselves Americans.

Religious diversity Each year, the colonies became less like Britain. Many immigrants came from other European countries. They brought with them new religions. Lutheran, Baptist, Presbyterian, and other Protestant churches sprang up in the colonies. Catholics and Jews had their places of worship. The Quakers became a large and important group in the colonies.

Different religious groups increased religious toleration. A movement started called the **Great Awakening.** This movement swept the colonies in the 1740s. It led people to demand a greater voice in running their churches. People spoke more about human rights. Some began to tolerate different ideas.

Self-government Other differences divided the colonists from the British. Colonists were used to making their own decisions. They ran their towns and villages. They elected local leaders. Most colonies had elected assemblies.

These assemblies increased their power over time. At first, laws were made by the colonial governors. The assemblies only approved laws. Later, assemblies won the power to pass their own laws. Colonists did not want the British government to tell them what to do.

Growing trade Colonists also did not want to obey British trade laws. These laws forced them to trade only with Britain. The colonists thought this was unfair. So by the 1700s, colonial merchants traded with many parts of the world.

Ships from New England sold fish and lumber in the West Indies and returned with sugar and molasses. Often, merchants bought molasses on French or Dutch islands. This was illegal. But it was cheaper there than on British islands.

The trade routes were called the **triangular** (try-ANG-gyoo-luhr) **trade.** These routes formed a triangle between Europe, the Americas, and Africa. Ships sailed from New England to Africa. They exchanged rum, cloth, and guns for slaves. The slaves were taken to the West Indies and the Southern Colonies.

Colonists also traded with each other. Ships sailed up and down the Atlantic coast. New England merchants traded with Southern plantations. This trade changed the colonies. They were no longer completely tied to Britain.

Educating the people The spread of education also made Americans different. Massachusetts took the lead. It ordered towns to set up public schools. Other colonies followed. By the mid-1700s, most adult males in New England could read and write. In the Middle Colonies, many churches founded schools. Education spread more slowly in the Southern Colonies. However, by about 1750, over half of the Southern free population could read and write.

Colonists read all kinds of materials. Newspapers were very popular. At first, all newspapers were published in Britain. In 1704, the *Boston News-Letter*, the first colonial newspaper, was founded. By 1765, there were 25 newspapers published in the colonies. Every colony, except New Jersey and Delaware, had at least one. These newspapers had an American point of view. Sometimes, they criticized colonial governments.

This could cause big trouble for newspaper publishers. John Peter Zenger published the *New York Weekly Journal*. He criticized New York's governor. The governor threw him in jail. In 1735, Zenger was put on trial. After a strong defense by his lawyer, Andrew Hamilton, Zenger was found innocent. The case helped set up a tradition of **freedom of the press.** This means that publishers are free from government control. Zenger's victory encouraged other newspaper publishers to print the truth as they saw it.

Differences widen   Between 1650 and 1750, Britain's 13 colonies changed a great deal. Population jumped from about 70,000 to over 1.5 million. By 1750, most colonists had been born in North America. Nationalism kept growing. It soon put the colonies on the road to independence.

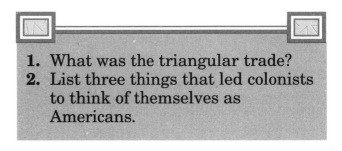

1. What was the triangular trade?
2. List three things that led colonists to think of themselves as Americans.

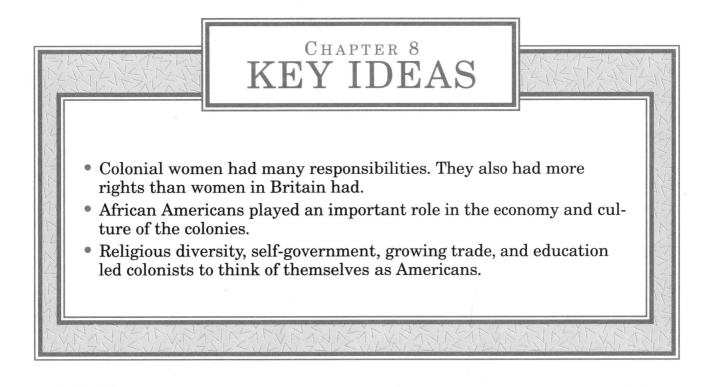

CHAPTER 8
KEY IDEAS

- Colonial women had many responsibilities. They also had more rights than women in Britain had.
- African Americans played an important role in the economy and culture of the colonies.
- Religious diversity, self-government, growing trade, and education led colonists to think of themselves as Americans.

REVIEWING CHAPTER 8

I. Reviewing Vocabulary

Match each word on the left with the correct definition on the right.

1. midwife
2. racism
3. assembly
4. Middle Passage
5. nationalism

a. a group that makes laws
b. belief that one group is superior to others, and the unjust treatment based on such beliefs
c. the journey across the Atlantic from Africa to the Americas in the slave trade
d. loyalty to or pride in one's country
e. someone who helps with childbirth

II. Understanding the Chapter

1. What kind of work did colonial women do?
2. What legal rights did colonial women have?
3. How did African Americans resist slavery?
4. Why were there fewer slaves in the colonies to the North?
5. Why did feelings of nationalism grow in the American colonies?

III. Building Skills: Reading a Map

1. Look at the triangular trade map on page 72. What did North American colonies ship to Europe?
2. List five regions in Africa that exported slaves.

IV. Writing About History

1. **What Would You Have Done?** If you published a colonial newspaper, would you have written an article supporting John Peter Zenger? Explain.
2. Imagine you are an enslaved African who survived the Middle Passage. Write a short story about the experience that you might tell your children.

V. Working Together

1. Meet in small groups. Your group should imagine the daily life of a colonist. You could pick a free African American business owner, a midwife, or a member of a colonial assembly. Then write a short skit about the person you selected.
2. **Past to Present** With a group, discuss the role of women in the 13 colonies. Then talk about the role of women today. As a group, list at least three similarities and three differences between colonial women and women today.

The French Set Up Colonies in North America. (1590-1763)

*How did France build and then lose
a vast empire in North America?*

LaSalle's trip down the Mississippi in 1682 was the first contact between many Native Americans and Europeans. Here he visits the Natchez people.

Looking at Key Terms
- French and Indian War

Looking at Key Words
- **Jesuit:** a member of a special Catholic order
- **coureurs de bois:** French fur traders
- **habitant:** a small farmer in New France

- **ally:** a person or group of persons who joins with others for a common purpose

STUDY

Make a chart listing each French explorer in one column and the territories he explored in the other.

HINT

Jacques Cartier (kahr-TYAY) sailed to explore North America in 1533. The king of France had ordered him to find gold, riches, and a short sea route to Asia. Between 1533 and 1542, Cartier made several trips. However, he did not find a route to Asia. However, his voyages were not in vain. Cartier discovered the St. Lawrence River and claimed land for France in what is today Canada. He called this territory New France. New France would soon grow to be a huge French empire in North America.

1 France Claims Land in the Americas.

How did the French explore North America?

After Cartier failed to find gold, riches, and a route to Asia, France lost

French traders, like this one, traded weapons for furs. They traveled deep into North America.

interest in North America for almost 50 years. Then, in the late 1500s and early 1600s, King Henry IV of France began to worry. England and other European nations were also exploring North America. The king of France wanted to protect his country's land claims in North America. He wanted more colonists to come to New France. He believed that only by settling the area would it remain French.

Henry IV made a deal with French merchants. He allowed them to trade for furs with Native Americans in New France. By doing this the merchants would be able to sell the furs in Europe for a huge profit. However, the French king said the merchants could take part in the fur trade only if they brought colonists to America. The merchants agreed and began forming French fur-trading companies.

First settlements Samuel de Champlain (sham-PLAYN), a geographer, worked for one such fur-trading company. In 1605, Champlain founded a trading post at Port Royal in Nova Scotia. It was the first permanent French settlement in North America.

In 1608, Champlain continued to explore the St. Lawrence River. At the point where the river narrowed, he had to stop. There he founded a fur trading fort called Quebec (kwih-BEHK). Quebec became the center of New France.

Champlain explored the territory around Quebec. He wanted to find Native Americans from whom he could buy furs. He met the Huron, a powerful Native American nation living near Quebec. Champlain made peace treaties with these people. The Huron sold their valuable furs to his company. As he traveled in Huron territory, Champlain studied the way of life of these Native Americans. Champlain described the Huron and their culture in his book *The Voyages*.

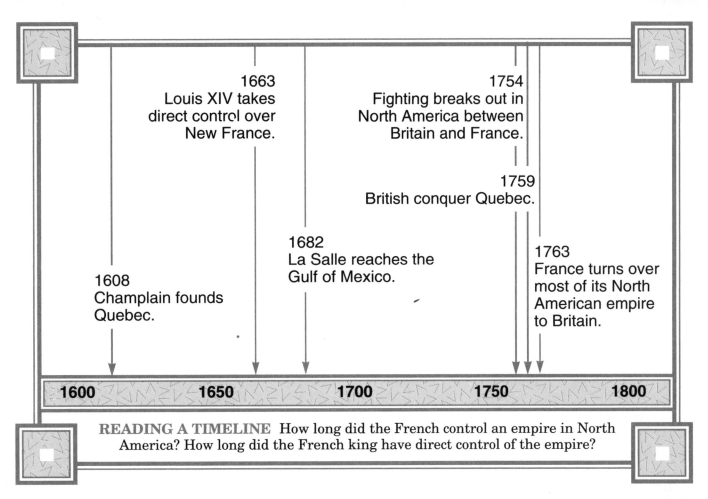

1663
Louis XIV takes direct control over New France.

1754
Fighting breaks out in North America between Britain and France.

1759
British conquer Quebec.

1682
La Salle reaches the Gulf of Mexico.

1608
Champlain founds Quebec.

1763
France turns over most of its North American empire to Britain.

| 1600 | 1650 | 1700 | 1750 | 1800 |

READING A TIMELINE How long did the French control an empire in North America? How long did the French king have direct control of the empire?

Champlain wanted to strengthen the friendship between the French and Huron nations. So he joined them in a battle against their enemies, the Iroquois (IHR-uh-kwoi). This began serious trouble for the French. The Iroquois nation was very powerful. They kept the French from expanding their settlements for many years.

Farther inland In 1663, King Louis XIV (Fourteenth) took direct control of settlements in New France. He sent troops to fight the Iroquois. The Catholic church also sent **Jesuit** (JEHZH-oo-iht) missionaries to New France. Jesuits were members of a special Catholic order. These missionaries tried to convert the Huron and other Native Americans. From the Native Americans, the missionaries learned of a large river to the west that might lead to the Pacific Ocean. The French hoped it was a sea route to Asia.

Louis Joliet (zhoh-lee-AY) and Father Jacques Marquette (mahr-KEHT) set off to find the large river. Joliet was an experienced fur trader. Father Marquette was a Jesuit priest. In 1673, they reached the river. They called it the Mississippi. At first, the river flowed west, but then it turned south. Joliet and Marquette traveled as far south as Arkansas. They turned back when they were sure that the Mississippi did not flow into the Pacific Ocean.

Marquette and Joliet brought back valuable information about the territory they explored. The French then built trading forts along the Mississippi. They also built forts near other rivers in the region.

South to the Gulf of Mexico Another French explorer continued where Joliet and Marquette had stopped. Robert Cavalier de La Salle (lah SAHL), aided by Native American guides, traveled farther down the

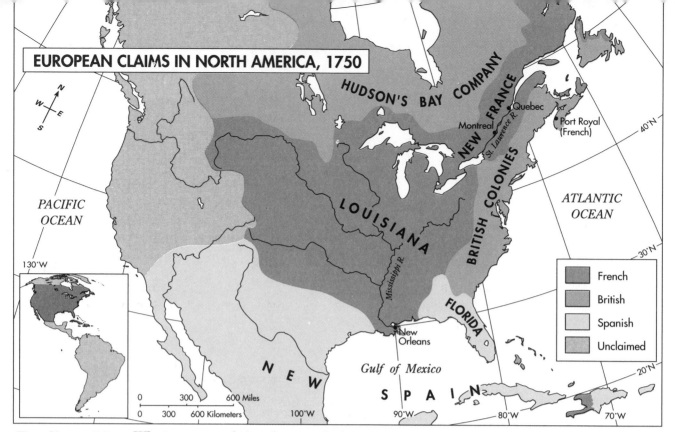

EUROPEAN CLAIMS IN NORTH AMERICA, 1750

PACIFIC OCEAN

HUDSON'S BAY COMPANY

NEW FRANCE

Quebec

Montreal

St. Lawrence R.

Port Royal (French)

BRITISH COLONIES

ATLANTIC OCEAN

LOUISIANA

Mississippi R.

FLORIDA

New Orleans

N E W   S P A I N

Gulf of Mexico

French
British
Spanish
Unclaimed

Reading a Map. What country claimed most of what is today the southern United States? What country claimed the Mississippi River valley?

Mississippi River. In 1682, he reached the Gulf of Mexico. La Salle called this entire region Louisiana, after King Louis XIV, and claimed it for France.

In 1718, the French built a city near the Gulf. They named it New Orleans. It became a major French trading center. New Orleans grew into one of the largest cities in the Americas.

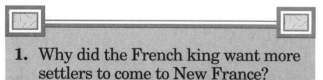

1. Why did the French king want more settlers to come to New France?
2. What river did the French follow to the Gulf of Mexico?

2 New France Depends on the Fur Trade.

Why was the fur trade more important than agriculture to New France?

A group of young French women came ashore in New France in the 1660s. In France, some had been homeless. Others were from large families that could not afford to care for them. They were called the "king's daughters" because King Louis XIV of France paid their fare across the Atlantic Ocean. They were met by crowds of men in New France. Within a few weeks, all the young women were married. The French king gave each couple a wedding present. They received a few farm animals, salted meat, and some money. Over the years, 1,000 of these young women came to New France.

Fur traders The king sponsored the "king's daughters" project because he wanted to encourage settlement in New France. The first colonists in New France had been men. They hoped to make money in the fur trade. Almost everyone in New France had something to do with the fur trade.

French fur traders were called **coureurs de bois** (koo-ROOR duh BWAH). This means "runners of the forest." The coureurs de bois traveled miles to trade with Native Americans. They used snowshoes and dog sleds to move furs through New France's snowy forests. Each spring, when the ice in the rivers melted, the traders brought furs in canoes to the trading posts.

However, the fur trade did not increase New France's population enough. By the 1660s, there were only 2,500 settlers in New France.

The French king tried many ways to increase New France's population. Sending the "king's daughters" to New France was one way. The French government also gave rewards to couples who had large families. It gave money to men who married by age 20 and to girls who married by age 16. Men who refused to marry were punished with heavy fines. By the 1680s, the French population of New France had reached 10,000.

Farming the land   The government of New France also tried to get colonists to become farmers. The government divided the land along the St. Lawrence River into large pieces. These pieces were given to nobles or retired army officers. These large landowners got colonists to farm smaller pieces of land.

These farmers of smaller pieces of land were called **habitants** (HAHB-ih-tuhntz). Farming in New France was not easy. The cold climate made farming difficult. New France's thick forests made it hard for habitants to clear the land. However, habitants raised farm animals and crops. These crops were sent to markets at trading posts.

The number of farmers slowly increased. However, their crops only supplied their families and the fur traders. The crops were not enough to send back to Europe. Therefore, the fur trade remained the colony's main source of money.

Government in New France

There was much less self-government in New France than in the British colonies. The top-ranking official in New France was the governor, appointed by the king.

The Catholic church played an important role in governing New France. It was the only religion in the colony. The bishop of the church ranked just below the governor in New France. The church also owned huge amounts of land. Its priests and nuns ran hospitals and schools. Missionaries also tried to convert the Native Americans.

Relations with Native Americans

The French usually got along well with Native Americans. The French did not threaten the Native Americans' way of life. Coureurs de bois lived among Native Americans and learned their languages. Some married Native American women.

The French also did not destroy the places where Native Americans hunted. Since fur-bearing animals lived in the forests, fur traders needed the forests. In New France, farms did not pay as well as the fur trade. So the French did not cut down much forest to make farms.

Another reason that the French got along with Native Americans was that the population of New France stayed small. New France had far fewer colonists than the British colonies did. By 1759, the population of New France was still only 80,000. There were more than 1 million colonists in the British colonies. Native Americans did not fear that the French would take their lands.

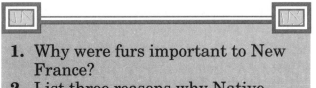

1. Why were furs important to New France?
2. List three reasons why Native Americans and the French got along.

Young George Washington led a mixed force of colonists and Native Americans in his invasion of the Ohio River valley during the French and Indian War. Here, before battle, he reads a prayer to the troops.

3 The British and the French Wage a War.

How did the British double the size of their territory in North America?

Great Britain and France were rivals. By the middle of the 1700s, they were the two most powerful nations in Europe. They fought each other in both Europe and North America. The name of the war in North America was called the **French and Indian War.** It began in 1754.

Taking sides The French found **allies** in their struggles against the British. An ally is a person or group of persons who joins with others for a common purpose. Many Native Americans worried about the thousands of farmers in the British colonies. Native Americans feared British colonists

would take their land. So the Native Americans sided with the French.

One important exception was the powerful Iroquois nation. The Iroquois did not forgive the French for joining the Huron in battles against them. In 1754, the British asked the Iroquois to side with them. At first, the Iroquois refused. They pointed out that the French and British were fighting over Iroquois land. However, later in the war, the Iroquois supported the British.

French successes The French goal in North America was to control the Ohio Valley. British fur traders had come to the region. The French intended to drive the British out.

The French had an important fort in the Ohio Valley. It was called Fort Duquesne (doo-KAYN). In 1754, a British force of 200 colonists marched into the valley. They were led by a 22-year-old colonel, George Washington. The British force was attacked by about 800 French and 400 Native Americans. The British colonists were badly outnumbered. Many were killed or wounded. George Washington had no choice but to surrender. The French allowed Washington and his troops to return home.

The French won a bigger victory in 1755. A large British force led by General Edward Braddock marched toward Fort Duquesne. George Washington warned him that the French and Native Americans would hide behind trees and attack in the forest. But Braddock did not listen. He expected the French to fight out in the open because that was how armies fought in Europe.

The French did exactly as Washington predicted. They destroyed Braddock's army. Braddock was killed in battle. Washington brought the survivors home. The French continued to win battles for the next two years.

British victory   In 1756, the British king named William Pitt as head of Britain's government. Pitt improved the army. The British began to win the war in North America. In 1759, the British conquered Quebec. Although there was fighting for another year, the British had won the war.

The British and French signed a peace treaty in 1763. The French gave up most of their North American territory. Spain, France's ally in the war, received French territory west of the Mississippi River. The British took all the territory between the 13 British colonies and the Mississippi. Only New Orleans remained out of British hands. This meant that British colonists could move westward.

The British also took control of Canada. However, large parts of what was once New France kept French traditions. French culture is still strong in those regions today.

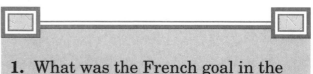

1. What was the French goal in the French and Indian War?
2. What was the result of this war?

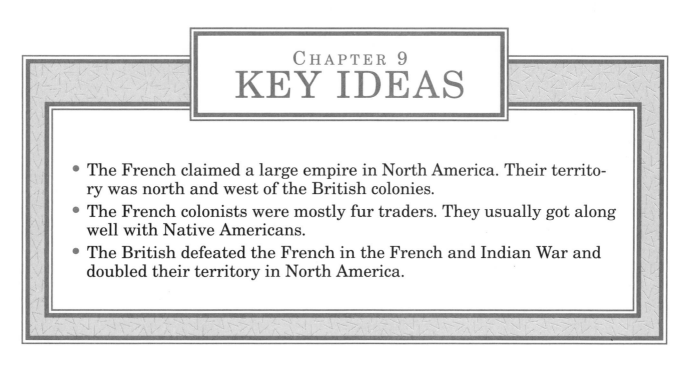

CHAPTER 9
KEY IDEAS

- The French claimed a large empire in North America. Their territory was north and west of the British colonies.
- The French colonists were mostly fur traders. They usually got along well with Native Americans.
- The British defeated the French in the French and Indian War and doubled their territory in North America.

REVIEWING CHAPTER 9

I. Reviewing Vocabulary

Match each word on the left with the correct definition on the right.

1. Jesuit

2. coureurs de bois

3. habitant

4. ally

5. French and Indian War

a. a person or group of persons who joins with others for a common purpose

b. a member of a special Catholic order

c. French fur traders

d. conflict between French and British in North America

e. a small farmer in New France

II. Understanding the Chapter

1. What were French explorers looking for in North America?

2. What source of money did New France depend on?

3. What did the French government do to increase the population of New France?

4. Why did the French usually get along with Native Americans?

5. What territory did the British gain from France as a result of the French and Indian War?

III. Building Skills: Reading a Map

1. Look at the map on page 78. Which river flows through New Orleans?

2. What area of North America did the French claim?

IV. Writing About History

1. **What Would You Have Done?** If you had been a Huron chief, would you have agreed to be an ally of the French? Explain.

2. Write a short skit about George Washington's warning to General Braddock.

V. Working Together

1. Form small groups of students. Choose an important event that occurred in New France between 1590 and 1763. For example, you could choose the explorations of La Salle or Louis XIV's "king's daughters" project. Then draw a mural that depicts the event you have chosen.

2. **Past to Present** With a group, discuss how your lives would be different if France had won the French and Indian War. Then, individually write a paragraph that describes the differences.

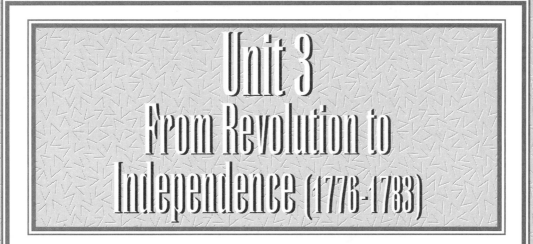

Unit 3
From Revolution to Independence (1776-1783)

Chapters

THE BRITISH TIGHTEN THEIR CONTROL. (1763-1766)

Why did hard feelings develop between colonists and the British?

Pontiac, a chief of the Ottawa nation, organized the Native Americans of the Ohio valley in a last-ditch war against the settlers moving west.

STUDY

As you read the chapter, make a list of the different British laws. Then write down how the colonists responded to each of them.

HINT

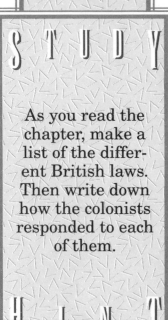

Looking at Key Terms

- Pontiac's War • Proclamation of 1763 • Navigation Acts
- Sugar Act • Parliament • Stamp Act • Stamp Act Congress
- Sons of Liberty

Looking at Key Words

- **import:** to bring goods into a country in order to sell them
- **smuggle:** to bring goods into a country illegally
- **representative:** an official elected to act and speak for others

- **boycott:** to refuse to buy, sell, or use goods from a particular person, business, or country
- **repeal:** to cancel

West of the 13 colonies lay a rich land. The soil was fertile. Beautiful forests stretched for miles. Great rivers cut through the forests. It seemed a perfect place for colonists to settle. They had only to cross the Appalachian Mountains. Then they could spread west as far as the Mississippi River.

1 The British Stop Colonists from Moving Beyond the Appalachians.

Why did the British forbid colonists to move westward?

After the British victory in the French and Indian War, the region west of the Appalachian Mountains seemed open for settlement. French control had ended. Settlers from the 13 colonies expected that they could move west. Some planned to hunt for furs. Others wanted to become farmers there. However, events did not go as the settlers had expected.

Pontiac's War   Native Americans living west of the Appalachians distrusted the British. Many had been allies of the French. After the war, the British raised the prices of goods traded to Native Americans. Native Americans felt cheated. They also feared that the British colonists would take their lands. The French had agreed that Native Americans owned the land. The British did not.

Many British colonists began to settle in the Ohio Valley. They cut down forests to make farms. Settlers and Native Americans clashed several times. Some Native Americans wanted to fight back.

By 1763, these Native Americans found a leader. He was Pontiac, an Ottawa chief. He spoke out against the settlers. Pontiac was skilled at winning allies. Soon, the Chippewa, Delaware, Shawnee, Miami, and Huron joined Pontiac.

In May 1763, **Pontiac's War** began. At first, the Native Americans were successful. Eight British forts fell within weeks. Pontiac's victories threatened settlements in New York, Pennsylvania, Virginia, and Maryland.

However, Pontiac ran into trouble. His forces failed to capture Detroit, the most important British fort in the region. Some of Pontiac's allies stopped fighting. By December, the fighting was over. More than 4,000 Native Americans and settlers had died.

Closing the frontier   Pontiac's War worried the British. They had just fought an expensive war with France. If colonists moved westward, it might cause more wars with Native Americans. The British did not want any more costly wars.

There was another reason that the British did not want settlers west of the Appalachians. These settlers would be too far away for the British to control. The settlers might start making all sorts of products. These products could compete with goods made in Britain.

To control settlement, the British government issued the **Proclamation of 1763.** A proclamation is an official announcement. It said that colonists could not settle on land between the Appalachians and the Mississippi River. It also said that Native Americans owned the land that they lived on.

Angry responses   The Proclamation of 1763 made colonists furious. Several colonies had claimed land west of the Appalachians. Some people already owned land there. They expected to sell it to small farmers at a profit. The Proclamation made this impossible.

Settlers who planned to go west were the angriest of all. Many just ignored

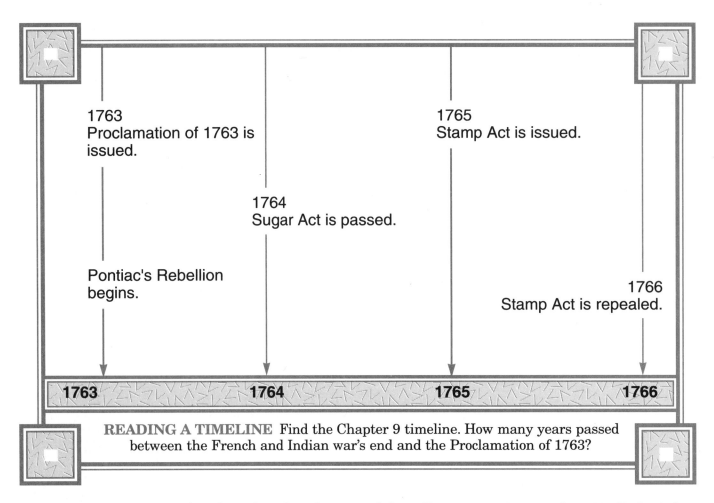

1763
Proclamation of 1763 is issued.

1764
Sugar Act is passed.

1765
Stamp Act is issued.

Pontiac's Rebellion begins.

1766
Stamp Act is repealed.

| 1763 | 1764 | 1765 | 1766 |

READING A TIMELINE Find the Chapter 9 timeline. How many years passed between the French and Indian war's end and the Proclamation of 1763?

the Proclamation. Settlers by the thousands moved west from Virginia and North Carolina. Towns grew up along the Tennessee and Kentucky rivers. No proclamation could stop the westward movement of American colonists.

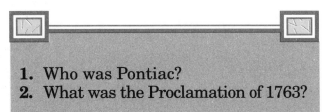

1. Who was Pontiac?
2. What was the Proclamation of 1763?

2 Britain Makes the Colonists Pay New Taxes.

How did the colonists respond to new taxes?

Great Britain had many problems after its victory over France. The French and Indian War was very expensive and left Britain with huge debts. Between 1754 and 1763, Britain's debt doubled.

Money problems The British government had to pay these debts. However, it could not keep raising taxes in Britain. Taxes in Britain were already very high and taxpayers were complaining. After the war was over, they demanded lower taxes.

Many people in Britain wanted the 13 colonies to pay their fair share. They believed that the colonies had not helped enough during the French and Indian War. They argued that the colonies had gained the most from the war. However, each colony sent money and troops only when it was in danger. British soldiers fought to protect *all* the colonies. But Britain paid most of the costs of the war.

British taxpayers also thought that the colonies should cover their own costs. The colonies had been expensive to govern.

By the mid-1700s, those costs were rising. The British had to organize the land that they had won from the French. Conflicts between settlers and Native Americans continued. More soldiers were needed to defend these territories. They had to be paid. Pontiac's War was also costly. The British government was spending more and more money on its American colonies.

A hated solution   King George III of Britain wanted to keep tight control over the 13 colonies. In 1763, he named a new leader of the British government. This leader was George Grenville, an expert on money matters.

Grenville disliked the American colonists. He said that they behaved like spoiled children. George III and Grenville believed that the colonists should pay more of their own expenses. They decided to enforce some laws that had long existed.

These laws were the **Navigation Acts.** The Navigation Acts had been passed in the 1660s to control trade. They required the colonists to sell only to Britain such products as cotton, sugar, indigo, and tobacco.

The acts also limited what products could be made in the colonies. The British government wanted the colonists to buy goods only from Britain. It wanted to strengthen British companies.

The colonies also **imported** goods from Europe, Africa, and Asia. To import is to bring goods into a country. The Navigation Acts required goods to go through Britain first. Then they could be shipped to the colonies.

For a century, the colonists had ignored the Navigation Acts. Instead, they **smuggled** goods into the colonies. To smuggle is to bring goods into a country illegally. Smugglers do not pay taxes on their goods. So the British collected very little money.

This made Grenville furious. In 1763, he sent navy warships to catch colonial smugglers. He had two goals. He wanted colonists to pay more taxes. He also wanted to show the colonists that Britain still controlled the 13 colonies.

Grenville also sent customs officers from Britain to colonial ports to collect the new taxes. This upset the colonists. They felt that the British were taking away their rights.

More taxes   Britain's next step was to pass the **Sugar Act** of 1764. The Sugar Act did several things. It added

Colonists in Boston gathered angrily at the docks when the British government sent 10,000 British troops to occupy the city.

Protests against the Stamp Act swept through the colonies. This picture shows colonists in Philadelphia protesting against the new taxes.

give British soldiers food and housing. Grenville sent 10,000 soldiers from Britain. They were supposed to defend the western frontier. However, most of them stayed in the eastern cities. Many colonists suspected that the soldiers were really sent to control the colonies.

The Stamp Act   The British were not satisfied. They wanted the colonists to pay even more taxes. The British announced the **Stamp Act** of 1765.

The Stamp Act taxed legal and other documents. It listed over 50 items to tax. Each item needed a stamp to show that the tax had been paid. These items included marriage licenses, land deeds, and wills. Even newspapers, playing cards, and dice were taxed. The tax ranged from one cent on newspapers to $10 on college diplomas.

The Stamp Act was a different kind of tax. Before, when Britain had taxed imports, only merchants paid import taxes. Colonists had paid import taxes indirectly by paying higher prices for taxed goods. But the Stamp Act put a direct tax on all colonists. Anyone who bought one of the items listed had to pay the tax.

Colonial outrage   The Stamp Act angered many colonists. They said that it went against British legal tradition. In Britain, voters had some control over taxes. Voters elected their own **representatives.** A representative is an official elected to act and speak for others. Representatives made up the **Parliament,** the British lawmaking body. It was Parliament that passed the Stamp Act.

The colonists argued that this taxation without representation went against their rights as British citizens. Because they did not elect representatives to Parliament, they had no

new rules for ships carrying goods to the colonies. These rules made it easier to catch smugglers. The act also put new taxes on many imports, such as sugar, molasses, coffee, and cloth.

There was already a tax on molasses. However, it was so high that no merchant paid it. The new tax cut the earlier tax almost in half. However, this time the British meant to enforce it. Grenville demanded that smuggling stop. He wanted these taxes to be paid. This made colonists angry.

Colonists also disliked the Quartering Act of 1765. This act forced colonists to

say in these new taxes. So the colonists said that Parliament had no right to tax them. They believed that only their colonial assemblies should have the right to tax them directly. Thus, their slogan was "No taxation without representation."

Taking action   Protests against the Stamp Act swept the colonies. Newspapers published articles attacking it. Merchants complained. Colonial assemblies met to protest.

Many colonists refused to accept the Stamp Act. They decided to meet to discuss what to do. They felt that the colonies had to unite against the act. Each colony was asked to send representatives to a meeting. Nine colonies sent representatives. The meeting was called the **Stamp Act Congress.**

The Stamp Act Congress sent letters to King George III and Parliament. In the letters the colonists demanded that both the Sugar Act and the Stamp Act be repealed. The colonists also argued that Parliament had no right to tax the colonies.

The colonists also **boycotted** British goods. To boycott is to refuse to buy, sell, or use goods from a particular person, business, or country in the hope of forcing change. Colonial merchants promised not to deal with British goods. Colonists did not buy taxed goods. Trade with Britain slowed. British businesses began to suffer.

Sons of Liberty   A new group of colonists formed to protest the Stamp Act. The group was called the **Sons of Liberty.**

British tax collectors faced the anger of the colonists. Sometimes, they were beaten and "drummed out" of a town. Hands and feet bound, this tax collector will be carried out of town and dumped on a road.

The Sons of Liberty were very strong in Massachusetts. Samuel Adams was a leader of the Sons of Liberty in Boston. He was a member of the Massachusetts assembly. Although Adams had been a tax collector, he often helped poorer people by not making them pay their taxes. In 1765, Adams asked these people to help the Sons of Liberty. Many rushed to join.

The Sons of Liberty used newspaper advertisements and articles to protest the Stamp Act. They organized marches and demonstrations. They burned piles of stamps in town squares.

Marchers sometimes turned into mobs. There were a number of riots. Angry crowds smashed the offices of stamp tax collectors. The property of some people who cooperated with the British was destroyed. Mobs attacked the houses of government officials. The house of the governor of Massachusetts was burned.

The Sons of Liberty also threatened British stamp officials. Angry colonists threw stones at British tax collectors. Mobs poured hot tar over some officials and covered them with feathers. This was painful and embarrassing.

A victory for the colonies The British could not enforce the Stamp Act. Most colonists refused to use the stamps. Newspapers and other products were bought and sold without the stamps.

In March 1766, the British Parliament **repealed,** or canceled, the Stamp Act. Colonists celebrated. However, Parliament said that it had the right to pass laws to govern the colonies. This would soon mean more trouble.

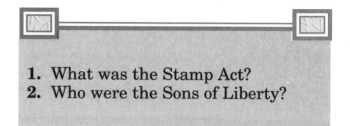

1. What was the Stamp Act?
2. Who were the Sons of Liberty?

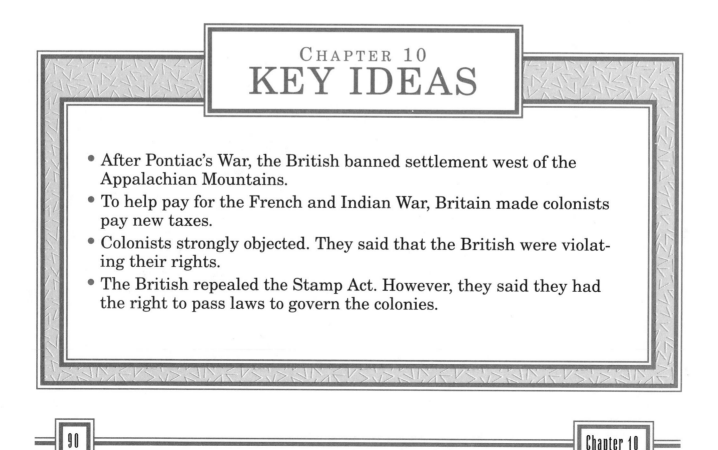

CHAPTER 10
KEY IDEAS

- After Pontiac's War, the British banned settlement west of the Appalachian Mountains.
- To help pay for the French and Indian War, Britain made colonists pay new taxes.
- Colonists strongly objected. They said that the British were violating their rights.
- The British repealed the Stamp Act. However, they said they had the right to pass laws to govern the colonies.

I. Reviewing Vocabulary

Match each word on the left with the correct definition on the right.

1. boycott
2. repeal
3. representative
4. smuggle
5. import

a. to bring goods into a country illegally
b. to bring goods into a country in order to sell them
c. to cancel
d. to refuse to buy, sell, or use goods from a particular person, business, or country
e. an official elected to act and speak for others

II. Understanding the Chapter

1. Why did the Proclamation of 1763 anger the colonists?
2. Why did Great Britain want the colonists to pay more taxes?
3. What was the Sugar Act?
4. Why did the Stamp Act anger the colonists?
5. How did the colonists respond to the Stamp Act?

III. Building Skills: Understanding Time

1. Which of these events happened first: Parliament passes the Stamp Act, the Proclamation of 1763, Parliament passes the Sugar Act?
2. Did Parliament repeal the Stamp Act before or after the Stamp Act Congress met?

IV. Writing About History

1. Imagine you were Pontiac. Write a short speech to convince other Native American leaders to go to war with the British.
2. **What Would You Have Done?** If you had been a colonist, would you have joined the Sons of Liberty? Explain your position in a short paragraph.

V. Working Together

1. Divide into small groups. Each group should divide itself into two sides for a debate. One side should defend the British point of view during 1763-1766. The other side should defend the colonial view. Each group should then hold a debate for 10 minutes in front of the rest of the class.
2. **Past to Present** In the mid-1700s, many colonists felt that they were unfairly taxed and the money taxes raised did not help them. Discuss with a group why the colonists felt that way. Then talk about taxes today. Are people being taxed unfairly? Does the money raised by taxes help citizens? As a group, make a list of all your opinions. Underline those that are similar to the ideas of the colonists.

THE COLONISTS FIGHT BACK. (1767-1775)

How did colonists protest new British taxes?

Dressed as Native Americans, Boston colonists boarded British ships in 1773 and destroyed valuable tea. This "Boston Tea Party" angered the king.

STUDY

On a sheet of paper, write down all of the colored phrases in the text (such as "New taxes" on page 93). Write a short sentence summarizing the text under each colored phrase.

HINT

Looking at Key Terms

- Townshend Acts • Daughters of Liberty • Boston Massacre
- Committee of Correspondence • Intolerable Acts
- Boston Tea Party

Looking at Key Words

- **duty:** a tax put on goods for sale
- **massacre:** the cruel killing of a great number of people
- **intolerable:** too terrible to bear
- **declaration:** an official announcement
- **militia:** a group of citizens who act as soldiers in an emergency

The people of Boston were furious. In June 1768, the British seized a ship called the *Liberty*. Customs officials said it was used for smuggling. The officials worried that colonists would take the ship back by force. So it was towed out of Boston harbor and anchored next to a British warship. There the *Liberty* was safe. But the officials were not. Mobs attacked them, and their homes were damaged. The frightened officials fled Boston. It was clear that the colonists were serious about their dispute with Britain.

1 The Colonists Protest New Taxes.

How did the colonists object to the Townshend Acts?

The repeal of the Stamp Act in 1766 was a victory for the colonists. But the victory did not last long. The British Parliament found another way to tax colonists.

New taxes   In 1767, Parliament passed a new set of taxes and rules called the **Townshend Acts.** These acts put taxes, called **duties,** on several products imported from Britain. Goods such as cloth, paint, glass, and paper were taxed. The British also placed a tax on tea.

British officials were sent to Boston to collect all import taxes in the colonies. Boston was a center of smuggling. People in Boston strongly opposed new British taxes.

The Townshend Acts gave the new tax collectors a great deal of power. The tax collectors could search the homes and businesses of colonists for smuggled goods. These searches could take place without any warning. The tax collectors did not even have to go to a judge for permission.

A storm of protest   The colonists protested the Townshend Acts. New England newspapers attacked the acts, saying that the acts violated the law.

By 1768, tempers in the colonies were hot. The Massachusetts assembly called on King George to repeal the Townshend Acts. It also asked other colonial assemblies to join the protest.

Virginia's assembly was the first to follow Massachusetts. The assemblies of

Reading a Chart. Which act placed a tax on legal papers in the colonies? Why did these taxes come after the end of the French and Indian War?

BRITISH LAWS AND TAXES IN THE COLONIES		
Act	**Date**	**Explanation**
Sugar Act	1764	taxed sugar and molasses coming from the West Indies to the colonies
Quartering Act	1765	forced colonists to provide food and housing for British troops
Stamp Act	1765	taxed newspapers, almanacs, playing cards, and all legal papers in the colonies
Townshend Act	1767	taxed manufactured goods shipped to the colonies, such as paper, glass, and paint
Tea Act	1773	allowed British East India Company to sell tea directly to colonies: made imported tea cheaper, hurting colonial merchants

New Jersey, Maryland, and Connecticut joined next. The protest movement grew quickly. By the end of 1768, New Hampshire, Pennsylvania, Rhode Island, Delaware, New York, and North Carolina joined the protest.

Meanwhile, demonstrations were taking place in the streets. Like several other cities and towns, Boston had a tree called the "Liberty Tree." In March 1768, the Sons of Liberty met at the Liberty Tree. Suddenly, it looked as if two British officials were hanging from the tree. A crowd gathered, and some people cheered. In fact, what looked like British officials were only dummies. This fake hanging did not hurt anyone. But it showed how angry the colonists were.

Boycott! Another form of protest did hurt the British. The colonists boycotted British goods. The boycott started in Boston. It quickly spread to the other large colonial ports.

Boycotting was not easy. Colonists wanted British goods, especially cloth and tea. The **Daughters of Liberty** came to the rescue. These colonial women opposed the Townshend Acts. They convinced people not to buy British goods.

The Daughters of Liberty spoke out against drinking tea. They suggested coffee. Some women made their own tea from local herbs. However, many colonists enjoyed imported tea too much to give it up. Instead, they smuggled in Dutch tea.

The Daughters of Liberty also refused to buy British cloth. They asked women to make their own cloth. Cloth made at home was called homespun. The Daughters of Liberty wore only homespun cloth and held cloth-making contests.

As opposition to the British rose, colonial women decided not to buy British cloth. Colonial women began to make their own cloth. Soon many colonists proudly wore clothing that had been spun at home.

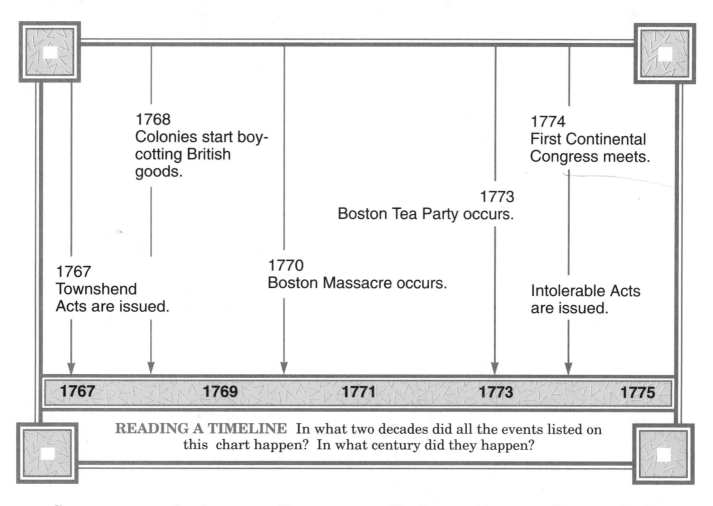

1768
Colonies start boy-
cotting British
goods.

1774
First Continental
Congress meets.

1773
Boston Tea Party occurs.

1767
Townshend
Acts are issued.

1770
Boston Massacre occurs.

Intolerable Acts
are issued.

| 1767 | 1769 | 1771 | 1773 | 1775 |

READING A TIMELINE In what two decades did all the events listed on this chart happen? In what century did they happen?

Soon, many colonists proudly wore homespun cloth. In fact, the boycott actually helped poorer colonial women and their families. They earned money making cloth. This money no longer went to the British. The Daughters of Liberty made the boycott of British cloth successful.

The boycott badly hurt British merchants. Colonists hoped that it would make the British government repeal the Townshend Acts. But it would take a tragedy to make the British change their minds.

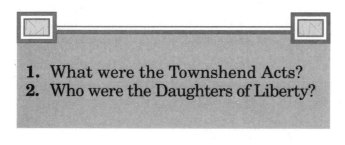

1. What were the Townshend Acts?
2. Who were the Daughters of Liberty?

2 The Boston Massacre Worsens Feelings Between the Colonists and the British.

How did the Boston Massacre make the situation in the colonies worse?

In 1768, when colonists protested the Townshend Acts, Britain sent more soldiers to Boston. The soldiers often did not get along with the citizens of Boston. The colonists felt that the soldiers were interfering in their lives. Sometimes, they insulted soldiers they met on the streets or in stores.

Bad feelings The British soldiers knew they were disliked. They, in turn, were rude to the citizens of Boston. The soldiers often played or sang a song called "Yankee Doodle." The people of New England thought the song was dis-

On a March evening in 1770, Crispus Attucks and four other colonists were shot by British troops. Anti-British feelings grew strong when people in other colonies found out about this "Boston Massacre."

respectful. Tension built up between the colonists and the soldiers.

On the night of March 5, 1770, the mood in Boston was ugly. A crowd gathered outside the customs house. Colonists surrounded the ten British soldiers who were guarding the customs house. One of the leaders of the crowd was Crispus Attucks, an African American sailor. He was a member of the Sons of Liberty. He and the other colonists began to insult the soldiers.

People in the crowd yelled at the British soldiers. They also threw mud, snowballs, oyster shells, and rocks. The crowd grew larger and angrier. Crispus Attucks shouted that the soldiers would not dare shoot.

Suddenly, a fight broke out. Attucks grabbed a gun from one of the soldiers. He cried out for the crowd to attack. The crowd surged forward, and the British soldiers were frightened. The officer in charge tried to keep the soldiers calm. But one of the nervous soldiers shouted "Fire!" First one and then the other soldiers fired into the crowd.

When the smoke cleared, Crispus Attucks and four other colonists lay dead. Most of those killed had not attacked the soldiers. They were only standing nearby watching.

The people of Boston were outraged. Blood had been spilled in their streets. They called the event the **Boston Massacre. A massacre** is the cruel killing of a great number of people. News of the Boston Massacre spread quickly through the colonies.

Crispus Attucks and the other colonists killed were heroes to the Americans. They were the first to die for freedom from British rule. Anti-British feelings grew as the news spread.

A murder trial Angry citizens in Boston wanted the soldiers arrested and put on trial. Others talked about attacking all British soldiers in the city. Many demanded that British troops leave Boston. The British official in charge in Boston wanted to avoid further violence. He removed British soldiers from the city. He also agreed to

put the soldiers involved in the Boston Massacre on trial.

The soldiers had a surprising defender. John Adams was well known in Boston. He strongly supported the rights of the colonists against the British. However, Adams thought that everyone deserved a fair trial. He also wanted to show that the Americans believed in justice for all, including British soldiers. So Adams served as the soldiers' defense lawyer. Through his arguments, most of the soldiers were found innocent.

Repeal of the Townshend Acts
The Boston Massacre had one positive result. The boycott against British goods had hurt the British. Now, this violence convinced the British government to repeal some taxes. In April 1770, most of the Townshend duties were repealed. But the duty on tea was not. The tea tax continued to be a sore spot between the British and the colonists.

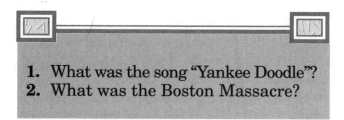

1. What was the song "Yankee Doodle"?
2. What was the Boston Massacre?

3 The British Colonies Unite.
Why did the Boston Tea Party take place?

Between 1770 and 1773, the colonies seemed quiet. Colonists celebrated the end of the Townshend Acts. The boycotts were over.

A calm before the storm
However, many colonists were still angry at the British. Colonists worried that the British might pass more taxes. A growing number of people wanted the colonies to break away from Britain.

One strong supporter of independence was Mercy Otis Warren.

Warren was a writer who criticized the British. Her poems and plays made fun of British officials. Warren also mocked colonists who were still loyal to the British. Her work was widely read in the colonies. Warren also held political meetings in her home. There, Samuel Adams and John Adams discussed plans to resist the British. Warren was unusual. Women were not expected to take part in politics at that time.

In 1773, Warren helped set up the Massachusetts **Committee of Correspondence.** Its job was to make sure that news from Massachusetts reached the other colonies. Soon every colony set up a committee of correspondence. These committees helped unite the colonists against the British.

Crisis over tea   Trouble broke out in 1773. The British Parliament passed the Tea Act. The act let the British East India Company decide which colonial merchants could sell their tea. Colonists did not want anyone telling them whom they could do business with. They soon let the British know how they felt.

Boston Tea Party   On December 16, 1773, three tea ships from India were docked in Boston harbor. Thousands of colonists protested. They demanded that the ships leave without unloading. The British governor ordered the ships to stay. When word of this order reached the crowd, there was an uproar.

Dressed as Native Americans, a band of colonists stormed onto the ships. They worked quickly, smashing chests of tea and tossing them overboard. Soon, more than 340 chests of valuable tea floated in Boston harbor. The events of that night became known as the **Boston Tea Party.**

Angry colonists also kept East India Company tea from being unloaded in New York and Philadelphia. However, after the Boston Tea Party, King George III and the British government felt that the colonists had to be punished.

Harsh punishment   In 1774, Parliament passed a series of acts to punish the colonists. One act closed the port of Boston. No ship could enter and no ship could leave. Another took away most of Massachusetts's right of self-government. A third act made much of the land west of the Appalachians part of Canada.

The colonists had never been angrier. Many who had supported the British now turned against them. They called these acts the **Intolerable Acts. Intolerable** means something that is too terrible to bear. The colonists decided to work together to defend themselves.

A call for united action   The colonies sent representatives to a meeting called the First Continental Congress. The Congress met in Philadelphia in September 1774. Every colony except Georgia was present.

Samuel Adams was there. So was Patrick Henry, a lawyer from Virginia. Another Virginian at the Congress was George Washington.

The First Continental Congress called for a boycott of all British goods. But the Congress went much further than a boycott. It passed a **declaration,** or official announcement, saying that the colonists had the right to govern themselves. The declaration also said that many of the laws that Parliament had passed since 1763 were illegal.

The First Continental Congress knew that its struggle with Britain was just beginning. It told each colony to set up a militia. A **militia** is a group of citizens who act as soldiers in an emergency. It also called for another meeting if the British did not end the Intolerable Acts. Britain and its 13 American colonies were about to split.

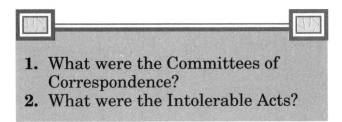

1. What were the Committees of Correspondence?
2. What were the Intolerable Acts?

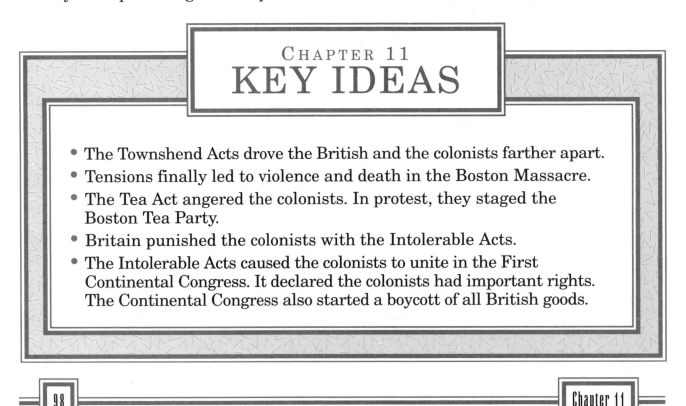

CHAPTER 11
KEY IDEAS

- The Townshend Acts drove the British and the colonists farther apart.
- Tensions finally led to violence and death in the Boston Massacre.
- The Tea Act angered the colonists. In protest, they staged the Boston Tea Party.
- Britain punished the colonists with the Intolerable Acts.
- The Intolerable Acts caused the colonists to unite in the First Continental Congress. It declared the colonists had important rights. The Continental Congress also started a boycott of all British goods.

REVIEWING CHAPTER 11

I. Reviewing Vocabulary

Match each word on the left with the correct definition on the right.

1. duty
2. massacre
3. intolerable
4. declaration
5. militia

   a. a group of citizens who act as soldiers in an emergency
   b. an announcement
   c. the cruel killing of a great number of people
   d. a tax put on goods being imported into a country
   e. too terrible to bear

II. Understanding the Chapter

1. What were the Townshend Acts?
2. How did the colonists protest the Townshend Acts?
3. Why did the Boston Massacre take place?
4. Why did British Parliament pass the Intolerable Acts?
5. What did the First Continental Congress call for?

III. Building Skills: Recognizing Cause and Effect

1. What came first, the repeal of the Townshend Acts or the Boston Massacre? Explain.
2. Did the First Continental Congress meet before or after colonists set up the Committees of Correspondence? Explain.

IV. Writing About History

1. **What Would You Have Done?** Imagine that you are a colonial merchant. The Townshend Acts affect you, but you make a living selling British tea. Will you join the boycott against British goods? Why or why not?
2. Write a short article about the Boston Massacre that could have appeared in a New England newspaper. Be sure to answer the questions *who? what? when? where?* and *why?*

V. Working Together

1. Form groups of three students. You are representatives to the First Continental Congress. You must decide what the colonies should do. Do you want a guarantee of the rights of the colonies? Perhaps you want the colonies to unite and act against Britain. Make a list of the arguments. Then present your arguments to the class. After all groups have presented their arguments, take a vote.
2. **Past to Present** In chapters 10 and 11, you read about ways the colonists protested against Britain. With a group, discuss these methods. Then talk about how people protest today. Together, make a chart of colonial ways of protesting still used today, ways people no longer use, and new ways to protest.

THE AMERICAN REVOLUTION IS LAUNCHED. (1774-1776)

How did the American Revolution begin?

When colonial men were shot down at Lexington and Concord, colonial women often rushed to take their places on the firing line.

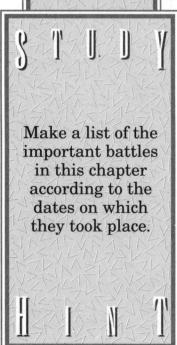

S T U D Y

Make a list of the important battles in this chapter according to the dates on which they took place.

H I N T

Looking at Key Terms

- American Revolution • Minutemen • Continental Army
- Battles of Lexington and Concord • Battle of Bunker Hill
- Second Continental Congress

Looking at Key Words

- **rebellion:** an armed resistance to a government
- **pamphlet:** a short booklet
- **tyrant:** a cruel ruler who takes away the rights of the people
- **debate:** a formal discussion in which opposing sides of a question are argued
- **delegate:** a person who represents others

It was the night of April 18, 1775. Two lanterns suddenly glowed in the steeple of Boston's North Church. They signaled that British troops had boarded boats and left Boston. The troops landed across the bay. They then marched toward the towns of Lexington and Concord. Their goal was to find and destroy guns and supplies that the colonists had hidden in Concord.

But colonists were watching for a signal from the North Church steeple across the bay. When they saw the two lanterns, they knew that the British were coming! Paul Revere and other colonists raced on horseback ahead of the marching troops. They rode to Lexington and Concord to warn that the British soldiers were on the way. When the British reached Lexington, colonial soldiers were waiting for them. The two sides faced each other. The **American Revolution,** the colonies' war for independence from Britain, was about to begin.

1 The Colonists Fight the First Battles of the Revolution.

Why were the battles of Lexington and Concord important?

By late 1774, King George III decided that the colonies were in **rebellion.** A rebellion is armed resistance to a government. Parliament agreed with the king. It was time to use force. The colonies had to learn to obey the British.

Neither side understood the other. King George III and Parliament believed that the colonists would back down. They thought that all Britain had to do was to send more troops to the colonies. They did not listen to General Thomas Gage, the British governor of Massachusetts. He warned that the colonists would fight. It turned out that Gage was right.

Most colonists thought that all they had to show was that they were willing to fight for their rights. Then Britain would change the way it treated the colonies.

Liberty or death However, other colonists thought that Britain would not change. They argued that the colonies would have to go to war with Britain. One such person was Patrick Henry of Virginia. In March 1775, he made a passionate speech before Virginia's assembly. Henry said that he was not afraid of war. He stated that the colonists would have to protect their freedom. Henry ended his speech by saying, "Give me liberty or give me death."

Patrick Henry was not alone. In Massachusetts, colonists also prepared for war. The British were sending more soldiers to Massachusetts. So the colonists organized their own forces and armed themselves. The colonists formed militias and began to train. The militia was supposed to be ready to fight with only a one-minute warning. Therefore, the members of the militia were called **Minutemen.**

The minutemen hid many of their weapons and supplies in Concord less than 20 miles from Boston. General Gage knew about the weapons. He wanted to destroy or capture them. On the night of April 18, 1775, he sent 700 soldiers to Concord. But Gage did not know that the colonists had been warned. The two lanterns in the Boston church warned colonists that the British were on the move.

First shots The village of Lexington was between Boston and Concord. The British force marched into Lexington early on the morning of April 19. A group of about 70 Minutemen stood waiting for them. The Minutemen did not intend to fight. Many were not even armed. They were there to show the British that they would stand up for their rights.

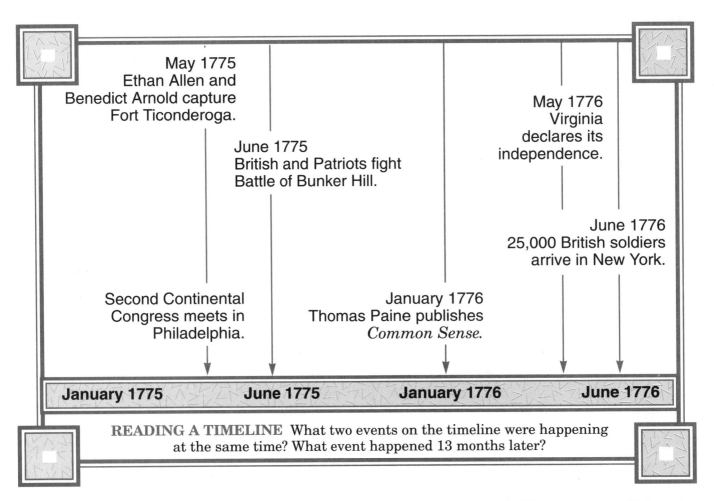

May 1775
Ethan Allen and
Benedict Arnold capture
Fort Ticonderoga.

June 1775
British and Patriots fight
Battle of Bunker Hill.

May 1776
Virginia
declares its
independence.

June 1776
25,000 British soldiers
arrive in New York.

Second Continental
Congress meets in
Philadelphia.

January 1776
Thomas Paine publishes
Common Sense.

| January 1775 | June 1775 | January 1776 | June 1776 |

READING A TIMELINE What two events on the timeline were happening at the same time? What event happened 13 months later?

The British troops advanced toward the colonists. The British commander ordered those Minutemen who had guns to lay them down. The Minutemen refused. However, most of the Minutemen began to walk away from the British troops. Suddenly, a shot rang out. No one knows who fired it. Other shots followed. When the firing stopped, eight colonists were dead. One British soldier was wounded. Only a few minutes had passed. However, the American Revolution had begun.

Fighting back   The British troops continued toward Concord. But the colonists had moved most of their military supplies. The British destroyed the supplies they were able to find. Then they moved out of town to look for more weapons. The British troops came to the North Bridge. About 300 colonists blocked their way.

This time, the Minutemen did not turn away. They could see a cloud of smoke rising from their town. The British had set fire to Concord's Liberty Tree. A Minuteman shouted, "Would you let them burn our town?" The colonists moved toward the British. A short battle followed. The British retreated back into Concord. People on both sides were killed.

The **Battles of Lexington and Concord** had ended. However, the fighting was not over. The British began to retreat toward Boston. They marched down the same road they had taken to Concord. More than 3,000 Minutemen, hiding behind trees and stone fences, were waiting for them. As the British marched along the road, the Minutemen shot at them. It was very hard for the British soldiers to shoot back.

In Lexington, 1,200 more troops joined the British army. The retreat

continued. Colonists shot at the British every step of the way. When the British finally reached Boston, 273 British troops were dead or wounded. The colonists had lost less than a hundred soldiers.

"The shot heard round the world"
The Battles of Lexington and Concord were very important. For the first time, American colonists had stood and fought against the British. The colonists fought for their ideas of freedom. People in Europe had discussed such ideas. But no one had dared to act on them before. The Battle of Concord sent the message that people were willing to die for their ideas of freedom. The colonists' message reached many countries all over the world. That is why people say that the minutemen at Concord fired the "shot heard round the world."

The battles were important in another way. They made it clear how far apart the colonists and the British were. It was going to be very hard to avoid war.

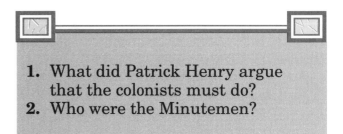

1. What did Patrick Henry argue that the colonists must do?
2. Who were the Minutemen?

2 Colonists Want Peace but Prepare for War.

What led the colonies to go to war with Great Britain?

Abigail Adams tossed more wood on the fire. The pot on the fire was now hot

An old print shows the British fleeing from the Americans after the first shots were fired at the battle of Lexington. How does this picture differ from the account of the battle in this chapter?

enough. She threw her silver spoons into the pot. They melted slowly. She explained to her young son, John Quincy Adams, that she was making bullets. Abigail Adams was married to John Adams (see page 97). She and her husband supported the colonists' struggle against the British. The colonists badly needed bullets, and some would use Adams's bullets to fight the British troops.

Reading a Map. After Lexington and Concord, the British retreated to Boston. In what battle did they try to drive the colonists from hills near Boston?

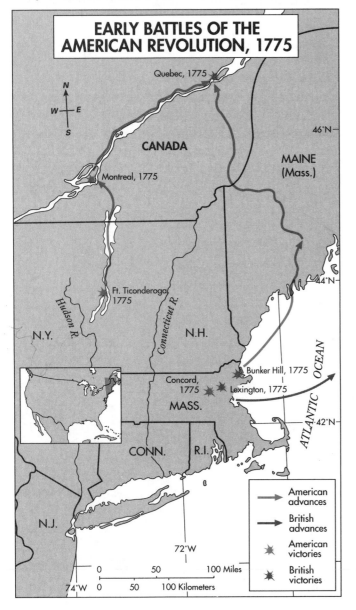

EARLY BATTLES OF THE AMERICAN REVOLUTION, 1775

Early colonial victory Colonial forces found other ways to get bullets and weapons. On May 10, 1775, a colonial force attacked Fort Ticonderoga (ty-con-deh-ROH-gah) in New York. They were led by Ethan Allen of Vermont.

It was not much of a battle. The fort was defended by fewer than 50 British soldiers, and its walls had giant holes. The colonists quickly captured the fort. No one was killed on either side.

The colonists seized the fort's weapons and military supplies. Among these weapons were cannons. The colonists badly needed these powerful weapons to fight the British.

Bloodiest battle As the British retreated from Concord, the colonists followed them to Boston. The colonists set up camps around the city. They also built defenses on two tall hills across the bay, Breed's Hill and Bunker Hill. From there, colonists could keep British troops from leaving Boston.

The colonists were camped near the farm of John and Abigail Adams. Many people living near Adams were afraid. They thought that the British might break through the colonial forces. Then the British could attack the towns around Boston. Many colonists, therefore, left their homes.

Abigail Adams refused to leave. She waited to see what would happen. Before dawn on June 17, she woke up suddenly. She heard firing cannons in the distance. She and her son went to watch. They saw the British firing at Charlestown on Breed's Hill. Soon, the town was on fire. The **Battle of Bunker Hill** had begun.

The British tried to drive the colonists from Breed's Hill. More than 2,500 British troops attacked about 1,200 colonists. The British charged straight up the hill. They expected the colonists to turn and run. But the

When the British Parliament voted to send 25,000 troops to the colonies, American anger exploded at the British. Here a mob of angry colonists in New York City pulls down a statue of King George the Third.

colonists fought bravely. The attacking British soldiers were easy targets. The colonists retreated only when they ran out of gunpowder. The British drove them first from Breed's Hill and then from Bunker Hill.

The Battle of Bunker Hill was the bloodiest battle of the entire American Revolution. In the battle, more than 1,000 British soldiers were killed or wounded. The colonists lost about 400. The British won the battle, but they paid a terrible price. One British general said the losses filled him with horror. Now the British knew that the colonists would fight.

Second Continental Congress
On May 10, 1775, the **Second Continental Congress** met for the first time in Philadelphia. At first, only 12 colonies sent **delegates.** A delegate is someone who represents others. Georgia was absent. In September, Georgia sent delegates. Then all 13 colonies had delegates at the congress.

Many of the most important leaders in the colonies were at the Continental Congress. These leaders included Benjamin Franklin of Pennsylvania, Thomas Jefferson of Virginia, and George Washington of Virginia.

Most delegates still did not want to break completely with Britain. They just wanted to defend their rights. However, fighting had started and the congress had to act. It voted to turn the different colonial militia into one army. It called this force the **Continental Army.** The Continental Congress appointed George Washington as army commander.

At first, the congress tried to prevent a final split with Britain. It sent a message to King George that listed the complaints of the colonists. The king tore up the message. Then Parliament voted to send 25,000 more soldiers to the colonies. It was the largest army that Britain had ever sent overseas. This huge force would arrive in New York in June 1776.

Meanwhile, British rule in the colonies was falling apart. In colony after colony, people refused to obey the British gover-

nors. Colonists forced British officials to leave their posts. Then the colonists set up governments of their own. Most colonists, however, still did not want to break completely with Britain.

A call for independence In January 1776, a **pamphlet,** or short booklet, was published that would change many colonists' minds. The pamphlet was *Common Sense.* The author was Thomas Paine.

Paine was a newcomer in America. He had arrived from Britain in 1774 with revolutionary ideas. He wrote that kings had no right to rule. He said that wherever kings ruled they destroyed the rights of the people. Paine called King George III a **tyrant,** a cruel ruler who takes away the rights of the people. He also wrote that the only good form of government is one elected by the people. Paine argued that the colonies had to declare independence from Great Britain.

Paine's pamphlet *Common Sense* had a huge influence on the American colonists. More than 120,000 copies of the pamphlet were sold during the first three months of 1776. Colonists everywhere read it. Newspapers praised it. *Common Sense* convinced thousands of colonists

that the time for independence had come. It also convinced many of the delegates at the Second Continental Congress.

Preparing to split with Britain Another event pushed the colonists toward independence. In May 1776, the colony of ~~Virginia~~ *Rhode Island* declared its independence from Britain. On June 7, a delegate asked the Second Continental Congress to declare independence from Britain for all the colonies.

Congress **debated** the question. A debate is a formal discussion in which opposing sides of a question are argued. However, congress still was not ready to declare independence. Instead, it formed two committees. One would make up a plan for a new government. The second would write a declaration of independence. These committees prepared for the final split from Britain. Their work would shape the future of the colonies.

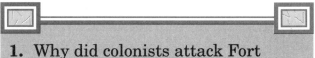

1. Why did colonists attack Fort Ticonderoga?
2. What effect did *Common Sense* have on the colonists?

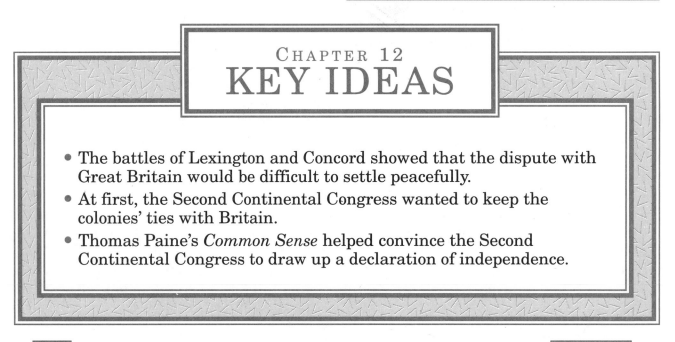

CHAPTER 12
KEY IDEAS

- The battles of Lexington and Concord showed that the dispute with Great Britain would be difficult to settle peacefully.
- At first, the Second Continental Congress wanted to keep the colonies' ties with Britain.
- Thomas Paine's *Common Sense* helped convince the Second Continental Congress to draw up a declaration of independence.

REVIEWING CHAPTER 12

I. Reviewing Vocabulary

Match each word on the left with the correct definition on the right.

1. pamphlet
2. rebellion
3. delegate
4. Second Continental Congress
5. tyrant

a. a cruel ruler who takes away the rights of the people
b. a person who represents someone else
c. an armed resistance to a government
d. a small printed booklet
e. the meeting of colonial leaders that began in May 1775

II. Understanding the Chapter

1. Why did the British send troops to Lexington and Concord?
2. Why were the Battles of Lexington and Concord important?
3. What happened at the Battle of Bunker Hill?
4. What did the Second Continental Congress do when it first met?
5. What was the mission of the Second Continental Congress?

III. Building Skills: Distinguishing Between Fact and Opinion

Tell whether each of the following statements is a fact or an opinion.

1. Britain should have let the colonies govern themselves.
2. The Battle of Concord has been called "the shot heard round the world."
3. *Common Sense* was the most important document ever published in the colonies.

IV. Writing About History

1. Imagine that you had been at the Battle of Concord, either as a Minuteman or a witness. Write a diary entry that describes the battle.
2. **What Would You Have Done?** If you had been asked to be a delegate to the Second Continental Congress, would you have accepted? Explain.

V. Working Together

1. Form small groups of students. Pick an important event that took place between April 1775 and June 1776. For example, you could choose the Battle of Lexington or the publication of *Common Sense*. Create a storyboard about that event for a TV show. A storyboard shows what happens in a TV show through a series of drawings. It is like an outline in pictures. Share your storyboard with the class.
2. **Past to Present** *Common Sense* had a huge influence on the American colonists. With a group, discuss which ideas in the pamphlet still influence Americans today. Write down two that are most important to you.

THE AMERICANS DECLARE THEIR INDEPENDENCE. (1776)

Why did the American colonies declare their independence from Great Britain?

When Americans celebrate the Fourth of July with parades such as this one in Illinois, they remember the day Americans declared themselves free.

Looking at Key Terms

• Declaration of Independence • Patriots • Loyalists

Looking at Key Words

- **treason:** the act of betraying one's country, including trying to overthrow the government
- **preamble:** an introduction

- **ideal:** an idea or goal that someone tries to live up to
- **consent:** to agree to something

STUDY

As you read, use the section titles and the subsection titles to make a brief outline of the chapter. Under each title, write one or two sentences that summarize the section or subsection.

HINT

It was June and very hot in Philadelphia. Thomas Jefferson was alone in his apartment. He wrote for days. Finally, he finished his work. The first draft of the colonies' declaration of independence from Britain was done.

The Second Continental Congress was still in session. Jefferson was on the committee that the congress set up. Its job was to draw up a declaration of independence. Benjamin Franklin, Roger Sherman, Robert Livingston, and John Adams were also on the committee. They had asked Jefferson to write the first draft. They reviewed it. The committee made a few changes. Then they presented the declaration to the congress.

About 100 miles (160 kilometers) away in New York, thousands of British troops were coming ashore. They were well trained and ready for battle. King George III sent them to control the colonies. Now the members of the Continental Congress had to decide. They must vote on whether to declare independence.

1 The Declaration of Independence Is Written.

Why did the Second Continental Congress vote to declare independence from Britain?

On a spring morning in June 1776, the Second Continental Congress came to order. Before the delegates voted, they discussed declaring independence. John Adams called this discussion the "great debate." The debate started in June. By July, it was time to finish that debate.

Reasons for independence   Most delegates at the congress were for independence. There were many reasons that the delegates felt this way. The colonists' anger toward the British continued to grow. Many colonial leaders no longer trusted Britain. The king and Parliament might promise something one day and take it away the next. The colonial leaders believed that their rights would never be safe if they remained part of the British Empire.

There was another important reason to declare independence. The colonists already were fighting the British army. They wanted help from Britain's enemies in Europe. They hoped that France and Spain would give them money, weapons, and even troops. But how could the colonists prove to France and Spain that they would not suddenly give in to Britain? The best way was to declare their independence.

The Great Debate   At first, it seemed that the Continental Congress would quickly vote for independence. However, some delegates opposed it. One of them was John Dickinson of Pennsylvania. He explained his views to the congress.

Dickinson believed declaring independence would hurt the colonies rather than help them. He argued that it would lead to a war that would cause great suffering. He did not think any European nation would help the colonies against Britain. Dickenson also believed that the colonies would not stay united if they won independence. He feared they would break up into separate states.

John Adams then gave a speech in favor of declaring independence. He agreed that a declaration would lead to difficult times. It would take a long time to build a new country. However, Adams also said that there was no other way out of the dispute with Britain.

It took courage to vote for independence. The delegates knew they were placing the colonies in danger. They faced a war with the most powerful country in Europe. Each delegate also was risking his own life. Those who voted for independence could be hanged for **treason** if the revolution failed. Treason is the act of betraying one's country, including trying to overthrow the government.

Declaring Independence Despite the risks, the Second Continental Congress voted for independence. On July 4, 1776, it adopted the **Declaration of Independence.** John Hancock was the president of the congress. He announced that the colonies were now states. They cut their ties with Great Britain.

The Declaration of Independence announced to the world the founding of a new nation. It is one of the most important documents in the history of the United States.

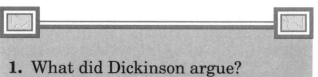

1. What did Dickinson argue?
2. List two reasons for delegates to have voted for independence.

2 The Declaration of Independence Continues to Guide Us.

What did the Declaration of Independence say?

The Declaration of Independence is divided into four parts. The first part is the **preamble.** A preamble is an introduction. The second part states the principles upon which the new nation will be based. The third lists the reasons for breaking away from Britain. The last

The signing of the Declaration of Independence was painted by American painter John Trumbull. John Adams, Thomas Jefferson, and Benjamin Franklin are shown at center, standing. Can you identify the three?

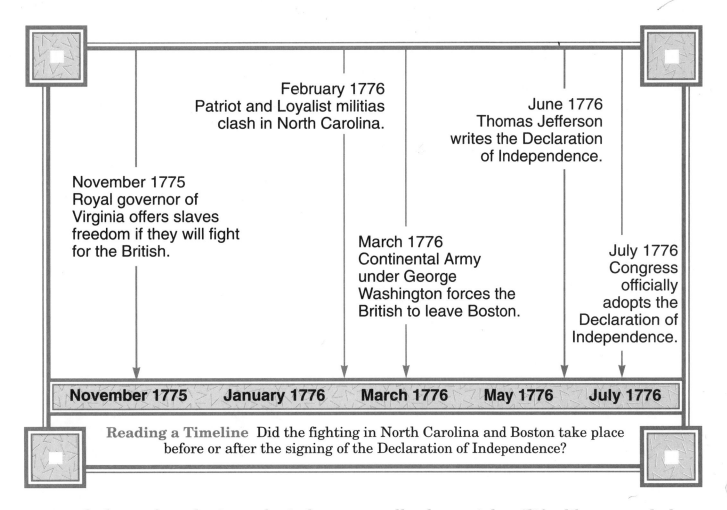

November 1775
Royal governor of Virginia offers slaves freedom if they will fight for the British.

February 1776
Patriot and Loyalist militias clash in North Carolina.

March 1776
Continental Army under George Washington forces the British to leave Boston.

June 1776
Thomas Jefferson writes the Declaration of Independence.

July 1776
Congress officially adopts the Declaration of Independence.

November 1775	January 1776	March 1776	May 1776	July 1776

Reading a Timeline Did the fighting in North Carolina and Boston take place before or after the signing of the Declaration of Independence?

part declares the colonies to be independent of Britain.

Preamble The preamble states why the declaration was written. It is only one sentence long. It says that sometimes a group of people is forced to break its ties with another group. Then the leaders of the newly independent group must explain why they made such a serious decision.

Principles of the new nation The Declaration's second part states the basic principles of democracy. These democratic **ideals** governed the new nation. An ideal is an idea or goal that someone tries to live up to. The declaration set high goals that no nation had ever met before.

The Declaration of Independence states that "all men are created equal." Everyone has the same basic rights. It calls those rights "life, liberty, and the pursuit of happiness." According to the declaration, the protection of these rights is the reason that people form governments. It is the job of government to protect these rights.

The second part of the declaration says what governments may and may not do. A government may stay in power only if it has the support of the people. The government gets its powers from "the consent of the governed." **Consent** is someone freely agreeing to something. People must agree to be ruled by the government. The government may never take away the people's rights. If it does so, the people should overthrow it. This is both their right and their duty.

Complaints against the British
The third part of the declaration tells how the British took away the colonists'

Americans did not address the issue of slavery when they fought for independence. This picture shows goods being unloaded in a Virginia town. The hardest work was left to enslaved African Americans.

rights. It blames King George III for these abuses. Many of these things were actually done by Parliament. However, Jefferson thought it would be more dramatic if he blamed the king.

The Declaration of Independence accuses the king of many things. It says that he destroyed colonial self-government. He tried to stop colonists from moving west. He kept British troops in the colonies during peacetime. He taxed colonists without their consent. He restricted trade with other countries. He denied trial by jury in many cases. Worst of all, he sent armies to fight the colonists.

The list gives more examples of how the British took away the colonists' rights. The Declaration says that the king "destroyed the lives of the people." It points out that the colonists protested against this treatment. The third part ends by saying that the king ignored these protests.

Officially independent   The fourth part of the declaration announces that the colonies are free. It says that they have the right to be free. The declaration calls the colonies "free and independent states." Equally important, it says those states are united. It promises that they will stick together in the struggle ahead. They are now the United States of America.

All men are created equal   The Declaration of Independence set high ideals for the United States. None was more important than "all men are created equal." Even in 1776, many people thought that this meant that all people should have equal rights. However, there was a serious problem. The delegates at the Continental Congress meant that only white men who could vote should be equal. This did not include many people. Women, African Americans, and other groups were not considered equal. Some people asked how the 13 states could fight for freedom from Britain and still allow slavery.

Many of the delegates who signed the Declaration owned slaves. One of them

was Thomas Jefferson, the author of the declaration. Jefferson was unusual. He owned slaves, but he hated slavery. He believed that slavery harmed everyone involved. Enslaved African Americans lost their freedom. Slavery turned some slave owners into cruel tyrants. Jefferson hoped that slavery would slowly disappear. Many people in New England and the Middle Colonies also hated slavery.

Jefferson attacked the slave trade in his first draft of the Declaration of Independence. He blamed the slave trade on the king. However, delegates from the Southern Colonies objected to Jefferson's statement. So the congress took it out of the final version. The declaration still said "all men are created equal." But it said nothing against slavery.

Since then, the meaning of these words has changed. Now, Americans believe *all* people are created equal. Many people keep working to live up to this ideal. This has been a long struggle, and the work is not yet complete. Equality for all Americans is still a goal to be reached.

The ideals of the Declaration of Independence have guided the United States for over 200 years. Americans believe these ideas. Each citizen deserves the same basic rights. All Americans have the right to "life, liberty, and the pursuit of happiness." The government must rule with the people's consent. It must protect the rights of all citizens. These ideals are as important today as they were in 1776.

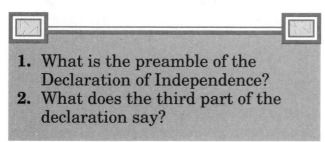

1. What is the preamble of the Declaration of Independence?
2. What does the third part of the declaration say?

3 The Nation Welcomes the Declaration of Independence.

How did most Americans react to independence from Britain?

As soon as the Second Continental Congress adopted the Declaration of Independence, it told the American people. The congress did not even wait until the official document was signed. It had copies of the declaration printed. These were given out throughout America. The first newspaper to publish the declaration was the *Philadelphia Evening Post*. It was published on Saturday, July 6, 1776.

Independence celebrations Most Americans were happy about the Declaration of Independence. Philadelphia was the first city to get the news. Officials announced the Declaration at the main government building in the city. A crowd of thousands cheered. Soldiers paraded through the streets. John Adams remembered that "bells rang all day and almost all night."

On July 10 in New York City, officers of the Continental Army read the declaration to their troops. The soldiers were excited. So were ordinary New Yorkers. That night, a crowd pulled down a statue of King George III. They planned to use the lead in the statue to make bullets. They needed the bullets for the war for independence.

Since then, the United States has celebrated the day that the declaration was adopted. On July 4 of each year, Americans celebrate Independence Day. Fireworks and parades mark the founding of our nation.

A nation divided Those who supported the Declaration of Independence

At the Battle of Bunker Hill, Peter Salem, a free African American, helped defend the hill from the Redcoats. During the battle, Salem cut down the British commander.

called themselves **Patriots.** The great majority of Americans were Patriots. This was true whether they were born in America, England, or other European countries. Most people from countries like Holland, Germany, France, and Sweden supported the Revolution. Like those of English descent, by 1776, people from other European countries had become Americans.

However, some people in the colonies remained loyal to England and King George III. They called themselves **Loyalists.** Loyalists made up about one-fifth of the total free population. There were Loyalists in all the colonies and among all groups of people. Families even split apart into Patriots and Loyalists.

Patriots and Loyalists were bitter enemies. They started fighting even before the congress adopted the Declaration of Independence. In February 1776, Patriots and Loyalists fought in North Carolina. The two sides also fought each other in Maryland.

After the Declaration of Independence, Patriots acted against Loyalists. They

accused Loyalists of treason. Sometimes, Patriot crowds beat up Loyalists. More often, state governments accused Loyalists of crimes and took away their property.

Some Loyalists fled from their homes during the war. In March 1776, the Continental Army forced the British army to leave Boston. About 1,100 Loyalists left with the British troops. At the end of the war, over 50,000 Loyalists left the United States. Many settled in Canada and in other British colonies. However, most Loyalists stayed in the United States. As time passed, people forgot the old divisions. Very few grandchildren of Loyalists knew which side their grandparents were on back in 1776.

African Americans on both sides
The British tried to get more supporters in the colonies. In November 1775, the royal governor of Virginia promised to free any slaves who fought for Britain. About 800 slaves joined the governor's forces. Later, thousands of African Americans served on the British side in the war. They served as soldiers, laborers, guides, sailors, and spies.

However, most African Americans sided with the Patriots. They supported the struggle for independence. Some were active in the Sons of Liberty. African American minutemen fought at both Lexington and Concord.

African Americans also volunteered to serve in the Continental Army. At first the congress turned them down. However, many states soon found themselves short of troops. They then allowed both free African Americans and slaves to serve as soldiers.

During the war, 5,000 African Americans served as soldiers with the Patriot forces. They served in units with white soldiers. Many of their officers praised their bravery. Another 2,000 served in the navy. Thousands more served as laborers, spies, and messengers. African Americans helped win the struggle for independence.

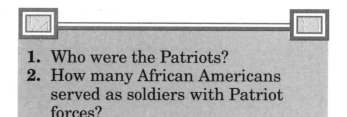

1. Who were the Patriots?
2. How many African Americans served as soldiers with Patriot forces?

CHAPTER 13
KEY IDEAS

- The Second Continental Congress voted for independence despite the great risks it knew the new nation faced.
- The Declaration of Independence stated the rights of Americans and listed the abuses of Great Britain against the colonies.
- Most Americans supported independence. A minority sided with Great Britain.

I. Reviewing Vocabulary

Match each word on the left with the correct definition on the right.

1. treason
2. ideal
3. Patriot
4. preamble
5. consent

a. an introduction
b. the act of betraying one's country, including trying to overthrow the government
c. when someone freely agrees to something
d. an idea or goal that someone tries to live up to
e. a colonist who supported independence from Britain

II. Understanding the Chapter

1. What were the main reasons that most of the delegates to the Second Continental Congress wanted to declare independence?
2. What were the arguments against declaring independence?
3. What basic rights did everyone have according to the Declaration of Independence?
4. What does the fourth part of the Declaration of Independence say?
5. What happened to some Loyalists after the Declaration of Independence was adopted?

III. Building Skills: Summarizing

On a separate sheet of paper, write two or three sentences that summarize each part of the Declaration of Independence as listed below.

1. the preamble of the Declaration of Independence
2. the second part of the Declaration of Independence
3. the third part of the Declaration of Independence
4. the fourth part of the Declaration of Independence

IV. Writing About History

1. Design a poster that announces the signing of the Declaration of Independence. Be sure to include details about the declaration.
2. **What Would You Have Done?** If you were an African American slave in Virginia in November 1775, would you have joined the British who offered freedom in return for fighting against the colonists? Explain.

V. Working Together

1. Break into small groups. Each group should prepare to debate whether or not the colonies should declare independence. Decide which position your group will take. List the reasons to support your position. Then the entire class should pretend it is the Second Continental Congress. Debate whether or not to declare independence.
2. **Past to Present** With a group, discuss the ideals expressed in the Declaration of Independence. Think about how the ideas influence people in the United States now. Then make a list of examples that show why these ideas are still important today.

THE COLONISTS FIGHT FOR INDEPENDENCE. (1776-1783)

How did the American colonists defeat the British and win independence?

In 1777, Sybil Ludington, aged 16, rode 40 miles through the night. She warned the people of Connecticut that the British were coming to attack.

Looking at Key Terms

- Hessians • Battle of Saratoga • Battle of Yorktown

Looking at Key Words

- **retreat:** to withdraw from or escape a battle
- **alliance:** a formal partnership between nations

STUDY HINT

Copy the time line onto a sheet of paper. Add events that are not already shown on the time line. Write a brief description of each event, and explain how it affected the outcome of the war.

The colonists knew that the fight for independence would be long and hard. At first, it appeared that they would lose the war. Slowly, their luck began to change.

1 Americans Lose Early Battles of the Revolution.

What were the key events in the months after the Declaration of Independence?

In the distance, the people of New York City saw the great fleet of British ships coming. Colonial soldiers were ready to defend the city. But the colonists were worried. The British had so many more soldiers than the Americans had.

The British attacked first on Long Island, east of New York City. They won the Battle of Long Island late in August 1776. Two weeks later, Britain's General William Howe captured New York City. The American army had to **retreat,** or withdraw from the battle. General George Washington barely escaped capture. He led his 5,000 soldiers into nearby New Jersey.

The British army The British were sure that they would win the war. Britain had 50,000 trained soldiers in the American colonies or on the way. Its navy ruled the seas. British ships could easily move supplies and soldiers to where they were needed. They could block ships that tried to supply the colonists. Britain could also count on help from Native Americans. Many Native Americans feared that the colonists would take away their lands.

Reading a Map. What British general invaded New York State after sailing up Canada's St. Lawrence River? When Lord Cornwallis left New York by ship, what Southern cities did he attack?

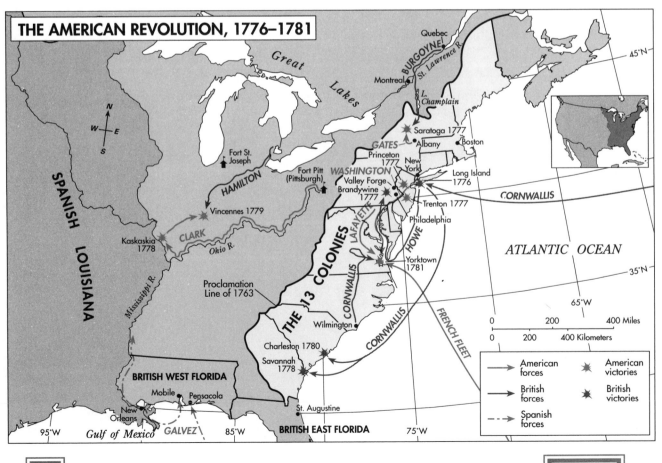

THE AMERICAN REVOLUTION, 1776–1781

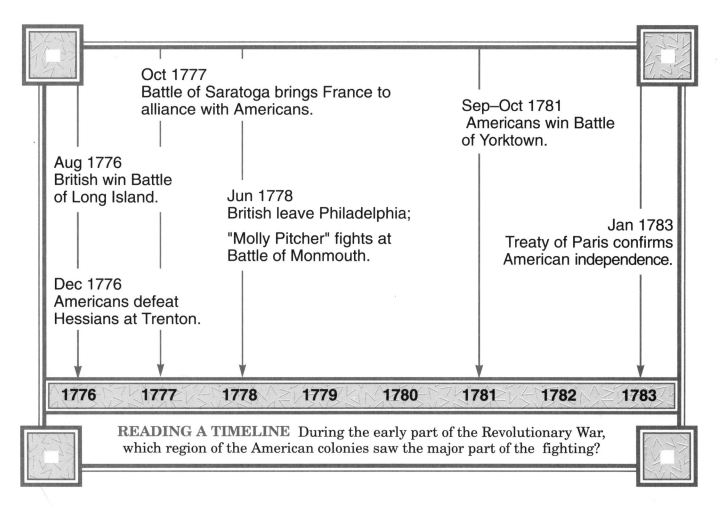

Oct 1777
Battle of Saratoga brings France to alliance with Americans.

Sep–Oct 1781
Americans win Battle of Yorktown.

Aug 1776
British win Battle of Long Island.

Jun 1778
British leave Philadelphia;

"Molly Pitcher" fights at Battle of Monmouth.

Jan 1783
Treaty of Paris confirms American independence.

Dec 1776
Americans defeat Hessians at Trenton.

| 1776 | 1777 | 1778 | 1779 | 1780 | 1781 | 1782 | 1783 |

READING A TIMELINE During the early part of the Revolutionary War, which region of the American colonies saw the major part of the fighting?

However, the British also faced some problems. Many people in Britain were against the war. They thought that the colonies should be allowed to go free. Another problem was the great distance that British ships had to sail to reach the colonies. The ocean was 3,000 miles (4,800 kilometers) wide. Finally, thousands of soldiers on the British side were **Hessians.** Hessians were German soldiers whom the British hired to fight. However, the Hessians did not feel great loyalty to the British cause.

The American army The colonists could not match the British in fighting power. The Americans had a very weak navy. They had only the small Continental Army. At most it numbered 10,000 men. Many of the American officers had little military training. The Continental Congress also had a hard time raising money to pay the army or to buy supplies.

The colonists had some big advantages, however. They were fighting for their freedom. They were defending their own homes and families. They were fighting on familiar ground. The colonists knew the trails and coastlines, the good lookouts, and the best places to hide. They also had excellent leaders.

George Washington George Washington was an impressive person at 6 feet 2 inches tall. He commanded respect even from his enemies. Washington was a wealthy planter from Virginia who owned many enslaved African Americans.

Washington had led a full life. He had commanded troops in the French and Indian War. Later, he served in the Virginia legislature and in the First and the Second Continental Congress. At the Second Continental Congress, Washington was the only delegate to

appear in a soldier's uniform. All the delegates voted "yes" when the congress elected Washington to command the Continental Army.

Washington's leadership was a key to the American victory. It was true that his soldiers lost more battles than they won. At times, his own officers plotted to have him replaced. However, Washington remained calm even during battle. In the end, his Continental Army won the war.

Early battles After the Battle of Long Island, the Americans fled into New Jersey. When the British followed, the Americans retreated to Pennsylvania. Washington feared that "the game was pretty nearly up." Still, he fought on.

On Christmas in 1776, Washington came up with a plan to take Trenton, New Jersey, from British hands. In the dark of night, Washington's men rowed silently across the icy Delaware River. Among the 2,400 soldiers in Washington's boats were two African Americans. One was Oliver Cromwell, a free man. The other was Prince Whipple, an enslaved man. The 1,400 Hessian soldiers in Trenton had settled down for the winter. They were not expecting an attack. The Americans easily took the Hessians by surprise and defeated them. A week later, Washington captured Princeton, New Jersey. These battles gave Americans hope of victory.

Burgoyne's plan British General John Burgoyne worked out a plan that he hoped would defeat the American colonies. Three British armies would move toward Albany, New York. Burgoyne would march one army south from Canada. General Howe would lead a second army north from New York City. A third army would approach Albany from the west. If the plan worked, New England would be totally cut off. It would fall into British hands like a ripe apple.

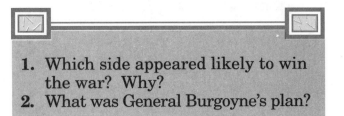

1. Which side appeared likely to win the war? Why?
2. What was General Burgoyne's plan?

2 The Tide Turns for the Americans.
Why was the Battle of Saratoga important?

General Burgoyne's plan might have worked if General Howe had cooperated. Instead of moving north, Howe's army went south. It attacked and occupied the American capital, Philadelphia. Now that the British forces were spread thinly, the Americans had a better chance in the north.

Victory at Saratoga General Burgoyne's army got off to a fast start. Burgoyne easily took back Fort Ticonderoga on Lake Champlain. Sure of victory, Burgoyne moved south toward Albany.

The big battle was fought near Saratoga, New York. There, an American force under General Horatio Gates won a clear victory over Burgoyne. On October 17, 1777, Burgoyne and his 5,000 soldiers gave up.

The **Battle of Saratoga** was a turning point. It blocked Britain's chances of cutting off New England from the other colonies. Still more important, it showed Europeans that the Americans had a chance to win. The victory convinced France to form an **alliance** with the Americans. An alliance is a formal partnership between nations. Before the alliance, France secretly had sent money and weapons to the Americans. However, it had not sent French soldiers or French ships. After Saratoga, France joined the Americans in making war on Britain.

Mary Ludwig Hays was helping her soldier-husband during a battle with the British. When her husband was wounded, Mary Hays took his place at the front lines. She loaded and fired cannon until the battle was won.

Winter at Valley Forge The victory at Saratoga did not end the Americans' troubles. The British now held the capital city, Philadelphia. The Continental Congress fled to York, Pennsylvania, 80 miles (130 kilometers) to the west. The Americans were desperate for new supplies.

Washington's poorly clothed and poorly fed troops spent the cold winter of 1777-1778 at Valley Forge, outside Philadelphia. Snow piled up, and icy winds ripped the soldiers' tents. The soldiers lacked clothing and supplies. Those without shoes lost their toes to frostbite. Some 3,000 of the 11,000 soldiers died during that terrible winter.

The next summer, new supplies came. The Americans and the British fought a fierce battle at Monmouth, New Jersey. At Monmouth, a woman named Mary Ludwig Hays became famous. Hays earned the name "Molly Pitcher" for carrying pitchers of water to Americans as they fought. When her husband fell, she took his place at a cannon. Like Hays, women throughout the colonies fought for the American cause.

War in the South Later in 1778, the war shifted to the South. Lord Cornwallis (korn-WOL-ihs) led Britain's Southern campaign. The British captured Savannah, Georgia. In 1780, they took Charleston, South Carolina. Loyalists in Southern states fought for the British cause.

Colonial soldiers fought bravely. They began to beat the British in quick battles. At last, the colonial soldiers succeeded in driving Lord Cornwallis back. Cornwallis retreated north to Yorktown, Virginia. There he built forts and waited for British ships to arrive. But to Cornwallis's surprise, French ships got there first.

Battle of Yorktown The combined American and French forces closed in on Cornwallis. French ships cut off the British navy so that it could not reach Yorktown. On land, American soldiers were led by a French noble, the Marquis de Lafayette (mahr-KEE deh lah-fih-YEHT). The Americans surrounded Cornwallis and his troops. James Armistead, an enslaved African

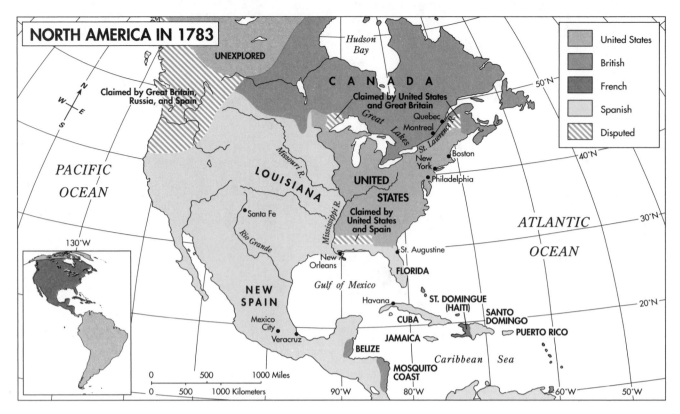

NORTH AMERICA IN 1783

	United States
	British
	French
	Spanish
	Disputed

UNEXPLORED

Claimed by Great Britain, Russia, and Spain

Hudson Bay

CANADA

Claimed by United States and Great Britain

Great Lakes

Quebec

Montreal

St. Lawrence R.

50°N

PACIFIC OCEAN

Missouri R.

LOUISIANA

UNITED

STATES

New York

Boston

Philadelphia

40°N

130°W

Santa Fe

Rio Grande

Mississippi R.

Claimed by United States and Spain

ATLANTIC

OCEAN

30°N

New Orleans

St. Augustine

FLORIDA

NEW SPAIN

Gulf of Mexico

Havana

ST. DOMINGUE (HAITI)

SANTO DOMINGO

20°N

Mexico City

CUBA

PUERTO RICO

Veracruz

JAMAICA

BELIZE

Caribbean Sea

MOSQUITO COAST

90°W

80°W

60°W

50°W

0   500   1000 Miles
0   500   1000 Kilometers

Reading a Map. When the American Revolution ended in 1783, who controlled most land east of the Mississippi River? What countries claimed land located at 50° N latitude and 120° W longitude?

American, risked his life to spy on the British for Lafayette. Years later, a grateful Virginia legislature set Armistead free. Other states also freed enslaved African Americans who had fought with the Continental Army.

The Battle of Yorktown in 1781 was a stunning American-French victory. General Washington brought 16,000 American and French soldiers from the north. Joining Lafayette's troops, they trapped Cornwallis and forced his 7,000 soldiers to surrender.

The American success at Yorktown ended British hopes for victory. When word of the battle reached London, the prime minister bowed his head. "It's all over! It's all over!" he said.

The Treaty of Paris was the peace agreement that ended the war. American and British officials signed the treaty in 1783. It gave the colonists most of what they wanted. Britain finally agreed to American independence.

The treaty set the new country's western border at the Mississippi River. (See the map above.) The country's borders did not include Florida. Florida belonged to Spain. Canada remained under British rule.

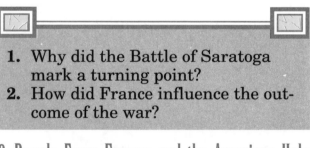

1. Why did the Battle of Saratoga mark a turning point?
2. How did France influence the outcome of the war?

3 People From Europe and the Americas Help the Colonists Defeat the British.

What help did Americans get from abroad?

The Americans owed part of their victory to Europeans. People from many lands fought for American independence. Without outside help, the

122

Chapter 14

chances of an American victory would have been slim indeed.

Baron von Steuben   Baron Frederick von Steuben (STOO-bin) was from Germany. He was a skilled general. Washington accepted von Steuben's offer to teach the Americans how to fight. During the terrible winter of 1777-1778, von Steuben arrived in Valley Forge. At first, he could not speak a word of English. Yet he made himself understood. Baron von Steuben turned American farmers into trained soldiers.

Bernardo de Gálvez   The Latino Bernardo de Gálvez (GAHL-vehz) also helped the American cause. Gálvez was from Spanish Louisiana. Spain declared war against Britain in 1779. As governor of Louisiana, Gálvez wanted to protect Spain's interests. However, Gálvez also wanted the Americans to win the war.

In 1779, Gálvez led a band of soldiers against British posts in West Florida. The soldiers included Latinos, African Americans, and Anglo Americans. He also helped Americans to sneak weapons past the British forts on the Mississippi River. In 1781, he led a Spanish fleet that took Pensacola, Florida, from the British.

Other friends of America   Thaddeus Kosciusko (kahs-ee-US-koh) was an engineer from Poland. He built forts on the Hudson River. Another Polish patriot was Count Casimir Pulaski. He led a group of Pennsylvania Germans in many battles. Pulaski died of battle wounds at Savannah, Georgia, in 1779.

Fighting beside the Americans at Savannah were hundreds of volunteers. They included 545 free Africans from French-ruled Haiti. The Haitians were part of a larger French unit. When the main French forces retreated, the Haitians moved forward. By holding the line, they prevented a French-American setback from becoming a crushing defeat.

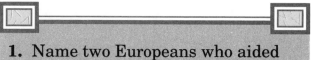

1. Name two Europeans who aided the Americans.
2. How did Bernardo de Gálvez help the American cause?

CHAPTER 14
KEY IDEAS

- Americans had major defeats in the early years of the Revolution.
- The American victory at the Battle of Saratoga was a turning point in the American Revolution. After Saratoga, France sent much-needed help. By 1783, the Americans were able to defeat the British.
- The Continental Army also received help from individuals such as Lafayette, von Steuben, Kosciusko, and Pulaski. Gálvez helped American troops in the South.
- After the war, Americans faced the task of building a strong new nation.

REVIEWING CHAPTER 14

I. Reviewing Vocabulary

Match each word on the left with the correct definition on the right.

1. retreat
2. Hessians
3. Continental Army
4. von Steuben
5. alliance

a. German soldiers hired by the British
b. German general who trained American soldiers
c. a formal partnership between nations
d. to fall back or withdraw
e. the American fighting force

II. Understanding the Chapter

1. What advantages and problems did each side have at the start of the American Revolution?
2. What qualities made George Washington a good military leader?
3. Why did General Burgoyne's plan fail?
4. Why was an alliance with France important to the Continental Army?
5. How did African Americans and Latinos contribute to the American victory?

III. Building Skills: Telling Facts from Opinions

Decide whether each statement below is a fact or an opinion. If it is an opinion, change the statement to make it a fact.

1. The British had far more soldiers than the Americans.
2. George Washington was wise to use foreign volunteers in the Continental Army.
3. The British should have followed Bourgoyne's original plan.

IV. Writing About History

1. Imagine that you are a colonial soldier in New York City in July 1776. You see a great fleet of British warships coming. Write a letter to your family telling how you feel and what you think will happen in the days ahead.
2. **What Would You Have Done?** If you were a Latino living in Florida or Louisiana, would you have joined Gálvez in fighting against the British? Explain.

V. Working Together

1. Form a small group. Imagine that you lived in one of the towns where the British and Americans fought. Prepare a skit showing how the war affected the people of the town. Tell whether the people of the town supported the British or the Americans and show how they helped the side they supported.
2. **Past to Present** People from several European countries helped the Americans defeat the British during the Revolutionary War. With a group, discuss why people from one country might fight for people from another country. Make a list of reasons. Then think of times when Americans have fought for people in foreign countries. Add these fights to your group's list.

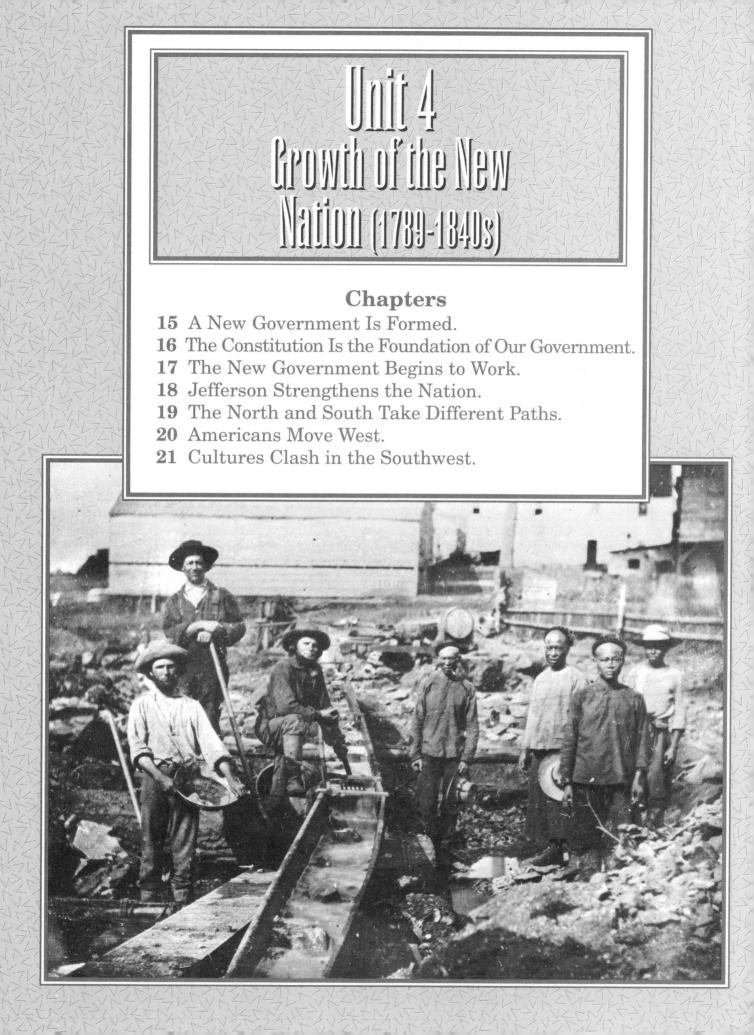

Unit 4
Growth of the New Nation (1789-1840s)

Chapters

A New Government Is Formed. (1781-1790)

How did the U. S. Constitution set up a government that has lasted more than 200 years?

With George Washington looking on, a delegate signs the U.S. Constitution. This document is the basis for the rights all Americans have.

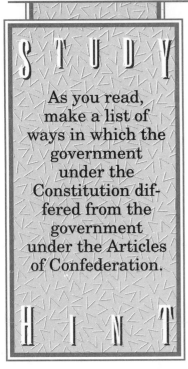

STUDY

As you read, make a list of ways in which the government under the Constitution differed from the government under the Articles of Confederation.

HINT

Looking at Key Terms

- Articles of Confederation • Constitutional Convention
- Federalists • Anti-Federalists • Bill of Rights

Looking at Key Words

- **constitution:** the basic laws under which a country operates
- **convention:** a meeting at which important decisions are made
- **republic:** a country where people choose their own leaders

- **compromise:** an agreement that gives each side part of what it wants
- **federal system:** a system of government in which the national government shares power with states or regions
- **ratify:** to approve
- **amend:** to change or revise

As the people of Philadelphia watched, a stream of men entered the red brick state house on May 25, 1787. Through the rain, they recognized the tall figure of George Washington. They saw James Madison, a short, slim man "no bigger than half a piece of soap." In all, 55 men entered the building. They represented 12 of the 13 states. Only Rhode Island did not send anyone.

These men were leaders in their states. They came to Philadelphia because they were worried about the problems facing the United States. Many of them thought that the national government was not working well. They met all summer long. In the end, they built a new plan of government. That plan is the U.S. Constitution—the basic laws of our land today.

1 A New Form of Government Is Needed.

Why was a constitution necessary?

In 1787, the United States had a very weak government. It had no President. It had no system of courts. All it had was a Congress in which each state had one vote.

Articles of Confederation During the American Revolution, the Continental Congress wrote a **constitution** called the **Articles of Confederation.** A constitution is a document that sets out the basic laws under which a country operates.

The Articles of Confederation created the first national government of the United States. The 13 states **ratified,** or approved, the Articles of Confederation in 1781. Congress could not **amend,** or change, the Articles of Confederation unless every state approved.

Under the Articles of Confederation, state governments had more power than the national government. The Articles of Confederation gave few pow-ers to Congress. Congress could make war. It could deal with foreign nations. It could print money and run a postal service. Congress could also set taxes, but the states collected the money. If the states refused to collect taxes, Congress had no way to get money.

Many weaknesses The weaknesses of the national government soon caused problems. The United States could not raise money to pay a navy. It could not pay back money it had bor-rowed during the Revolution.

Other nations took advantage of the United States' weakness. Britain had promised to remove its soldiers from the Great Lakes region. But it kept them there. Spain refused to allow U.S. citizens to use the Mississippi River. That hurt western farmers and fur traders. They needed the river to get their products to market. Across the Atlantic Ocean, pirates looted U.S. ships off the north coast of Africa.

Calling a convention People began to realize that the United States needed a stronger national government. They decided to call a **convention** to suggest changes in the Articles of Confederation. A convention is a meeting at which people make important decisions.

Congress asked each state to send delegates to a convention in Philadelphia. The delegates to the convention were powerful people. They were lawyers, merchants, and planters. All delegates were white, Christian men. There were no women delegates. Nor were there any African American, Latino, or Jewish delegates.

Writing a new constitution Within five days, the delegates decided to throw out the Articles of Confederation. They began the task of writing an entirely new constitu-

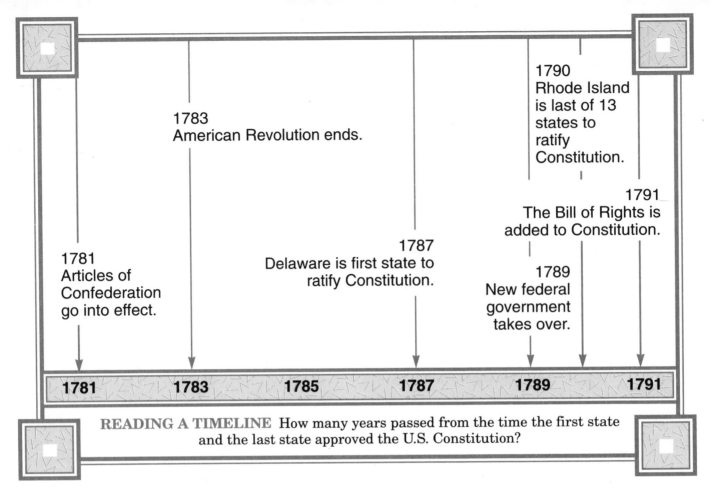

1790
Rhode Island is last of 13 states to ratify Constitution.

1791
The Bill of Rights is added to Constitution.

1783
American Revolution ends.

1787
Delaware is first state to ratify Constitution.

1789
New federal government takes over.

1781
Articles of Confederation go into effect.

| 1781 | 1783 | 1785 | 1787 | 1789 | 1791 |

READING A TIMELINE How many years passed from the time the first state and the last state approved the U.S. Constitution?

tion. Today, the historic meeting in Philadelphia is called the **Constitutional Convention.**

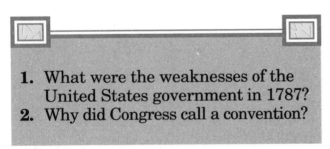

1. What were the weaknesses of the United States government in 1787?
2. Why did Congress call a convention?

2 Important Compromises Help to Create the Constitution.

What issues divided delegates to the Constitutional Convention?

"If men were angels, no government would be necessary," James Madison said. But people are not angels. Government *is* necessary. That was one idea, at least, on which the delegates could agree. That, and the need for a more powerful national government.

Choosing leaders The delegates also agreed on the basic form of the government. They wanted the United States to remain a **republic.** A republic is a country where the people elect their leaders. Americans did not want a king like Britain's King George.

Compromises On many other points, the delegates argued loudly. Some got so angry that they left and went home. But others stayed and kept talking. They worked out a series of **compromises,** or agreements in which each side got part of what it wanted.

The key compromises were between Northern and Southern states. The Northern and Southern states had different needs and interests. Northern states had the most citizens. People there owned few slaves. Southern states

had fewer free citizens than the Northern states. But they had many slaves. Slavery was central to the Southern economy. White southerners saw slavery as part of their way of life.

How could the delegates overcome these differences? Three big compromises settled the issues.

A federal system The delegates chose a **federal system** of government. In a federal system, the federal, or national, government shares power with state governments.

The delegates in Philadelphia wanted the national government to be more powerful than it was. However, they wanted to be sure that it did not become *too* powerful. Southern delegates in particular wanted to limit the national government. In that way, they hoped to protect slavery.

Big states and small states The delegates also had to decide how to divide power between big states and small states. The states with the most votes in Congress would have the most power. The delegates asked: Should the states have equal votes, as they did under the Articles of Confederation? Smaller states wanted it that way. Or should states with more people have more votes in Congress? That's what the big states wanted.

The delegates compromised. They created a Congress with two houses. In the House of Representatives, states with the most people would have the most votes. In the Senate, the states would be equal. Each state would have two senators and, therefore, two votes.

Counting slaves The last big compromise dealt with how enslaved people

This print shows a Southern plantation in the 1800s. One group of Americans who were not protected by the Constitution were African Americans. The writers of the U.S. Constitution allowed slavery to continue.

should be counted. Under the law, enslaved African Americans were considered "property." But delegates from the Southern states wanted them to be counted as "people"—even though they did not want to grant them the same rights as free people. Some Southern states had almost as many enslaved people as free citizens. If slaves and nonslaves counted the same, those states would have extra power in voting. Some Northern delegates thought that was wrong. They did not want slaves to count at all. As a compromise, the delegates decided to count each slave as three-fifths of a free citizen.

The delegates did not try to end slavery. However, they did allow a tax on the slave trade. They also agreed that after 1808, Congress might stop Americans from bringing in new slaves. Some delegates, to be sure, believed that holding people in slavery was wrong. But they knew that the new Constitution would never be adopted without the support of Southern delegates. Therefore, they also agreed that all states would be requested to return runaways to their owners.

1. What form of government did the delegates agree to have?
2. On what three main issues did delegates compromise?

3 The Constitution Is Adopted.

What issues divided supporters and opponents of the new Constitution?

On September 17, 1787, the delegates approved the new U.S. Constitution. As delegates signed the document, Benjamin Franklin told delegates his thoughts about the convention. For months he had been looking at a painting of the sun on the chair in which George Washington sat. Was it a rising sun—a sign of a hopeful future? Or was it a setting sun? "Now at last," Franklin said, "I know it is a rising sun."

State conventions The delegates were proud of what they had done. But would the nation approve? Before the Constitution could take effect, 9 of the 13 states had to ratify it. Each state held a convention to decide whether to say "yes" or "no."

Opinion was sharply divided. Supporters of the Constitution were called **Federalists.** Opponents were known as **Anti-Federalists.**

The Federalists James Madison, Alexander Hamilton, and John Jay strongly favored the Constitution. They wrote a series of essays supporting the Constitution. They argued that the United States needed a stronger government. A strong government would be able to promote trade and protect U.S. citizens. If the states rejected the Constitution, they said, the United States might break apart.

Other important Americans shared those opinions. George Washington and Benjamin Franklin were among the Federalists.

The Anti-Federalists Anti-Federalists did not trust government. A strong federal government could be dangerous. The President could become a tyrant—a cruel ruler. Congress could take away people's rights. Anti-Federalists like Patrick Henry and Samuel Adams wanted the United States to remain a loose grouping of states.

Approval Many people shared the fear that the new government would take away people's rights. To win their

support, the Federalists made a promise. If the Constitution was ratified, then Congress would add a bill of rights that guaranteed basic freedoms. You will read more about the **Bill of Rights** in the next chapter.

After that promise, support for the Constitution grew. The vote was close in many states. However, in June 1788, New Hampshire became the 9th state to ratify the Constitution. In 1790, Rhode Island became the 13th and last state to ratify the new union.

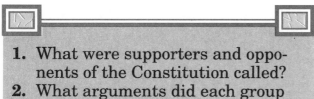

1. What were supporters and opponents of the Constitution called?
2. What arguments did each group make?

4 The Constitution Is Based on Ideas of Justice and Liberty.

How does the Constitution provide for a government that is fair to the people?

The rules laid down in the Constitution have shaped our national life for more than 200 years. The Constitution has been successful because it is a "living" document. The rules have grown and changed as people's ideas of justice and liberty have changed. Our freedoms today are rooted in the Constitution.

The Constitution is flexible "Liberty and Slavery—Heaven and Hell—are both in the Constitution," wrote Frederick Douglass. Douglass

Women at the polls in New Jersey. During the early years of the country, women were allowed to vote in some states. By the beginning of the 1800s, the states had taken the right to vote away from women.

was an African American. He was born into a system of slavery that the Constitution protected. The writers of the Constitution had ignored the rights of slaves. They had paid little attention to the rights of women. The Constitution made the United States a democracy. However, at first only about one person in ten could vote.

The Constitution kept up with the times. In the middle of the 1800s, it was changed to outlaw slavery. At the beginning of the 1900s, it was changed to grant women the vote. Today, all U.S. citizens have a say in our democracy.

The Constitution allows for change. It describes how people can amend, or change, rules. The Federalists kept their promise to add the Bill of Rights to the Constitution. By 1791, the states ratified 10 amendments. The amendments guarantee freedom of religion, freedom of speech, and many other freedoms. In all, Americans have added 27 amendments to the Constitution.

Ideas of the Constitution The Constitution contains many powerful ideas. First, it says that all the powers of government flow from the people. If people are not satisfied with the government, they can change it.

Second, the Constitution protects individual rights. For example, people in the United States may follow any religion they please.

Third, the federal government has only certain powers. The Constitution lists those powers. The 10th Amendment says that the powers that do not belong to the federal government belong to the states, or "to the people."

The Constitution is a living document that affects our lives every day. You will read more about it in the next chapter.

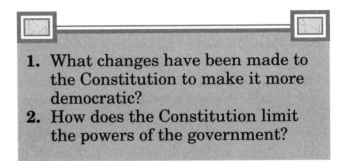

1. What changes have been made to the Constitution to make it more democratic?
2. How does the Constitution limit the powers of the government?

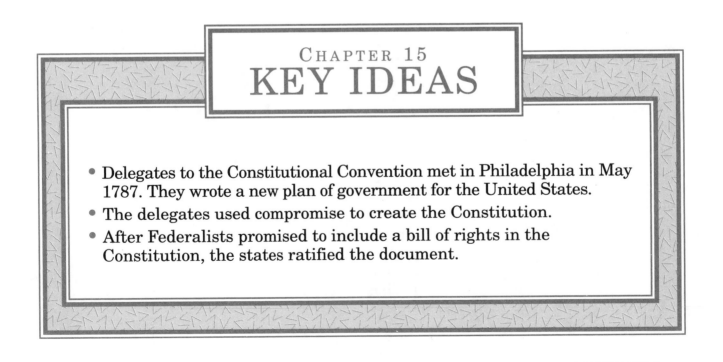

CHAPTER 15
KEY IDEAS

- Delegates to the Constitutional Convention met in Philadelphia in May 1787. They wrote a new plan of government for the United States.
- The delegates used compromise to create the Constitution.
- After Federalists promised to include a bill of rights in the Constitution, the states ratified the document.

I. Reviewing Vocabulary

Match each word on the left with the correct definition on the right.

1. republic   **a.** the basic laws under which a country operates
2. constitution   **b.** an agreement that gives each side part of what it wants
3. compromise   **c.** a country where people choose their own leaders
4. ratify   **d.** to change or revise
5. amend   **e.** to approve

II. Understanding the Chapter

1. Why was it hard for the United States to keep an army and navy under the Articles of Confederation?
2. Which compromises at the Constitutional Convention pleased the Southern states? Why?
3. How did the Constitution satisfy both the large states and the small states?
4. What arguments did Anti-Federalists make against the Constitution?
5. How has the Constitution become more democratic since 1787?

III. Building Skills: Making a Chart

Make a chart that lists the three main compromises at the Constitutional Convention. In Column 1, label them: Federalism, Representation, and Counting Slaves. In Column 2, list who was involved in the compromise. In Column 3, describe the compromise and how it worked.

IV. Writing About History

1. Imagine that you are a newspaper reporter in Philadelphia in September 1787. The delegates have just finished their work and you wish to interview some of them. Write a list of five questions that you want to ask the delegates.
2. **What Would You Have Done?** Imagine that you are a free African American living in a Northern state in 1787. Would you have supported the new Constitution? Why or why not?

V. Working Together

1. Choose two or three classmates to work with. Together, select a person in the United States in 1787. The person can be real (perhaps a delegate to the convention) or imaginary (a farmer or a slave). Write a brief description of the person. Then tell whether he or she supports the Constitution and why or why not.
2. **Past to Present** With a group, discuss why compromises were important. (You might look at the charts you made in Building Skills for information.) Then, list some situations today—in your school, community, or state—that are problems. Create compromises you think are necessary to solve the problems.

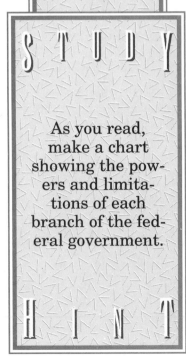

CHAPTER
16

THE CONSTITUTION IS THE FOUNDATION OF OUR GOVERNMENT.

How is the U.S. government organized under the Constitution?

The right to vote is one of the important rights the Constitution gives Americans. Above, the scene at a New York City polling place.

Looking at Key Terms

- separation of powers • checks and balances • Cabinet
- impeachment • due process

Looking at Key Words

- **legislative:** the branch of government that makes laws; Congress
- **majority:** more than half
- **veto:** to refuse to sign (a bill passed by the legislature)
- **unconstitutional:** against or not permitted by the Constitution

- **bill:** a proposed law
- **executive:** the branch of government, headed by the President, that carries out the laws
- **judicial:** the branch of government headed by the Supreme Court; the courts

STUDY HINT

As you read, make a chart showing the powers and limitations of each branch of the federal government.

In Chapter 15, you learned why the Constitution was written. In this chapter, you will learn how the Constitution organizes our government.

The U.S. Constitution divides the national government into three parts. The three parts, or branches, are Congress, the President, and the courts.

The Constitution creates a **separation of powers** among the three branches. Separation of powers means that each branch has its own duties. The members of Congress write the laws. The President carries out the laws. The judges of the Supreme Court and other federal courts settle disputes about the laws. The courts also make sure that the laws are carried out fairly.

Each branch of government can take actions that check, or limit, the powers of the other branches. The writers of the Constitution were careful to include this system of **checks and balances.** It keeps any part of government from becoming too powerful.

1 Congress Is Our Lawmaking Body.
What kinds of laws can Congress pass?

The main job of Congress is to write the nation's laws. Congress is the **legislative,** or lawmaking, branch of government. Congress is made up of two houses. The two houses are the House of Representatives and the Senate.

The House of Representatives As a result of the compromise between large and small states (see page 129), the House of Representatives is based on population. The states with the most people have the most votes.

The seven states with the smallest populations have only one representative. California, the state with the largest population, has 52. Today, the House has 435 members. Each member represents about 600,000 people in a congressional district. Representatives are elected by the voters of a district. The members of the House serve two-year terms.

The Senate Every state has the same number of senators, two. Tiny Vermont has as many senators as giant California. Senators serve six-year terms. Senators represent an entire state and not just one part of a state.

Making laws Congress passes many different types of laws. Some laws are passed to collect taxes. Other laws allow the government to spend money to build highways or keep an army. Still others involve help for senior citizens and the sick.

Congress cannot pass just any law. It must follow the rules of the Constitution. That is because the Constitution is "the supreme law of the land." This means that the Constitution is more important than any of Congress's laws. It is a "law above laws."

The Constitution lists many kinds of laws that Congress can pass. For example, Congress can set taxes. It can control trade between the United States and foreign countries. It can declare war and create an army and a navy. The Constitution also lists kinds of laws that Congress *cannot* pass. Congress cannot pass a law to punish a person without a trial.

Becoming a law Each law begins as a **bill,** or proposed law. A member of Congress introduces the bill. To introduce a bill means to put it up for discussion. In order to become law, a bill must receive a **majority** of votes in both houses of Congress. That means at least half of those voting in each house must support the bill. Then the President must sign it.

Checks on Congress The President and the Supreme Court have the power to check the actions of Congress. For example, suppose Congress passes a bill that the President does not support. The President may **veto,** or refuse to sign, the bill. After the President vetoes the bill, Congress can take another vote on it. However, now two thirds of each house must vote yes to pass it over the President's veto.

The Supreme Court also has the power to check Congress. It can declare a law **unconstitutional.** An unconstitutional law is one that goes against the rules of the Constitution. If a law is found to be unconstitutional, it is canceled.

The Congressional Black Caucus is made up of African American men and women who are members of the U.S. Senate and House of Representatives.

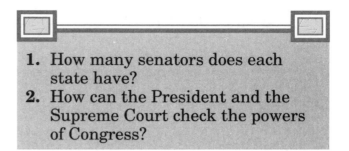

1. How many senators does each state have?
2. How can the President and the Supreme Court check the powers of Congress?

2 The President Heads the Government.

What part does the President play in our government?

Watch the news almost any evening. You will see the President making a speech. You may see the President visiting a distant land. You might hear about a bill that the President supports. Whatever the President does is news because the President is the top figure in U.S. government. The President heads the **executive** branch. The executive branch executes, or carries out, the laws.

The President also has other duties or powers. One duty is to be commander in chief of the armed forces. Another is to direct the nation's foreign policy. As the top figure in government, the President may propose new laws.

The President, along with the Vice-President, is elected by the people and serves a term of four years. Under the 22nd Amendment, a President can serve only two terms.

The Cabinet The President needs a variety of people to help carry out the duties of the office. The most important of these people are the leaders of the 14 departments of the executive branch. Those leaders belong to the President's **Cabinet.**

The secretary of state is one of the top members of the Cabinet. This official directs the work of the State Department, which deals with other nations. Other members of the Cabinet

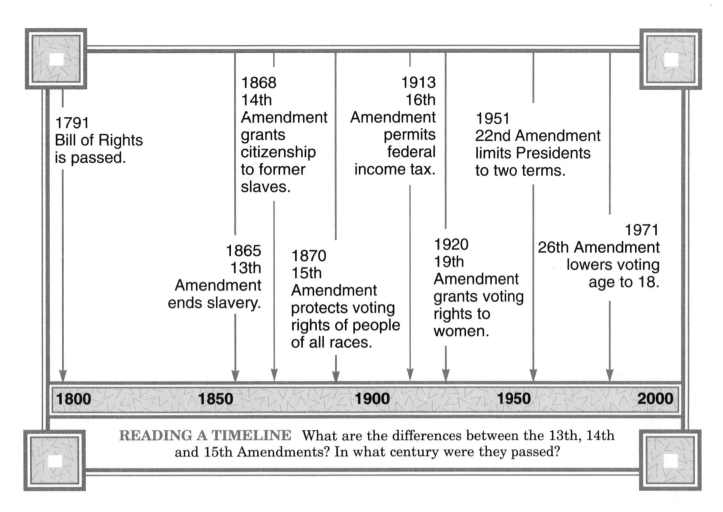

1791
Bill of Rights
is passed.

1868
14th
Amendment
grants
citizenship
to former
slaves.

1913
16th
Amendment
permits
federal
income tax.

1951
22nd Amendment
limits Presidents
to two terms.

1865
13th
Amendment
ends slavery.

1870
15th
Amendment
protects voting
rights of people
of all races.

1920
19th
Amendment
grants voting
rights to
women.

1971
26th Amendment
lowers voting
age to 18.

1800   1850   1900   1950   2000

READING A TIMELINE What are the differences between the 13th, 14th and 15th Amendments? In what century were they passed?

include the heads of the departments of defense, justice, and education.

Checks on the President Both Congress and the Supreme Court can limit the President's actions. You have read how Congress can pass a law over the President's veto. Congress also controls the money that the government spends. The executive branch cannot spend money unless Congress approves first.

The President chooses key people in the executive branch and in the courts. For example, the President appoints members of the Cabinet. The President also names members of the Supreme Court and judges of lower federal courts. But the Senate must approve the President's appointments. It can block any appointment it does not agree with.

Congress has one more very important power. It can remove the President from office through a process known as **impeachment.** Congress has used this power only once, in 1868.

The Supreme Court makes sure that the President obeys the Constitution. The Supreme Court also makes sure that the executive branch follows the laws passed by Congress. In one Supreme Court case, U.S. citizens sued the government. They said that part of the executive branch, the Environmental Protection Agency, was doing too little to enforce antipollution laws. The Supreme Court agreed. It ordered the agency to follow the law.

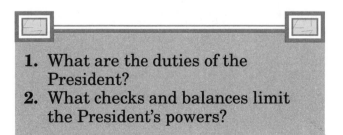

1. What are the duties of the President?
2. What checks and balances limit the President's powers?

Thousands of Americans gathered to watch Bill Clinton become President in 1993. The President is the head of the executive branch of government.

3 The Courts Decide Issues of Law.

What part does the judicial branch play in our government?

The federal courts make up the third branch of the federal government. This is known as the judiciary, or the **judicial** branch. The words come from the same root as "judge."

The Supreme Court   The Constitution says that the U.S. government must create a Supreme Court. In addition, Congress created a system of lower courts. At the head of the Supreme Court is the chief justice of the United States. Since 1986, that person has been William H. Rehnquist (REN-kwist).

The chief justice and eight associate justices are appointed by the President and approved by Congress. They hold office for life.

Visitors to the nation's capital can see the Supreme Court in action. Today, there are seven men and two women on the Supreme Court. The justices sit in a row behind a bench. Lawyers stand in front of the bench to argue their cases. After the arguments have been made, the justices decide the case. The side that convinces the majority of justices to agree with it wins the case.

A pyramid of courts   The federal judiciary is organized like a pyramid. The Supreme Court is a point at the top. Beneath it are layers of lower federal courts. In addition, each state has its own courts, separate from the federal courts.

Most federal cases start and end at the bottom layer. There are more than 100 federal district courts. Each state has from one to four such courts.

Above the district courts is a second layer, made up of 12 courts of appeals. Appeals courts do not conduct trials, as district courts do. Instead, they hear cases that have been appealed, or submitted for review, from lower courts. How does this happen? If someone who loses in a lower court feels that the decision was unfair, the loser may appeal the case.

Those who lose a federal case may ask the Supreme Court to review decisions of the appeals courts. Most of the cases that reach the Supreme Court start in the lower courts.

A Supreme Court case   The Supreme Court hears cases that have to do with constitutional issues. In the case of *Brown* v. *Board of Education of Topeka,* the Supreme Court was asked to decide whether the 14th Amendment was being followed.

During the 1950s, many towns in the United States had separate schools for African American and white students. Oliver Brown, an African American, decided to sue the board of education of Topeka, Kansas. The town would not allow Brown's daughter to attend an all-white school near their home.

The 14th Amendment states that all citizens must have equal protection under the law. The Supreme Court had to decide whether separate schools based on skin color could provide equal education. In 1954, the Supreme Court decided that separate schools could not provide equal education. The Supreme Court's decision outlawed separate schools in the United States.

Checks on the courts The judiciary, too, is subject to checks and balances. As you have read, the President appoints federal judges. Congress has a

say in this. If judges do not act properly, Congress can remove them from office.

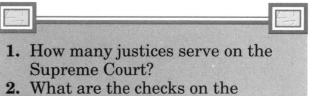

1. How many justices serve on the Supreme Court?
2. What are the checks on the Supreme Court?

4 The Bill of Rights Protects Individual Liberties.
What rights does the Bill of Rights protect?

The first ten amendments to the Constitution are the Bill of Rights. These amendments protect many rights of citizens. They protect your right to practice any religion you choose. They allow people to express their opinions freely. They forbid the government from putting a person in jail for years without a trial. It is important for all citizens to know their rights under the Bill of Rights.

Reading a Chart. Each of the three branches have powers that limit the other two branches. Name one way the judicial branch can check the legislative.

THE THREE BRANCHES OF THE U.S. GOVERNMENT: CHECKS AND BALANCES		
EXECUTIVE BRANCH	**LEGISLATIVE BRANCH**	**JUDICIAL BRANCH**
Carries out the laws	**Makes the nation's laws**	**Interprets the laws**
• can veto bills	• may remove President from office	• can declare laws unconstitutional
• appoints judges	• must approve President's appointments	• resolves disputes and punishes lawbreakers
• can call special sessions of Congress	• must approve treaties	• can declare President's actions unconstitutional
	• can pass laws over President's veto	

Americans have rights—but they have responsibilities. One is to participate in the life of their community. Above, Pennsylvania teenagers at a cleanup project.

Freedom of religion and speech The 1st Amendment protects several important freedoms. One is freedom of religion. The federal courts often have to decide what this means. The Supreme Court has said that public schools may not start the day by reading a prayer. However, the Supreme Court has allowed Congress to have prayers at its meetings.

The 1st Amendment also protects freedom of speech and of the press. Freedom of speech means the right to voice unpopular opinions in public. Freedom of the press means the right to publish those opinions.

The right to keep arms The 2nd Amendment protects the right to have arms, or weapons. The amendment links this right to the need of state governments to have a militia, or armed force. The 2nd Amendment is often mentioned when people discuss gun-control laws. Such laws would set limits on buying or owning guns. People who oppose such laws say that the laws go against the 2nd Amendment. People who favor such laws disagree. So far the courts have not made a clear ruling on the question.

No unreasonable searches The 4th Amendment protects people against

"unreasonable searches and seizures." This means that police can only search a car or house when they have a good reason. In many cases, they must first explain their reason to a judge to get permission.

Rights of the accused   Nothing is more frightening than to be arrested for a crime you did not commit. The 5th Amendment protects the rights of people accused of crimes. If the police suspect that someone committed a crime, they cannot just send that person to trial. First, they must present evidence to a group of citizens called a grand jury. Only if the grand jury believes that there is enough evidence can someone go to trial.

The 5th Amendment also protects a suspect's rights during and after a trial. You do not have to answer questions if your answers would make you seem guilty. The amendment also states that if a jury finds you not guilty, the decision is final. You cannot be tried again on the same charges.

The 5th Amendment says that the government cannot take your life, liber-ty, or property without **due process** of law. This means that the government must follow rules that are the same for everyone. It cannot treat white people one way and African American people another. It cannot treat rich people differently from poor people.

Other rights   The Bill of Rights covers many other freedoms. The 6th Amendment requires trial by jury. It states that trials must be speedy, public, and fair. The 8th Amendment bars "cruel and unusual punishments." Finally, the 10th Amendment refers to the powers of the states. The states—or the people—keep all the powers "not delegated [given] to the United States by the Constitution."

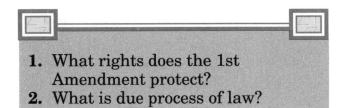

1. What rights does the 1st Amendment protect?
2. What is due process of law?

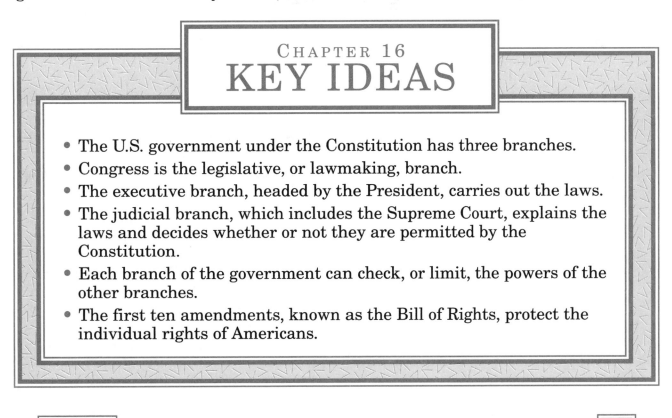

CHAPTER 16
KEY IDEAS

- The U.S. government under the Constitution has three branches.
- Congress is the legislative, or lawmaking, branch.
- The executive branch, headed by the President, carries out the laws.
- The judicial branch, which includes the Supreme Court, explains the laws and decides whether or not they are permitted by the Constitution.
- Each branch of the government can check, or limit, the powers of the other branches.
- The first ten amendments, known as the Bill of Rights, protect the individual rights of Americans.

REVIEWING CHAPTER 16

I. Reviewing Vocabulary

Match each word on the left with the correct definition on the right.

1. legislative	**a.**	the branch of government headed by the President
2. unconstitutional	**b.**	to refuse to sign (a bill)
3. executive	**c.**	the branch of government headed by the Supreme Court
4. judicial	**d.**	the branch of government that makes laws
5. veto	**e.**	against the Constitution; not permitted

II. Understanding the Chapter

1. How does the Constitution limit the types of laws that Congress can pass?

2. How can each of the three branches have a say in making the nation's laws?

3. What is the difference between the federal district courts and the federal appeals courts?

4. How would you decide whether to file a court case in a state court or in a federal court?

5. How does the Bill of Rights protect the rights of people accused of crimes?

III. Building Skills: Using Primary Sources

Find the 1st Amendment in a reference book. Read it over. On a sheet of paper, do the following:

1. Make a list of difficult words in the amendment. Find the words in a dictionary. Write their definitions beside them. (You may also want to refer to the discussion of the 1st Amendment on page 140.)

2. Summarize the amendment's major points.

IV. Writing About History

1. What Would You Have Done? Imagine that you were a justice on the Supreme Court during the case of *Brown* v. *Board of Education of Topeka*. How would you have ruled in that case? Write a brief paragraph explaining your decision.

2. Design a poster that explains one of the first ten amendments to the Constitution. The poster should relate the amendment to everyday life.

V. Working Together

1. Form a group of four students. Have each person in your group read a section of the chapter. Then, ask each person to write a brief summary of the main points covered in his or her section. Finally, share your summaries with one another to learn about the chapter.

2. Past to Present With a group, review the summaries of the 1st Amendment that you wrote in Building Skills. Discuss how the summaries are similar and different. Then, as a group, write a paragraph telling how your life might be different if the 1st Amendment did not exist.

THE NEW GOVERNMENT BEGINS TO WORK. (1789-1800)

What challenges did the first U.S. Presidents face?

On April 30, 1789, crowds gathered in the streets of New York. They were there to see George Washington take the oath as first President of the U.S.

Looking at Key Terms

- Democratic Republican • Whiskey Rebellion
- Farewell Address • 12th Amendment

Looking at Key Words

- **precedent:** an act or a decision that sets an example for later actions
- **tariff:** a tax on goods
- **Cabinet:** a group of advisers that help the President
- **neutral:** not taking sides in an argument

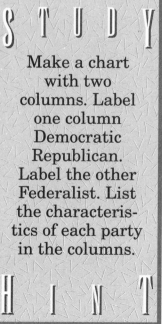

STUDY

Make a chart with two columns. Label one column Democratic Republican. Label the other Federalist. List the characteristics of each party in the columns.

HINT

The United States today is the most powerful nation on earth. It has a strong government and economy. It has two main political parties that most U.S. citizens support. It may seem that the United States was always powerful. But as you will read, that was not true in the nation's early days.

1 George Washington Becomes the First President.

How did George Washington help make democracy strong in the United States?

When George Washington became the first U.S. President in 1789, the country was not strong. Other nations did not respect the United States.

Reading a Chart. How did the two parties differ in their view of strong central government? Which party was pro-British? Which was pro-French?

THE FIRST POLITICAL PARTIES	
Federalists	Jeffersonian Republicans
★ Led by Alexander Hamilton	★ Led by Thomas Jefferson
★ Wealthy and well-educated should lead nation	★ People should have political power
★ Strong central government	★ Strong state governments
★ Emphasis on manufacturing, shipping, and trade	★ Emphasis on agriculture
★ Loose interpretation of Constitution	★ Strict interpretation of Constitution
★ Pro-British	★ Pro-French
★ Favored national bank	★ Opposed national bank
★ Favored protective tariff	★ Opposed protective tariff

Early difficulties The United States faced many difficulties. The people of the United States were not united. They were loyal to their state or region first. They called themselves Virginians or New Yorkers. The United States was their second loyalty.

Then there was a problem with money. The government had borrowed large amounts of money to pay for the American Revolution. It had to find ways to pay this debt.

The biggest question of all was: Would democracy work? The idea of democracy was an experiment. Democracy had failed in other places. Could it work in a country as large and diverse as the United States?

Taking office If there was anyone who could make democracy work, it was George Washington. Washington had not wanted to be President. He had accepted only because his friend James Madison persuaded him to take the office.

In April 1789, Washington left his home in Virginia. He was bound for New York City to be sworn into office. As Washington traveled north, crowds of people gathered to cheer him. Near the end of his trip, he crossed New York harbor in a boat painted red, white, and blue. He was rowed by 13 people, one for each state in the Union.

Washington looked very serious as he took the presidential oath. As the first President of the United States, he faced the toughest job of his life. Washington knew that he needed to unite Americans into a strong country.

Yet, Washington also realized that everything about his job was new. Any action that Washington took as President would be a first. Whatever he did would set a **precedent**. A precedent is an action that sets an example for later actions.

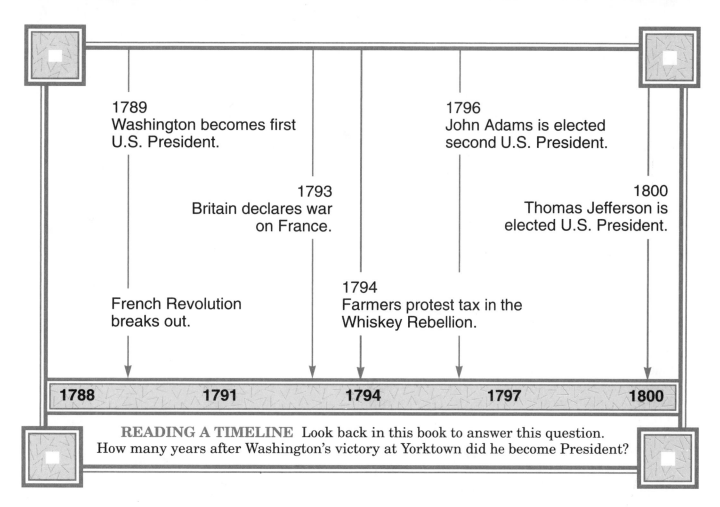

1789
Washington becomes first U.S. President.

1796
John Adams is elected second U.S. President.

1793
Britain declares war on France.

1800
Thomas Jefferson is elected U.S. President.

French Revolution breaks out.

1794
Farmers protest tax in the Whiskey Rebellion.

| 1788 | 1791 | 1794 | 1797 | 1800 |

READING A TIMELINE Look back in this book to answer this question. How many years after Washington's victory at Yorktown did he become President?

Choosing the first Cabinet

Washington's first job was to find able people to help him. He asked a few people to head the different departments of government. Washington's most important advisers became known as his **Cabinet**. The Constitution does not say there should be a Cabinet. Yet, every President since Washington has had a Cabinet.

Washington chose his Cabinet wisely. He did not care if the members of his Cabinet did not agree with him. He did not even care if they agreed with each other. What he wanted were good ideas about how to organize the nation.

One member of Washington's Cabinet was Thomas Jefferson. Jefferson was the first secretary of state. Jefferson believed that the United States should be ruled by rich and poor alike. He trusted farmers and workers to vote wisely and protect their freedom. Jefferson also believed that state governments should have more power than the national government.

Another member of Washington's Cabinet was Alexander Hamilton. Hamilton served as secretary of the treasury. He would decide how to raise money for the country. Hamilton believed that wealthy and educated people could run the nation best. He also believed that the national government should be stronger than the state governments.

The first political parties

When Washington took office, there were no political parties. As time went on, members of Congress started to disagree about ways to govern the country. Some members of Congress supported Hamilton's ideas. Others supported Jefferson's.

Those who supported Hamilton were called Federalists. Jefferson's support-

The Whiskey Rebellion of 1794 began because the U.S. government enforced a high tax on whiskey that was sold. This made Western farmers angry. Only George Washington's firm action helped end the violence.

ers were known as **Democratic Republicans**. These two groups were the first political parties in the United States.

The Federalists were in the majority in Congress. Therefore, in 1791, Congress began passing Hamilton's plans for the economy.

Hamilton convinced Congress to set up a bank to print money. He also persuaded Congress to pass certain tax laws. One of these laws put a **tariff,** or tax, on all foreign goods that came into the country. Another tax was placed on whiskey This whiskey tax was supposed to raise money. Instead, it led to a rebellion.

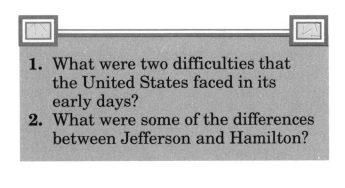

1. What were two difficulties that the United States faced in its early days?
2. What were some of the differences between Jefferson and Hamilton?

2 Washington Serves a Second Term.

Why was Washington's second term important for the nation?

During the early days of the nation, the settlements between the Appalachian Mountains and the Mississippi River were growing. Farmers west of the Appalachians raised corn and other grains. It was hard to ship these crops to market over rough mountain roads. It was easier to turn the corn into whiskey and ship it in jugs.

Whiskey became a very valuable product on the frontier. In many places, it was as good as money. Farmers traded it for things they needed.

The Whiskey Rebellion When the U.S. government enforced an existing tax on whiskey in 1794, farmers felt that the tax was unfair. Many farmers west of the Appalachians rebelled. They refused to pay the tax. Some also attacked tax collectors. Washington ordered the farmers to stop the attacks. The farmers refused. Thousands of farmers joined in a huge march.

Washington knew he had to act quickly. He called up 12,000 soldiers and took command. Faced with this show of strength, the farmers surrendered peacefully.

Washington's action was important to the new government. It showed that people had to obey all laws, even laws they did not like.

A new capital for the nation The first capital of the United States was in New York City. Later, the capital was moved to Philadelphia. But the leaders of the nation wanted to build a new capital that would show that the United States was a first-rate power.

Washington chose a team to build a city with wide streets and beautiful buildings. He asked French engineer Pierre L'Enfant (lahn-FAHN) to draw up plans for the city. L'Enfant's chief assistant was Benjamin Banneker. Banneker was a free African American who lived in Baltimore. Banneker was a gifted inventor. Once, he built his own clock, carving all the pieces out of wood.

The new capital city was complete in 1800. The city was named Washington in honor of George Washington. It was not a part of any state. The area around Washington was made part of the District of Columbia, or D.C., for short.

A neutral nation Washington agreed to serve a second term. During Washington's second term, the United States was still a new nation trying to survive. The last thing it needed was to be swept into Europe's wars. In 1789, revolution broke out in France. Soon, the king of France was overthrown.

At first, Americans were thrilled by the news of revolution in France. They believed that democracy would spread to France. Then France went through a

terrible time known as the Reign of Terror. During this time, many French people were beheaded, including the king and queen of France.

Other kings and queens in Europe were worried about their power. They decided to end the French Revolution. In 1793, Britain declared war on France.

Americans were divided over which country to back. The Democratic Republicans cheered the spread of democracy. The Federalists worried that the violence might spread to the United States. They wanted the United States to back Britain.

Washington did not agree with either side. He felt that Europe would always have its quarrels. The United States

This is a page from Benjamin Banneker's Almanac, which was popular in the 1790s. Banneker also helped design the new national capital, Washington, D.C.

After serving two terms as President, George Washington decided to retire. Here he is shown in 1796, bidding farewell to the officers who had served with him years before in the American Revolution.

was still weak. It should devote its energies to making itself strong. He said that the United States would trade with both France and Britain. However, it would not fight either country. It would remain **neutral** in the war. To be neutral is to refuse to take sides.

Farewell Address After his second term, the people wanted Washington to serve as President again. Washington set another precedent. He said that he would not serve a third term. No President served more than two terms until 1940.

When he left office, Washington gave a **Farewell Address**, or speech. He warned against political parties. He said parties would cause quarrels among Americans. He also told the American people to stay out of Europe's wars.

Washington's health was failing as he retired. He wrote a friend: "I now compare myself to the weary [tired] traveler who seeks a resting place." The American people mourned when he died in 1799.

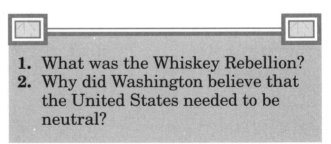

1. What was the Whiskey Rebellion?
2. Why did Washington believe that the United States needed to be neutral?

3 The United States Struggles to Keep Out of War.
How did President John Adams's actions cause divisions in his political party?

In 1796, John Adams was elected the second President of the United States. Adams was an able leader, although he never became very popular. He worked hard to keep the United States out of war. In the end, he was successful. However, it ruined his career.

Many people pressured Adams to declare war. Both the French and British were seizing U.S. ships. The French even demanded a bribe to stop the attacks. Americans were angry when they heard about the demand. Some called for war with France.

Still Adams held out. People in his own Federalist party wanted war with France. They were so angry that they split from the party. This gave the Democratic Republicans the chance to win the election of 1800. Democratic Republicans chose Thomas Jefferson to run for President. They also named Aaron Burr to run for Vice-President. The Federalists named John Adams and Charles Pinckney.

An odd election The election of 1800 was the strangest election in U.S. history. The Constitution said that the person with the most electoral votes would become President. The person who came in second would become Vice-President. In the election, both Jefferson and Burr received the same number of electoral votes.

Who would be President, Jefferson or Burr? The Constitution said that when the electoral vote was tied, the House of Representatives would choose the President.

The House voted 35 times. Each time, the vote was a tie. On the 36th try, some votes shifted. Jefferson became President. Burr became Vice-President.

The election of 1800 caused Congress to amend, or change, the Constitution. It passed the **12th Amendment**. The amendment says that electors must vote separately for President and Vice-President. There can be no more elections like the one of 1800.

1. Who ran for President and Vice-President in 1800?
2. How did the 12th Amendment change the way the President and Vice-President are elected?

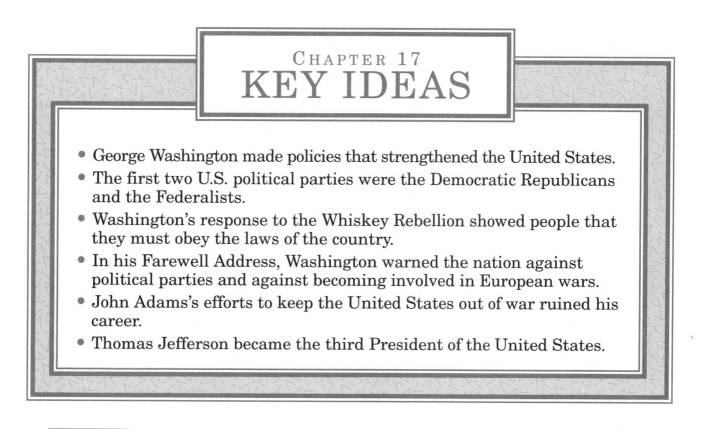

CHAPTER 17
KEY IDEAS

- George Washington made policies that strengthened the United States.
- The first two U.S. political parties were the Democratic Republicans and the Federalists.
- Washington's response to the Whiskey Rebellion showed people that they must obey the laws of the country.
- In his Farewell Address, Washington warned the nation against political parties and against becoming involved in European wars.
- John Adams's efforts to keep the United States out of war ruined his career.
- Thomas Jefferson became the third President of the United States.

REVIEWING CHAPTER 17

I. Reviewing Vocabulary

Match each word on the left with the correct definition on the right.

1. debt
2. precedent
3. Cabinet
4. tariff
5. neutral

a. a group of advisers that help the President
b. not taking sides in an argument
c. money that is owed
d. an act or a decision that sets an example for later actions
e. a tax on goods coming from another country

II. Understanding the Chapter

1. What was one precedent that George Washington set?
2. Explain how the first two political parties in the United States began.
3. Why did farmers west of the Appalachians rebel against the tax on whiskey in 1794?
4. Why did some Americans support the French Revolution? Why were some against it?
5. How did the Democratic Republicans gain a chance to win the presidency in 1800?

III. Building Skills: Understanding Cause and Effect

Understanding causes and effects is important in studying history. Causes are events or conditions that lead to a major event or development. Effects are the results of the major event or development. Answer the questions below to learn more about cause and effect.

1. What was the cause of the 12th Amendment?
2. What was one effect of the amendment?

IV. Writing About History

1. Imagine that George Washington has asked you to help him choose a Cabinet. Make a list of at least five qualities or characteristics that you think Cabinet members should have.
2. **What Would You Have Done?** Would you have joined the Federalists or the Democratic Republicans? Explain.

V. Working Together

1. Choose two or three classmates to work with. Imagine that you have been asked to design a new capital city for the United States. Include in your design buildings for the two houses of Congress, the Supreme Court, the Treasury Department, and other departments of government. Design a house for the President.
2. **Past to Present** George Washington's Farewell Address was a warning to the nation. With a group, discuss what Washington was concerned about. Then talk about dangers to the United States today. As a group, make a list of warnings that could be included in a farewell speech now.

JEFFERSON STRENGTHENS THE NATION. (1800-1814)

How did the new nation double in size and defend its territory?

Lewis and Clark led a group that included the African American, York, across the continent. They were guided by the Shawnee woman, Sacajawea.

Looking at Key Terms

- Northwest Territory • Land Ordinance of 1785
- Northwest Ordinance • Battle of Tippecanoe
- Louisiana Purchase • Lewis and Clark Expedition
- War Hawk • War of 1812

Looking at Key Words

- **territory:** an area that is not yet a state
- **ordinance:** a law
- **diary:** a daily record of notes and information

- **impressment:** forced service, especially in a navy or other armed force
- **embargo:** a government order preventing trade

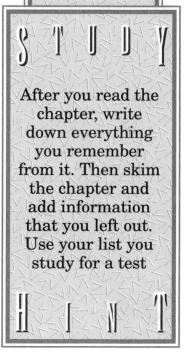

STUDY

After you read the chapter, write down everything you remember from it. Then skim the chapter and add information that you left out. Use your list you study for a test

HINT

After the American Revolution, pioneers such as Daniel Boone led settlers to Tennessee and Kentucky. Thousands set out for the **Northwest Territory.** A **territory** was an area that was not yet a state. The Northwest Territory was located north of the Ohio River and west of the Appalachian Mountains. Settlers wanted its rich land. But, so many arrived that conflicts broke out.

1 Americans Move Westward.

How did the Congress organize territory in the West?

By 1785, many people had moved into the Northwest Territory. Rules were needed for settling this region. So Congress passed the **Land Ordinance of 1785.** This **ordinance** (OHR-duhn-

uhns), or law, called for the land to be divided into sections. Each section would have land set aside for a school.

A second law, called the **Northwest Ordinance,** was passed in 1787. This law set up rules for government in the territories. It outlawed slavery there. It also guaranteed freedom of religion and trial by jury. In addition, the Northwest Ordinance set up a way in which the territory could be organized into states.

A territory could ask Congress to be admitted as a state when there were 60,000 "free people" living there. However, free people did not include Native Americans or enslaved African Americans.

Five states were carved from the Northwest Territory. They were Ohio, Indiana, Illinois, Michigan, and Wisconsin. Later, other territories followed the same rules to be admitted as states. The Northwest Ordinance created a way for new states to enter the United States.

Growing conflicts Settlers streamed into the Northwest Territory in the 1790s. But Native Americans already lived there. They had signed treaties with the U.S. government. These treaties were supposed to protect Native American land. Yet the settlers ignored the treaties. They cut down trees to set up farms. This made it hard for the Native Americans to hunt. The Native Americans and the settlers soon clashed. Each hoped to drive the other off the land.

Tecumseh's plan Two Shawnee brothers wanted to stop the settlers from taking more land. The two were Tecumseh (tih-KUM-suh) and Tenskwatawa (tehn-SKWAH-tah-wah), who was also known as the Prophet. The brothers began to unite many Native American groups to push back the settlers.

Reading a Map. Into what river does the Ohio River flow? Name five of today's states that were carved from the Northwest Territory.

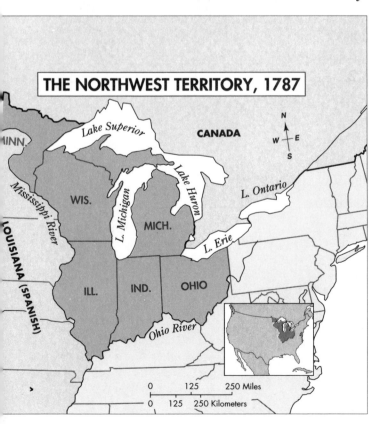

THE NORTHWEST TERRITORY, 1787

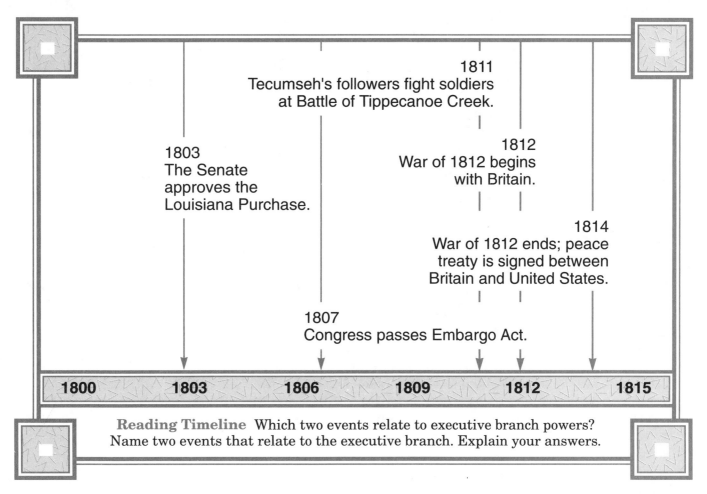

1811
Tecumseh's followers fight soldiers
at Battle of Tippecanoe Creek.

1803
The Senate
approves the
Louisiana Purchase.

1812
War of 1812 begins
with Britain.

1814
War of 1812 ends; peace
treaty is signed between
Britain and United States.

1807
Congress passes Embargo Act.

| 1800 | 1803 | 1806 | 1809 | 1812 | 1815 |

Reading Timeline Which two events relate to executive branch powers? Name two events that relate to the executive branch. Explain your answers.

Tecumseh was a powerful speaker and a great leader. He traveled many miles visiting different Native American groups. He urged them to unite against the settlers. He convinced many Native American nations to join his campaign.

Battle of Tippecanoe Many settlers worried that Tecumseh's plan would stop settlement. Governor William Henry Harrison of Indiana took action. In 1811, he marched 1,000 soldiers to Tecumseh's village on Tippecanoe (TIP-uh-kah-noo) Creek in Indiana. The soldiers and Native Americans, led by Tecumseh's brother Tenskwatawa, fought a bloody battle. Neither side was a clear winner. Yet many people in the East celebrated the **Battle of Tippecanoe** as a victory for the settlers. This battle was only the beginning of a long war between Native Americans and settlers.

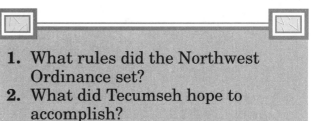

1. What rules did the Northwest Ordinance set?
2. What did Tecumseh hope to accomplish?

2 The United States Grows Larger.
Why did President Jefferson buy the Louisiana Territory?

Thomas Jefferson became the third President of the United States in 1800. By this time, one million settlers lived between the Appalachians and the Mississippi. Most were farmers. They needed to ship their crops down the Mississippi to New Orleans. (See map on page 155) This city was a key link to markets in the East and in Europe. New Orleans, however, did not belong to the United States.

An old print shows the Battle of Tippecanoe in 1811. At this battle, the American forces under William Henry Harrison fought the Native Americans led by Tenskwatawa, the brother of the absent Shawnee chief, Tecumseh.

The Louisiana Purchase In 1800, France owned Louisiana, which included New Orleans. Jefferson decided to try to buy New Orleans from the French. He sent agents to France with an offer of $10 million. The French government surprised the Americans. They were not just interested in selling New Orleans. They wanted to sell all of the giant Louisiana Territory. The shocked Americans agreed on a price of $15 million.

A constitutional issue Jefferson was eager to purchase the Louisiana Territory. The land would double the size of the United States. It would also place the port of New Orleans under U.S. control. The price that France asked for all this land was low. Yet Jefferson had one major concern. Did the Constitution allow the President to buy land from another country?

In the end, Jefferson decided that he had the right to buy land. After all, the Constitution stated that the President could make treaties. The Senate agreed. In 1803, it approved the **Louisiana Purchase**. A huge amount of land west of the Mississippi was now part of the United States.

Exploring the new land In 1803, a small group of Americans set out on a dangerous trip to study the new U.S. territory. Meriwether Lewis and William Clark led the group. Jefferson asked them to bring back all the information they could about the new land. He wanted them to go beyond the Louisiana Territory. He hoped they would find a route through the Rocky Mountains to the Pacific Ocean.

The Lewis and Clark Expedition set out from St. Louis in 1804. (See map on page 155.) Lewis and Clark kept **diaries** of what they saw. A diary is a daily record of notes and information. They wrote about flat stretches of land that seemed to go on forever. They described large herds of buffalo and deer. They told about the Native Americans who offered them friendship.

Among the group was York, an enslaved African American. York proved to be a valuable member of the expedition. He was an excellent hunter. He traded with many Native Americans for food that kept the group alive.

The explorers traveled 1,600 miles (2,560 kilometers) up the Missouri River. There, they met **Sacajawea** (sahk-uh-juh-WEE-uh), a Shoshone (shoh-SHOH-nee) Native American. She and her husband guided the expedition westward. Finally, the group reached her homeland in the Rocky Mountains. There, Sacajawea convinced her people to give the explorers food, horses, and a guide.

The group continued through the mountains. Then they took canoes down the rough Columbia River. Many times, they almost smashed into rocks. On November 7, 1805, Lewis and Clark saw a great body of water. At last, they had found the Pacific Ocean.

Lewis and Clark brought back important information about the Louisiana Purchase and the land west of the Rockies. They made detailed maps of the region. In years to follow, 15 states were created from the Louisiana Purchase.

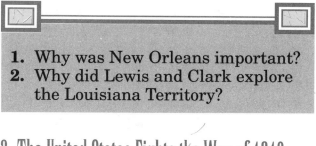

1. Why was New Orleans important?
2. Why did Lewis and Clark explore the Louisiana Territory?

3 The United States Fights the War of 1812.
What events led to the War of 1812?

At the beginning of the 1800s, the United States grew stronger. However, events in Europe soon slowed the young nation's growth. In 1803, war broke out again between France and Britain. Jefferson did not want the United States to get involved. He declared that the country would stay neutral.

Staying neutral Merchant ships from the United States continued to

trade with both countries. These U.S. ships provided many of the supplies that France and Britain needed. So both France and Britain tried to stop the United States from trading with the other. The French navy captured U.S. trading ships bound for Britain. The British seized U.S. merchant ships on their way to France. Both sides stole valuable cargoes and sometimes even the ships themselves.

U.S. merchants were furious. Even worse, sailors captured on U.S. ships were often forced into the British navy. This practice was called **impressment,** or forced service. The British impressed thousands of U.S. sailors.

Then, in 1807, a British warship opened fire on a U.S. ship right off the

Reading a Map. What was the border of the Louisiana territory on the west? What nation controlled most of the American West at the time?

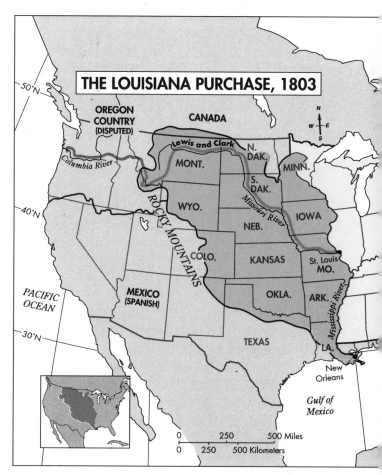

THE LOUISIANA PURCHASE, 1803

During the War of 1812, the British sailed up the Chesapeake to attack and set fire to the new American capital at Washington, D.C. The British burned many government buildings, including the home of the President.

coast of Virginia. Many Americans demanded that the United States declare war on Britain. Instead, Jefferson asked Congress to pass an **embargo,** or a government order stopping trade. In 1807, Congress passed the Embargo Act. This act made it illegal for U.S. merchants to import or export any goods. Jefferson thought an embargo would hurt Britain and France.

But the Embargo Act did not work as Jefferson expected. It hurt the United States more than it hurt Britain or France. Thousands of sailors were out of work. Farmers could not sell their crops. Merchants lost money. Congress had to replace the Embargo Act with a law that was not as strict.

James Madison easily won the 1808 presidential election. President Madison hoped to avoid war. However, Britain continued to attack U.S. trading ships and impress U.S. sailors.

Pressure for war   By this time, many more Americans wanted war with Britain. In 1810, this prowar feeling affected who was elected to Congress. A group of new representatives from the Middle West and the South pushed hard for war. They said British attacks on U.S. ships showed that Britain had lost respect for the United States. This group was called the **War Hawks.**

The War Hawks feared that Britain might try to win back control of the United States. They were convinced Britain was behind Native American attacks on settlers in the Middle West.

The War Hawks also wanted more land for the United States. They thought the United States could get it by winning a war. Many settlers in the South wanted Florida. This land was owned by Spain, Britain's ally. The War Hawks also wanted to conquer Canada.

The War of 1812   Finally, in June of 1812, Madison gave in to the War Hawks' pressure. The President asked Congress to declare war on Britain.

Early in the War of 1812, U.S. troops invaded Canada. The Canadian troops were joined by British soldiers and several Native American groups. The U.S. invasion failed. The British even gained control of parts of the Northwest Territory. Later, U.S. forces won back this territory.

In 1813, the British fleet controlled the Great Lakes. They captured the city of Detroit on Lake Erie. U.S. Captain Oliver Hazard Perry was ordered to remove the British. Perry had no ships when he received the order. Over several months, Perry and a team of local helpers secretly built nine small ships. Then Perry's troops sailed out to face the British warships. After a fierce battle, Perry won control of Lake Erie. His victory message proudly declared, "We have met the enemy and they are ours."

The war between Britain and France was over in 1814. Britain was able to send more troops to fight in the United States. British forces attacked the capital of the United States, Washington, D.C. As the British neared, Dolley Madison, the President's wife, risked her life to save important papers. She escaped just in time. The British burned many government buildings—including the President's house.

By the end of 1814, it seemed that neither the United States nor Britain was winning the war. In late December, a peace treaty was signed. The War of 1812 was over.

However, news traveled slowly. Both armies continued to fight. U.S. forces, led by Andrew Jackson, crushed a British attack on New Orleans. One of the greatest U.S. victories was won after the war had already ended!

The War of 1812 did not really change much between the United States and Britain. U.S.-British relations simply returned to the way they had been before the war. However, many Americans felt that the young United States had made the European nations have more respect. The war proved that the United States could defend itself.

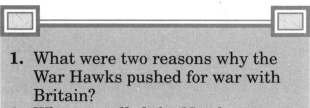

1. What were two reasons why the War Hawks pushed for war with Britain?
2. Who controlled the Northwest Territory after the War of 1812?

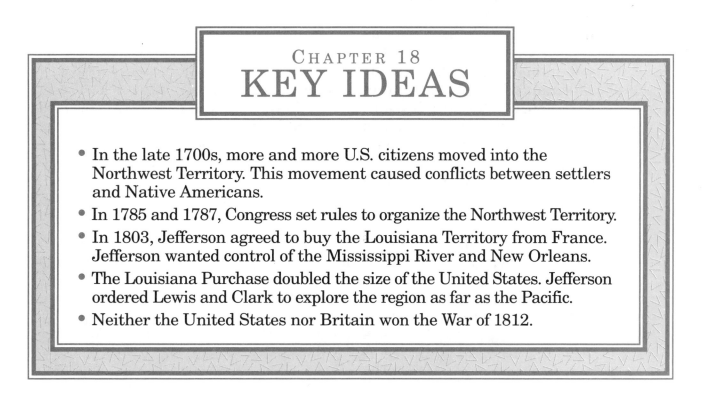

CHAPTER 18
KEY IDEAS

- In the late 1700s, more and more U.S. citizens moved into the Northwest Territory. This movement caused conflicts between settlers and Native Americans.
- In 1785 and 1787, Congress set rules to organize the Northwest Territory.
- In 1803, Jefferson agreed to buy the Louisiana Territory from France. Jefferson wanted control of the Mississippi River and New Orleans.
- The Louisiana Purchase doubled the size of the United States. Jefferson ordered Lewis and Clark to explore the region as far as the Pacific.
- Neither the United States nor Britain won the War of 1812.

REVIEWING CHAPTER 18

I. Reviewing Vocabulary

Match each word on the left with the correct definition on the right.

1. territory
2. embargo
3. Northwest Territory
4. impressment
5. ordinance

a. forced service, especially in a navy
b. land bordered by the Ohio River and the Appalachian Mountains
c. a law
d. a government order preventing trade
e. an area that is not yet a state

II. Understanding the Chapter

1. What two laws did Congress make to organize the Northwest Territory?
2. Why was New Orleans important to the settlers in the West?
3. What was the purpose of Lewis and Clark's trip?
4. What was the effect of the Embargo Act?
5. What did many Americans feel was a result of the War of 1812?

III. Building Skills: Time Check

1. Did the flood of settlers moving to the Northwest Territory begin before or after the Land Ordinance of 1785? How do you know?
2. Did the Louisiana Purchase come before or after Lewis and Clark crossed the continent? Explain your answer.

IV. Writing About History

1. **What Would You Have Done?** Imagine that you are a leader of a Native American nation in 1810. Tecumseh tells you that the only way to stop settlers from taking more land is to unite with other Native Americans. Some of the Native American groups joining Tecumseh have attacked you in the past. Would you tell your people to follow Tecumseh? Explain.
2. Imagine that you are an explorer with Lewis and Clark. Write at least three entries in a diary. Write down what you see and feel as you cross the Rockies and canoe down the Columbia River.

V. Working Together

1. Form a small group with some of your classmates. In your groups, think of an important event that occurred during the early years of the United States. Create storyboards about that event for a movie. A storyboard is a series of drawings and captions that show the order of scenes to be shot for television or the movies.
2. **Past to Present** The first three Presidents of the United States wanted the country to be neutral. Decide, with a group, if you agree with the three Presidents' ideas. Then discuss whether the United States should be neutral today. Explain your group's most important opinions in a class discussion.

THE NORTH AND SOUTH TAKE DIFFERENT PATHS. (1793-1840)

How did the North and South begin to grow apart?

An 1858 photograph shows African Americans working as slaves in cotton fields on a Georgia plantation. This work brought the South great wealth.

Looking at Key Terms

- Industrial Revolution • cotton gin • Vesey Conspiracy

Looking at Key Words

- **textile mill:** a factory where cloth is made
- **boardinghouse:** a house where room and meals can be purchased
- **overseer:** the person who watches over slaves' work

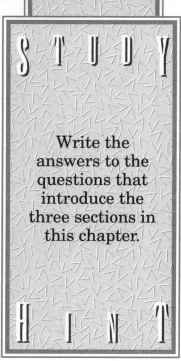

S T U D Y

Write the answers to the questions that introduce the three sections in this chapter.

H I N T

In the 1700s, most American families made or grew almost everything they needed. If they could not make or grow it, they bought it. People made goods such as shoes, candles, and cloth in their own homes. By the end of the century, that would change.

1 Factories Are Built in the North.

Why were thousands of factories built in the North beginning in the 1800s?

During the 1700s, a great change was taking place in Great Britain. Today, this change is called the **Industrial Revolution**. This was not a revolution with fighting and bloodshed. Rather, it was a peaceful change in the way people made goods.

The Industrial Revolution   The change started when people began to use the power of water to run machines. Later, people invented other machines that ran by steam power.

The new machines could make goods much faster than people could make them. However, the machines were very expensive. Only wealthy people could afford to buy them and start businesses.

At first, Britain was the only country with the new machines. That put Britain in a strong position. Cotton grown in the United States was shipped to Britain to be made into cloth for clothing. The cloth was then shipped back to the United States and sold. This brought big profits to British factory owners. It also made clothing very expensive for Americans.

To protect their profits, the British would not allow the machines out of the country. They also would not allow the plans to build the machines out. The gov-

Work conditions were grim in the new mills of the Northeast. Women and children worked from before dawn until late into the night in the first cloth mills. Their wages? Usually, workers earned less than $2 per week.

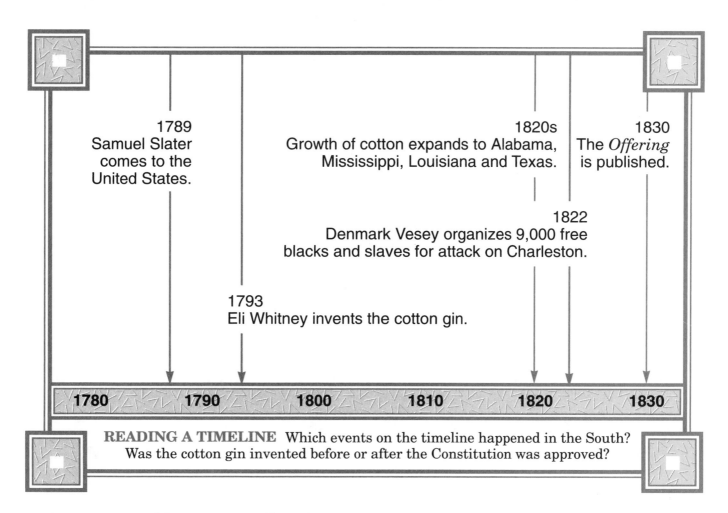

1789
Samuel Slater comes to the United States.

1793
Eli Whitney invents the cotton gin.

1820s
Growth of cotton expands to Alabama, Mississippi, Louisiana and Texas.

1822
Denmark Vesey organizes 9,000 free blacks and slaves for attack on Charleston.

1830
The *Offering* is published.

1780   1790   1800   1810   1820   1830

READING A TIMELINE Which events on the timeline happened in the South? Was the cotton gin invented before or after the Constitution was approved?

ernment would not even allow factory workers to leave. However, wealthy Americans offered large rewards to anyone who would bring them plans for the machines. There were some people who were willing to risk jail to win this reward.

The first U.S. factory   Samuel Slater was a young factory worker who decided to take a risk. Slater knew that the British would search his baggage if he left. They would throw him in jail if they found the plans for machines. So Slater spent years memorizing every part of every machine in the factory. Then he told the British he was a farmer and left by boat for the United States.

In New York, Slater wrote to Moses Brown, a wealthy merchant in Providence, Rhode Island. Slater said: "If I do not make as good yarn as they make in England, I will take no money for my services, and I'll throw every-

thing I build over the bridge." Brown could not refuse such an offer.

Slater built a complete cotton mill from memory in Rhode Island. Later his wife, Hannah developed a way to make thread stronger so it would not snap. The Slaters made so much money that other Americans started building their own **textile mills** in the Northern states. A textile mill is a place where cloth is made. Within 20 years, 165 mills were operating in New England.

Factory workers   Without workers, there could be no factories. At first, most workers came from small farms. Later, many factory workers came from other countries. (See Chapter 22.)

Factory work was hard. Workers labored 12 to 14 hours a day, six days a week. Most workers earned less than two dollars a week. Running the machines was dangerous. People who

were injured simply lost their jobs. They received no money or help from factory owners.

Factories were not pleasant places to work. Factories were unbearably hot in summer. In winter they were cold, and the air was thick with smoke from lamps. Throughout the year, the factories were terribly noisy. As time went on, workers were forced to operate three and sometimes four machines at the same time. They were given little time to eat. Workers could be fired just for laughing.

The "Lowell girls"   Young women and children did most of the work in the factories. They were hired because they would work for less money. Often, they received less than half what a man earned for doing the same work.

A wealthy factory owner named Francis Cabot Lowell wanted to hire women as workers. He realized that he would have to make factory work respectable. That would encourage parents to allow their daughters to work for him. Lowell started by building **boardinghouses** for the women workers. A boardinghouse is a place where people can rent a room and get a meal. The Lowell boardinghouses were supervised by older women. That way, parents knew their daughters were safe.

A day in a Lowell factory started early and ended late. The factory bell rang at 4:00 A.M. to call the young women to work. Looms were ready by 5:00 A.M. At 7:30 A.M., workers were allowed to eat breakfast. At noon, there was a 30-minute lunch break. Finally, at 7:30 P.M., a bell released the young women to go home. The final bell of the day rang at 10:00 P.M. for lights out in the boardinghouses. The factories were closed only on Sundays.

In their time off, the women could attend lectures and go to school. They wrote poetry and even published their own magazine, called the *Offering*. In fact, the first factory workers felt like pioneers. They were opening up new ways for women to support themselves. They gave women a freedom they had not had before.

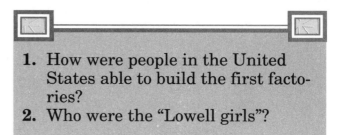

1. How were people in the United States able to build the first factories?
2. Who were the "Lowell girls"?

2 The South Becomes a Slave Society.
Why did the growth of cotton increase the demand for slaves?

Two different worlds were developing in the United States during the early 1800s. The North had busy cities. It had many factories and farms. It had railroads, roads, and canals to carry people and goods from one place to another.

A different way of life grew in the Southern states. It was a world dominated by slavery. Most whites in the South did not own slaves. In fact, in 1860 only about 40,000 of the 8 million people in the South owned 20 or more slaves. Still, slavery affected all people who lived there.

The cotton gin   A new machine played a key role in making slavery important. The person who developed this machine was a young teacher named Eli Whitney. Whitney had a talent for invention. While traveling in the South, he became interested in a problem that Southern cotton planters had.

The problem was cotton seeds. Before cotton could be made into yarn, the seeds had to be removed. The seeds were tough and sticky. Because it was hard to

Eli Whitney's cotton gin is shown in this picture. By removing seeds much quicker than it could be done by hand, the cotton gin made cotton growing more profitable. What effect did this have on slavery?

remove them, a person could clean only a few pounds of cotton a day. The planters wanted to speed up this process.

Whitney decided to invent a machine that would help the planters. He worked day and night for six months. Whitney hid behind a locked door in a small basement room so he would not be disturbed. In 1793, he produced a simple machine to remove seeds. He called his invention a "cotton engine," or "cotton gin" for short. The new cotton gin was an instant success. It sped up work tremendously. Now a person could pick the seeds from about 1,000 pounds of cotton in a single day.

Whitney's machine changed farming in the South. Cotton farming became so profitable that most Southern farmers stopped growing tobacco and began growing cotton. Within one year, cotton production went up 12 times. Within eight years, it had increased more than 250 times.

Growing slavery To grow such large crops, plantation owners planted more land with cotton. They expanded to new lands in Alabama, Mississippi, Louisiana, and Texas. Soon, white Southerners were saying: "Cotton is king."

Huge numbers of workers were needed to grow so much cotton. Who were these workers? White Southern farmers chose to use enslaved African Americans. Slavery had long been a part of life in the South. With the new importance of cotton, many more slaves were needed. Slaves were sent from islands in the Caribbean. Enslaved African Americans in tobacco areas were also sold to cotton planters. The planters did not care if they broke up families. All they wanted were more workers for their cotton crops.

Where did all this cotton go? Most of the cotton went to the textile mills in the North. There, it was made into yarn and then into cloth. The Northern mills could

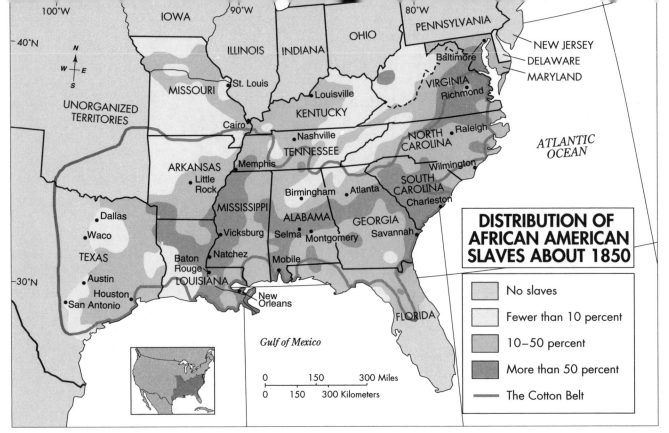

Reading a Map. Which state had a larger percentage of slaves in its population: North Carolina or South Carolina? Which large cities shown on the map were outside the Cotton Belt?

not have produced so much cloth without Southern cotton raised by enslaved African Americans. So Northern factory owners also became rich because African Americans were enslaved.

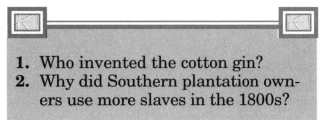

1. Who invented the cotton gin?
2. Why did Southern plantation owners use more slaves in the 1800s?

3 Enslaved African Americans Fight for Their Freedom.

What were living conditions like for enslaved African Americans?

How did it feel to be enslaved on a plantation in the South? Slavery differed from place to place. However, the worst conditions were on cotton plantations.

Solomon Northup was a free African American who was kidnapped and sold into slavery. He was forced to work in the cotton fields for 12 years. After he won his freedom in 1853, Northup wrote about his years as a slave.

The workers are required to be in the cotton fields as soon as it is light in the morning. They are only given 10 or 15 minutes at noon to swallow some cold bacon. They are then not allowed to be idle [rest] until it is too dark to see. When the moon is full, they often work until the middle of the night.

Enslaved African Americans were controlled by an **overseer,** the person who watched over and directed the slaves' work. If the overseer did not think the slaves were working hard enough, he could whip them. "The lash [whip] flew from morning to night," said Northup.

Each evening, weary slaves came home to still more chores. They hauled water, chopped wood, and cared for their

small gardens. Then they built fires in their own cabins and cooked their supper. After they ate, they went to bed. An hour before dawn, a horn woke them to begin another day of labor.

Learning to survive   Nothing could make African Americans forget the pain of slavery. However, enslaved African Americans developed their own culture that helped them survive. To forget the cruelty of their daily lives, slaves turned to activities that reminded them of their homeland. Music, dancing, and storytelling provided a break from hard work. The family was the greatest defense against the cruelties of slavery. Enslaved African Americans created a feeling of closeness among themselves by calling one another "brother" and "sister" even when they were not related.

Slaves knew that at any point a mother, a sister, a son, or a father could be sold to a slave owner far away. They probably would never see that loved one again. Slave owners would even sell parents away from their children. To deal with this horror, everyone took part in caring for children. All the slaves acted as mothers or fathers to the young.

African Americans also had strong religious beliefs. They held secret meetings to practice their faith. They developed religious songs, or spirituals. These spirituals expressed their hatred of slavery. The songs proclaimed that all people are equal in the eyes of God.

Fighting slavery   From colonial times, African Americans rose up against slavery. Free African Americans as well as slaves fought against it. There were uprisings wherever there was slavery. There was one

This old print shows a slave market from the 1850s. African American slaves dreaded the idea that someone in the family might be taken away and sold. Those who were sold might never see their families again.

in New York City in 1712. New York then had more slaves than any other city except Charleston, South Carolina. New York had another uprising in 1741. In each case, officials executed the rebels and passed tough new laws.

The Vesey conspiracy   With the rise of cotton farming in the South, slave conditions got worse. This caused many new uprisings in the South. One of the most important was led in 1822 by a former slave named Denmark Vesey. Vesey had bought his freedom for $600 after he won a lottery. He then became a carpenter in Charleston, South Carolina.

Despite his good fortune, Vesey continued to hate slavery. He vowed to take over Charleston. He held meetings in his house to develop a plan for the uprising. Vesey knew there were seven key points in the city. If the group could capture these seven points, the plotters would control the city.

Vesey thought he had kept the plot secret. However, at the last moment, one of his partners revealed the plans. Officials arrested Vesey and about 130 other African Americans. Vesey and 45 others were executed. The rest were put in prison or sent to slavery on islands in the Caribbean. South Carolina also passed strict laws limiting the rights of free African Americans.

Other uprisings like Vesey's failed. Still, the uprisings continued until the Civil War. These uprisings showed just how much African Americans hated slavery. Whether free or enslaved, African Americans suffered. The will to be free burned brightly within all African Americans.

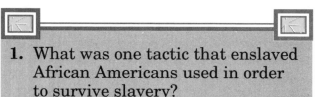

1. What was one tactic that enslaved African Americans used in order to survive slavery?
2. Who was Denmark Vesey?

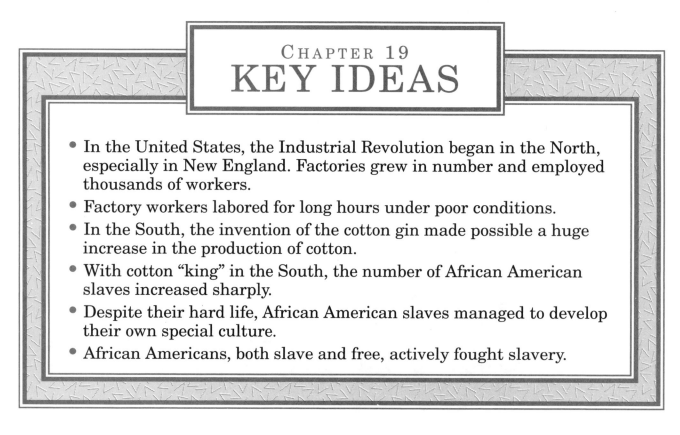

CHAPTER 19
KEY IDEAS

- In the United States, the Industrial Revolution began in the North, especially in New England. Factories grew in number and employed thousands of workers.
- Factory workers labored for long hours under poor conditions.
- In the South, the invention of the cotton gin made possible a huge increase in the production of cotton.
- With cotton "king" in the South, the number of African American slaves increased sharply.
- Despite their hard life, African American slaves managed to develop their own special culture.
- African Americans, both slave and free, actively fought slavery.

I. Reviewing Vocabulary

Match each word on the left with the correct definition on the right.

1. Industrial Revolution
2. boardinghouse
3. cotton gin
4. overseer
5. textile mill

a. a factory where cloth is made
b. a machine for removing seeds
c. the time when many goods began to be produced by machines in factories
d. the person who watches over and directs the slaves' work
e. a house where rooms and meals can be purchased

II. Understanding the Chapter

1. How was Samuel Slater able to build the first factory in the United States?
2. Why did factory owners like to hire women and children as workers?
3. How did Eli Whitney's invention change farming in the South?
4. How were Northern mills and Southern plantations connected?
5. What were some of the things that enslaved African Americans did to forget the cruelty of their daily lives?

III. Building Skills: Reading a Map

Study the map on page 164. Then answer the following questions:
1. What states were part of the cotton belt?
2. Which states had the highest percentage of African American slaves?
3. What does this tell you about the relationship between slavery and cotton?

IV. Writing About History

1. **What Would You Have Done?** If you had been a young person living on a farm in New England, would you have become a factory worker? Explain your reasons.
2. Enslaved African Americans created songs and spirituals that expressed their longing for freedom. Write the words to an original song that tells of a deep desire for freedom.

V. Working Together

1. Choose several classmates to work with. Together you will create a mural showing what life was like in the early 1800s. Your mural could show a factory town, people working at the machines, slaves laboring in a cotton field, or something else. After you have finished your mural, write a title that informs viewers about your subject.
2. **Past to Present** In the 1800s, many inventions changed the way people in the United States lived. With a group, discuss the inventions and the changes that they made. Make a list of new inventions that have changed peoples' lives today.

AMERICANS MOVE WEST. (1820-1860)

*What happened as the
United States spread westward?*

In 1838, the Cherokee people were forced from their homes in the U.S. Southeast. They had to move west in a march known as "The Trail of Tears."

Looking at Key Terms
- Erie Canal • Oregon Country • Indian Removal Act
- Indian Territory • Trail of Tears

Looking at Key Words
- **frontier:** the edge of a country next to a wilderness
- **canal:** waterway dug by people to connect two bodies of water

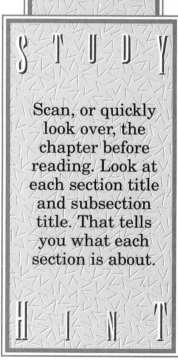

"Westward ho!" called the wagon master as the stream of wagon trains left for the lands of the **frontier.** A frontier is the edge of a country next to a wilderness. In the 1800s, the lands west of the Mississippi River were known as the frontier.

Many of the people on the wagon trains had been encouraged by the words of a New York newspaperman named Horace Greeley. In 1846, Greeley printed an article that advised people to go west. Searching for a chance to build better lives, thousands of men and women took Greeley's advice. They looked forward to building their homes and making their fortunes in the West. To them, the West seemed open and unsettled. But there were thousands of Native Americans and Mexicans living on land that the new settlers would soon claim.

1 Travel Becomes Easier and Cheaper.

How did new ways of travel help people moving west?

Americans had been moving west since colonial times. Early settlers built communities near rivers. The rivers provided an easy way to move people and goods from place to place.

Improving transportation   As more people moved west, the land near the rivers became crowded. Settlers began moving farther away from the rivers. Far from rivers, they had to use dirt roads to move goods to market. But these roads made travel slow and more expensive. Settlers needed a better way to reach the rivers.

Reading a Map. In what section of the country were most of the major railroads located? In what directions did most of the major roads go, north and south, or east and west? Why was this so?

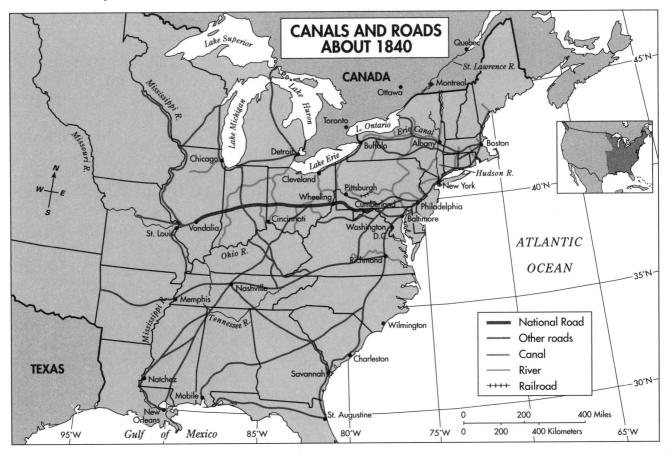

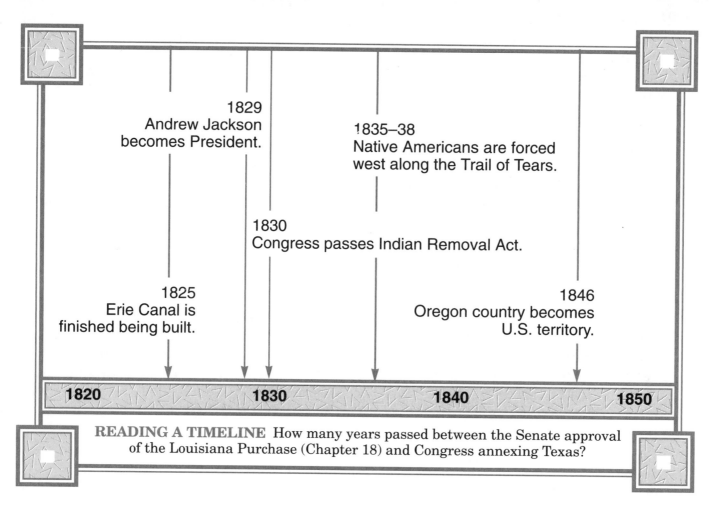

1829
Andrew Jackson becomes President.

1835–38
Native Americans are forced west along the Trail of Tears.

1830
Congress passes Indian Removal Act.

1825
Erie Canal is finished being built.

1846
Oregon country becomes U.S. territory.

1820   1830   1840   1850

READING A TIMELINE How many years passed between the Senate approval of the Louisiana Purchase (Chapter 18) and Congress annexing Texas?

To solve their problem, settlers began building **canals.** Canals are waterways dug by people to connect two bodies of water. To build a canal, workers dug a deep passageway in the earth between rivers or lakes. They filled the passageway with water and used it to ship goods to market. Settlers who lived near canals no longer needed to rely on roadways.

Building canals was not easy. It was also expensive. But once canals were built, they proved to be one of the most efficient ways to move people and goods.

The Erie Canal For many years, New Yorkers had dreamed of a canal that would connect the Hudson River with Lake Erie. Their dreams were realized when the Erie Canal was built.

The Erie Canal was an engineering wonder. Nothing like it had ever been done before. Workers began digging the canal in 1817. Using only shovels and scoops, they dug 363 miles (584 kilometers) from Albany, New York, on the Hudson River to Buffalo, New York, on Lake Erie. (See map on page 171.)

The Erie Canal took eight years to build and cost $7 million. It was the longest canal in the world. People and goods traveled the canal on barges. Mules and horses walked along the edge of the canal and pulled the barges.

Advantages of the canal The canal made it possible to ship goods between New York City and the Great Lakes region. The barges carried such things as furniture and clothing west. They brought grain and lumber east.

The Erie Canal made transporting goods much cheaper. Before the canal was built, it cost $100 to send a ton of wheat from the Midwest to the East. Using the canal, it cost only 8 dollars a ton for the same trip.

Towns and cities along the canal grew quickly. New cities like Syracuse and Rochester sprang up. Buffalo grew into a busy city. New York City became the largest city in the United States.

By 1840, there were many other canals. The people of Pennsylvania and Ohio built large canals of their own. Canals connected the Great Lakes with the Ohio and Mississippi rivers. Towns such as Cleveland and Cincinnati became important cities. Canals helped more people to move west and allowed western products to move east.

Going farther west   Trails such as the Oregon Trail and the Santa Fe Trail became important routes. The journey from Independence, Missouri, to the West Coast could last up to six months. Settlers traveled in covered wagons. The wagons were organized into wagon trains for safety. Sometimes, as many as 120 wagons were part of a train. Stagecoaches began to carry people over long distances. By 1858, stagecoaches made regular trips from the East to California.

Many settlers moved to **Oregon Country.** (See the map below.) Oregon Country was occupied by Britain and the United States. In 1846, they divided Oregon. Settlers also moved to lands that were part of Mexico. These lands included California, New Mexico, and Texas.

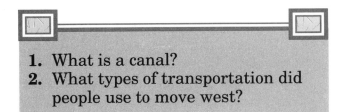

1. What is a canal?
2. What types of transportation did people use to move west?

Reading a Map. Where did the Mormon Trail begin? Where did the Oregon Trail end? If you had gone from St. Louis to Los Angeles during this time what trails would you take and what towns would you pass through?

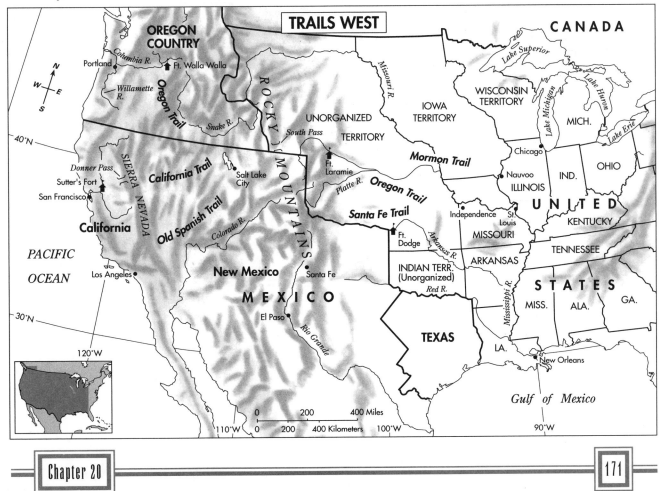

2 Settlers Build New Lives in the West.

How was life in the West different from that in the East?

Once settlers arrived in the West, they began to build new lives. The first things they needed were food and shelter.

Life on the frontier   Living on the frontier was hard and dangerous. First, the land had to be cleared of trees, bushes, and large stones. Settlers used the trees they cut to build their first homes. These homes were often simple shelters.

A frontier family's first real house was usually a log cabin. It was no more than a box made of trees and mud. Neighbors would come from miles around to help new settlers build their homes.

After the trees were cut down, grass could grow on the land. Cattle and other farm animals could then feed on the grass. The rest of the land was used for growing crops.

Family members usually did all the farmwork themselves. They raised animals, hunted for food, cleared more land, and planted crops. They made their own furniture, clothes, and tools.

As more people moved west, towns began to grow. Some towns sprang up where rivers met. Others appeared along important roads. As towns grew, schools, churches, and stores were built. Even with everything that a town supplied, life on the frontier was still hard.

Democracy in the West   The people who moved west were from all parts of the United States and the world. Some were poor people from the South. Others were people who had lived in the East and wanted to leave the growing cities. Some were Northern farmers who wanted better land to grow their crops. There were also immigrants from other countries who hoped to have land of their own.

The settlers all shared the same hardships and fears. Because of this, settlers often saw themselves as equals. The way they governed themselves reflected their belief that all were equal.

The settlers set up governments based on those in the East. However, more people could participate. Community problems were discussed at town meetings where all white men over the age of 21 had a vote. In the East, only white men who owned property could vote. But women, African Americans, Native Americans, Latinos, and Asians could not vote in the East or the West.

When white male factory workers and others in the East heard about the voting rules in the West, they wanted to vote too. Many of the Eastern states changed their laws and allowed all white men to vote. This made the United States more democratic.

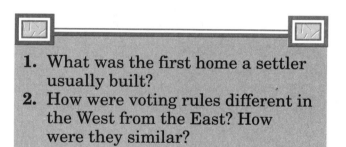

1. What was the first home a settler usually built?
2. How were voting rules different in the West from the East? How were they similar?

3 Native Americans Are Forced to Move.

How did settlement of the Western lands affect Native Americans?

As you learned in Chapter 18, the United States went to war with Great Britain in 1812. At the beginning of the war, the government asked the Cherokee nation to fight the British. Many Cherokee hoped that the U.S. government would stop taking their lands if they fought on the side of the Americans. So they joined with the United States in the War of 1812.

Hundreds of Cherokee served under the command of General Andrew Jackson. During one battle, a Cherokee named Junaluska (joo-nah-LOC-skah) saved Jackson's life. Despite this brave act, after the war was over, Jackson turned against his Native American allies.

Andrew Jackson became President of the United States in 1829. By that time, many Native Americans from the East had moved west. They were forced off lands in the East by settlers. Only about 125,000 Native Americans still lived east of the Mississippi River. Most of them lived in the southeastern states. Many of these Native Americans accepted the customs of white settlers. They hoped to live in peace with white Americans. One of the most important of these groups was the Cherokee.

The Cherokee nation   The Cherokee had a written constitution. It declared the Cherokee an independent nation within Georgia. The constitution set up a separate Cherokee government.

The Cherokee constitution was written in the Cherokee language. The Cherokee writing system was developed by a silversmith named Sequoyah (suh-kwoi-uh).

Sequoyah took 12 years to develop the Cherokee alphabet. Sequoyah spoke no English and knew little about writing. Yet he realized that written language would be a great tool for the Cherokee.

Using Sequoyah's alphabet, Cherokee leaders created schools where young Cherokee learned to read and write. The Cherokee wrote down their history, beliefs, and treaties. They printed books and published a newspaper.

Reading a Map. What Native American groups shown on the map were forced from their homelands? Using the distance scale, about how many miles were the Seminole people forced to travel? In what direction did they go?

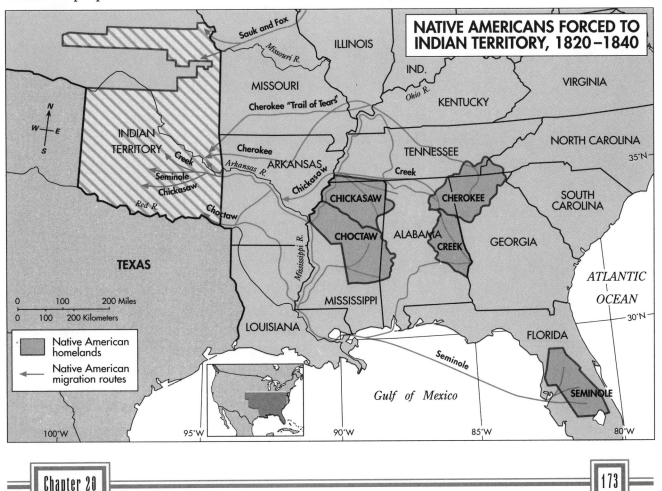

NATIVE AMERICANS FORCED TO INDIAN TERRITORY, 1820–1840

The Cherokee and other Native Americans wanted to live in peace with their white neighbors. Unfortunately, Cherokee land was good for growing cotton, so the settlers wanted it. Then gold was discovered on Cherokee land. The settlers wanted the land even more.

President Jackson supported the settlers. He urged Congress to put aside land in the West for Native Americans. In 1830, Congress passed an act that did what Jackson wanted. The **Indian Removal Act** stated that Native Americans had to move west of the Mississippi River. The land where they were to settle was called the **Indian Territory.** But the Cherokee people did not want to leave their lands.

The Cherokee appealed to the U.S. Supreme Court. In 1836, the Court ruled in favor of the Cherokee. The court victory did not help the Cherokee, however. President Jackson said he would push the Native Americans out no matter what the Supreme Court had ruled. Junaluska, who had saved Jackson's life, cursed himself for not allowing a bullet to cut Jackson down.

The Trail of Tears The Cherokee and other Native Americans were forced to leave. U.S. soldiers took men, women, and children from their homes at gunpoint. The Native Americans were put in prison camps. The crowded camps soon became deathtraps filled with disease.

In the fall of 1838, Native American leaders began guiding their people to the Indian Territory. First, they suffered under a blazing sun. People died by the hundreds. Then came the bitter winter. Frostbite and hunger claimed thousands more. Graves lined the trail. Nearly one fourth of the Native Americans died on the journey.

The Cherokee called the tragic march the **Trail of Tears.** When it ended, the Cherokee nation and other Native Americans who survived faced a difficult task. They had to build a new life in a strange land.

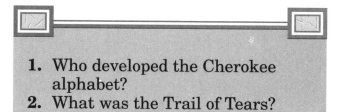

1. Who developed the Cherokee alphabet?
2. What was the Trail of Tears?

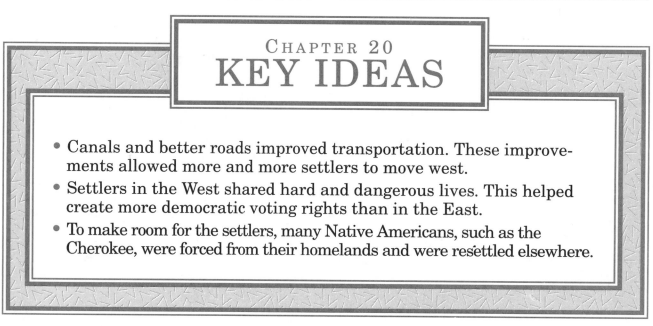

CHAPTER 20

KEY IDEAS

- Canals and better roads improved transportation. These improvements allowed more and more settlers to move west.
- Settlers in the West shared hard and dangerous lives. This helped create more democratic voting rights than in the East.
- To make room for the settlers, many Native Americans, such as the Cherokee, were forced from their homelands and were resettled elsewhere.

REVIEWING CHAPTER 20

I. Reviewing Vocabulary
Match each word on the left with the correct definition on the right.

1. frontier
2. canal
3. Oregon Country
4. Indian Territory
5. Trail of Tears

a. land that became part of the United States in 1846
b. land west of the Mississippi River put aside for Native Americans
c. the edge of a country next to a wilderness
d. forced journey for the Cherokee to land in the West
e. a waterway built by people to connect two bodies of water

II. Understanding the Chapter
1. How did canals improve transportation?
2. Why was life hard and dangerous for frontier families in the West?
3. Why was there more democracy in the West than in the East?
4. What were two ways in which the Cherokee were helped by their alphabet?
5. Why did the U.S. Congress pass the Indian Removal Act?

III. Building Skills: Summarizing
1. List two or three of the most important ideas from Section 1 entitled "Travel Becomes Easier and Cheaper."
2. Use your list to write a short paragraph that summarizes the section.

IV. Writing About History
1. **What Would You Have Done?** If you had been living in one of the crowded cities of the East during the 1840s, would you have moved to the western frontier? Explain.
2. Imagine that you are the lawyer who defended the Cherokee people in the Supreme Court. Write a short speech that you would give to the judges to convince them that the Cherokee should not be removed from their lands.

V. Working Together
1. Choose two or three classmates to work with. Imagine that you and your friends decide to move west and start a new life. As a group, make your travel plans. When you finish, present your plans to the entire class and ask for their comments.
2. **Past to Present** American ideas about democracy expanded as settlers moved west. With a group, discuss what changes took place. Then talk about how ideas about democracy have changed from the mid-1800s to the present. Make a list that shows how the United States has become more democratic.

CULTURES CLASH IN THE SOUTHWEST. (1821-1850)

How did life in the Mexican borderlands change when the U.S. took it over?

San Antonio, Texas, a few days after Texas joined the United States in 1845. After Texas became a state, Mexican Americans faced discrimination.

STUDY HINT

Make a chart comparing life in California, Texas, and New Mexico before and after the U.S. take-over. Review the chapter to help you fill in the chart.

Looking at Key Terms

- Treaty of Guadalupe Hidalgo • Mexican Cession • Gold Rush
- Foreign Miners' Tax of 1850 • Land Act of 1851

Looking at Key Words

- ***tejanos:*** Spanish-speaking residents of Texas
- **annex:** to add onto a nation
- **cadet:** a soldier in training
- ***californios:*** Spanish-speaking residents of California
- **prejudice:** dislike of people who are different
- **discrimination:** when people are treated differently because of their cultural background, religion, or because they are male or female
- **irrigation:** a system of bringing water to crops through ditches

Mexico won its independence from Spain in 1821. Almost immediately, the new nation began to worry about the United States. The United States was Mexico's neighbor to the north. The northern part of Mexico had few people. One region called Texas was a frontier land. It was not well defended. Land-hungry settlers from the United States were eager to settle there.

1 Texas Becomes an Independent Republic.

Why did U.S. settlers in Texas break away from Mexico?

Stephen Austin and the first group of U.S. settlers arrived in Texas in 1821. Austin had been granted a large piece of land by the Mexican government. Mexico wanted to have settlers in the region. Americans were willing to settle there. Everyone seemed to be getting what they wanted.

U.S. immigrants and *tejanos* At first, the Spanish-speaking residents of Texas, or ***tejanos*** (teh-HAH-nohz), welcomed the settlers. Austin and the settlers agreed to follow the rules set by the Mexican government. U.S. settlers could stay in Texas if they became Mexican citizens. They also had to become Roman Catholics. Finally, they had to obey Mexican laws.

Austin soon brought hundreds of U.S. families to Texas. Mexico gave Austin and other U.S. settlers more land. The population of Texas began to skyrocket. Soon the U.S. settlers outnumbered the *tejanos.*

Gradually, the *tejanos's* feelings toward the U.S. settlers began to change. Many U.S. settlers refused to follow the rules set by Mexico. They refused to become Mexican citizens. They did not convert to the Catholic faith. Others did not follow Mexican laws. In addition, many of the U.S. settlers considered themselves superior to the *tejanos* and treated them badly.

The Mexican government tried to slow immigration from the United States. They were afraid that the U.S. settlers might try to make Texas part of the United States. In 1830, the Mexican government outlawed U.S. immigration to Texas. However, this law was hard to enforce. It did not stop the flow of U.S. immigrants.

The Texas rebellion Gaining control of Texas was only one of Mexico's concerns. Mexico was also trying to form a stable government. During the 1830s, General Antonio López de Santa Anna came to power. Santa Anna declared himself dictator of Mexico in 1834. Then, Santa Anna threw out the Mexican constitution. Many *tejanos* and U.S. settlers turned against him. The U.S. settlers rebelled. Some *tejanos* joined them.

The rebels fought several battles against the Mexican army. Then, in 1835, Texan rebels surrounded Mexican troops at the Alamo. The Alamo was an abandoned mission in San Antonio. The Mexicans fought back. But after 41 days they surrendered. The Texans took the Alamo. However, a large Mexican force led by Santa Anna was on its way.

In 1836, Santa Anna's soldiers surrounded the Texans at the Alamo. Hundreds of Mexicans and Texans lost their lives in the battle. Finally, Santa Anna's troops captured the Alamo. All the Texan defenders were put to death.

The Republic of Texas While this battle was raging, the rebels declared their independence from Mexico. They created the Republic of Texas. Soon after, a large force of Texan rebels surprised Santa Anna's troops at the San Jacinto River. Santa Anna was forced to surrender and sign a treaty that recognized the independence of Texas.

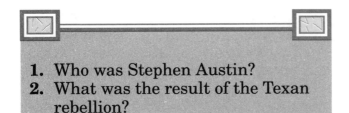

1. Who was Stephen Austin?
2. What was the result of the Texan rebellion?

2 The United States and Mexico Go to War.

What events led to a war between Mexico and the United States?

The independence of Texas did not bring peace for long. Mexico and Texas began arguing about the southern border of Texas shortly after the war. Texas claimed its border was the Rio Grande. Mexico argued that the border of Texas was the Nueces (noo-AY-cees) River. Mexican and Texan troops fought several times at the border.

Annexing Texas   Most of the U.S. settlers in Texas wanted to join the United States. Many in the United States also wanted to **annex,** or add on, Texas. Mexico warned that if Texas was annexed, Mexico would declare war on the United States. So for nine years, Texas stayed independent.

By the 1840s, more people in the United States supported the idea of annexing Texas. Many also wished to gain Mexico's territories of California and New Mexico. If the United States gained that territory, its borders would reach to the Pacific Ocean.

Mexico was aware of U.S. desires. Mexico was especially alarmed when James Polk was elected U.S. President in 1844. The Mexicans knew Polk supported expansion. In 1845, Congress finally decided to annex Texas. Mexico was furious, but did not declare war.

Reading a Map. The Texas fight for independence was brief, but bloody. Who won the battle at Goliad? In what direction did Mexican forces move after the battle at the Alamo?

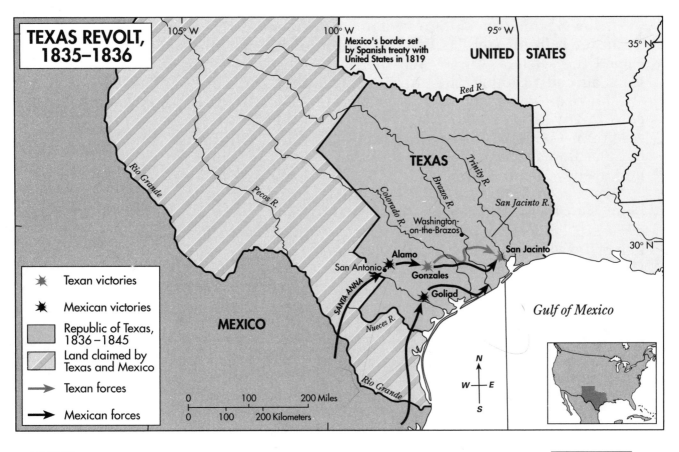

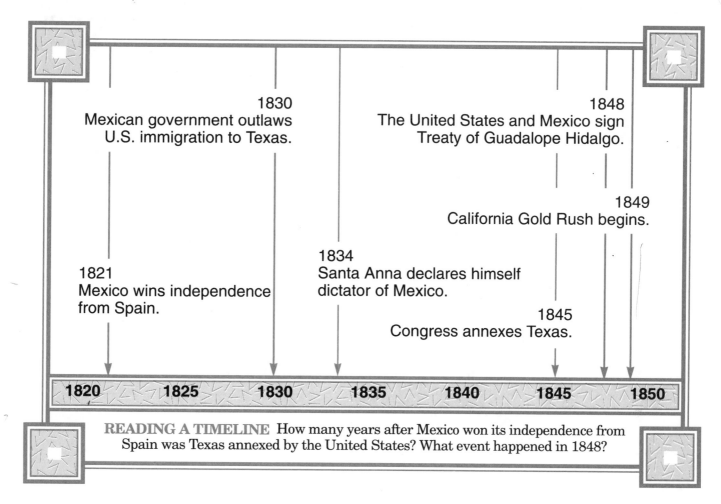

1830
Mexican government outlaws
U.S. immigration to Texas.

1848
The United States and Mexico sign
Treaty of Guadalope Hidalgo.

1849
California Gold Rush begins.

1834
Santa Anna declares himself
dictator of Mexico.

1821
Mexico wins independence
from Spain.

1845
Congress annexes Texas.

| 1820 | 1825 | 1830 | 1835 | 1840 | 1845 | 1850 |

READING A TIMELINE How many years after Mexico won its independence from Spain was Texas annexed by the United States? What event happened in 1848?

The road to war As you read in Chapter 20, many U.S. settlers were moving west onto Mexican lands during the early 1800s. These settlers had no loyalty to Mexico. They thought of themselves as U.S. citizens.

Polk thought Mexico might want to sell California and New Mexico. He offered Mexico $30 million for the territories. Mexico refused. It did not want to lose any more land.

War breaks out Polk was determined to gain land from Mexico. In 1846, he decided to send troops to the Rio Grande—the river that the United States claimed as the border of Texas. Polk knew this might start a war. But he was sure the United States would win.

U.S. troops soon clashed with Mexican soldiers. Polk persuaded Congress to declare war on Mexico. The two nations prepared for war.

U.S. forces attacked Mexico from three sides. The troops at the Rio Grande defeated a large Mexican army led by Santa Anna. Another U.S. force took control of California in 1847. A third force landed on the coast of Mexico at Veracruz. They captured the fort there. Then they marched on to Mexico City. Santa Anna's troops rushed to defend the capital city.

The U.S. force greatly outnumbered the Mexican defenders. Santa Anna's troops fell back before heavy gunfire. Fighting was fierce. Soon the only place that the Mexicans still held was Chapultepec (chuh-POOL-tuh-pek) Castle. This building was Mexico's National Military Academy. **Cadets,** or soldiers in training, were defending the building. Some were as young as 13. These brave young men fought until all were killed. Finally, Chapultepec fell to the U.S. troops. In 1847, Mexico City was conquered.

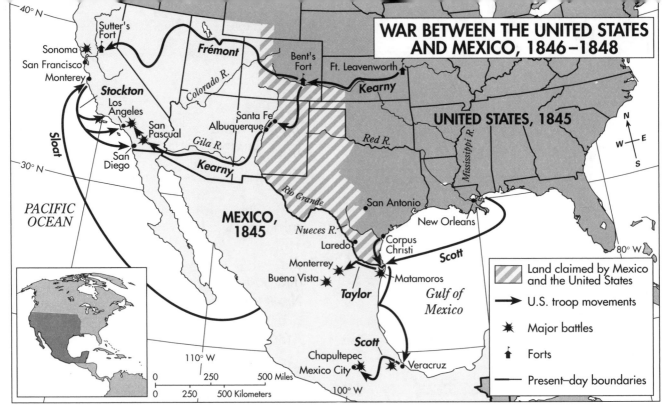

WAR BETWEEN THE UNITED STATES AND MEXICO, 1846–1848

UNITED STATES, 1845

MEXICO, 1845

PACIFIC OCEAN

Gulf of Mexico

Land claimed by Mexico and the United States

→ *U.S. troop movements*

✴ *Major battles*

⬧ *Forts*

— *Present–day boundaries*

Reading a Map. Mexico and the United States had a dispute over the territory shown in cross hatching. Name three of today's states that were in the territory that the two countries fought over.

The peace treaty Mexican and U.S. officials signed a peace treaty ending the war in 1848. The **Treaty of Guadalupe Hidalgo** (gwah-dah-LOO-peh ee-DAHL-goh) gave the United States almost half of Mexico's land. (See the map on page 182.) These lands are called the **Mexican Cession.**

Mexican officials insisted on one condition before they signed the treaty. They were concerned about the Mexicans who lived in the areas that had been given up. The United States had to promise to treat these people fairly. The United States agreed that those who stayed would have all the rights of U.S. citizens. However, this promise was not always kept.

1. Who led the Mexican army in the war against the United States?
2. What did the United States promise in the Treaty of Guadalupe Hidalgo?

3 California Becomes a State.

How did the discovery of gold affect California?

Only nine days before Mexico signed the Treaty of Guadalupe Hidalgo, gold was discovered in northern California. News of the discovery spread like wildfire. Soon people from all over the world were rushing to California.

Gold in California Thousands traveled to California hoping to get rich. People came from Mexico, South America, Europe, and even China. Some *californios,* or Spanish-speaking residents of California, moved from the south to the north. But most of the newcomers were from the eastern part of the United States. So many people came during the **Gold Rush** that California's population increased from 10,000 in 1848 to 110,000 in 1849. New towns sprang up overnight.

Conflict in the gold fields The goldseekers did not want any competition. They demanded that the U.S. government pass laws to limit "foreigners" from mining gold. One such law was the **Foreign Miners' Tax of 1850.**

The miners' tax forced all foreign miners to pay 16 dollars a month. This was a large sum of money at the time. According to the law, "foreigners" included *californios*. These people had lived all their lives in California. They were U.S. citizens according to the treaty. *Californios* began to feel like foreigners in their own land.

Passing laws was not the only way that eastern U.S. miners tried to limit competition. Some formed mobs and attacked *californios* and foreigners. Chinese miners were a major target. Gangs of U.S. miners burned cabins and mining equipment owned by the Chinese. You will read more about Chinese immigrants in Chapter 22.

New opportunities Some of the foreigners returned to their countries. Others stayed but stopped mining. Many Chinese, Mexicans, and *californios* opened new businesses. Some became merchants who sold food and goods to miners. Others took jobs as cooks and laborers.

Although many immigrants stopped mining, the mob violence continued. This violence was based on **prejudice,** or a dislike of people who are different. Mobs destroyed Chinese-owned businesses. Native Americans were murdered. *Californios* were driven off their lands. African Americans were threatened.

Becoming a state Despite the hard life, people continued to come to California. California soon had enough people to become a state. In 1850, Congress made California the 31st state.

An African American gold miner stands by his claim in 1849. The California gold fields attracted many people in 1849. Some African Americans became gold miners, but others made livings as merchants or restaurant owners.

THE UNITED STATES GAINS SPANISH AND MEXICAN LANDS

Reading a Map. What territories shown on this map were lost by Mexico as a result of the war between Mexico and the United States? What lands on this map were purchased from Mexico in the 1850s?

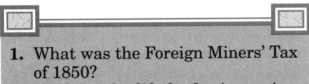

1. What was the Foreign Miners' Tax of 1850?
2. Explain why life for foreigners in California was hard.

4 A New Culture Develops in the Southwest.

What was life like in the Southwest under U.S. rule?

U.S. rule of Texas, California, and New Mexico caused many changes. U.S. settlers were hungry for land. They often ignored the rights of the people who already lived in these areas. U.S. settlers forgot the promises of the treaty.

Losing land Many *californios* and other people of Mexican heritage lost their land when the United States took over. Settlers from the East wanted land in the new territory.

In response, the government passed the **Land Act of 1851.** This law allowed U.S. officials to review land ownership in California. Landowners had to prove they owned their land.

This was often difficult to prove. Some documents had been lost. Other claims were old and unclear. It was also very expensive to prove a land claim.

The U.S. government also began a review of land claims in New Mexico. These reviews dragged on for years. Just as in California, many people lost their land.

Unfair laws Land reviews were not the only problem that Spanish-speaking people of the Southwest faced. Laws were passed that **discriminated**

against people of Mexican descent. Discrimination occurs when one treats people differently based on their cultural background, religion, or because they are male or female. One such law did not allow Native American to be witnesses in court. Most people of Mexican descent were *mestizos,* or part Native American. So this law kept them from testifying in court.

A new culture   People of Mexican heritage continued to play an important role in the Southwest despite discrimination. Over time, a new culture developed. This culture blended U.S. culture with the culture of people of Mexican descent.

English was the main language of U.S. settlers in the Southwest. However, many Spanish and Native American words became part of the English language. Such words include *rodeo, bronco, lazo* (lasso), and *sombrero* (wide-brimmed hat).

Mexican ways of farming were also adopted. People of Mexican descent taught their new neighbors how to **irrigate** their crops. Irrigation is the system of bringing water to crops through ditches.

Settlers from the East had little experience dealing with rights to water in a dry land. Therefore, California followed Spanish and Mexican practices. California also passed a property law based on Spanish traditions. It gave married women greater rights over property than women had in other parts of the United States.

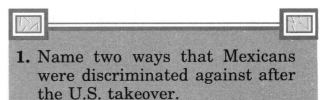

1. Name two ways that Mexicans were discriminated against after the U.S. takeover.
2. Which Spanish or Mexican laws became new laws in the U.S.-controlled Southwest?

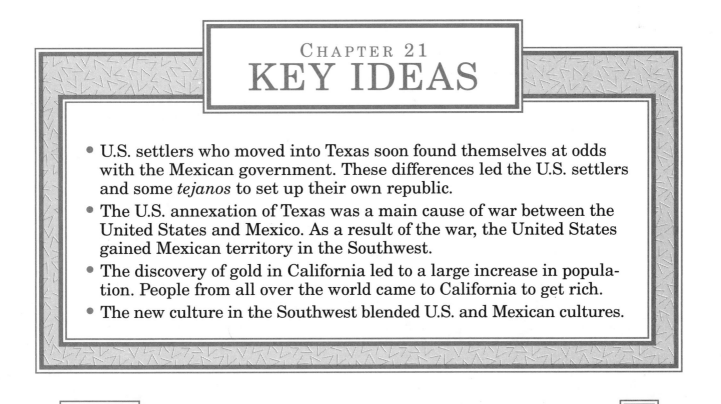

CHAPTER 21
KEY IDEAS

- U.S. settlers who moved into Texas soon found themselves at odds with the Mexican government. These differences led the U.S. settlers and some *tejanos* to set up their own republic.
- The U.S. annexation of Texas was a main cause of war between the United States and Mexico. As a result of the war, the United States gained Mexican territory in the Southwest.
- The discovery of gold in California led to a large increase in population. People from all over the world came to California to get rich.
- The new culture in the Southwest blended U.S. and Mexican cultures.

REVIEWING CHAPTER 21

I. Reviewing Vocabulary
Match each word on the left with the correct definition on the right.

1. prejudice   **a.** soldier in training
2. annex   **b.** when people are treated differently
3. discrimination   **c.** to add onto a nation
4. cadet   **d.** a dislike of people who are different
5. irrigation   **e.** a system of bringing water to crops

II. Understanding the Chapter
1. Why did Mexico want to stop people from the United States from settling in Texas?
2. What events led to the war between Mexico and the United States in 1846?
3. Why did the population of California increase so quickly after 1848?
4. How did many Mexicans lose their land after the United States took over the Southwest?
5. How did Mexican culture influence the new culture of the U.S. Southwest?

III. Building Skills: Making a Time Line
Make a time line divided into five-year periods: 1820, 1825, 1830, 1835, 1840, 1845, and 1850. Fill in the dates and events listed below on your timeline.

1821 Mexican government grants land in Texas to Stephen Austin.

1830 Mexico outlaws all U.S. immigration to Texas.

1836 Texas wins independence from Mexico.

1845 The United States annexes Texas.

1846 The United States declares war on Mexico.

1848 War between Mexico and the United States ends. Gold is discovered in California.

1850 California becomes a state.

IV. Writing About History
1. **What Would You Have Done?** If you were a *tejano* who was angry with the Mexican government, would you choose to fight for independence? Explain.
2. Imagine that you are the head of a family of landowners in California in the 1850s. Your ranch is being taken over by settlers. Write several entries in a diary describing what is happening and your feelings.

V. Working Together
1. Your class will produce a TV news program. Work with several classmates to create one part of the show. Choose an event to report or person to interview. Write a script with an anchorperson, a reporter or expert to tell the story, and people to give eyewitness accounts. Add costumes and props. Rehearse your news segment. Then present it as part of the class's TV news program.
2. **Past to Present** With a group, discuss how Mexican heritage has influenced the way Americans live today. Make a list that shows evidence of Mexican cultural influence in your community.

Unit 5
A Nation Divided;
A Nation United (1840s-1876)

Chapters

IMMIGRANTS FLOCK TO THE UNITED STATES. (1840s-1860s)

How were new immigrants from Europe and Asia accepted in the United States?

Irish immigrants are pictured withdrawing money from a New York bank. The money was sent to relatives who were suffering from famine back in Ireland.

Looking at Key Terms

• Great Famine • fong • native-born • Know-Nothing party

Looking at Key Words

• **evict:** to force someone out of his or her home
• **slum:** a poor area of a city
• **immigrant:** someone who leaves his or her homeland to settle in a new country

• **prejudice:** dislike of people who are different
• **peddler:** traveling salesperson

On a hot day in July 1845, an Irish farmer was looking at his potato crop. He noticed strange black spots on his potato plants. In a few days, the leaves of the plants blackened and crumbled. Within weeks, there was a sickening smell in the fields. It was the smell of potatoes rotting in the ground.

This was the beginning of the **Great Famine.** During the Great Famine, more than 750,000 Irish people died from hunger and disease.

1 Irish and Germans Find New Homes in the United States.

Why did the Irish and Germans leave their homelands in the mid-1800s?

The disease that destroyed the potato crop affected farmers throughout Europe. It had the worst effect in Ireland. There, most of the land was owned by British landlords. Irish farmers were allowed to rent only a few acres. Farmers could grow a great many potatoes on just a little land. Therefore, they raised almost nothing but potatoes on their farms. When the potato crop died, farmers had nothing to sell. So most farmers had no money. Families who could not pay their rent were **evicted,** or thrown out of their homes.

The suffering during the Great Famine was beyond belief. Most Irish people depended on potatoes as their main source of food. When the potato crop failed, they had almost nothing to eat. Millions of people became hungry and ill. A visitor in one town saw people who were as thin as skeletons. So many people died that the supply of coffins ran low. Bodies were placed in coffins with hinged bottoms. After the funeral, the body was dropped into the grave and the coffin was used again.

Leaving Ireland For many Irish, the only hope of surviving was to leave Ireland. They sold everything they had for a ticket to the United States. Between 1845 and 1860, more than 1.5 million Irish came to the United States.

It was not easy for people to leave Ireland. Before they left, many Irish held what they called "American wakes." They gathered with friends and family for one last meal. They spent the evening telling stories and singing sad songs. Then they said goodbye. They knew they would never see these people again.

The Irish in the United States The Irish had been farmers in Ireland. Yet most could not afford to buy land in the United States. Instead, many settled in the cities where their ships landed. Thousands of Irish families moved into Boston, New York, Philadelphia, and Baltimore. Here Irish neighborhoods grew up in **slums,** or poor areas of the city.

The jobs that the newcomers found were low paying and dangerous. Irish men worked on docks and in factories. They built canals and roads. They also built thousands of miles of railroad lines. Irish workers were well known for their courage and hard work.

Irish women found jobs also. Many became servants in middle-class homes. These women often worked seven days a week. Their workday usually began at 6:00 A.M. and ended at 11:00 P.M. Some felt like prisoners in these homes because they had no time for themselves.

Still, working in people's homes paid better than working in mills. Working conditions in these factories were dangerous. Hours were long. The work was tiring.

Although the work was hard, the **immigrants** were glad to have jobs. An immigrant is someone who leaves his or her homeland to settle in a new country. These jobs gave young Irish women money for shelter, food, and clothing.

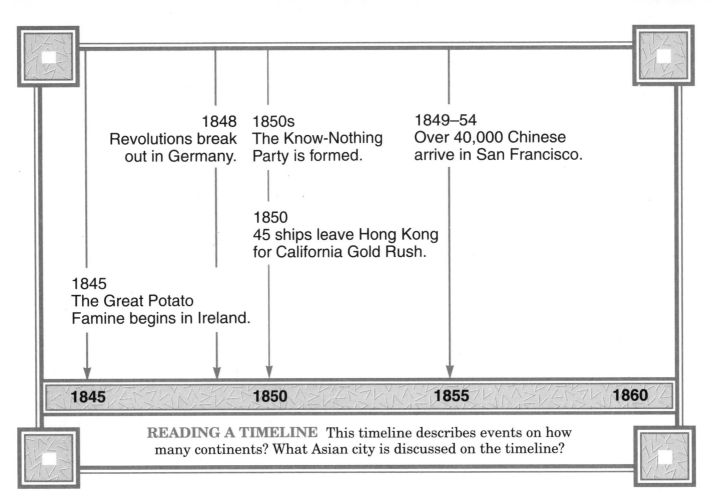

1848
Revolutions break
out in Germany.

1850s
The Know-Nothing
Party is formed.

1849–54
Over 40,000 Chinese
arrive in San Francisco.

1850
45 ships leave Hong Kong
for California Gold Rush.

1845
The Great Potato
Famine begins in Ireland.

| 1845 | 1850 | 1855 | 1860 |

READING A TIMELINE This timeline describes events on how many continents? What Asian city is discussed on the timeline?

The work also gave the women something they had not had in Ireland: a sense of independence.

Other Europeans leave The Irish were not the only newcomers. Between 1820 and 1860, 8 million immigrants came to the United States from countries in Europe. Besides Ireland, people came from countries such as England, Norway, Sweden, and Germany.

Revolutions broke out in many parts of Germany in 1848. The rebels fought for democracy. When they failed, thousands had to escape to save their lives. Almost 1 million Germans arrived in the United States between 1848 and 1860.

Other Germans came to make a better life for themselves. Those with enough money often bought farms in the Midwest. Others settled in Midwestern cities. By the 1850s, large numbers of Germans lived in St. Louis, Cincinnati, and Milwaukee.

Immigrants from Europe added much to the United States. The Germans brought new music, Christmas trees, and kindergarten to the United States. The Swedes taught native-born Americans how to build log cabins. The Irish became leaders in politics, the Catholic church, and labor unions. Immigrants from many countries worked in factories. They built railroads and canals. Europeans helped the cities grow and the nation prosper.

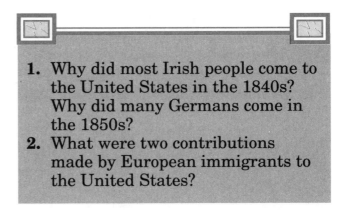

1. Why did most Irish people come to the United States in the 1840s? Why did many Germans come in the 1850s?
2. What were two contributions made by European immigrants to the United States?

2 Asians Arrive in California.

Why did the Chinese come to the United States?

In the summer of 1848, villages in eastern China buzzed with news of the "land of the golden mountain." Gold had been discovered in California, more than 7,000 miles (11,270 kilometers) away.

Some villagers doubted the story at first. They did not become believers until 1850. In that year, some gold seekers returned to China with gold in their pockets. This created "gold fever" in eastern China. Thousands of young Chinese men decided to go to California. In 1850 alone, 45 ships left Hong Kong for San Francisco. Each carried 500 passengers.

The land of the golden mountain
Within a few years, thousands of Chinese had reached California. Between 1849 and 1854, more than 40,000 Chinese arrived in San Francisco. Most of the Chinese immigrants were men. They expected to make their fortunes in the United States and then return to China. Some did, but many stayed.

The Chinese came to California with other men from their villages. They worked together. They helped one another in times of trouble. The Chinese tended to keep to themselves. Yet they were not unfriendly. They were willing to share their knowledge and skills with others.

One miner, Ah Sang, became a legend in the goldfields. In China, Ah Sang had studied medicine. In California, other Chinese would come to him when they were ill. Before long, his skill attracted other miners as well. His cures were so

Reading a Map. Were there more Chinese living in the United States East or West in 1880? Why was this so? Name four states that had more than 2,000 Chinese living there in 1880.

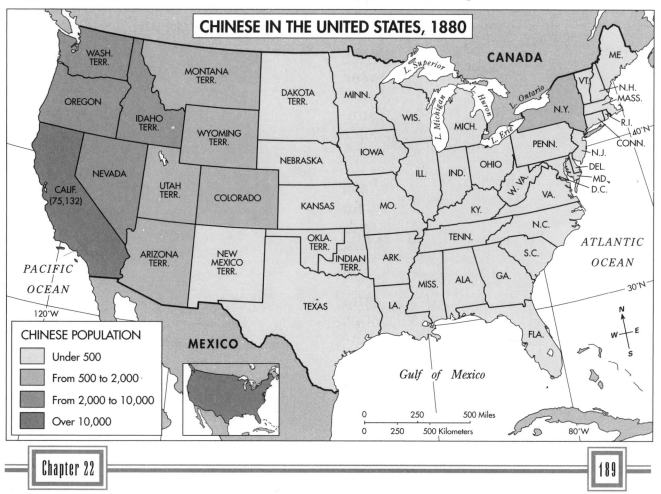

CHINESE IN THE UNITED STATES, 1880

CHINESE POPULATION
- Under 500
- From 500 to 2,000
- From 2,000 to 10,000
- Over 10,000

Chinese and Anglo gold miners are shown in this 1852 photo of a California gold mining claim. When gold was discovered in 1848, people rushed to the fields from all over the world. Few struck it rich.

successful that he decided to give up his search for gold and start a clinic.

Ah Sang's first clinic was in a hotel. His practice soon grew. In time, he built a hospital with 50 beds. It became one of the leading hospitals in California.

Other ways to earn money Other Chinese who came to San Francisco had no interest in digging for gold. They saw better ways to earn money. Many became merchants. They sold food, tools, clothing, and supplies to the miners. Another opportunity was in construction. Near the goldfields, villages were growing. Chinese carpenters built hundreds of houses in these villages.

Still other Chinese immigrants looked beyond the goldfields. Chinese farmers turned swampland into farmland in California. They created one of the richest farming regions in the United States. Some opened laundries and small shops. Others made a living as **peddlers**, or traveling salespeople.

As more and more Chinese came to California, a Chinese neighborhood grew in San Francisco. It became known as "Chinatown." By the 1850s, it covered 15 city blocks. It contained dozens of stores, restaurants, boarding-houses, and butcher shops. It was a place where workers could relax in the evening after long hours in factories, stores, and on the docks. In Chinatown, the immigrants formed family and town groups. The groups, or **fongs**, ran club-houses for meetings and parties.

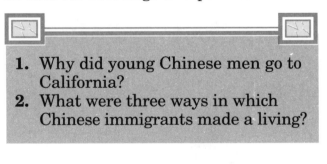

1. Why did young Chinese men go to California?
2. What were three ways in which Chinese immigrants made a living?

3 The Newcomers Are Not Welcomed.

Why were some Americans prejudiced against foreigners?

The United States was a land of promise to immigrants from Europe and

Asia. However, the newcomers faced discrimination. Discrimination occurs when people are treated differently or unfairly because of their cultural background, religion, or because they are male or female.

Facing prejudice   Why did **native-born** Americans, those who were born in the U.S., dislike the immigrants? Some thought that the new immigrants were strange. Others claimed that the immigrants were taking jobs from native-born Americans. The Irish, the Chinese, and many other newcomers were poor. They often took the most difficult and dangerous jobs. They were also forced to work for the lowest wages. Native-born Americans claimed that this kept wages low.

Immigrants also faced **prejudice,** dislike of people who are different. The Irish and German Catholics faced religious prejudice. Most of the Irish and some of the Germans were Catholic. Most people in the United States were Protestant. In some places, business owners advertised for workers with signs that read, "Irish Need Not Apply." Asians faced ethnic prejudice. They could not testify in court against a white person.

Prejudice against Asians was worst in California. There were riots against Chinese and Japanese. Mobs killed innocent people. Laws barred Asians from becoming U.S. citizens. They could not even own property.

The Know-Nothing party   In the 1850s, a new political party was formed by people who disliked immigrants. The party was called the **Know-Nothing party**. The "Know-Nothings" got this name because members were pledged to

Cartoons in American newspapers showed prejudice towards the new immigrants. This one, printed in 1848, shows prejudice towards two groups. Which two groups are shown? What false stereotypes does the cartoon show?

secrecy. When asked about the party, they replied, "I know nothing." The Know-Nothings wanted to reduce immigration. They also wanted to raise the waiting period for immigrants to become citizens to 21 years.

The Know-Nothing party soon died out. However, the movement showed that under the surface there was a fear of foreigners. This fear would continue in the United States for many years.

Yet the United States could not have made progress without immigrants. Their work helped the cities grow. The newcomers introduced better ways to farm. They helped build the world's strongest economy. They made the culture of the United States the most varied of any nation in the world.

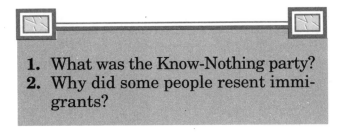

1. What was the Know-Nothing party?
2. Why did some people resent immigrants?

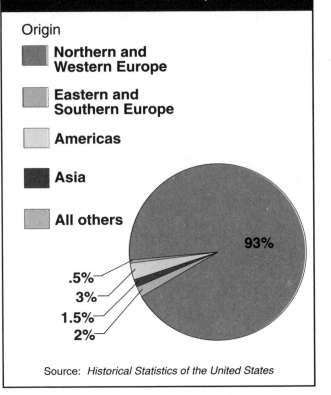

ORIGIN OF IMMIGRANTS TO THE UNITED STATES, 1840–1860

Origin

- Northern and Western Europe
- Eastern and Southern Europe
- Americas
- Asia
- All others

93%

.5%
3%
1.5%
2%

Source: *Historical Statistics of the United States*

Reading a Chart. From what portion of the world did the great majority of immigrants to the United States come in the period 1840-1860?

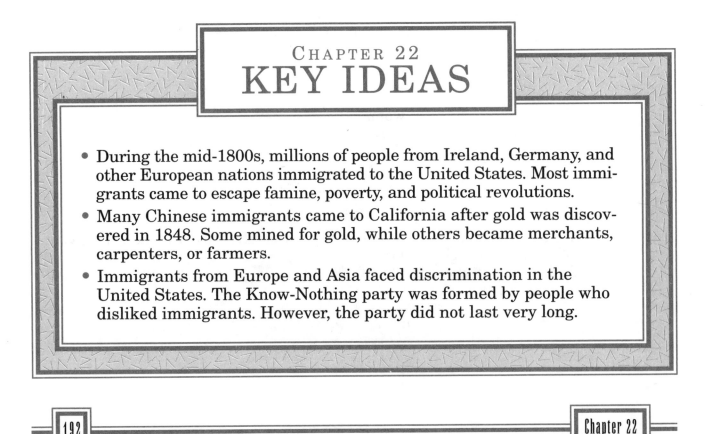

CHAPTER 22
KEY IDEAS

- During the mid-1800s, millions of people from Ireland, Germany, and other European nations immigrated to the United States. Most immigrants came to escape famine, poverty, and political revolutions.

- Many Chinese immigrants came to California after gold was discovered in 1848. Some mined for gold, while others became merchants, carpenters, or farmers.

- Immigrants from Europe and Asia faced discrimination in the United States. The Know-Nothing party was formed by people who disliked immigrants. However, the party did not last very long.

I. Reviewing Vocabulary

Match each word on the left with the correct definition on the right.

1. evict	**a.** a time when there is not enough food for people
2. slum	**b.** to force someone out of his or her home
3. famine	**c.** disliking someone for no good reason
4. immigrant	**d.** a poor area of a city
5. prejudice	**e.** someone who leaves his or her homeland to settle in a new country

II. Understanding the Chapter

1. What effects did the Great Famine have on Ireland?

2. Why did many Irish immigrants settle in cities?

3. Why did many Germans come to the United States between 1848 and 1860?

4. To which region in the United States did most Chinese immigrate? Why?

5. How did members of the Know-Nothing party feel about immigrants? Explain.

III. Building Skills: Analyzing Primary Sources

A ballad is a poem or song that tells a story. Read these lines from a ballad written by Irish immigrants. Then answer the questions.

> *When I lay me down to sleep, the ugly bugs around me creep.*
> *So bad that I can barely sleep.*
> *While working on the railroad.*

1. What do these lines tell you about the working conditions of railroad workers?

2. Write three more lines for this ballad that describe the life of U.S. immigrants.

IV. Writing About History

1. Imagine that you are an Irish woman who is a factory worker. Write a letter home describing your work and your new sense of independence.

2. **What Would You Have Done?** If you had been asked to join the Know-Nothing party, what would you have done? Explain.

V. Working Together

1. Work with four classmates to develop a television talk show. One person in your group will be the host. The others will be immigrants from Ireland, Germany, and China. Make a list of questions for the host to ask. Then, think of answers that the immigrants might give.

2. **Past to Present** People from many different places came to the United States in the mid-1800s. With a group, discuss why each group came. Then research the people living in your community. Find out why they or their relatives came to this country. Report your findings to the class.

WOMEN FIGHT FOR REFORM. (1820-1860)

How did women fight for reform in the 1800s?

The struggle for women's suffrage was long. In the early 1800s, Victoria Woodhull argued for women's suffrage before bored members of Congress.

Looking at Key Terms

- women's rights ● Seneca Falls Convention
- Declaration of Sentiments ● abolition movement
- temperance movement

Looking at Key Words

- **reform:** change, improvement
- **suffrage:** the right to vote

- **feminist:** a supporter of the women's rights movement

STUDY HINT

Make a list of all the individuals mentioned in this chapter. Write a brief phrase explaining why each person was important.

During the 1800s, women such as Elizabeth Cady Stanton and Susan B. Anthony began to work for **women's rights.** It seemed clear to them that women were not treated fairly. For one thing, women could not vote. In many states, they could not own property. Other women saw that issues such as slavery and education needed **reform,** or change. Between 1820 and 1860, many women joined together to fight for reform.

1 Women Organize a Meeting at Seneca Falls.

How did the women's rights movement begin?

Young Elizabeth listened in silence as her father, a judge, ruled on a case. Judge Cady was telling a woman that she had no right to the property her parents had given her. According to the law, she could not own property. The property belonged to her husband. Outraged, Elizabeth promised herself that she would change things. Someday, the law would be different.

Seneca Falls   Elizabeth Cady Stanton kept her promise. She became a leader in the fight for women's rights. Stanton was one of the chief organizers of the **Seneca Falls Convention** in 1848.

The purpose of the Seneca Falls Convention was to discuss women's rights. Women came from miles around to attend. Men came too, eager to see what sorts of "rights" these women might want. The meeting marked the beginning of an organized movement for women's rights.

Declaration of Sentiments   The main goal of the Seneca Falls Convention was to change unjust laws. The convention approved a document called the **Declaration of Sentiments.** It rang with phrases from the Declaration of Independence:

We hold these truths to be self-evident [obvious]: that all men and women are created equal. . . .

History is full of injuries on the part of man toward woman. . . .

He has refused her the right to vote. . . . He has made her, if married, "dead" in the eyes of the law. . . . He has kept to himself all the best jobs. . . . He has denied her a thorough education. . . .

We insist that women receive all rights and privileges which belong to them as citizens of the United States.

The right to vote   Stanton insisted that the women demand **suffrage,** or the right to vote. Many were shocked by the idea. Lucretia Mott, another of the organizers, thought it went too far. Mott said: "Thee [You] will make us ridiculous. Thee moves too fast. We must go slowly." However, Stanton had her way.

Without the right to vote, women had few ways to influence the men who wrote the laws. They could not vote men out of office. Only their sons, husbands, and male friends could do so.

Spreading the word   Many more women's rights conventions took place between 1848 and 1860. A small band of women devoted their lives to the cause of women's rights. These people were called **feminists.** They had two main tasks. One was persuading other women—and men—to support the movement. The other was persuading men to change the laws.

The feminists had to overcome strong feelings against their cause. Many religious leaders opposed the feminists. Some preachers warned people not to listen to the feminists.

Susan B. Anthony went from door to door telling women about the movement. Often, women slammed the door

in her face. But some women welcomed her. They told her their troubles. Anthony collected these stories about unfair treatment of women.

Another feminist, Lucy Stone, gave speeches in town after town. Often, boys and men tried to break up the meetings. Once, someone threw a book that struck her in the head. That was so not bad, Stone said. "I never had bad eggs thrown at me the way Abby Kelley [another woman speaker] did."

Fighting against slavery Many feminists were also active in the movement to end slavery. The fight to end slavery was called the **abolition movement.** You will read more about it in the next chapter.

Many feminist women compared the position of the American woman to that

Speaking in favor of women's rights, Lucretia Mott faced an angry mob of men. Here she has to be protected by armed men as she leaves after a speech.

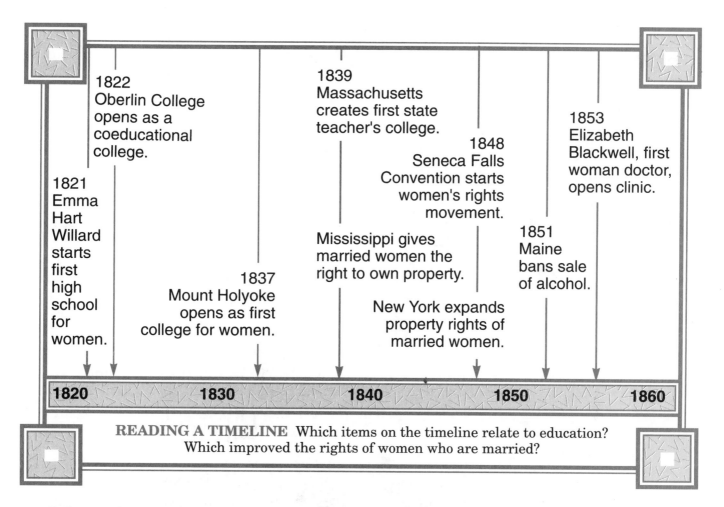

1822
Oberlin College opens as a coeducational college.

1821
Emma Hart Willard starts first high school for women.

1837
Mount Holyoke opens as first college for women.

1839
Massachusetts creates first state teacher's college.

Mississippi gives married women the right to own property.

1848
Seneca Falls Convention starts women's rights movement.

New York expands property rights of married women.

1851
Maine bans sale of alcohol.

1853
Elizabeth Blackwell, first woman doctor, opens clinic.

1820   1830   1840   1850   1860

READING A TIMELINE Which items on the timeline relate to education? Which improved the rights of women who are married?

of the enslaved African American. "She too," wrote Stanton, "sighs and groans in her chains; and lives but in the hope of better things to come."

1. Why was the Seneca Falls Convention important?
2. What rights did feminists demand?

2 Women Gain Limited Rights.

What rights did the women's movement win?

By 1860 the women's movement was beginning to make advances. The feminists still had many battles to fight. It would be years before women won the right to vote. But they were more determined than ever to succeed.

New legal rights Gradually, several states gave women more rights. In 1839, Mississippi gave married women the right to control their own property. New York did so in 1848.

Unsatisfied with this limited gain, Elizabeth Cady Stanton made a bold move. She spoke before a committee of New York lawmakers. No woman had ever done that before. Most Americans were shocked by the thought of a woman speaking at a public meeting of any sort. Stanton politely asked the lawmakers to change more laws. Her speech won great applause—but no new laws.

Six years later, Stanton again addressed the committee. This time, New York did pass new laws. It gave married women the right to keep any money they made by working. It allowed married women to sue in court for the right to their money. The legislature also gave women equal rights to custody of their children.

Sojourner Truth could neither read nor write. But she was a superb public speaker. She spoke forcefully for an end to slavery and equal rights for women.

African American women   Although these laws were passed to protect "women," many only applied to white women. Free African American women were denied many of the rights that white women had. Those who were enslaved had no rights at all.

Sojourner Truth was a former slave who won her freedom. She worked to free slaves and to gain rights for women. Truth made speeches to women's rights conventions. She denied that women were weak, as many men believed. She said to one group, "The man over there says women need to be helped into carriages and lifted over ditches. Nobody ever helps me into carriages or over puddles—and ain't I a woman? Look at my arm! I have

ploughed and planted, and no man could head [do better than] me—and ain't I a woman?" Her listeners applauded loudly.

Women with special rights   In some parts of the country, women had more rights. California became a state in 1850. It had laws based on Spanish traditions. It gave married women more rights over property than other states did (see page 183).

In some Native American groups, women had far greater rights. The women of the Seneca nation in western New York State were one such group. Women chose their group's rulers, who were male. In 1848, the Senecas adopted a new constitution. It gave equal voting rights to women and men. All decisions had to be approved by three fourths of all voters and three fourths of all mothers.

More job opportunities   Women began to seek new job opportunities. Most educated women went into teaching. A few brave individuals became lawyers or doctors.

Elizabeth Blackwell was the nation's first woman doctor. At medical school, teachers at first did not allow her to study the human body alongside male students. Still, she finished first in her class. Refused the right to practice in hospitals, she opened a clinic for poor people in New York in 1853.

Maria Mitchell was an astronomer, someone who studies stars and planets. From the roof of her house, she spotted an unknown comet in 1847. Scientists named it Mitchell's comet. They also admitted Mitchell into the Academy of Arts and Sciences.

Women authors   During these years, several women writers became famous. One of them was Louisa May Alcott, author of *Little Women*. Another was Harriet Beecher Stowe. She wrote

Uncle Tom's Cabin, a story about cruel slave owners and desperate slaves.

Sarah Josepha Hale made her mark another way. She edited *Godey's Lady's Book*, the leading women's magazine of the time. It sold 150,000 copies each month.

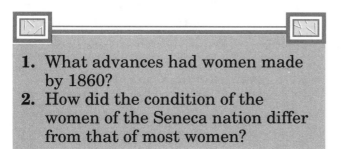

1. What advances had women made by 1860?
2. How did the condition of the women of the Seneca nation differ from that of most women?

3 Women Reformers Bring About Change.

What changes did women seek to bring about?

Many women and men saw ills in society that they wanted to cure. They promised to reform, or improve, both individuals and society.

Reforming society   Most reformers were members of the middle class. These reformers had two chief goals. They wanted to reform society so that it worked better. They also wanted to reform individuals so that they became better people.

Prisoners and the mentally ill   A shocking experience made Dorothea Dix a reformer. She went to a prison one Sunday to give lessons to female prisoners. She discovered that some prisoners were women who had committed no crime. They were there because of mental illnesses. Dix found them crammed into a dark basement without heat. Outraged, she filed suit to force the prison to provide heat. Finally, it did.

Dix felt strongly that people with mental illnesses should not be put in with criminals. All over Massachusetts, she visited prisons and asylums. Everywhere, she took a notebook. She jotted down notes about what she saw—naked people, people in chains, people who had been beaten. She told the state lawmakers. They too were shocked. The state built new institutions for the mentally ill. Later, Dix carried her crusade to every state east of the Mississippi River.

The temperance movement   Other reformers saw beer, wine, and liquor as a source of evil. Many women had suffered at the hands of drunken husbands. Men and women formed what was called the **temperance movement.**

Some temperance groups promoted temperance, or moderation, in drinking. Others opposed all drinking. They aimed to stop all sales of alcohol. Maine banned

Mary Edwards Walker was a doctor and a long-time fighter for women's rights. During the Civil War, she served as a surgeon with the Union army.

the sale of alcohol in 1851. A few more states tried such laws but then abandoned them. Other states allowed each community to decide for itself whether to allow the sale of alcohol.

Free public education   A third group of reformers worked to get free public schools. Massachusetts had long been a leader in education. Horace Mann headed that state's board of education. He built a strong system of public elementary schools. In 1839, Massachusetts opened the first state teacher's college. Very slowly, women began to replace men as elementary school teachers.

The idea of public high schools caught on more slowly. By 1860, about 300 such schools existed. Most were in Massachusetts and New York.

Education for women   At this time, most colleges did not admit women. Even getting a high-school education was a challenge for women. In 1821, Emma Hart Willard started Troy Female Seminary. Located in Troy, New York, it was the first high school for women. Willard believed that women should learn math and science—the same subjects that men learned.

Catharine Beecher started schools that trained hundreds of women teachers. Her school in Cincinnati sent teachers to schools all over the Western United States.

Oberlin in Ohio was the first college to admit both men and women. It did so in 1833. But women and men at Oberlin were not equal. When Lucy Stone attended Oberlin in the 1840s, she fought for more equality. Teachers selected her and a few other honor students to prepare essays for the graduation ceremonies. Only male students were allowed to read their essays out loud. It was "out of place," Stone was told, for a woman to speak in public. A man would read her essay. In protest, Stone refused to write an essay at all.

In 1837, Mary Lyon started the first college for women. It was Mount Holyoke in Massachusetts. In the first class entered that November. There were 80 students attending. The following April, 116, students enrolled. Mt. Holyoke continued to grow. Today, the college is very well respected.

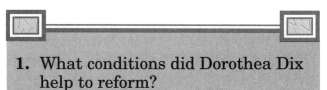

1. What conditions did Dorothea Dix help to reform?
2. What other reforms did women seek?

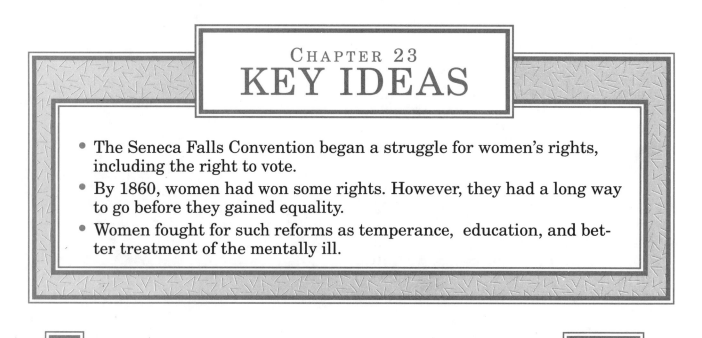

CHAPTER 23
KEY IDEAS

- The Seneca Falls Convention began a struggle for women's rights, including the right to vote.
- By 1860, women had won some rights. However, they had a long way to go before they gained equality.
- Women fought for such reforms as temperance, education, and better treatment of the mentally ill.

I. Reviewing Vocabulary

Match each word on the left with the correct definition on the right.

1. suffrage   **a.** the fight to end slavery
2. feminist   **b.** the right to vote
3. abolition movement   **c.** a drive to change people's drinking habits
4. reform   **d.** change, improvement
5. temperance movement   **e.** a supporter of the women's rights movement

II. Understanding the Chapter

1. What obstacles did feminists face in struggling to win more rights for women?
2. What important points did the Declaration of Sentiments make?
3. Describe the rights that American women had in 1860. What had changed since 1820?
4. How did the opportunities for women to get an education improve between 1820 and 1860?
5. What were Elizabeth Blackwell's important achievements?

III. Building Skills: Generalizing

1. Read the excerpts from the Declaration of Sentiments on page 195. On a sheet of paper, tell whether you think the following sentence is either a good or a poor generalization about the Declaration: *The signers believed that women deserve the same rights as men.*
2. Read the excerpt from Sojourner Truth's speech on page 198. Write two titles for the speech. Tell why you think each title is a good generalization about the speech's contents.

IV. Writing About History

1. **What Would You Have Done?** Imagine you are a woman in 1855. Susan B. Anthony comes to your door to tell you about the women's movement. What questions would you ask her? Would you join the movement? Why or why not?
2. Suppose you are a feminist of the 1850s who visits a Seneca settlement. You are amazed at the important place that women hold in Seneca society. Write a letter to a friend describing your experience.

V. Working Together

1. Choose two or three classmates to work with. Choose one of the women mentioned in this chapter. Work together in the school library to find out more about that woman. Then, tell your class what you found out.
2. **Past to Present** Women in the mid-1800s worked hard to improve life in the United States. With a group, create a list of all the changes that reformers wanted to make. Then discuss what you would like to improve today. Choose one reform and create a plan of action. Present your action plan to the class.

The Fight Against Slavery Gains Ground. (1820-1860)

How did the opponents of slavery fight to bring it to an end?

Late in her life, Harriet Tubman, left, posed with a few of the hundreds of slaves she had led to freedom on the Underground Railroad.

Looking at Key Terms

- Drinking Gourd • Underground Railroad

Looking at Key Words

- **abolition movement:** the campaign to abolish slavery
- **abolitionist:** someone who fought to end slavery
- **militant:** aggressive; ready to take risks in support of a cause

STUDY

As you read the chapter, make a list of the people mentioned. Then, write a description of each person's role in the abolition movement.

HINT

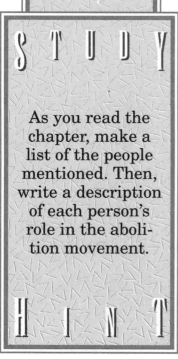

The struggle to end slavery was one of the most important movements in the United States in the early 1800s. The **abolition movement,** or the campaign to end slavery, began in the 1830s. Until then, most **abolitionists,** or people who fought to end slavery, had worked slowly and quietly. Now, the debate turned angry and often violent.

1 Some Americans Fight Against Slavery.

How did the abolitionists work to end slavery?

The abolition movement found its voice in 1831. On the first day of that year, 26-year-old William Lloyd Garrison, a white man, started a fiery antislavery newspaper in Boston. Garrison called his weekly paper the *Liberator*. He said he would speak out against the evils of slavery until all slaves were free. Garrison wrote: "I will not retreat a single inch—AND I WILL BE HEARD."

A new goal: Abolition now Garrison was not content to work for a gradual end to slavery. He wanted abolition right away.

Most of Garrison's first readers were African Americans. James Forten, who owned a sail-making factory in Philadelphia, sent $54 for 27 subscriptions. Other African Americans also subscribed. At first, few whites even knew of the paper. Then a slave rebellion in Virginia made Garrison a national figure.

Nat Turner's rebellion Nat Turner was an enslaved African American who lived on a plantation. He believed that he had seen God in a vision. In his vision, God told him to kill white people who enslaved African Americans.

Turner's bloody revolt in August 1831 made national headlines. First, Turner and eight other slaves went to the home of Turner's owner. They killed everyone there. More slaves joined them. They moved on to other plantations. In all, they killed some 60 whites. White Virginians hunted the rebels down. They killed many outright. After a trial, the authorities hanged Turner and 16 others.

Angry and scared, Southern whites blamed abolitionists for the revolt. In particular, they blamed Garrison. In fact, Garrison had nothing to do with the slave revolt. However, the attacks against him helped him win more followers.

A new organization Garrison started a new antislavery group. It was called the American Anti-Slavery Society. The society held its first convention in Philadelphia in 1833. Sixty-three delegates from 11 states attended. Several African Americans were present. One was James Forten. Another was James C. McCrummell, a Philadelphia dentist. Still another was James G. Barbadoes, who owned a Boston clothing store.

The American Anti-Slavery Society demanded an immediate end to slavery. The Society quickly grew. By 1838, as many as 250,000 members had signed up. Most were white, but a number were African Americans.

Women abolitionists At first, women played a small role in the abolition movement. They held meetings and talked with other women. Some formed antislavery societies for women.

Angelina Grimké (GRIHM-kee) broadened the role of women abolitionists. Both she and her sister, Sarah, were from South Carolina. They moved north to fight against slavery. Both also became active feminists. Angelina decided to speak at abolition meetings where both men and women were present. The idea of a woman speaking in public shocked many people. In 1837, Sarah wrote a booklet defending Angelina's speeches.

Lucretia Mott and Elizabeth Cady Stanton (see page 195) were abolitionists before they were feminists. The two met at a world antislavery convention in London in 1840. The convention did not allow women to participate fully. Women had to sit in the audience and watch. That experience made Mott and Stanton angry. It started them thinking about women's rights.

Different approaches Many abolitionists admired William Lloyd Garrison. Others thought he was too extreme. For one thing, he supported the movement for women's rights. Few male abolitionists were willing to go that far. In addition, Garrison disagreed with the U.S. Constitution because it allowed slavery. He even burned a copy of the Constitution in public. He called it "a bloodstained document."

By 1840, the abolition movement had split. Garrison and his group refused to vote in U.S. elections or to run for office. Other abolitionists formed political groups and nominated candidates for office (see Chapter 25). Finally, more **militant,** or aggressive, abolitionists were willing to use violence. They urged slaves to stage more revolts.

Anger at abolitionists Many people hated the abolitionists. Southern whites feared that the abolitionists would start slave revolts. Even many Southern whites who did not own slaves resented the abolitionists' attacks on slavery.

In the North, too, the abolitionists made people angry. Many Northerners had business ties to the South. They

Frederick Douglass was speaking at an 1860 anti-slavery meeting in Boston when the police broke up the meeting. Why do you think the police and opponents of abolition tried to stop Douglass from speaking?

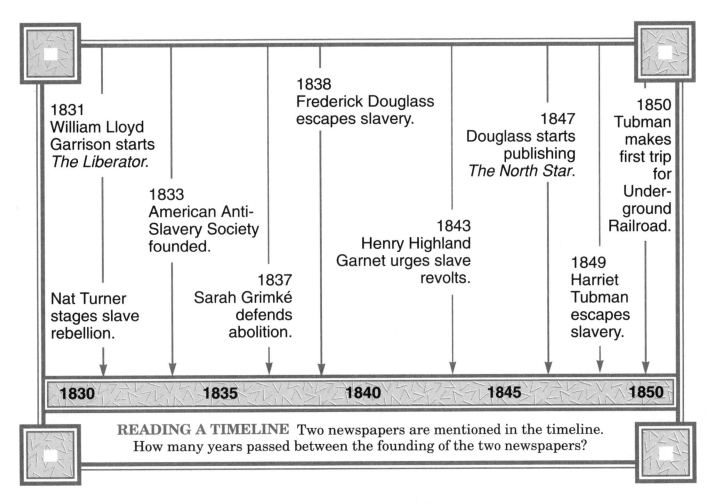

1831
William Lloyd
Garrison starts
The Liberator.

Nat Turner
stages slave
rebellion.

1833
American Anti-
Slavery Society
founded.

1837
Sarah Grimké
defends
abolition.

1838
Frederick Douglass
escapes slavery.

1843
Henry Highland
Garnet urges slave
revolts.

1847
Douglass starts
publishing
The North Star.

1849
Harriet
Tubman
escapes
slavery.

1850
Tubman
makes
first trip
for
Under-
ground
Railroad.

1830   **1835**   **1840**   **1845**   **1850**

READING A TIMELINE Two newspapers are mentioned in the timeline.
How many years passed between the founding of the two newspapers?

feared that the abolition movement might divide the country. That, they knew, would hurt their businesses. Many working-class Northerners opposed the abolitionists, too. They saw African Americans as competitors for jobs. Freeing the slaves, they felt, would hurt their own chances for jobs.

Angry mobs often attacked people who spoke out against slavery. In 1834, a mob in New York City burned the homes of 20 African American abolitionists. Three years later, a mob in Alton, Illinois, killed a white newspaper editor named Elijah Lovejoy.

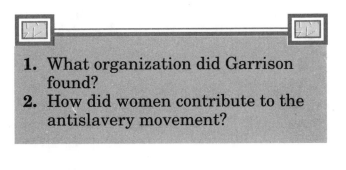

1. What organization did Garrison found?
2. How did women contribute to the antislavery movement?

2 African Americans Take Risks to Win Freedom.

How did enslaved African Americans escape from the South?

Many enslaved African Americans risked their lives trying to escape from slavery. African American and white abolitionists helped thousands of slaves to reach freedom. Helping slaves to escape was not only personally risky. It was illegal. Strict laws made helping runaways a crime.

Following the North Star For enslaved African Americans who escaped, leaving their master was only the first step. The journey to freedom was long and dangerous.

First, they had to escape immediate capture. Slave owners often used packs

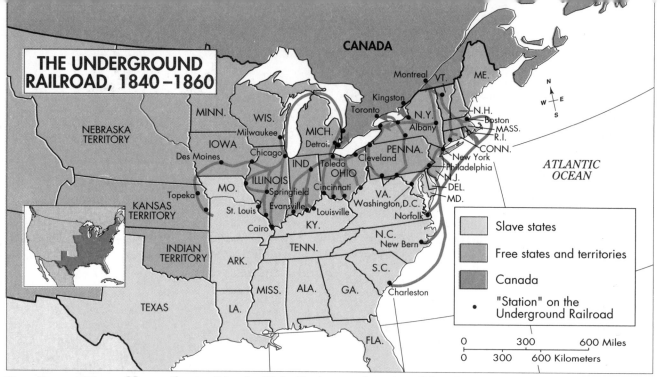

THE UNDERGROUND RAILROAD, 1840–1860

Slave states

Free states and territories

Canada

• **"Station" on the Underground Railroad**

0   300   600 Miles
0   300   600 Kilometers

Reading a Map. Name three cities in Ohio that were "stations" for the Underground Railroad. Why did many African Americans who escaped slavery choose to live in Canada, rather than in the United States?

of dogs to hunt down runaways. If the runaways refused to halt, their pursuers might shoot them. Some slaves chose to die rather than be caught. They knew how cruel masters could be. Slave owners might cripple runaways so that they could not escape again.

Planters tried to keep slaves ignorant of geography. However, enslaved African Americans knew the magic word *North*. To them, North meant freedom. Runaways searched the night sky for the stars in the Drinking Gourd, or Big Dipper. One edge of the Big Dipper points toward the North Star. That star became their guide to the North.

A dangerous operation Abolitionists helped runaways in many ways. They hid the escaped slaves in barns or in secret rooms inside their homes. They tucked them under loads of hay and drove them past roadblocks in wagons.

Quakers and other opponents of slavery offered such help to runaways as early as the 1700s. As time passed, more and more people joined in. By the

1830s, abolitionists had a secret network of people helping runaways as they fled northward.

The network worked so well that many slave owners found it impossible to follow a runaway. One Kentucky slave owner trailed a runaway into Ohio. Suddenly, the trail vanished. The slave owner said that the runaway "must have gone off an underground road."

The Underground Railroad The secret network of helpers came to be called the **Underground Railroad**. It was not under the ground, and it was not a railroad. But it might just as well have been.

The "tracks" of this railroad were country roads, backwoods trails, and rivers. Its "stations" were homes where runaways could find food and shelter. Its "conductors" were abolitionists, both African American and white, who guided slaves to freedom.

Harriet Tubman The most famous conductor of all was an escaped African

American slave named Harriet Tubman. She was born on a Maryland plantation in 1820. When she was 29 years old, she escaped to Philadelphia. However, she was not satisfied with freedom for herself.

Tubman returned to the South again and again. She led others to freedom. First, she rescued one of her sisters and her two children. A month later, she led one of her brothers and two men out of Maryland. In all, she made 19 trips to the South. She led more than 300 people north. Tubman proudly stated that she had never let "a train run off the track." That meant she had never lost any of the people she was rescuing.

Slave owners placed a $40,000 price on Tubman's head. But, no one ever collected. During the Civil War, Tubman served as a scout and spy for the Union army. She lived to the age of 92.

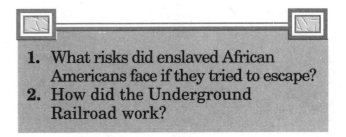

1. What risks did enslaved African Americans face if they tried to escape?
2. How did the Underground Railroad work?

3 Free African Americans Battle Slavery.

How did free African Americans fight against slavery?

African Americans who had escaped from slavery knew the evils of slavery firsthand. At abolitionist meetings, they told their stories. Their speeches made people imagine the lash of the whip and the grief of a mother who saw her child sold away.

Frederick Douglass The most well-known African American in the

Henry Brown, an enslaved African American, escaped slavery in 1848 by hiding in a box sent to the North. What did Brown's escape from slavery show about African Americans' desire for freedom?

Frederick Douglass escaped slavery to become a leading fighter against slavery. Douglass became world famous for speaking out against slavery.

abolition movement was Frederick Douglass. Douglass was born a slave. Although it was against the law, he struggled to learn to read and write. As a child, he tricked white playmates into teaching him the alphabet. Later, his owner's wife helped him learn to read.

At 21, Douglass disguised himself as a sailor and ran away. He went to Massachusetts. When he discovered Garrison's newspaper, the *Liberator*, Douglass said, "My soul was set all on fire." He threw himself into the fight against slavery.

Douglass often spoke at antislavery meetings. He would begin: "I stand before the immense [large] assembly this evening as a thief and a robber. I stole this head, these limbs [arms and legs], this body from my master, and ran off with them."

Douglass published his own newspaper to promote the cause of abolition. It was called *North Star*. African Americans put out more than a dozen papers in the fight against slavery.

Henry Highland Garnet Another African American abolitionist was Henry Highland Garnet. He too fled slavery. He got an education and became pastor of a church in Troy, New York.

Garnet believed that slaves should grab their freedom by force. At a convention of African American abolitionists in 1843, he urged, *"Rather die freemen than live to be slaves."* However, the convention did not accept Garnet's call for slave revolts. He lost by one vote.

African American churches African American churches played a key role in the fight against slavery. Many times, they opened their doors to abolitionists who were not allowed to meet in other places.

Free African Americans started their own churches because they did not feel welcome at white churches. Many churches made African Americans sit apart from white worshipers. In 1794, Richard Allen founded the Mother Bethel African Methodist Episcopal (AME) Church. It was begun in Philadelphia. Later, African Americans started Baptist and other churches, too.

African American churches often acted as stations on the Underground Railroad. Allen's Mother Bethel Church was one station. Allen hid runaways there until his death in 1831. The church continued to help runaways until the Civil War.

African American churches also gave African Americans faith in a better future. They taught people to stand up for what was right.

Mary Ann Shadd African American abolitionists carried their struggle beyond the borders of the United States. Some went to Canada. There, men of African heritage could vote and own property. Women could live free. Children could go to school.

Mary Ann Shadd was one of 15,000 African Americans who moved to Canada during the 1850s. She opened a school there for fugitive slaves. She also started a newspaper. Shadd tried to persuade abolitionists to send more African Americans to Canada. However, many believed African Americans should stay in the United States to fight slavery.

Successes and failures Free African Americans had to struggle to survive. In the South, they lived in the shadow of slavery. In the North, they were disliked by many whites. Most African Americans barely survived. But a few managed to build successful businesses.

In the South, many free African Americans became craftpersons. In 1850, Charleston's African American workers included 122 carpenters, 87 tailors, and 30 shoemakers. A number of free African Americans became wealthy.

There were business opportunities in the North, too. James Forten became wealthy making sails. Thomas L. Jennings made a fortune by inventing a way of cleaning clothes. John Jones became rich as a tailor in Chicago. All these men contributed to the abolition movement.

A new image African American successes helped to open other Americans' eyes. They gave African Americans a new and more positive image. In the struggle to end slavery, African Americans would eventually succeed. However, it would be a long, tough fight.

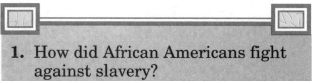

1. How did African Americans fight against slavery?
2. What role did African American churches play in the abolition movement?

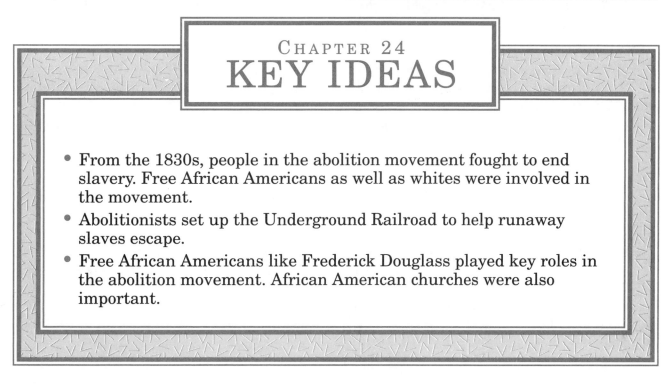

CHAPTER 24
KEY IDEAS

- From the 1830s, people in the abolition movement fought to end slavery. Free African Americans as well as whites were involved in the movement.
- Abolitionists set up the Underground Railroad to help runaway slaves escape.
- Free African Americans like Frederick Douglass played key roles in the abolition movement. African American churches were also important.

I. Reviewing Vocabulary
Match each word on the left with the correct definition on the right.

1. abolitionist
2. abolition movement
3. Underground Railroad
4. militant
5. conductor

a. aggressively active in support of a cause
b. someone who joined in the fight to end slavery
c. a network of people helping runaway slaves
d. a person who helped lead slaves to freedom
e. the campaign to put an end to slavery

II. Understanding the Chapter
1. How did the abolition movement differ from earlier antislavery movements?
2. Why did people have different views of William Lloyd Garrison?
3. Why did many Americans oppose the abolitionists?
4. What risks did runaways and their helpers in the Underground Railroad face?
5. Why might a runaway slave go to Canada? Why might a runaway stay in the United States?

III. Building Skills: Analyzing a Map
Study the map on page 206, and answer the following questions.
1. What slave states are shown on the map?
2. How many "stations" are shown in Illinois?
3. List three "stations" in the South.
4. If you were a slave fleeing Georgia, what route would you choose? Why?

IV. Writing About History
1. **What Would You Have Done?** Imagine that you live in a community near the Underground Railroad. A neighbor is helping a group of runaway slaves and asks you to let some of them spend the night in your barn. What will you say? Why?
2. Write a newspaper story that describes an abolitionist meeting at which Angelina Grimké spoke. Tell what Grimké said and how the audience responded.
3. Create a drawing or painting that shows the Underground Railroad in action. Write a caption for your picture that explains the action.

V. Working Together
1. Form a group with two or three classmates. Together, write a skit about one of the people discussed in the chapter. Discuss what story you want to tell in your skit. Then write the dialogue. Perform your skit for the class.
2. **Past to Present** With a group, discuss the different ways abolitionists fought against slavery. Discuss how successful these methods would be today. Write a sentence or two summarizing your discussion.

SLAVERY DIVIDES THE NATION. (1820-1860)

What were the reasons for the bitter feeling between the North and the South?

Even before the Civil War, there was war over slavery in the state of Kansas. Here, pro-slavery forces are shown on their way to plunder Lawrence, Kansas.

Looking at Key Terms

- Missouri Compromise • Free-Soiler • Compromise of 1850
- Fugitive Slave Act • Kansas-Nebraska Act
- Bleeding Kansas • Dred Scott decision

Looking at Key Words

- **fugitive:** someone who runs away to escape the law; a runaway slave
- **arsenal:** a place where weapons are stored

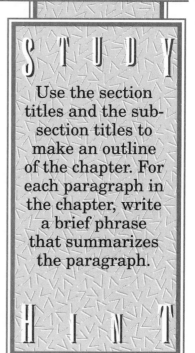

S T U D Y

Use the section titles and the sub-section titles to make an outline of the chapter. For each paragraph in the chapter, write a brief phrase that summarizes the paragraph.

H I N T

The debate over slavery grew more and more bitter. Increasingly, it set the North and the South against one another. People began to fear that the United States might split apart.

1 Slavery Spreads to the South and West.

What was the reason for the spread of slavery?

Settlers poured over the Appalachian Mountains during the early 1800s. Some began farms near the Mississippi River. Others crossed the river and settled the Plains. Cheap land drew thousands of people from the North and the South. Many Southerners took their slaves to the West. Northerners were against slavery in the West.

Slave country To Southern slave owners, most of the western lands were good slave country. The lands from the Gulf of Mexico to present-day Missouri were just right for plantation farming. The climate was warm and humid—perfect for cotton. Slave owners began growing cotton. Enslaved African Americans did the back-breaking work.

Slave owners were moving west for the same reasons as Northern farmers.

After years of use, the lands in the East were wearing out. New lands were richer. Plus, new lands were cheaper.

Slave states and free states Slavery in the West raised an important issue. The issue concerned the balance of power between the North and the South. In 1819, there were 22 states in the United States. Eleven were slave states—states that allowed slavery. Eleven were free states—states that forbade slavery. The slave states were located in the South. The free states were located in the North. (See the map below.)

Southern slave owners wanted the Western territories to allow slavery. Then the territories could be organized into slave states. New slave states would mean more support in Congress for the goals of the South. Slave owners feared that without such support the free states would become too powerful.

Missouri applied to be the 23rd state in 1819. The settlers of Missouri wanted to make it a slave state. Northerners objected. Missouri would be the first slave state west of the Mississippi River. Northerners wanted to stop slavery at the Mississippi.

Most Northerners did not want to end slavery where it already existed. They

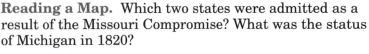

Reading a Map. Which two states were admitted as a result of the Missouri Compromise? What was the status of Michigan in 1820?

THE MISSOURI COMPROMISE, 1820

MAINE admitted as a free state

MISSOURI admitted as a slave state

MISSOURI COMPROMISE LINE

Latitude 36°30'N

Louisiana Purchase, 1803
Free states
Free territories
Slave states and territories

0   300   600 Miles
0 300 600 Kilometers

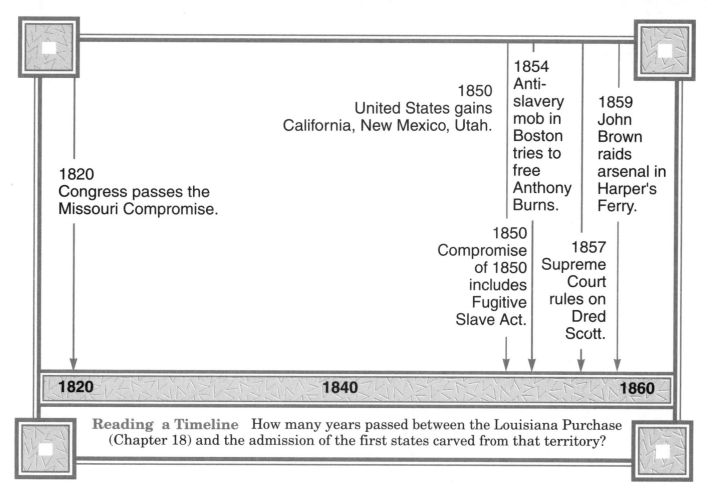

1820
Congress passes the
Missouri Compromise.

1850
United States gains
California, New Mexico, Utah.

1854
Anti-
slavery
mob in
Boston
tries to
free
Anthony
Burns.

1859
John
Brown
raids
arsenal in
Harper's
Ferry.

1850
Compromise
of 1850
includes
Fugitive
Slave Act.

1857
Supreme
Court
rules on
Dred
Scott.

1820   1840   1860

Reading a Timeline How many years passed between the Louisiana Purchase (Chapter 18) and the admission of the first states carved from that territory?

were only against the spread of slavery to new areas. Southerners, however, believed that they had a right to own slaves anywhere.

The Missouri Compromise After months of debating, Senator Henry Clay of Kentucky worked out a compromise. Clay's agreement was called the **Missouri Compromise** of 1820. It had two main parts. First, two new states entered the Union. As the South wanted, Missouri became a slave state. Maine, which had been part of Massachusetts, entered as a free state. The balance between free and slave states remained.

The second part of the compromise dealt with slavery in the rest of the Louisiana Purchase. Congress drew an imaginary line running westward from Missouri's southern border. North of that line, Congress forbade slavery completely, except in Missouri. (See the map on page 212.)

Many hoped that the Missouri Compromise would settle the question of slavery in the territories. They would be sadly disappointed.

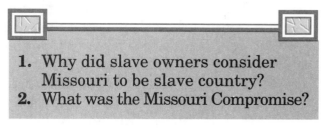

1. Why did slave owners consider Missouri to be slave country?
2. What was the Missouri Compromise?

2 The Slavery Debate Heats Up.
Why did the compromise over slavery fail?

After the war with Mexico (1846-1848), the United States expanded. (See Chapter 21.) The new territories were not part of the Missouri Compromise. Congress had to decide whether the new territories would be free or slave.

Three opinions U.S. opinion divided three ways on slavery in the territo-

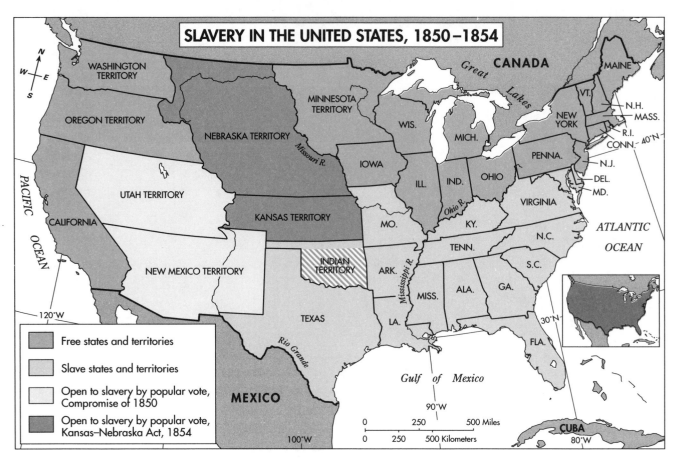

SLAVERY IN THE UNITED STATES, 1850–1854

Legend:
- Free states and territories
- Slave states and territories
- Open to slavery by popular vote, Compromise of 1850
- Open to slavery by popular vote, Kansas–Nebraska Act, 1854

Reading a Map. Was the New Mexico territory free or slave in 1850? What river was a dividing line between free and slave states in the Midwest?

ries. One group believed Congress had no right to ban slavery in any new territories. This was the position of slave owners. Many other Southerners agreed.

A second group wanted slavery barred completely from all new territories. People in this group were known as **Free-Soilers.** Abolitionists supported this position, but so did many people who were not abolitionists.

A third group wanted to let the people decide. It argued that Congress should allow the settlers in each territory to choose whether to permit slavery.

Once again, tempers in Congress rose as the members debated. Even within the same political party, people disagreed. At the time, the two major parties were the Democrats and the Whigs. The antislavery members of both parties began to split away in 1848. The splits grew deeper as time went on.

Compromise of 1850 Henry Clay of Kentucky worked out another compromise. But this time, he had to work much harder. In the end, his compromise angered as many people as it pleased.

The **Compromise of 1850** made California the 16th free state. That upset the balance because there were only 15 slave states. The compromise created two new territories, New Mexico and Utah. There, settlers would vote on whether to allow slavery. In addition, the compromise put an end to the slave trade in the nation's capital. That pleased abolitionists.

To please the South, a tough new federal law made it easier for slave owners to claim runaway slaves. This was the **Fugitive Slave Act** of 1850. A **fugitive** is someone who has run away. The law set a six-month jail term and a $1,000 fine for anyone helping a slave to escape. It also said that the courts had

to take the word of a slave owner who claimed an African American as his or her slave. African Americans would no longer get a chance to tell their side of the story to a jury.

No one was more pleased with the compromise than Stephen A. Douglas. Douglas was a Democratic senator from Illinois. The slavery question was settled for good, Douglas said. "Let us . . . stop the debate, drop the subject."

Anger in the North But the Fugitive Slave Act was too much for many Northerners to take. The act made it all too easy for slave catchers to enslave free African Americans.

Anthony Burns was an African American enslaved in Virginia. He escaped to Boston. However, one day in 1854, Burns was caught. Law officers took him to a federal courthouse. He was to be sent back into slavery.

Rescuing Anthony Burns African American and white abolitionists tried to free Burns. They stormed the courthouse with axes and revolvers. Using a large beam, the mob bashed in a door. A shot rang out. A law officer fell dead. But other officers beat the abolitionists back. The rescue attempt failed.

President Franklin Pierce sent soldiers to Boston. They stood guard around the courthouse. Finally, 1,500 soldiers marched Burns away. The soldiers put Burns on a U.S. gunboat and sent him back to Virginia.

In the end, however, Burns got his freedom. A group of Northerners bought him and set him free. Burns went to college. He became a minister and moved to Canada.

Anger in the South It was not just abolitionists who hated the Compromise of 1850. Some Southerners felt just as angry. In their view, the government had a duty to protect the rights of slave owners. They felt the North controlled the government.

Bleeding Kansas A new fight over slavery broke out in 1854. Congress passed the **Kansas-Nebraska Act.** It created a Kansas Territory and a Nebraska Territory. (See the map on page 214.) The act let voters in the two territories decide whether or not to allow slavery. That angered many Northerners. It went against the Missouri Compromise. The 1820 compromise had barred slavery in that area.

Kansas became a battleground. People who opposed slavery rushed to settle in Kansas. So did people who owned slaves. Each side wanted the most voters. Battles broke out. So much violence occurred in 1856 that the territory was called **Bleeding Kansas.**

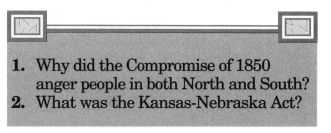

1. Why did the Compromise of 1850 anger people in both North and South?
2. What was the Kansas-Nebraska Act?

3 Two Events Push the North and South Farther Apart.

How did the nation respond to the Dred Scott decision and John Brown's raid?

In 1857, all eyes turned toward the Supreme Court. It was about to make a major decision about slavery. Both the North and the South were worried about the outcome to be known as the **Dred Scott decision.**

Dred Scott The case before the court had to do with an enslaved African American named Dred Scott. In 1833, Scott's owner had taken him from Missouri (a slave state) into Illinois (a

John Brown is shown leaving the jail on his way to the gallows. How can you tell that the painter is sympathetic to Brown?

free state). Later, he took Scott to the Minnesota Territory. That was in the part of the Louisiana Purchase where Congress had forbidden slavery. Finally, the owner took Scott back to Missouri.

In 1846, after the owner died, Scott went to court to claim his freedom. Scott argued that he became free when his owner took him where slavery was not allowed. For more than 10 years, the case inched its way through the courts.

The Court's decision   Finally, in 1857, the Supreme Court ruled on Dred Scott's fate. The decision ruled on three points. On all three, Scott lost.

First, according to Chief Justice Roger B. Taney, Scott had no right to sue in court. Scott was of African descent. Therefore, he was not a U.S. citizen.

Next, the fact that Scott had lived on free soil did not make him free. The Supreme Court ruled that because Scott was a slave, he was the property of his owner. People had a right to take their property anywhere.

Finally, the Supreme Court said that the Constitution gave Congress no power to bar slavery in U.S. territories. To do so would rob slave owners of property rights that the Constitution protected. The Court ruled that the Missouri Compromise was unconstitutional.

Responses to the decision   Most whites in the South greeted the ruling with great joy. The decision meant that people could take slaves into all U.S. territories.

In the North, however, many people were outraged. They felt that they no longer had any way to keep slavery from spreading. Abolitionists vowed to fight even harder against slavery.

John Brown's plan A fiery abolitionist named John Brown decided it was time to attack slavery head on. "Talk! Talk! Talk! That will never free the slaves," he said. "What is needed is action—action!" In Kansas, Brown had led armed men against the forces of slavery. Many abolitionists thought of him as a hero.

Brown wanted to start a slave uprising. His idea was to seize land in the Virginia mountains for a nation of free African Americans. In August 1859, he met with Frederick Douglass. Brown asked Douglass to join the uprising. But Douglass said no. He said Brown's plan "would set the whole country against us." However, Brown decided to go ahead with his plan.

Raid on Harpers Ferry Brown launched his uprising on the night of October 16, 1859. With a band of 18 men, he attacked a federal **arsenal** at Harpers Ferry, Virginia. An arsenal is a storage place for weapons.

Although the men captured the arsenal and many weapons, their raid failed. No slaves joined them. Soldiers quickly surrounded the arsenal. After two days of battle, the soldiers seized Brown and several of his men. Most of the others died in the fighting.

Reactions Brown's raid shocked the nation. In the North, most people condemned Brown as a madman. Many abolitionists, however, saw Brown as a man of courage. They admired the way he stood up for his beliefs at his trial. Brown was convicted and hanged. To many abolitionists, he was a hero of the fight against slavery.

White Southerners were outraged—first by the raid itself and then by the praise that Brown received in the North. How could the South continue to live with the North? Some thought it could not. More and more people believed that the time had come for an open break between North and South. But could such a break come peacefully?

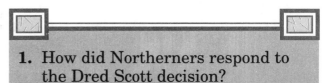

1. How did Northerners respond to the Dred Scott decision?
2. How did Southerners respond to John Brown's raid?

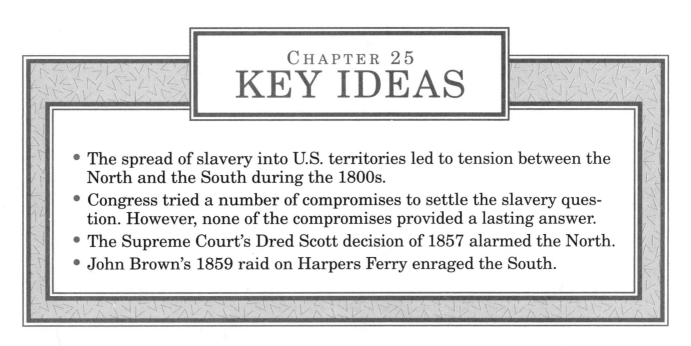

CHAPTER 25
KEY IDEAS

- The spread of slavery into U.S. territories led to tension between the North and the South during the 1800s.
- Congress tried a number of compromises to settle the slavery question. However, none of the compromises provided a lasting answer.
- The Supreme Court's Dred Scott decision of 1857 alarmed the North.
- John Brown's 1859 raid on Harpers Ferry enraged the South.

REVIEWING CHAPTER 25

I. Reviewing Vocabulary

Match each word on the left with the correct definition on the right.

1. fugitive
2. Free-Soiler
3. abolitionist
4. compromise
5. arsenal

a. believed slavery should be barred from new territories
b. believed in ending slavery
c. a place where weapons are stored
d. a runaway
e. an agreement giving each side part of what it wants

II. Understanding the Chapter

1. Why did Southerners want to have at least as many slave states as free states?
2. How did Free-Soilers differ from abolitionists?
3. What were the advantages and disadvantages of letting each territory choose?
4. What part of the Compromise of 1850 most angered Northerners? Why?
5. How did John Brown's raid drive the North and South farther apart?

III. Building Skills: Predicting

Predict the result or outcome of each set of facts.

1. The Missouri Compromise applied only to the Louisiana Purchase.
   The United States gained new territories in the war against Mexico.
   Both the South and the North felt strongly about slavery in U.S. territories.
2. The Missouri Compromise failed to end the debate over slavery.
   The Compromise of 1850 failed to end the debate over slavery.
   By 1859, hatred was growing between the South and the North.

IV. Writing About History

1. **What Would You Have Done?** Imagine that you had seen the crowd attacking the courthouse where Anthony Burns was held. What would you have done? Why?
2. Suppose you are an assistant to Chief Justice Taney. Write a memo to help him decide his position on the Dred Scott case. Explain the pros and cons of each recommendation you make.

V. Working Together

1. Form a small group to create an illustrated time line. First, choose five events from this chapter. Next, decide how you want to organize the time line. Then draw the time line. Place the events on the time line and draw a picture for each event.
2. **Past to Present** With a group, discuss the compromises that were made from 1820—1860. Then talk about issues that exist in your school, community, state, or the country. Suggest compromises that might help solve the problems.

THE CIVIL WAR BEGINS. (1860-1863)

What were the goals of the North and the South as the Civil War began?

Confederate gunners fire cannons across Charleston Harbor at Fort Sumter. The Confederate attack on the fort began the long and bloody Civil War.

Looking at Key Terms

- Confederacy • Civil War

Looking at Key Words

- **states' rights:** the idea that states have the right to decide certain issues without the involvement of the federal government
- **secede:** to leave or withdraw from
- **blockade:** shut off a nation's ports from trade
- **draft:** law requiring people to serve in the military

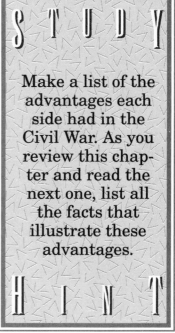

STUDY

Make a list of the advantages each side had in the Civil War. As you review this chapter and read the next one, list all the facts that illustrate these advantages.

HINT

The issue of slavery was splitting the United States apart. In 1860, the election for President showed how divided the nation had become. Even before the votes were counted, a number of Southern states threatened to leave the union. The nation stood on the edge of war.

1· The War Gets Under Way.
How did the Civil War begin?

Slavery was the main issue in the 1860 election. Many people in the North believed there should be some limits on slavery. At the very least, they believed it should be kept out of new territories. Most white Southerners thought they had a right to own slaves and take them where they wanted.

Splitting the Union Four political parties named candidates for President.

Republican Abraham Lincoln won the contest. But all his electoral votes came from states of the North and the West. He was not even on the ballot in ten Southern states.

Lincoln's election frightened many white Southerners. Lincoln believed that slavery was wrong. But he knew it would be hard to end slavery in states that already allowed it. Instead, he wanted to stop slavery from spreading to any new states.

Most white Southerners were sure that Lincoln and the Republicans in Congress would try to end slavery everywhere. These Southerners believed the federal government should not make decisions about slavery. They felt that these decisions were matters of **states' rights**. States' rights means that the states have the power to act without interference by the federal government.

On March 4, 1861, Abraham Lincoln became President. The United States he governed was smaller by seven states, which had left to form their own nation. Lincoln warned he would defend the Union if the South attacked it.

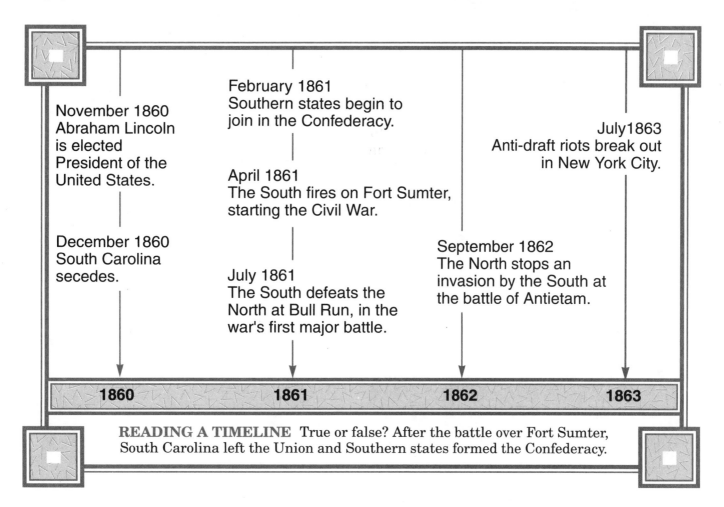

November 1860
Abraham Lincoln is elected President of the United States.

December 1860
South Carolina secedes.

February 1861
Southern states begin to join in the Confederacy.

April 1861
The South fires on Fort Sumter, starting the Civil War.

July 1861
The South defeats the North at Bull Run, in the war's first major battle.

September 1862
The North stops an invasion by the South at the battle of Antietam.

July 1863
Anti-draft riots break out in New York City.

| 1860 | 1861 | 1862 | 1863 |

READING A TIMELINE True or false? After the battle over Fort Sumter, South Carolina left the Union and Southern states formed the Confederacy.

Some white Southerners went a step further. They believed that under states' rights, a state could **secede**, or withdraw, from the Union. On December 20, 1860, South Carolina became the first state to secede. Less than six weeks later, Mississippi, Florida, Alabama, Georgia, Louisiana, and Texas had also seceded.

The Confederacy The seven Southern states decided to form a new nation. Delegates from those states met in Montgomery, Alabama, in February 1861. There, they drew up a new plan of government for their nation. They called that nation the Confederate States of America. It was also known as the **Confederacy**.

The delegates chose Jefferson Davis of Mississippi as the nation's president. They also invited the other Southern states to join their nation.

The road to war Abraham Lincoln became President of the United States on March 4, 1861. Lincoln did not believe that the Southern states had the right to secede. When Lincoln took office, he told the Southern states, "We are not enemies, but friends. We must not be enemies." But he also warned them that he was ready to defend the Union.

The Southern states did not rejoin the Union. Instead, those states began to take over federal forts, post offices, and buildings within their borders. By April, the Union held only four forts in all the Confederate States.

Fort Sumter Fort Sumter was one of those four Union forts. The Confederates needed Fort Sumter to protect Charleston, South Carolina. They demanded that the fort surrender.

At 4:30 on the morning of April 12, the skies over Charleston harbor lit up.

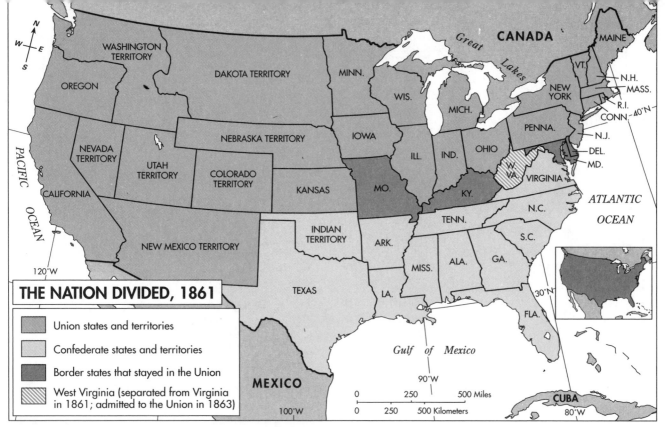

THE NATION DIVIDED, 1861

Union states and territories

Confederate states and territories

Border states that stayed in the Union

West Virginia (separated from Virginia in 1861; admitted to the Union in 1863)

Reading a Map. How many states joined the Confederacy during the Civil War? Which border states stayed in the Union? On which side did West Virginia fight? Which territories did not leave the Union?

The Confederates had begun firing at Fort Sumter. For almost 40 hours, Confederate shells rained down on the fort. Late on April 13, the Union commander surrendered.

No lives were lost in the battle for Fort Sumter. The Confederates had won an easy victory. But they had also begun a war–the **Civil War**.

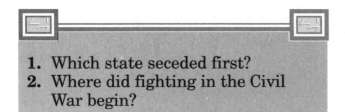

1. Which state seceded first?
2. Where did fighting in the Civil War begin?

2 Many Groups of People Fight for Each Side.

How was the Civil War a war of many different kinds of Americans?

News of Fort Sumter stirred excitement in the North and the South. Four

other slave states—Virginia, North Carolina, Arkansas, and Tennessee—decided to join the Confederacy. Both sides prepared for war.

The North   The North seemed to have most of the advantages on its side. It had 22 million people. This was almost two and a half times as many people as the South had.

The North also had most of the nation's factories. These factories could turn out the guns and supplies needed by the army.

Most of the nation's railroads were in the North as well. These railroads could transport troops and supplies quickly.

Finally, the North had most of the nation's ships. It also had the shipyards where new boats were built. This meant that the Union navy could control the seas.

The South   The South had only about 8 million people. About a third of these were enslaved African Americans.

The South did not want these African Americans in its armed forces.

Even with fewer people, the South did have some advantages. Many Southerners had been raised in the country. They already knew how to ride and shoot.

Also, many of the best officers in the U.S. Army were Southerners. When war broke out, most of them quit the Union army. They became Confederate officers instead.

White Southerners were also fighting for their homes and their way of life. The North had to invade the South and beat its armies on their home ground to win.

Joining up   When war broke out, volunteers rushed to join the armed forces on both sides. They came from all the many different peoples who had settled in the United States. The Irish Brigade won fame in the North's Army of the Potomac. German Americans made up several regiments in the Union army.

Latinos fought for both sides in the struggle. Confederate troops under Colonel Santos Benavides (beh-nah-VEE-des) drove Union forces out of Laredo, Texas. Farther east, Captain Federico Fernández Cavada (kah-VAH-dah) joined the Union army. Cavada went high over battle lines in hot-air balloons. From his post in the sky, he drew maps that showed the movements of enemy troops.

Native Americans fought as well. Colonel Stand Watie's Cherokee cavalry served the Confederates in the West. Ely Parker of the Seneca nation was one Native American who fought for the North. He became a top aide to Union commander Ulysses S. Grant.

African Americans   One group of people especially helped the Union side. They were African Americans. More than 180,000 African Americans served in the Union army and navy. Many had escaped from slavery in the South to fight for freedom.

African Americans who fought for the Union faced danger in battle. They also faced hardship behind their own lines. They were paid less than white soldiers. White soldiers usually did not treat them as equals. Often, they were given the hardest, dirtiest jobs. They also had to prove their courage.

One group that did was the 54th Massachusetts Volunteer Infantry. It was an African American regiment in the Union army. On July 18, 1863, the 54th led an attack on a fort that was protecting Charleston, South Carolina. Confederate bullets and cannon shells rained on the soldiers. The troops held out for about an hour. The 54th paid a heavy price for staying. Almost half the soldiers were killed. However, they showed that African American soldiers would fight bravely under fire.

African Americans served with honor. U.S. Secretary of War Edwin Stanton praised them to President Lincoln. He said they "have proved themselves among the bravest of the brave." Twenty African Americans won the Congressional Medal of Honor for bravery. Almost 40,000 died in the war.

Women and the war   Women were important to the war efforts of both sides. Many helped the armies as nurses.

Clara Barton became famous as the North's "Angel of the Battlefield." She tried to aid the wounded "anywhere between the bullet and the hospital." Barton later founded the American Red Cross.

Other women worked in army hospitals. Phoebe Yates Pember, a Jewish widow, was head nurse in the South's largest hospital. Before the war, Harriet Tubman helped African Americans escape from the South. During the war, she was head nurse at a Union hospital for African Americans.

Some women joined the armies. Sara Edmonds dressed up as a man. She served for two years with the Union army.

Loreta Velázquez also disguised herself as a man to fight for the South. She served as a lieutenant at the Battle of Bull Run. Later, officers discovered she was a woman, so she was discharged from the army. Velázquez joined the army again. At the Battle of Shiloh, a bullet hit her. Then doctors found her out once more. She had to leave the army for good. Velázquez later spied for the South in Washington, D.C.

Even far from the battlefields, women helped the war effort. They made clothing and supplies to send to the troops. They ran farms and businesses when husbands and sons went to war. Many took jobs in factories. There, they made guns and other vital supplies. Others took jobs as clerks in government offices.

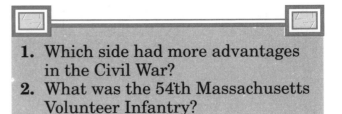

1. Which side had more advantages in the Civil War?
2. What was the 54th Massachusetts Volunteer Infantry?

3 Both Sides Have Victories and Defeats.

Why did the South gain an early advantage in the war?

People in both the North and the South expected the war to be a short one. Each side expected a quick victory. Few guessed how long and bloody the war would be.

Military goals The North had a three-part plan to win the war. First, it wanted to take control of the Mississippi River. This would split Arkansas, Louisiana, and Texas from the rest of the South.

These soldiers from the 4th U.S. Colored Infantry played a part in the defense of Washington, D.C. About 40,000 African American troops died in the war. Many died because of poor medical care.

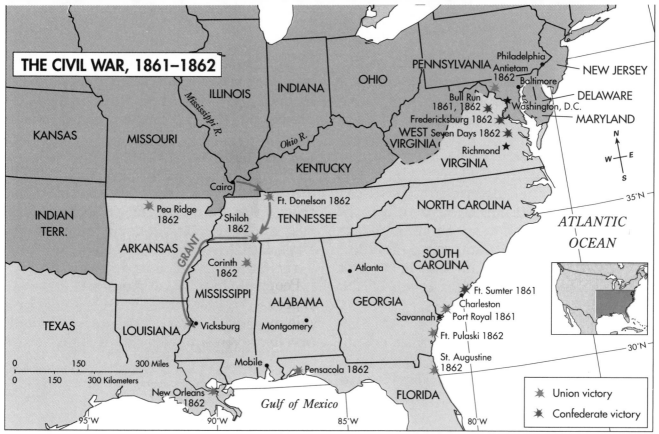

THE CIVIL WAR, 1861–1862

Reading a Map. What was the capital of the Union? What was the capital of the Confederate states? What Union general led the capture of Vicksburg? Name two Union victories and two Confederate victories.

Second, the North wanted to capture Richmond, Virginia. That city had become the Confederate capital.

Third, the Union navy wanted to **blockade** the South. This meant its ships would shut off Southern ports. The South's money came from selling cotton in Europe. Since it had few factories, it also had to buy needed supplies there. If its ports were closed, it would have neither money nor supplies.

The South's plan was simply to hold off attacks from the North. If it did, people in the North might grow tired of the war. They might accept the Confederacy as a nation.

People in the South also hoped France and England would help the Confederacy in its fight. France and England used Southern cotton in their factories. If they needed cotton badly enough, they might aid the South. However, the South had to win battles to convince those nations that the Confederacy meant to succeed.

Campaigns in the East In the early years of the war, the Union army in the East faced hard times. The Union soldiers were as brave as the Confederates. They had more supplies. But they lacked good generals.

The South, meanwhile, had found a great general. Robert E. Lee of Virginia took charge of Confederate troops in the East in 1862. He was helped by able officers such as Thomas "Stonewall" Jackson, James Longstreet, and J.E.B. Stuart.

The North tried to capture Richmond. Again and again, Union generals moved their troops south. Each time, Lee found a way to defeat them.

Lee had such success that he decided to invade the North. In September 1862, Union General George McClellan learned of Lee's plans by accident. He rushed to meet Lee.

The two armies clashed at Antietam (an-TEE-tum) Creek in Maryland. It was the war's bloodiest day. Together, both sides

lost more than 26,000 men. McClellan stopped Lee's invasion. But he would not chase the retreating Southerners. Lee's army survived to fight again.

Campaigns in the West   Things went better for the Union in the West. In February 1862, Union General Ulysses S. Grant captured two forts in Tennessee. Grant's army then fought its way south. (See the map on page 225.) By late 1862, the Union had control of much of Tennessee and of much of the Mississippi River.

A long war   By 1862, most people knew that the war was going to be a long one. Armies in the North and South needed more men. There were not enough volunteers to meet the need.

Both the North and the South turned to the **draft.** Under a draft, people are required by law to serve in the armed forces.

The draft laws were not popular. One part of the law made many people angry in both the North and the South. It let people pay for substitutes to take their place in the armed forces.

In the North, the draft law led to riots. The worst one was in New York City in July 1863. Many poor whites there felt they were being forced to fight to end slavery. They took out their anger on the city's free African Americans. They murdered almost 100 in four days of riots.

Despite anger over the draft, it stayed in effect. The armies of North and South grew larger. Battles grew bloodier. No end to the war was in sight.

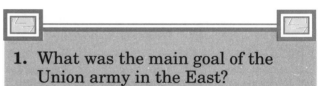

1. What was the main goal of the Union army in the East?
2. How did the North and the South get soldiers for their armies?

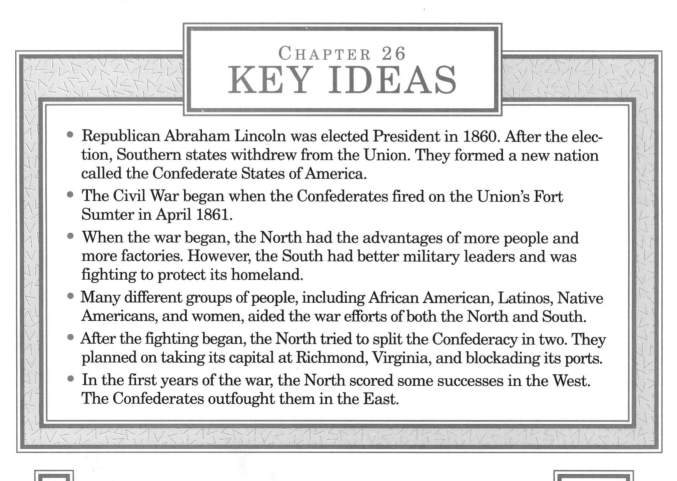

CHAPTER 26
KEY IDEAS

- Republican Abraham Lincoln was elected President in 1860. After the election, Southern states withdrew from the Union. They formed a new nation called the Confederate States of America.

- The Civil War began when the Confederates fired on the Union's Fort Sumter in April 1861.

- When the war began, the North had the advantages of more people and more factories. However, the South had better military leaders and was fighting to protect its homeland.

- Many different groups of people, including African American, Latinos, Native Americans, and women, aided the war efforts of both the North and South.

- After the fighting began, the North tried to split the Confederacy in two. They planned on taking its capital at Richmond, Virginia, and blockading its ports.

- In the first years of the war, the North scored some successes in the West. The Confederates outfought them in the East.

REVIEWING CHAPTER 26

I. Reviewing Vocabulary

Match each word on the left with the correct definition on the right.

1. blockade
2. secede
3. states' rights
4. draft
5. Confederacy

a. leave or withdraw from
b. states that withdrew from the Union
c. shut off a nation's ports from trade
d. idea that states could decide certain issues on their own
e. law requiring people to serve in the military

II. Understanding the Chapter

1. Why were many white Southerners upset by the election of Abraham Lincoln as President?
2. Why did the Confederates open fire on Fort Sumter?
3. How did women far from the battlefields aid the war efforts of both sides?
4. How did the South hope to defeat the North in the Civil War?
5. Why did the North face many setbacks in the East in the first years of the war?

III. Building Skills: Summarizing

On a separate sheet of paper, write two or three sentences that summarize each of the topics below.

1. Lincoln's attitude toward slavery.
2. The role of women in the Civil War.
3. The advantages of the North in the Civil War.

IV. Writing About History

1. Imagine that you are going to speak to a group of women in a small American town in 1861. Your subject is "How Women Can Help the War Effort." Write out the speech that you will give.
2. **What Would You Have Done?** Imagine that you are a free African American living in New York City in 1862. Would you join the Union army or avoid fighting? Explain.

V. Working Together

1. Form small groups of students. In your groups, prepare illustrated time lines showing events that led to the Civil War as well as events in the war itself. Your group can continue adding to its time line as you read the next chapter.
2. **Past to Present** During the Civil War, each side had rules about who could fight in its army. Some people were not supposed to fight at all. With a group, discuss why the Union and the Confederacy chose to make those rules. Then talk about who can fight in the armed forces today. Make a list of similarities and differences between the two time periods.

THE UNION IS SAVED. (1863-1865)

*What were some of the results of the
Union's victory in the Civil War?*

The 54th Massachusetts Regiment is shown storming Fort Wagner,
South Carolina, in 1863. The 54th lost nearly half its men in the battle.

Looking at Key Terms

- Emancipation Proclamation • Gettysburg Address

Looking at Key Words

- **border state:** slave state
  that remained loyal to the
  Union
- **emancipate:** to free from
  slavery
- **assassination:** murder of
  a public person

- **total war:** a war in which
  an army tries to destroy
  everything that can help
  an enemy army

S T U D Y

Review Chapters
26 and 27. As you
do, make a list of
the five most
important events
in the Civil War.
Briefly note why
each event is on
your list.

H I N T

Abraham Lincoln had one main goal in the Civil War. He wished to save the Union. But by summer 1862, the war was going badly for the North. Lincoln needed to weaken the South. He also needed to inspire Northerners to continue the fight.

1 Many Enslaved African Americans Win Freedom.

Why did Lincoln end slavery in the South?

Lincoln decided to follow the advice of abolitionists. He decided to free enslaved African Americans in the Confederacy.

Early steps From the start of the war, free African Americans had urged Lincoln to end slavery. White abolitionists had also pressed him. Lincoln, however, resisted.

Lincoln was worried about the **border states.** Those were the four slave states—Missouri, Kentucky, Maryland, and Delaware—that stayed in the Union. If Lincoln ended slavery, the border states might leave the Union.

Yet Lincoln did take some steps to limit slavery. He backed a bill to free enslaved African Americans in Washington, D.C. In June 1862, Lincoln signed a law that barred slavery in the territories. He also approved a law that struck at Southern slave owners. Under it, African Americans who escaped Confederate owners and reached Union-held land would be free.

A new goal In midsummer, Lincoln decided to issue an order to **emancipate,** or free, slaves in the South. He thought doing so would weaken the South. The order would encourage enslaved African Americans to flee from their owners. With less slave labor, the South would have a harder time raising food and getting work done.

Lincoln also knew that the South was trying to get aid from Great Britain and France. He felt that those nations would be less likely to help the South if the war was being fought to end slavery.

Finally, Lincoln believed the order would give Northerners a new reason to go on fighting. They would now be fighting to save the Union *and* win justice for African Americans.

The Emancipation Proclamation After the Union victory at Antietam (see page 225), Lincoln announced his plans to issue a proclamation, or order, concerning slavery. On January 1, 1863, he issued the **Emancipation Proclamation.** The proclamation freed slaves in those areas fighting against the United States. That meant that enslaved African Americans in areas held by the Confederates would be free.

The order did not free enslaved African Americans in the border states. Nor did it free slaves in parts of the South already held by Union troops.

Time of joy Still, African Americans welcomed the order. Frederick Douglass (see page 207) said, "We shout with joy" at the news. It was a major step toward the final end of slavery.

Celebrations broke out in Northern cities. In Washington, D.C., whites and African Americans filled the streets. They shook hands and sang together. They marched to the White House to cheer President Lincoln.

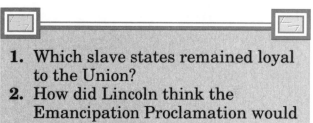

1. Which slave states remained loyal to the Union?
2. How did Lincoln think the Emancipation Proclamation would hurt the South?

2 The War Comes to an End.

How did the North win the Civil War?

After setbacks in the first years of the war, many Northerners grew discouraged. Victory seemed far away. But by 1863, the North's advantages slowly began to give it the upper hand.

Success in the West Union forces continued to have their greatest success in the West. The Union navy, under Latino commander David Farragut, played a major role. In 1862, Farragut's ships took New Orleans. They then sailed up the Mississippi River. This brought much of the river under Union control.

Meanwhile, the Union army under General Ulysses S. Grant fought its way south from Tennessee. By late 1862, Grant's troops reached the state of Mississippi. They were stopped by a strong Confederate force at Vicksburg. The cannons in the city gave the Confederates control of the river there.

Grant was determined to take Vicksburg. For months, Union guns bombarded the city. Union soldiers cut off food and supplies. Finally, in July 1863, Vicksburg surrendered. The Union now controlled the whole Mississippi River. The South had been cut in two. (See the map on page 232.)

Battles in the East Union troops had less success in the East. Union generals tried to take Richmond. But Lee beat back the larger Union armies.

These victories made Lee confident. He decided to invade the North again. He hoped that if the South won a victory there, the North would quit.

These African Americans are escaping from slavery to safety behind Union lines. As the Union armies fought their way into the South, African Americans took great risks to escape slavery.

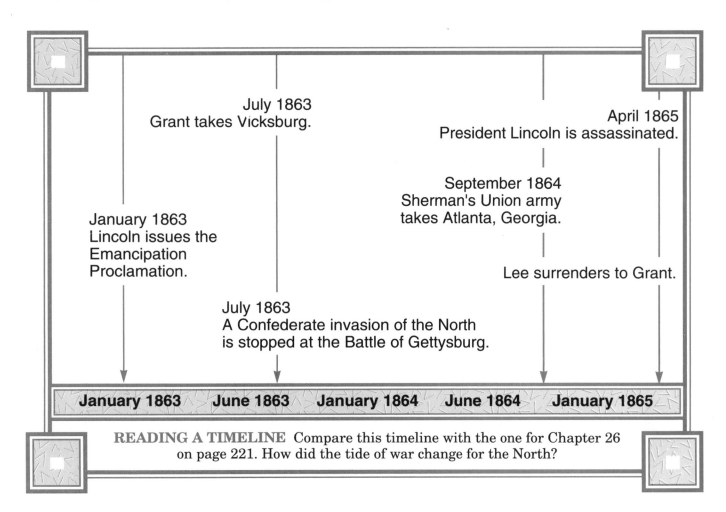

July 1863
Grant takes Vicksburg.

April 1865
President Lincoln is assassinated.

September 1864
Sherman's Union army
takes Atlanta, Georgia.

January 1863
Lincoln issues the
Emancipation
Proclamation.

Lee surrenders to Grant.

July 1863
A Confederate invasion of the North
is stopped at the Battle of Gettysburg.

| January 1863 | June 1863 | January 1864 | June 1864 | January 1865 |

READING A TIMELINE Compare this timeline with the one for Chapter 26 on page 221. How did the tide of war change for the North?

Gettysburg Lee's army reached Pennsylvania before Union troops caught up with him. The two armies clashed at the small town of Gettysburg on July 1, 1863. Three days of bitter fighting followed.

The Battle of Gettysburg was a brief but bloody fight. On the first day, the Confederates pushed Union troops back. But on the next two days, the Union turned back all attacks. On July 3, Lee sent 13,000 troops to charge Union lines. Almost one third of them were killed. The rest were driven back. The next day, Lee's army began to retreat south.

Lee had lost the Battle of Gettysburg. His defeat ended the South's hope of winning the war.

Four months later, President Lincoln came to Gettysburg. In a short speech, he praised the soldiers who had fought there. In his **Gettysburg Address,** he used simple words to remind his listeners what the war was all about:

We here highly resolve [promise] that these dead shall not have died in vain [without purpose]–that this nation, under God, shall have a new birth of freedom–and that government of the people, by the people, for the people shall not perish [be wiped out] from the earth.

Beginning of the end There was still much hard fighting after Gettysburg. After Vicksburg, Grant moved his army east. He won two battles near Chattanooga, Tennessee. Then the Union army got ready to push into Georgia.

President Lincoln recognized that Grant was a fine general. Lincoln made Grant head of all Union armies. Grant then took charge of the Union army in the East. He planned a new drive on Richmond.

Meanwhile, Grant put General William Tecumseh Sherman in charge of the Union army in the West.

THE CIVIL WAR, 1863–1865

Reading a Map. As the end of the war neared, which side won most of the battles? Describe the activities of Union General Sherman after the battle of Chickamauga. What cities did Sherman attack?

Sherman aimed his army at Atlanta, Georgia. After a summer of bitter battles, he captured that city in September 1864. Then Sherman led his troops toward Savannah, on the coast.

For weeks, the Union army marched across Georgia. Sherman's soldiers burned farms and destroyed crops. They left a path of ruin behind them. This was **total war.** In total war, an army destroys everything that the enemy army could use to help it. In December, the Union army took Savannah. From there, Sherman began a drive into South Carolina.

Road to victory In spring 1864, Grant began a move toward Richmond. The Union army suffered huge losses in battles in Virginia. But Grant would not stop. He knew the Union army could get more soldiers and more supplies.

Lee's army, on the other hand, kept shrinking. Lee kept retreating. In March 1865, Grant began a final drive on Richmond. By this time, Lee's army was too weak to hold out. Lee retreated, and in early April, Grant took Richmond.

Grant then chased Lee's army farther west into Virginia. Union soldiers caught up to the Confederates near the small town of Appomattox. Lee knew that to fight on would just mean more killing. On April 9, 1865, Lee surrendered to Grant.

When Grant's troops heard of Lee's surrender, they began to cheer and fire off their guns. Grant ordered his soldiers to be quiet. He told them, "The war is over, and the rebels are our countrymen again."

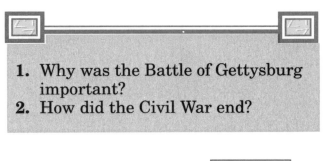

1. Why was the Battle of Gettysburg important?
2. How did the Civil War end?

3 The War Takes a Heavy Toll.

How did the Civil War affect both the North and the South?

The Civil War had ended. But the cost of that war had been high for both the North and the South. The nation would feel its effects for many years to come.

Death of Lincoln The news of Lee's surrender spread joy all over the North. But that joy did not last long.

On April 14, 1865, President Lincoln and his wife Mary went to a theater in Washington. As they watched a play, an actor named John Wilkes Booth crept up behind them. He aimed a pistol at the President's head and fired. Lincoln died a few hours later from the wound.

Booth had been a supporter of the South in the war. His **assassination,** or murder, of the President, stirred anger across the North. His act was a sign that the bitterness between the North and the South would not end soon.

Effects in the South The cost of the war was especially high in the South. (See chart on page 234.) About 260,000 Confederate soldiers were killed. Many civilians also lost their lives.

Much of the South lay in ruins. Its largest cities—Richmond, Atlanta, Charleston—were in ashes. Union armies had burned farms and plantations. They had wrecked railroads and factories. The South's old way of life was gone. Many people had no idea how they would build a new one.

Freed African Americans The war had freed 4 million enslaved African Americans. Of all Southerners, they had the most reason to celebrate the North's victory. At first, they did.

Then they began to think of their futures. One African American woman from Mississippi told what happened after the celebrations. "It was sad then. So many folks dead, things torn up, and nowhere to go and nothing to eat, nothing to do."

With slavery gone, African Americans began building a new life. They had to find work and places to live. The future seemed uncertain, but at last they were free.

Effects in the North The North escaped the ruin that the South faced. But even in the North, the war had brought great suffering and change.

The cost in lives was much higher in the North. About 360,000 Union soldiers had been killed. As in the South, many of the wounded who lived were disabled for life.

At Appomatox, Virginia, Robert E. Lee surrendered to Ulysses S. Grant. Do you think the artist thought both men were heroes or villains?

ECONOMIC EFFECTS OF THE CIVIL WAR

	NORTH	SOUTH
Number of Lives Lost During War	360,000 lives	260,000 lives
Difference in Wealth, 1860-1870	73% increase	48% decrease
Difference in Agriculture, 1860-1870	• corn: 22% increase • wheat: 52% increase • hay: 24% increase	• cotton: 50% decrease • corn: 44% decrease • hay: 64% decrease

Source: "The Economic Incidence of the Civil War in the South," Ralph Andreano, *The Economic Impact of the American Civil War*, 1967.

Reading a Chart. Which side lost more troops during the Civil War? How many more troops did that side lose? Why didn't that side win the war?

Little damage had been done to the North's factories and railroads. But the war still brought change to its economy. Since its birth, the nation had an economy that depended on farming. The war helped set the stage for a new economy. This one would be based on industry and big business.

Changes in government The war also changed the relationship between the federal government and the states. Now, it was clear that the federal government was supreme over the states. The states also had no right to secede.

During the war, the federal government had begun to play a larger role in the nation's economy. For example, Congress passed a bill to give free public lands to farmers. It also backed the building of a railroad all the way to the Pacific coast.

The war also left the federal government with a new job. It had to bring a divided nation back together. As you will read in the next chapter, this would be its hardest task.

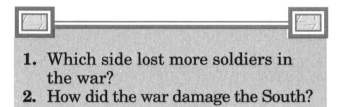

1. Which side lost more soldiers in the war?
2. How did the war damage the South?

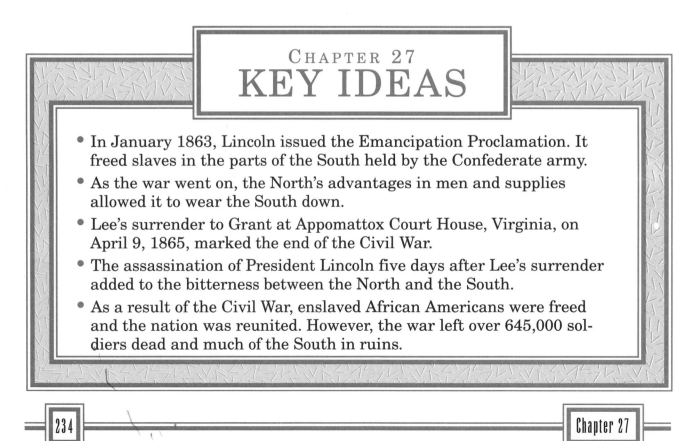

CHAPTER 27
KEY IDEAS

- In January 1863, Lincoln issued the Emancipation Proclamation. It freed slaves in the parts of the South held by the Confederate army.

- As the war went on, the North's advantages in men and supplies allowed it to wear the South down.

- Lee's surrender to Grant at Appomattox Court House, Virginia, on April 9, 1865, marked the end of the Civil War.

- The assassination of President Lincoln five days after Lee's surrender added to the bitterness between the North and the South.

- As a result of the Civil War, enslaved African Americans were freed and the nation was reunited. However, the war left over 645,000 soldiers dead and much of the South in ruins.

REVIEWING CHAPTER 27

I. Reviewing Vocabulary
Match each word on the left with the correct definition on the right.

1. emancipate
2. total war
3. Emancipation Proclamation
4. border state
5. assassination

a. it freed slaves in those areas in rebellion against the United States
b. area that permitted slavery but remained loyal to the Union
c. to free from slavery
d. murder of a public person
e. attempt to destroy everything that can be of use to an enemy

II. Understanding the Chapter
1. Why did President Lincoln at first hesitate to take action to end slavery?
2. What were some of the limits of the Emancipation Proclamation?
3. How did the Union army manage to split the Confederacy in two?
4. Why did General Lee decide to surrender?
5. What effects did the Civil War have on the relationship between the federal government and the states?

III. Building Skills: Generalizing
Write information from the chapter that supports each gerneralization below.
1. African Americans experienced gains and losses as a result of the Civil War.
2. The federal government played a larger role in the nation's affairs because of the Civil War.
3. Both the North and the South paid a terrible price for the Civil War.

IV. Writing About History
1. **What Would You Have Done?** If you were a U.S. senator from a border state, would you support or oppose the Emancipation Proclamation? Explain.
2. Review the selection from the Gettysburg Address on page 231. Write a brief paragraph in which you express Lincoln's ideas in your own words.
3. Imagine that you are an editor at a newspaper in a Northern or a Southern city. Write an editorial expressing your reaction to Lincoln's assassination.

V. Working Together
1. With a group, design a memorial to one person or group mentioned in the chapter. The memorial might include a statue or a plaque. The memorial should make clear why the person or group is being honored.
2. **Past to Present** With a group, discuss the cost of the Civil War for the people of the North and the South. Talk about how the effects of the Civil War might compare to the effects of a war today. List any that you think are similar. Then list the effects that might be different.

THE NATION REBUILDS. (1865-1877)

What were the gains and setbacks for African Americans after the Civil War?

What does this scene tell you about the desire of newly-freed African Americans to educate themselves and their children?

Looking at Key Terms

- Freedmen's Bureau • 13th Amendment • Reconstruction
- Black Codes • 14th Amendment • 15th Amendment

Looking at Key Words

- **freedmen:** enslaved African American men, women, and children set free during and after the Civil War
- **impeach:** formally accuse a President or other high official of breaking the law
- **carpetbagger:** Northerner who moved to the South after the Civil War
- **sharecropper:** farmer who pays a part of his or her crops to a landowner as rent
- **lynch:** killing by mob action

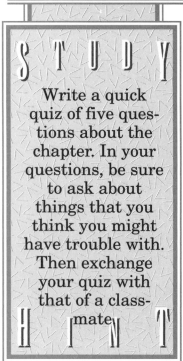

STUDY HINT

Write a quick quiz of five questions about the chapter. In your questions, be sure to ask about things that you think you might have trouble with. Then exchange your quiz with that of a classmate.

The Civil War was over. But the North and South had been enemies for four bloody years. How would they become one nation again? What would happen to the 4 million newly freed African Americans in the South? During the 12 years after the Civil War, great changes took place in the United States. These changes were especially great for African Americans.

1 African Americans Struggle to Build New Lives.

What was life like for African Americans in the South just after the Civil War?

After the Civil War, African Americans in the South faced some very tough challenges. Slavery was gone. Often, the jobs and homes of African Americans were gone as well. How would they survive?

Freedmen The African American men, women, and children released from slavery were called **freedmen**. Before the war, Southern laws and Southern slave owners had controlled their lives. After the war, the freedmen set out to build new lives.

During slavery, thousands of African American families had been broken up. Husbands, wives, and children were often sold to faraway owners. With freedom, many African Americans set out on the roads. They went in search of their families. One freedman walked over 600 miles looking for his wife and children.

New churches Before the war, African Americans in the South had few churches of their own. They often had to worship in separate parts of white churches.

After the war, new African American churches rapidly sprang up. Many were Baptist. African Methodist Episcopal and African Methodist Episcopal Zion churches opened as well.

These churches became centers of African American life. Members met in them to plan political campaigns. Parties were given there. Churches opened schools in their buildings.

Education Those school classes were an important part of life for freedmen. Few slave owners had let African Americans learn to read and write. Laws in some states barred slaves from doing so.

After the war, African Americans wanted education for themselves and their children. One North Carolina freedman put the feelings of many into words. He said a schoolhouse would be "the first proof of true independence." African Americans thus gladly raised money to buy land, build schools, and pay teachers.

New work Now, African Americans had a chance to work where they wanted and earn wages. One freedman stated that he felt like the richest man in the world after he received a dollar for working on the railroad. However, earning a living in the ruined South turned out to be very hard.

Help from the U.S. government Before the war ended, the U.S. government stepped in to aid African Americans.

The U.S. government also set up the **Freedman's Bureau** in 1865. The Bureau helped former slaves find jobs and homes. It also aided them in tracking down missing family members.

The Bureau played a major role in educating freedmen. By 1867, it had set up almost 4,500 schools. Some 250,000 pupils attended those schools.

Setbacks The Freedmen's Bureau offered much aid to African Americans.

Yet, it could not solve all their problems. Some of the worst problems were caused by state and local governments in the South.

After the Civil War, Congress made plans for **Reconstruction.** The purpose of Reconstruction was to put the United States back together. To do this, Southern states had to come back into the Union. President Lincoln had wanted to make it easy for them to return.

In 1865, Congress passed the 13th Amendment. The amendment banned slavery in the United States. By the end of 1865, it was part of the Constitution. Under Lincoln's plan, Southern states had to agree to the 13th Amendment.

Like other Southern cities, Charleston, South Carolina lay in ruins after the Civil War. Food and water were short and there were few jobs.

Then they could rejoin the Union. Most of them did. But the Southern states did not want to give African Americans real freedom.

Governments in the South began passing **Black Codes**. These were laws that took away many of the rights of the freedmen. Under Black Codes, African Americans could not vote. The codes also kept them from serving on juries. It was a crime for an African American to be without a job. Yet, the codes said freedmen could hold jobs only as servants or farm workers.

The codes angered African Americans and many people in the North. The Union had just fought a bloody war to end slavery. Now it seemed that Southern states were using Black Codes to set up a new kind of slavery.

1. What group was formed to set up to help former slaves adjust to freedom?
2. How did governments in the South attempt to control freedmen?

2 African Americans Take Part in Reconstruction Governments.

What part did African Americans play in Southern state governments?

Republicans from the North controlled the U.S. Congress. Many disagreed with Lincoln's Reconstruction plan. They believed that the South should be punished for starting the Civil War. They also did not want to see former Confederates regain power in the South. Most also believed the government had a duty to help the freedmen. They thought Congress should not allow the Southern

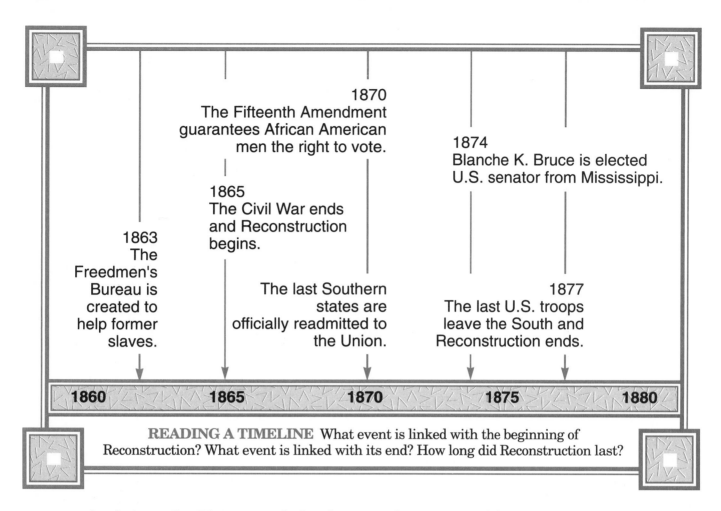

1870
The Fifteenth Amendment guarantees African American men the right to vote.

1874
Blanche K. Bruce is elected U.S. senator from Mississippi.

1865
The Civil War ends and Reconstruction begins.

1863
The Freedmen's Bureau is created to help former slaves.

The last Southern states are officially readmitted to the Union.

1877
The last U.S. troops leave the South and Reconstruction ends.

| 1860 | 1865 | 1870 | 1875 | 1880 |

READING A TIMELINE What event is linked with the beginning of Reconstruction? What event is linked with its end? How long did Reconstruction last?

states back into the Union until the former leaders had been punished.

Congress in action Congress tried to guarantee rights for freedmen. It wrote a new amendment to the Constitution. This **14th Amendment** said all people born in the United States were citizens. Under it, freedmen had equal rights with all other citizens. States that tried to take away those rights could be punished.

A new plan The South continued to ignore the rights of African Americans. Riots broke out in New Orleans late in 1866. In them, white mobs killed many freedmen. Elections were also held in November 1866 throughout the South. In them, most freedmen were kept from voting. Large numbers of former Confederates won office in the South.

Angry Republicans in Congress then drew up a new plan of Reconstruction in 1867. This plan set up five districts in the South. The U.S. Army ruled in those districts.

Before a Confederate state could rejoin the Union, it had to guarantee African American men the vote. It had to bar former Confederate officials from holding office. The state also had to approve the 14th Amendment.

Trial of President Johnson President Andrew Johnson vetoed Congress's plan. Congress then passed it over his veto. This was not his first veto. Johnson had vetoed several earlier bills. Members of Congress were growing tired of his vetoes.

In 1868, they tried to get rid of President Johnson. The House of Representatives **impeached** him. To impeach means to accuse an official of crimes. The House

Scenes of Southern life are on the outside of this 1881 print. The three men at center are Senators Blanche K. Bruce and Hiram Revels, and the great abolitionist, Frederick Douglass. At bottom, center, is John Brown.

said Johnson's crime was failing to carry out laws passed by Congress. The U.S. Senate then tried Johnson.

Johnson was saved from a guilty verdict by one vote. However, he no longer had any political power. In the 1868 election, voters chose war hero Ulysses S. Grant as President. Grant was ready to support Congress's plans.

New state governments   Many of Congress's ideas were already in action. Freedmen took part in writing new constitutions in Southern states. New African Americans voters also rushed to the polls in the South. By 1870, all the Southern states were back in the Union.

More than 600 African Americans served in Southern state governments during Reconstruction. Some held such high offices as lieutenant governor or treasurer. In Louisiana, P.B.S. Pinchback became the first African American governor in U.S. history.

New programs   For the first time, state governments in the South paid attention to the needs of African Americans. New programs brought new services to freedmen. Often, poor whites got those services for the first time as well.

Public schools and hospitals opened throughout the South. In South Carolina, a new plan brought medical care to the needy. In Alabama, a program gave legal aid to poor people accused of crimes. In all states, Black Codes were ended.

The new governments also approved a new amendment to the U.S. Constitution in 1870. This **15th Amendment** said that the right to vote could not be taken away from African Americans by any state.

Freedmen in federal government   During Reconstruction, African Americans held federal offices for the first time. Twenty served in the House of Representatives. On February 25, 1870, Hiram Revels became a senator from Mississippi. He was the first African American to serve in the U.S.

Senate. Blanche K. Bruce of Mississippi also served in the Senate.

Bruce was a slave who escaped to freedom. He worked as a printer and attended college in the North. After the war, Bruce moved south to Mississippi. He was elected to the Senate in 1874. African Americans respected him as a leader second only to Frederick Douglass.

Complaints The new state governments did not please all Southerners. Many whites complained Northerners played too large a role. They called Northerners who came South **carpetbaggers**. This name came from a kind of suitcase travelers carried.

State governments in the South spent a lot of money. The war had ruined roads, bridges, and railroads. The costs of rebuilding were high. Programs for freedmen and poor whites added to the tax burden. New taxes to pay for the spending upset voters.

What many white Southerners were really upset about was another change that Reconstruction made. These people knew that the days of slavery were over. But they did not want to share power with freedmen.

1. What two acts made African Americans citizens?
2. Why did Congress try to remove President Johnson from office?

3 Reconstruction Leaves Many Unsettled Problems.

Why did Reconstruction disappoint African Americans?

Reconstruction brought many changes to the lives of African Americans. When those years ended, however, most freed-

Many sharecroppers could not afford animals to plow their lands. They worked in the burning heat, plowing with the strength of their own bodies.

The Ku Klux Klan was a terror group that tried to keep rights from African Americans. They wore white sheets to make themselves look frightening.

men found that promises made to them had not been kept.

A bitter disappointment   Before the war, enslaved African Americans had worked for their owners on the owners' land. After the war, they hoped to work for themselves.

Many freedmen dreamed of having farms of their own. At the end of the war, a rumor spread through the South. It said that the federal government would give freedmen "40 acres and a mule." This would let them become independent farmers.

The rumor proved false. Freedmen did not get land or mules. In fact, laws in many states kept African Americans from owning land.

Sharecropping   To make a living, many freedmen became **sharecroppers**. A sharecropper farmed a piece of land that belonged to someone else. The farmer gave a share of the crop to the owner as rent.

Often, sharecroppers did not have money for seed, farm animals, or tools. Owners would lend the money in return for a larger share of the crops. Often, harvests were too small to pay what was owed. Sharecroppers fell deep into debt.

State laws kept people with debts from leaving their land until they paid what they owed. Freedmen thus faced a new kind of slavery. Poor whites shared their problems. Many had also become sharecroppers after the war.

A time of terror   Sharecropping kept African Americans from enjoying economic freedom. Many white Southerners wanted to keep them from enjoying other freedoms.

Soon after the war ended, new white organizations grew up in the South. One of these groups was the Ku Klux Klan. They aimed to keep freedmen "in their place." They would do this through terror, violence, and murder.

The groups burned African American homes, churches, and schools. One freedman said, "The government built schoolhouses, and the Ku Klux Klan went to work and burned them down." The terror groups tried hard to keep freedmen from voting.

Fighting back   African Americans fought back against the terrorists. Some formed militia groups. Others fought back individually. A mob in Marianna, Florida, attacked a white teacher at his

African American school. Freedmen came quickly to help him. The mob ran away. The next night the mob returned. "Forty colored men armed to protect themselves" drove the crowd away once more.

In the end, the African Americans could not stop the attacks. They had few guns. They had little money. They had very little government protection. African Americans who fought back were whipped or beaten. Many were **lynched**, or murdered by mobs.

The end of Reconstruction Fearing death, African Americans stayed away from the polls. Without the support of African Americans, Republicans could not win elections. White Democrats won office. Reconstruction governments fell.

By 1877, white Democrats were in power in all the one-time Confederate states. The last U.S. troops pulled out of the South. Reconstruction was over.

Reconstruction had brought the nation together again. During it, new constitutional amendments made former slaves citizens and said they had equal rights with whites. But African Americans faced many years of struggle before they could enjoy those rights.

1. How did sharecroppers pay for the land they farmed?
2. What was the aim of groups like the Ku Klux Klan?

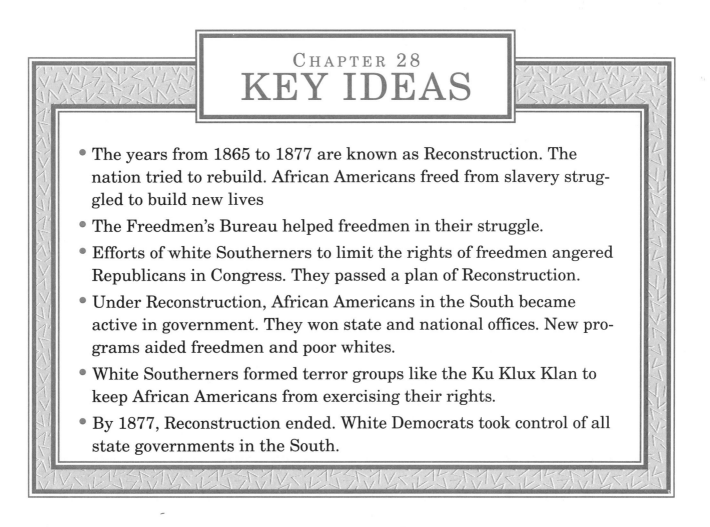

CHAPTER 28
KEY IDEAS

- The years from 1865 to 1877 are known as Reconstruction. The nation tried to rebuild. African Americans freed from slavery struggled to build new lives

- The Freedmen's Bureau helped freedmen in their struggle.

- Efforts of white Southerners to limit the rights of freedmen angered Republicans in Congress. They passed a plan of Reconstruction.

- Under Reconstruction, African Americans in the South became active in government. They won state and national offices. New programs aided freedmen and poor whites.

- White Southerners formed terror groups like the Ku Klux Klan to keep African Americans from exercising their rights.

- By 1877, Reconstruction ended. White Democrats took control of all state governments in the South.

REVIEWING CHAPTER 28

I. Reviewing Vocabulary

Match each word on the left with the correct definition on the right.

1. sharecropper
2. freedmen
3. impeach
4. lynch
5. carpetbagger

a. to murder by mob action
b. Northerner who moved to the South after the Civil War
c. farmer who pays part of a crop to a landowner as rent
d. to accuse an official of a crime
e. formerly enslaved African Americans

II. Understanding the Chapter

1. How did the Freedmen's Bureau aid African Americans in the South after the Civil War?
2. What were the key parts of Congress's plan for Reconstruction?
3. What steps did Reconstruction governments in Southern states take to aid African Americans?
4. Why did groups like the Ku Klux Klan try to keep freedmen from voting?
5. How did the period of Reconstruction come to an end?

III. Building Skills: Time Check

1. Did the impeachment of Andrew Johnson come before or after the election of Ulysses S. Grant? How do you know?
2. Did passage of Congress's plan of Reconstruction come before or after Southern states passed Black Codes? Give dates to support your answer.
3. What is the correct order of these events: passage of the 14th Amendment, pullout of all U.S. troops from the South, creation of the Freedmen's Bureau?

IV. Writing About History

1. **What Would You Have Done?** Imagine that you are an African American sharecropper in a Southern state in 1870. You have just learned that the Ku Klux Klan has burned the cabin of a friend of yours. Elections are going to be held next week. Will you vote? Explain your decision.
2. Imagine that you work for a newspaper in the North. Write an editorial giving your opinion of the Black Codes passed by Southern states.

V. Working Together

1. Form small groups of students. Imagine that you are freedmen in a small Southern town. You are planning to build a school for your community. Decide who can attend the school. Then decide what subjects should be taught in the school. Next, design the school and grounds. Share your group's school plans with the rest of the class.
2. **Past to Present** The high taxes raised by the Reconstruction governments upset many Southerners. Discuss in your group what voters today feel about taxes. With your group, write a paragraph that explains which government services you think are necessary even if the cost is high.

Unit 6
Challenges, Opportunities, and Achievements (1876-1900)

Chapters

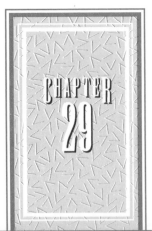
AFRICAN AMERICANS FACE A HOSTILE WORLD. (1877-1900)

How did African Americans in the South lose their rights after Reconstruction?

An African American minister visits a family in this 1881 painting. Ministers were highly respected members of African American communities.

Looking at Key Terms

- Jim Crow • *Plessy* v. *Ferguson*

Looking at Key Words

- **segregate:** to separate people by races

- **civil rights:** rights given to all citizens by the Constitution

S T U D Y

As you read, take notes that will help you answer the chapter-opening question above. Read the captions for more information to add to your notes.

H I N T

In 1884, an African American writer living in the North looked south. T. Thomas Fortune saw how African Americans lived there. He then told the world about their lives.

Fortune wrote that African Americans were more completely "under the control of the Southern whites than under the slave system." African Americans had won freedom in the Civil War. They had been promised rights during Reconstruction. What had gone wrong?

1 Jim Crow Laws Attack African Americans.

How did new laws in the South take away rights from African Americans?

In Chapter 28, you read how Reconstruction ended. White Democrats once again took over Southern governments. These officials set out to make sure that African Americans had no part in government.

Losing the vote   Groups like the Ku Klux Klan used terror to keep African Americans from voting. They kept many African Americans away from the polls.

Still, some African Americans would not be scared off. They continued to elect African Americans to office. For example, 104 African Americans held state office in North Carolina between 1876 and 1895.

White lawmakers in the South now came up with another idea. If terror could not keep African Americans from voting, new laws would. Those lawmakers knew that the federal government had lost interest in protecting the African Americans. It would not step in if the Southern states passed laws to limit African American rights. In the 1880s, the Southern states began to pass such laws.

None of the new laws said that African Americans could not vote. After all, the 15th Amendment said that no state could keep African American men from voting. (See Chapter 28.) But the new laws gave officials other ways to stop African Americans from voting. The chart below shows some of those laws.

The new laws worked. The number of African Americans in the South who voted fell sharply. In one state, the number dropped from 130,000 to under 5,000. As the numbers fell, African American elected officials vanished from the South.

Jim Crow   The voting laws kept African Americans out of the voting booths. But white lawmakers in the South wanted to keep African

Reading a Chart. Why did the Southern states create these barriers. Why didn't they simply rule that African Americans could not vote?

STATE BARRIERS TO VOTING BY AFRICAN AMERICANS

Poll Tax	A fee a voter must pay in order to vote; in effect, a voting tax that many African Americans were too poor to pay
Property Test	Requirement that a man must own a certain amount of property in order to vote; a test that few African Americans and poor whites could meet
Literacy Test	Requirement that to vote, a man must be able to read; white election registrars decided who passed the test
Grand-father Clause	Waived literacy and property tests for those men whose grandfathers had been eligible to vote before the Civil War, a test that few African Americans could meet
White Primary Elections	Primary, or nominating election, from which Southern Democrats could ban African American men because such elections were not covered by the 15th Amendment, which had given African Americans the vote

Americans out of much more than that. They passed laws to **segregate** whites and African Americans. To segregate means to separate by race.

Under these laws, African Americans had to ride in different railway cars from whites. They had to sit in separate parts of theaters. They could not use the same water fountains. They could not stay in the same hotels. Their children had to go to separate schools. Those who did not obey the laws could be fined or thrown in jail.

The system that these laws put in place was called **Jim Crow**. The name came from a popular song that made fun of African Americans.

Protesting Jim Crow African Americans hated Jim Crow. They thought the Jim Crow laws themselves broke the law. After all, the 14th Amendment said that all citizens had "equal protection of the laws." They felt that Jim Crow laws did not give them protection.

Many African Americans protested Jim Crow laws. One did more than protest. His name was Homer Plessy.

On a train trip in Louisiana, Plessy sat in a whites-only car. A conductor told him to move. Plessy refused. The conductor called the police. They arrested Plessy.

A Louisiana court found Plessy guilty of breaking the Jim Crow law. Plessy did not give up. He fought the case all the way to the U.S. Supreme Court.

In 1896, the Supreme Court reached its decision. It ruled against Plessy in the case known as ***Plessy v. Ferguson.*** The Court said that segregation was legal as long as African Americans and whites had use of equal services.

The Supreme Court's decision supported segregation for more than 50 years. White and African American schools, parks, and cemeteries dotted the South. They were separate places, but they were rarely equal. Places for whites were almost always far better than those for African Americans.

Lynch law Voting laws and Jim Crow laws were not enough for some white Southerners. At times, they went beyond the laws to try to control African Americans.

Reading a Chart. In which section of the country were most of the Jim Crow laws passed? In which two decades were most of the Jim Crow laws passed? What do you think it was like living with Jim Crow laws?

SOME JIM CROW LAWS, 1870–1965

Date/Place		Intent of Law	Date/Place		Intent of Law
1870	Georgia	separate schools	1915	Oklahoma	separate phone booths
1891	Georgia	separate seating in railroad cars	1915	S. Carolina	unequal spending for education
1900	S. Carolina	separate railroad cars	1922	Mississippi	separate taxicabs
1905	Georgia	separate parks	1932	Atlanta	separate baseball fields
1906	Alabama	separate streetcars	1935	Oklahoma	no boating or fishing together
1910	Baltimore	separate residential blocks	1937	Arkansas	segregation at race tracks
1914	Louisiana	separate entrances and seating at circuses	1944	Virginia	separate airport waiting rooms
1915	S. Carolina	separate entrances and work areas in factories	1965	Louisiana	no state money for schools not segregated

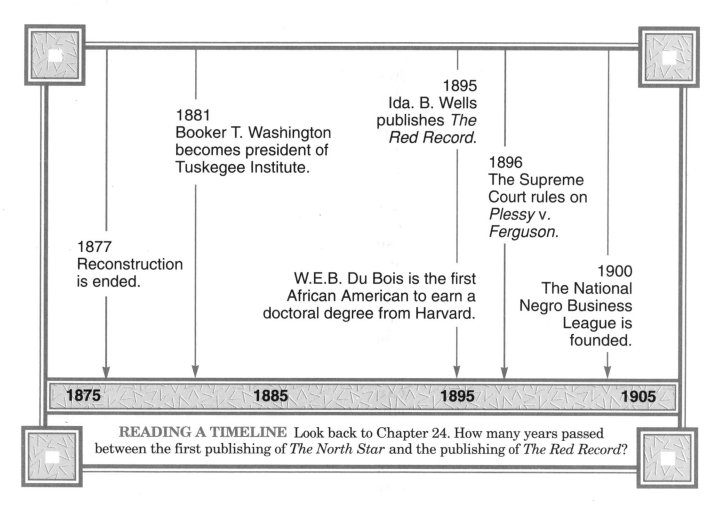

1877
Reconstruction
is ended.

1881
Booker T. Washington
becomes president of
Tuskegee Institute.

1895
Ida. B. Wells
publishes *The
Red Record.*

1896
The Supreme
Court rules on
Plessy v.
Ferguson.

W.E.B. Du Bois is the first
African American to earn a
doctoral degree from Harvard.

1900
The National
Negro Business
League is
founded.

| 1875 | 1885 | 1895 | 1905 |

READING A TIMELINE Look back to Chapter 24. How many years passed between the first publishing of *The North Star* and the publishing of *The Red Record*?

African Americans who protested unjust laws risked death. So did African Americans who fought for their rights. One day in 1892, a gang of whites attacked a store owned by three African Americans in Memphis, Tennessee. The owners fought back. When they did, they were arrested. As they waited for trial, a mob of whites stormed the jail. They dragged the three out and shot them to death.

Murders like that became common in the South. Thousands of African Americans were lynched in the late 1800s. Some white Southerners believed that terror was the best way to make African Americans act as they wanted them to.

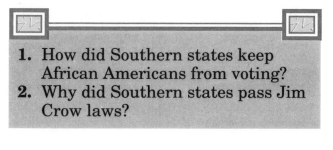

1. How did Southern states keep African Americans from voting?
2. Why did Southern states pass Jim Crow laws?

2 African Americans Fight Jim Crow.

How did African Americans try to overcome Jim Crow laws?

T. Thomas Fortune said, "It is time to face the enemy and fight inch by inch for every right he denies us." Many African Americans did fight Jim Crow. Some, like Homer Plessy, fought in courts. Others found different ways to fight.

Organizing African American clubs worked against Jim Crow. They asked the U.S. Congress and the states to protect the **civil rights** of African Americans. Civil rights are those rights given to all U.S. citizens by the Constitution.

The groups had some success. Fifteen states in the North passed stronger civil rights laws. Yet, Jim Crow stayed in place in the South.

Booker T. Washington, left, and W.E.B. DuBois had different views of how African Americans could win rights. Washington believed in education first. DuBois said that African Americans could not wait for equal rights.

Direct action   Other African Americans took more direct action against Jim Crow. They called for boycotts of places that practiced segregation.

In over 20 Southern cities, African American protesters took action against streetcar companies. They boycotted companies with segregated streetcars. One African American newspaper encouraged its readers to boycott. It stated, "Do not trample on our pride by being 'jim crowed.' Walk!"

Not all boycotts succeeded. But in some cities, Jim Crow streetcar companies went out of business. In a few places, African Americans started their own streetcar companies.

Attack on lynching   Some African Americans fought against the terror of lynching. One of them was Ida B. Wells.

Wells had been born into slavery in Mississippi. After the war, she taught school. In 1891, she became editor and part owner of a newspaper in Memphis, Tennessee.

In Memphis, a friend of Wells's died at the hands of a lynch mob. Wells then attacked lynching in the pages of *Free Speech*, her newspaper. Angry whites wrecked her printing presses. They threatened to hang her as well. Wells had to flee.

She settled in Chicago. There she carried on her fight. She wanted the whole nation to know about the lynchings. She thought that if enough people knew and spoke out, lynchings would stop.

Wells wrote articles for newspapers all over the country. In 1895, she also brought out *The Red Record*. This was a book about recent lynchings in the United States.

Wells did not end lynching. But after she started her fight, the number of lynchings dropped sharply. Wells would carry on her battle until her death in 1931.

A national leader Not all African Americans protested Jim Crow laws in public. Booker T. Washington was one who worked in another way. Washington was born into slavery in Virginia in 1856. After the war, he studied and taught at Hampton Institute in Virginia. This was a small college founded for newly freed African Americans.

In 1881, Washington got a job as head of a new school for African Americans in Alabama. The school was called Tuskegee Institute. It trained African Americans for jobs in farming and industry.

Washington built Tuskegee into the nation's leading school for African Americans. As he did, he became a national leader for African Americans. Many whites believed that he was the spokesperson for all African Americans.

Washington did not favor public protests about Jim Crow laws. He believed that African Americans should first work at getting educations and jobs. Once they had these, they could try to win other rights.

Another view Washington's views upset some African Americans. They felt that without equal rights, they would have no chance of good educations or good jobs.

W.E.B. DuBois (doo-BOYZ) was one of those concerned people. He was born in Massachusetts in 1868. A brilliant student, DuBois became the first African American to earn a doctoral degree from Harvard University. He taught history and wrote many books. DuBois would become an important African American leader in the early 1900s.

DuBois said African Americans could not wait for equal rights. They had to take action *now*! They should resist Jim Crow laws peacefully but firmly. They should demand the vote. They should also seek higher education. If they wanted to win their rights, jobs as farm or factory workers were not enough. They had to become teachers, lawyers, and doctors as well.

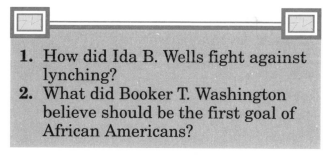

1. How did Ida B. Wells fight against lynching?
2. What did Booker T. Washington believe should be the first goal of African Americans?

3 African Americans Succeed in Business.

How did African Americans become successful in business despite Jim Crow laws?

Booker T. Washington and W.E.B. DuBois did agree about some things. Both felt that business ownership was

Madame C.J. Walker built a successful business from her beauty products. By 1910, her company employed 5,000 workers around the world.

important to African Americans. The more business owners there were, the more those people could help make things better for all African Americans.

African American businesses After the Civil War, African Americans opened many small businesses in the South. They ran food stores, drugstores, and cigar stores. They owned restaurants, barbershops, and beauty parlors. Most of these places were in African American neighborhoods of cities and towns.

African Americans owned larger businesses as well. African American banks opened across the South. By 1900, there were 50 of these. African Americans also owned insurance companies. The North Carolina Mutual Life Insurance Company was the biggest African American-owned business in the country.

A success story A woman founded one of the larger businesses. Sarah Breedlove had a job washing clothes in Missouri. One day, she thought of a new kind of hair conditioner. She mixed some up and sold it door to door. Her supply quickly sold out.

Encouraged, she made and sold more conditioner. Soon, she was making other beauty products. Then, she opened a chain of beauty parlors.

By this time, she had changed her name to Madame C. J. Walker. In 1910, her company had sales of over $1,000 a day. More than 5,000 people around the world worked for her.

Problems and opportunities Difficulties such as lack of money and poor locations made it hard for African American businesses to succeed. Despite problems, businesses struggled on.

From those business owners came the beginning of an African American middle class. This middle class wanted better schools for its children. It also wanted the chance to compete equally with white-owned businesses. Members of this middle class would support new groups pushing for equal rights as the 1900s began.

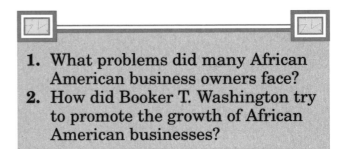

1. What problems did many African American business owners face?
2. How did Booker T. Washington try to promote the growth of African American businesses?

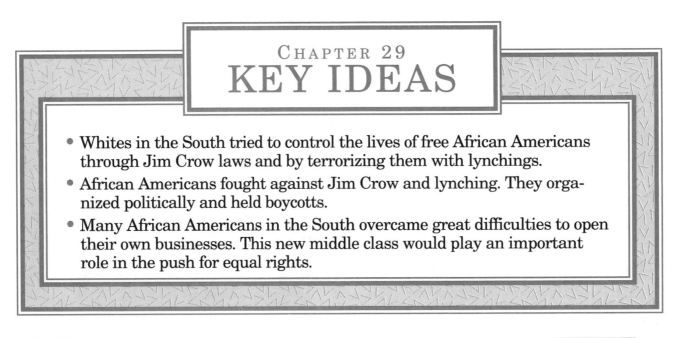

CHAPTER 29
KEY IDEAS

- Whites in the South tried to control the lives of free African Americans through Jim Crow laws and by terrorizing them with lynchings.
- African Americans fought against Jim Crow and lynching. They organized politically and held boycotts.
- Many African Americans in the South overcame great difficulties to open their own businesses. This new middle class would play an important role in the push for equal rights.

REVIEWING CHAPTER 29

I. Reviewing Vocabulary

Match each word on the left with the correct definition on the right.

1. segregate
2. Jim Crow
3. boycott
4. *Plessy* v. *Ferguson*
5. civil rights

a. protest by refusing to buy or use goods or services
b. things guaranteed to U.S. citizens by the Constitution
c. separate people by their races
d. system that kept African Americans and whites apart
e. Supreme Court decision that said separating people by race was legal

II. Understanding the Chapter

1. How did Southern laws keep African Americans from voting?
2. What was the purpose of Jim Crow laws?
3. How did African Americans in many Southern cities attempt to end segregation on streetcars?
4. What was the major difference in the views of Washington and DuBois on civil rights for African Americans?
5. Why were African American business owners important to the African American community in the United States?

III. Building Skills: Cause and Effect

For each cause below, give at least one effect.

1. Despite the efforts of groups like the Ku Klux Klan, African Americans in the South continue to vote.
2. The Supreme Court announces its decision in *Plessy* v. *Ferguson*.
3. Ida B. Wells tells the U.S. public about the lynching of African Americans.

IV. Writing About History

1. Imagine that you are an African American living in 1896. You have just heard of the decision in *Plessy* v. *Ferguson*. Write a letter to the editor of a local paper giving your response to the decision.
2. **What Would You Have Done?** If you were an African American living in 1895, who would you agree with Booker T. Washington or W.E.B. DuBois? Explain.

V. Working Together

1. Form a group of students. Imagine that your group is planning a boycott of Jim Crow streetcars in a Southern city in the late 1800s. Think of ways to encourage African Americans to join the boycott. Share your group's results with the class.
2. **Past to Present** Jim Crow laws stopped African Americans from voting. With a group, discuss other ways African Americans were kept away from the polls. Also discuss reasons why some people do not vote today.

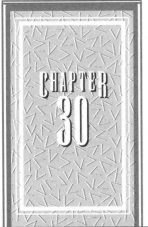

AMERICANS SETTLE ON THE GREAT PLAINS. (1865-1900)

How did U.S. settlers on the Great Plains change the way of life there?

An 1879 photo shows African American pioneers leaving Nashville, Tennessee, for Kansas. They called themselves Exodusters, after the book of Exodus.

Looking at Key Terms

- Homestead Act • Exodusters • Cattle Kingdom • Dawes Act

Looking at Key Words

- **transcontinental:** something that crosses the continent
- **homesteader:** person who got free government land on which to build a farm
- **sod:** top layer of earth made tough by grass roots
- **vaquero:** Spanish word for *cowhand*

- **cattle drive:** method developed in the mid 1800s for taking cattle from ranches to railroads and then to markets
- **rustler:** cattle thief
- **reservation:** land set aside for Native Americans

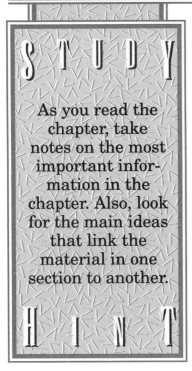

STUDY HINT

As you read the chapter, take notes on the most important information in the chapter. Also, look for the main ideas that link the material in one section to another.

Willianna Hickman stared out the window as her train chugged along. Before her lay a world very different from the hills and trees of Kentucky. That was where Willianna, her husband, and their six children had come from.

Now the African American family was headed for a new home in Kansas. The train carried them across miles and miles of flat land covered with tall grass. Willianna could not see a single tree. The land looked so empty. What would life be like here, she asked herself. How could they live?

Many other Americans asked questions like these after the Civil War. In those years, thousands of people moved to the Great Plains. There, they built new ways of life. But they also helped end some older ways.

1 Settlers Farm on the Great Plains.

What challenges did farmers face on the Great Plains?

The Hickmans planned to become farmers on the Great Plains. Laws passed by the U.S. government had helped the Hickmans and families like them decide to go west.

New railroads   During the Civil War, the federal government had backed the building of a railroad to California. Work on the railroad began in 1863. Crews mainly of Irish workers laid track west from Nebraska. Crews, largely of Chinese, worked east from California. In 1869, the crews met in Utah. This first **transcontinental** railroad linked the Atlantic and Pacific coasts. Transcontinental means something that crosses the continent.

Other transcontinentals followed. The government gave railroad companies huge amounts of land for building the railroads. The companies then sold the land at low prices. They wanted settlers who would use the railroads.

The railroads made moving west easier. People could reach their homes on the Great Plains more quickly. The railroads could also carry market crops that the new settlers raised.

Free land   The federal government helped settlement in another way. In 1862, it passed the **Homestead Act.** The act gave 160 acres (65 hectares) of land free to anyone who would farm it for five years.

Thousands of people took the offer. They became known as **homesteaders.** Homesteaders came from all over the United States. Some even traveled from Norway, Sweden, and Germany. In the six months after the act was passed, homesteaders took almost 250,000 acres (101,000 hectares) in Kansas and Nebraska alone.

Leaving the South   Willianna Hickman and her family were part of a special group. As you read in Chapter 29, African Americans in the South faced hard times at the end of Reconstruction. As Jim Crow laws came in, many African Americans gave up on the South. As one said, in the South "there was no hope for us and we had better go."

Many went west. African Americans formed groups and companies. They planned towns and colonies on the Plains. Agents toured the South selling Western land.

Some 80,000 African Americans headed for the Plains in the late 1870s. This movement was called the Exodus of 1879. That name came from a Bible story. In it, the Hebrews left slavery in Egypt for freedom in Israel. The

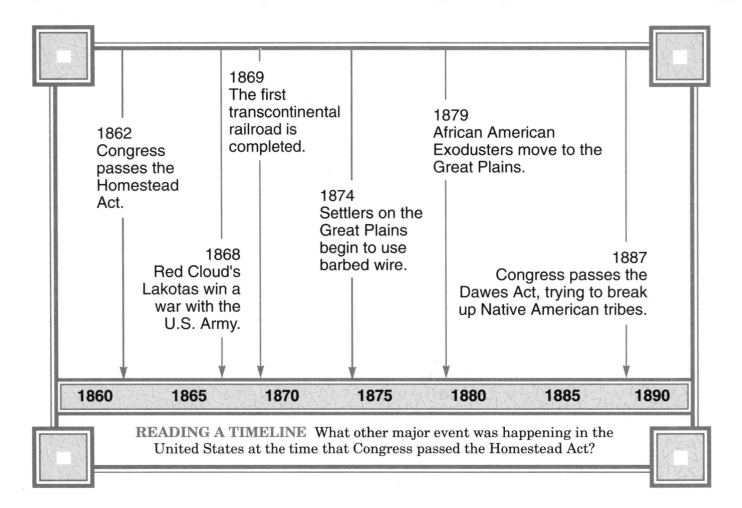

1862
Congress passes the Homestead Act.

1869
The first transcontinental railroad is completed.

1879
African American Exodusters move to the Great Plains.

1874
Settlers on the Great Plains begin to use barbed wire.

1868
Red Cloud's Lakotas win a war with the U.S. Army.

1887
Congress passes the Dawes Act, trying to break up Native American tribes.

| 1860 | 1865 | 1870 | 1875 | 1880 | 1885 | 1890 |

READING A TIMELINE What other major event was happening in the United States at the time that Congress passed the Homestead Act?

African Americans who went west were called **Exodusters.**

A hard life New settlers—Exodusters and whites—faced a harsh world on the Plains. Hot sun baked the Plains in summer. In winter, howling blizzards pushed snow over rooftops.

Grass was everywhere. It offered plenty of food for farm animals. But its roots wove together in a tough top layer of earth called **sod.** That sod made it hard to plant crops.

Still, the settlers stayed on. They learned to use new steel plows to cut the sod. They could then plant crops. They also learned to cut the sod into bricks. From these, they built shelters called sod houses.

Rainfall was scarce. To make up for a lack of water, the settlers learned ways of farming with less water. They also drilled to find water deep underground. New windmills pulled this water to the surface.

Without enough trees for wood fences, settlers used metal. A new product, barbed wire, came onto the market in 1874. Barbed-wire fences kept animals from trampling on or eating crops.

With all the hardships, settlers still hung on. They did so because they farmed some of the richest soil in the world. They slowly built up their farms, plowing more and more land. By the 1900s, farms of the Great Plains fed much of the world.

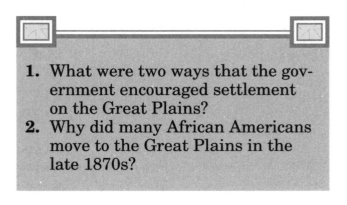

1. What were two ways that the government encouraged settlement on the Great Plains?
2. Why did many African Americans move to the Great Plains in the late 1870s?

2 Ranchers Prosper in the West.

How did ranching speed the development of the West?

Railroads aided more than farming in the West. They also helped cattle ranching grow there.

Roots of the cattle business   Cattle ranching had started hundreds of years before the first railroads were built. The first cowhands to ride the Plains were Latinos. They were called *vaqueros.* *Vaqueros* herded cattle in Texas in the 1700s, when it belonged to Spain.

By the 1800s, the ranching industry had grown greatly. Many people wanted to buy Texas beef. They included people in the growing cities of the East and Midwest. People in mining towns of the West also wanted beef. How could the ranchers get the cattle to those people? By railroad. But how could ranchers get the cattle to the railroad?

The long drives   The answer was the **cattle drive** run by cowhands. About a third of the cowhands were African Americans or Mexican Americans.

Cowhands would round up a rancher's cattle. Then they would drive the herd north. Cowhands would lead the herd to one of the towns that grew up on the new railroad lines. Such towns included Dodge City, Wichita, and Abilene. From the towns, railroad cars carried the cattle to market.

A cattle drive was hard work. Herds were driven from 500 to over 1,000 miles. Often, a drive was boring. Just as often, it could turn dangerous. Rivers might flood. Thunderstorms might start stampedes. **Rustlers,** or cattle thieves, might raid the herds.

The cattle drives proved a great success. The demand for beef kept growing. Some ranchers became rich. More peo-ple entered the business. By 1880, some 4.5 million cattle grazed from Kansas to Montana. The Great Plains became known as the **Cattle Kingdom.**

A changing business   As the business grew, it changed. More railroad lines crossed the Plains. More ranches were thus close to railroads. There was less need for long cattle drives.

More farmers were also settling on the Plains. They used barbed wire to protect their crops from cattle. At first, this led to fights between farmers and ranchers. The ranchers wanted their herds to roam freely. But slowly, the ranchers began to build their own fences.

Many of the cowhands in the U.S. West were Latinos. These Latino cowhands are shown at a New Mexico ranch during the 1890s.

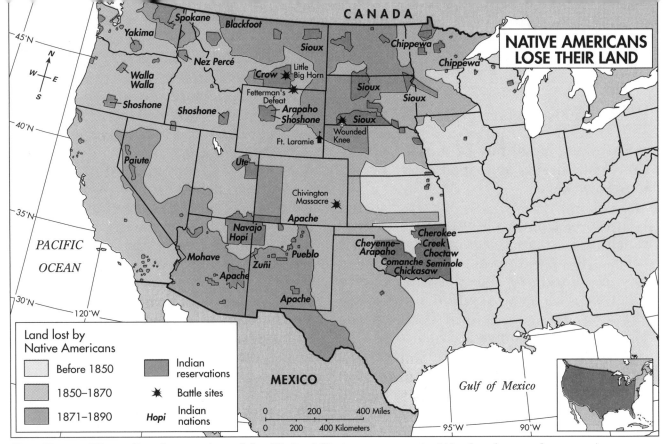

NATIVE AMERICANS LOSE THEIR LAND

Land lost by Native Americans

- Before 1850
- 1850–1870
- 1871–1890
- Indian reservations
- ✴ Battle sites
- *Hopi* Indian nations

Reading a Map. In what region of the United States was most of the land owned by Native Americans lost during the period 1871-1890? Name two Native American groups that still hold land in today's state of Montana.

Meanwhile, more and more people raised cattle. There were so many cattle that the price of beef fell sharply. By the 1890s, the great days of the Cattle Kingdom had ended.

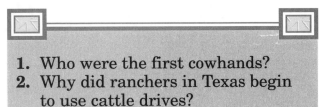

1. Who were the first cowhands?
2. Why did ranchers in Texas begin to use cattle drives?

3 Native Americans Fight for Their Way of Life.

How did the way of life of Plains Native Americans change with the coming of U.S. settlers?

Railroads, ranches, mines, and farms in the U.S. West changed the lives of many people. Among them were the first settlers of the Plains. They were the Native Americans.

Buffalo people   Long before the first whites arrived, Native Americans built a special way of life on the Plains. That way of life was based on the buffalo. Millions of the huge animals grazed the Plains at the time.

From spring to fall, groups of Native Americans followed the buffalo herds. (See Chapter 2.) At first, Native Americans hunted the herd on foot. Then they learned to use wild horses that had escaped from Spanish settlers. Horses made hunting buffalo much easier. Native American warriors also became skilled at fighting on horseback.

The people of the Plains became known as the "horse nations." They included the Blackfeet, Cheyenne, Lakota, and Comanche. In the late 1700s, they ruled the Plains.

Pressure of U.S. settlement   In the 1840s, the U.S. government wanted to

make the Plains into one big reservation. A reservation is land set aside for Native Americans. In many treaties, the government promised Native Americans that this land would be theirs "as long as grass grows, or water runs."

In the early 1800s, people of the United States thought that the Plains were worthless desert. By the 1860s, U.S. citizens began to realize that the Plains were valuable land. More and more railroads crossed them. More ranchers grazed cattle there. More farmers plowed the earth.

All these newcomers took Native American land. Native Americans protested. The U.S. government did not stop the new settlers. Instead, it pressed the Native Americans to live on smaller reservations.

Wars on the Plains Often, the Native Americans chose to fight instead. In 1866, the U.S. government wanted to build a road to new goldfields in Montana. The road would cross land belonging to the Lakota people in what is now Wyoming. The Lakota, however, did not want the road. The government began to build it anyway.

The Lakota then went to war. Under their leader Red Cloud, they fought for two years. In 1868, the U.S. government gave up. The Lakota had won. Red Cloud's War was the only war that Native Americans would ever win against the U.S. government.

For the next 20 years, Native Americans across the West fought to hold on to their land. The Comanche fought on the southern Plains. The Apache struggled in New Mexico and Arizona. The Cheyenne and Lakota went to war on the northern Plains.

Native Americans won some battles. In 1876, Lakota and Cheyenne warriors gath-

This famous picture shows the frozen body of the Lakota chief Big Foot. It lies on the snow-covered battle field at Wounded Knee, South Dakota. The Lakota were victims of a U.S. Army massacre in 1890.

ered near the Little Bighorn River in what is now Montana. Under Sitting Bull and Crazy Horse, they defeated a U.S. Army force led by George Armstrong Custer. Some 265 U.S. soldiers were killed.

Defeat   Such victories were rare for Native Americans. The U.S. Army had more soldiers. It also had more and better weapons.

The U.S. Army also had some unexpected help. As the railroads were being built, hunters shot buffalo to feed work crews. Then gangs of hunters began to shoot buffalo for their skins. In the early 1800s, there had been more than 60 million buffalo. By the 1880s, they were almost all gone.

Without buffalo, the Plains people lost their main source of food. Their whole way of life was vanishing. One after another, the peoples of the Plains were forced to surrender.

By the 1880s, most Native Americans lived on reservations. Up to that time, the government had let the Native Americans live in peace. But then it tried to break up the groups in which they lived. In 1887, Congress passed the **Dawes Act.** This broke up reservations into small plots of land. Each family got only about 160 acres (65 hectares) of land to live on. Any land left over was to be sold off. Under the act, Native Americans lost some 83 million acres (33.6 million hectares) of land.

A way of life had ended in the West. Now, the region's resources would help build a new way of life. That new way would take shape in the nation's cities and factories.

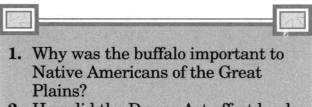

1. Why was the buffalo important to Native Americans of the Great Plains?
2. How did the Dawes Act affect lands of Native Americans in the West?

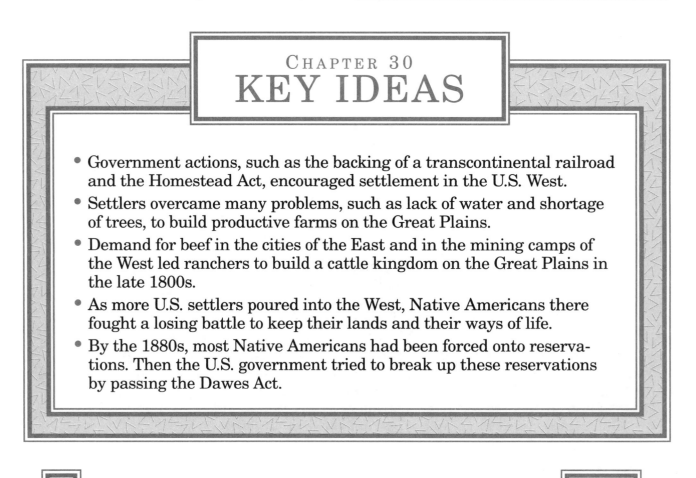

CHAPTER 30
KEY IDEAS

- Government actions, such as the backing of a transcontinental railroad and the Homestead Act, encouraged settlement in the U.S. West.

- Settlers overcame many problems, such as lack of water and shortage of trees, to build productive farms on the Great Plains.

- Demand for beef in the cities of the East and in the mining camps of the West led ranchers to build a cattle kingdom on the Great Plains in the late 1800s.

- As more U.S. settlers poured into the West, Native Americans there fought a losing battle to keep their lands and their ways of life.

- By the 1880s, most Native Americans had been forced onto reservations. Then the U.S. government tried to break up these reservations by passing the Dawes Act.

I. Reviewing Vocabulary

Match each word on the left with the correct definition on the right.

1. homesteader
2. sod
3. *vaquero*
4. reservation
5. rustler

   a. cattle thief
   b. land set aside for Native Americans
   c. person who built a farm on free government land
   d. one of the first cowhands on the Plains
   e. tough top layer of soil

II. Understanding the Chapter

1. What did the Homestead Act do?
2. How did settlers overcome hardships to build farms on the Great Plains?
3. What factors helped bring the Cattle Kingdom to an end?
4. Why did Native Americans of the Great Plains go to war in the later 1800s?
5. Why were Native Americans at a disadvantage in the struggle for the Plains?

III. Building Skills: Distinguishing Between Fact and Opinion

Read each sentence below and decide whether it states a fact or an opinion.

1. The soil of the Great Plains was good for farming.
2. Cowhands were very brave people.
3. The U.S. government made a mistake in passing the Dawes Act.
4. Native Americans won some battles but few wars in their struggle for the West.

IV. Writing About History

1. Write a short skit in which a Kansas rancher and a homesteader discuss the homesteader's plan to build a barbed-wire fence around her crops.
2. **What Would You Have Done?** Imagine that you are a Lakota in 1866. You have learned that the government wants to build a road across Lakota land. What would you say to U.S. representatives to protest that plan?

V. Working Together

1. Form small groups of students. Imagine that you are African Americans living in the South in the late 1870s. You have learned that some African Americans in a nearby town are planning to move to Kansas. Discuss whether to stay where you are or to go west. Make a list of arguments for staying or for going. You may wish to review Chapter 29 before starting your lists. Then take a vote to arrive at your decision. Share your group's arguments and its decision with the class.
2. **Past to Present** After the Civil War, many Americans moved westward from the South and the East. With a group, compare the settlers' reasons for going west to the reasons people today move from one part of the country to another. Make a chart that shows the similarities and the differences.

THE UNITED STATES BECOMES AN INDUSTRIAL NATION. (1865-1900)

Why did industry grow rapidly in the United States?

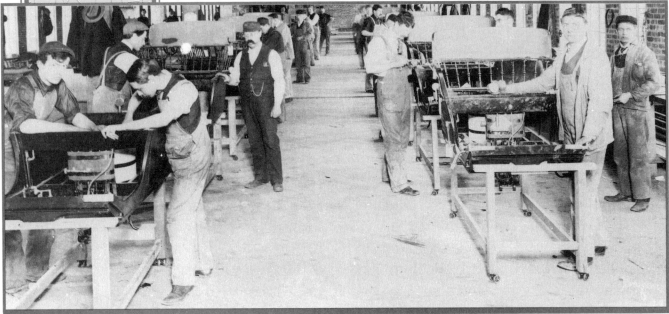

This photo shows an early assembly plant for "horseless carriages," or cars. In the late 1800s, new inventions made U.S. industry grow.

Looking at Key Terms

- Knights of Labor • Haymarket Riot
- American Federation of Labor (AFL)

Looking at Key Words

- **mass production:** way of making large amounts of a product quickly and cheaply
- **corporation:** company that raises money by selling shares in the business
- **stock:** a share in a corporation

- **monopoly:** a company with almost complete control of a good or service
- **strike:** refusal of workers to work until demands are met

STUDY HINT

Make an outline with these headings: New Technology, New Ways to Organize Business, New Ideas About Labor. Enter items you read about under each heading.

In Chapter 30, you learned how the U.S. West changed in the years after the Civil War. In the same years, great changes also swept the states of the East and the Midwest.

1 Industry Forges Ahead.

What part did railroads play in the growth of industry?

New railroads helped new farms, ranches, and mines in the West grow. Those railroads also helped new businesses and industries in the East grow.

New railroad companies Railroad building boomed after the Civil War. By 1900, the United States had six times more railroad track than it had in 1860. Before the Civil War, many small companies had built and run railroads. After the war, that changed. Business leaders bought up small railroad companies. They joined them into large companies. The Pennsylvania Railroad, for example, took in 73 smaller companies.

The big new companies made shipping and travel easier. Passengers and goods no longer had to change from one railroad line to another. This made shipping and traveling cheaper, too. The cost of shipping goods from New York to Chicago was cut in half. Now, a factory owner in New Jersey could sell goods across the country.

Just building the railroads helped industry grow. For every mile of track, 2,500 wooden ties had to be cut and placed. Workers dug tons of coal to power railroad engines. Thousands of workers also made steel for railroad engines and railroad tracks.

Steel Steelmaking became one of the nation's most important industries. In the 1850s, William Kelly in the United States and Henry Bessemer in

Great Britain had found simpler, cheaper ways to make steel. New steel mills sprang up in the United States. Pittsburgh, Pennsylvania, developed into the nation's steelmaking capital.

Steel became the key building material of many new industries. Now, railroads could afford to use steel for rails. Steel beams could hold up the walls of taller buildings. Strong steel plates could be made into huge ships.

New sources of power Railroads and steel helped industry grow. So did new sources of power. New inventions, for example, brought electric power to many people. Electric motors soon drove massive machines in factories. In 1879, Thomas Edison developed the electric light. Electric streetcars and elevators became common sights in cities.

Oil became another source of power. Scientists in the mid-1800s learned how to turn thick, black crude oil into a clear fuel for lamps. This set off a boom as people raced to drill oil wells.

The oil industry would grow still bigger. By the late 1800s, inventors had made new engines. These small, powerful motors used another form of oil–gasoline.

In 1893, Frank and Charles Duryea (DUR-ee-ay) used the gasoline engine to make what they called a "motor wagon." This was the beginning of the U.S. automobile industry. That industry would soon grow into the nation's largest.

Age of invention Edison and the Duryeas were just three of the many U.S. inventors of the late 1800s. One government official proudly said, "America has become known as the home of invention."

Here are a few examples of how many important inventions dated from these years. Edison also invented the

phonograph, the mimeograph machine, and the storage battery. Alexander Graham Bell invented the telephone in 1876. Gustavus Swift developed a refrigerated railroad car. This made it possible to ship fresh meat long distances.

African Americans such as Jan Matzeliger and Elijah McCoy also took part in the age of invention. Matzeliger made a machine that fastened the upper parts of shoes to their soles. Before Matzeliger's invention, shoes were sewn together by hand. Now, shoe companies were able to produce thousands of shoes in less time.

Elijah McCoy created a device to keep moving parts of engines oiled. This was a valuable invention for factory owners. Before McCoy's invention, machines had to be shut down several times a day so that they could be oiled. The automatic oiling device allowed machines to run almost constantly.

Ideas like these changed old industries or led to new ones. Some helped make bigger profits for businesses. Others made daily life easier or more pleasant. They also helped the U.S. economy grow.

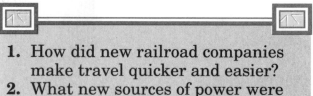

1. How did new railroad companies make travel quicker and easier?
2. What new sources of power were developed in the late 1800s?

2 Business Develops New Methods of Production.

How did U.S. industries increase their output during the late 1800s?

New inventions gave business owners many new products to sell. New rail-

Railroads tied the fast-growing United States together. This old print shows the station at Omaha, Nebraska, as the daily train arrived. What evidence does it show of Omaha as a multicultural city?

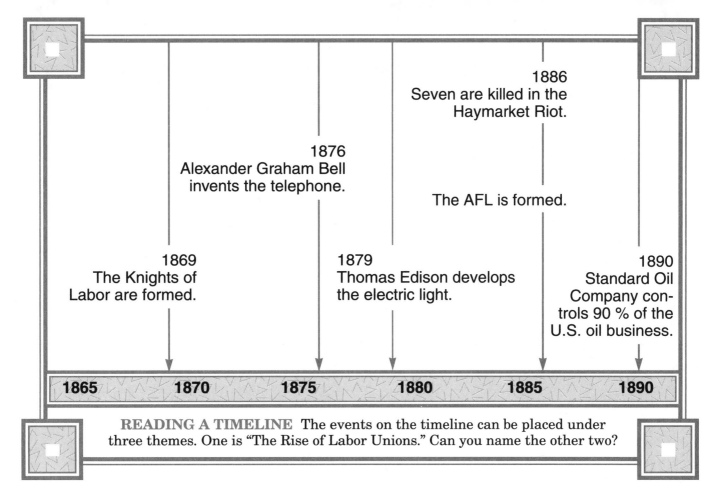

1886
Seven are killed in the Haymarket Riot.

1876
Alexander Graham Bell invents the telephone.

The AFL is formed.

1869
The Knights of Labor are formed.

1879
Thomas Edison develops the electric light.

1890
Standard Oil Company controls 90 % of the U.S. oil business.

| 1865 | 1870 | 1875 | 1880 | 1885 | 1890 |

READING A TIMELINE The events on the timeline can be placed under three themes. One is "The Rise of Labor Unions." Can you name the other two?

road lines let owners reach bigger markets than ever before. Now, owners looked for ways to turn out more and more products.

Making more goods   Before the Civil War, most workers had labored in small shops. Both owners and employees were usually skilled craftspeople. Often, they worked side by side.

Growing numbers of workers now labored in large factories. Making a product was broken down into many simple steps. Workers carried out the same steps over and over. They were told how much and how fast they should work. This process is called **mass production.** That is a way of making large numbers of goods quickly and cheaply. More and more U.S. businesses turned to mass production in the late 1800s.

Big business   Mass production made goods cheaply. But setting it up cost

money. Large buildings, costly machines, and many workers were needed.

Business owners looked for new ways to raise money. More and more of them did so by forming **corporations**. Corporations are businesses that raise money by selling shares, called **stock,** in the company. People who buy the stock get a share of the company's profits in return.

New business leaders   Some business leaders set out to gain complete control of their industries. In the 1870s, Andrew Carnegie built a steel mill near Pittsburgh. With the mill's profits, he bought iron and coal mines. Iron and coal were used in steel making. Carnegie bought ships to carry the iron and coal to his mills. He bought railroads to carry steel to market.

Carnegie thus controlled all parts of the steel-making business. This let him keep prices low. He drove many rival

The growing importance of women in U.S. labor is shown by the number of women delegates to the 1886 convention of the Knights of Labor. The women were concerned that the union did not represent them well.

companies out of business. By 1900, Carnegie's company made more steel than all the mills in Great Britain.

John D. Rockefeller became a leader in the oil business. In 1863, he bought a plant where crude oil was changed into kerosene. He kept his costs low and sold his products for less than rival companies. Soon, he began to buy up those companies. By 1890, Rockefeller's Standard Oil Company controlled 90 percent of the nation's oil business.

A company like Standard Oil is called a **monopoly**. A monopoly is a company that has almost complete control over a good or service. With no rivals in its field, a monopoly could easily raise prices for its products. By 1900, giant corporations controlled the oil, steel, and meat industries in the nation.

1. How did many businesses raise money to begin mass production?
2. How did Andrew Carnegie try to keep the costs of making steel low?

3 Workers Seek to Improve Working Conditions.

How did labor unions try to improve conditions for the nation's workers?

Businesses of the late 1800s tried to sell their goods at lower prices than their rivals did. One way to do this was to hold down costs. One of the costs they found easiest to control was what they paid for labor.

Many workers One reason why business owners could hold down wages was that there were many workers. Men and women were leaving farms to look for jobs in cities. African Americans were moving to the East and the Midwest to escape Jim Crow laws. As you will read in Chapter 32, many people were moving to this nation from other lands.

These people needed work. They would accept whatever wages and hours owners offered. Often, the workday was 10 or even 12 hours. Usually, workers toiled six days a week, sometimes seven.

Skilled workers might earn $12 a week. Unskilled workers would be lucky to earn $6. As the chart shows, women workers earned less than white men. The same is true for African American and child workers.

Conditions   Owners spent little on the safety and comfort of workers. This was another way to hold down costs. Most workers had no paid holidays or vacations. They could be fired at any time. They had no insurance if they lost a job or were hurt on the job.

On-the-job injuries were common. Factories, mines, and mills were dark, noisy, dangerous places. Steelworkers risked burns from hot metal. Textile workers breathed fibers that caused lung disease. Workers could lose their limbs or their lives in the machines.

Organizing   Poor pay and working conditions led many workers to join unions. By working as a group for better conditions, they would have more chance of success. Workers also had another weapon—the **strike.** In a strike, employees refuse to work until their demands are met.

Workers formed the first U.S. unions early in the 1800s. Most of them failed. Business owners claimed that unions slowed or stopped trade. Courts usually sided with the owners. They ruled that much union activity was illegal.

A national union   A new union formed in 1869. It was called the **Knights of Labor.** Most earlier unions only took skilled workers as members. The Knights took in skilled and unskilled workers. They also accepted women, African Americans, and immigrants.

The Knights pushed for better pay and shorter working hours. They also wanted equal pay for men and women workers and an end to child labor.

The Knights got the U.S. government to set up the Department of Labor. They also won some strikes against powerful railroad companies.

Reading a Chart. Which job shown on the chart provided the highest yearly wages for children? Name four occupations in which the average annual wage for men was more than double the annual wage for women.

AVERAGE EARNINGS OF MEN, WOMEN, AND CHILDREN IN SELECTED OCCUPATIONS IN THE 1870s

Occupation	Average Daily Wages			Average Yearly Wages		
	Men	Women	Children	Men	Women	Children
Farm laborers	$1.58	$1.00	$0.50	$328	$200	$100
Domestics		1.00			300	
Store workers	2.00	1.25	.20	600	375	60
Shoemakers	3.50	1.50	.75	625	375	188
Button makers	2.37	.92		711	276	
Cotton workers	1.67	1.05	.55	501	315	165
Woolen workers	1.57	1.04	.58	471	312	174
Cigar makers	3.00	1.25		900	375	
Pottery workers	2.50	.92		750	276	
Glassmakers	2.00	.75	.67	600	225	201
Bookbinders	3.00	1.00		750	250	
Felt makers	2.00	.83	.70	600	249	210
Chair makers	2.25	.87	.37	675	261	111
Sewing silk	2.50	1.15	.75	750	336	225
Tailors	3.50	1.25		875	313	

Violence In 1886, the Knights held a workers' rally at Haymarket Square in Chicago. During the rally, someone threw a bomb. The blast killed seven police officers and injured many more. There was no proof that the union was involved in the bombing. Yet people blamed the Knights anyway. Membership in the Knights fell sharply after the **Haymarket Riot.**

Strikes called by other unions turned violent in the late 1800s. Violence slowed the growth of unions. Still, it did not stop the unions. Workers needed some way of improving their lives. Unions offered the only hope.

New unions During the late 1800s, new unions formed. In 1886, the **American Federation of Labor** (AFL) started up. The AFL was made up of many different unions of skilled workers. It pushed for higher wages, shorter hours, and safer workplaces. By 1900, the AFL had more than a million members.

Many unions still would not take women or minorities as members. Often, these workers had to form their own unions. In 1903, skilled women workers formed the National Women's Trade Union League. Cuban American cigar makers started a union in Florida in the late 1800s. Mexican American miners joined unions in the Southwest.

The unions did help some workers win better wages and shorter hours. However, there were only 440,000 union members in the whole nation in 1897. That was less than 10 percent of the industrial workforce. Workers still had a long way to go.

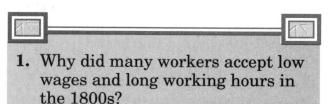

1. Why did many workers accept low wages and long working hours in the 1800s?
2. What setback did the Knights of Labor suffer in 1886?

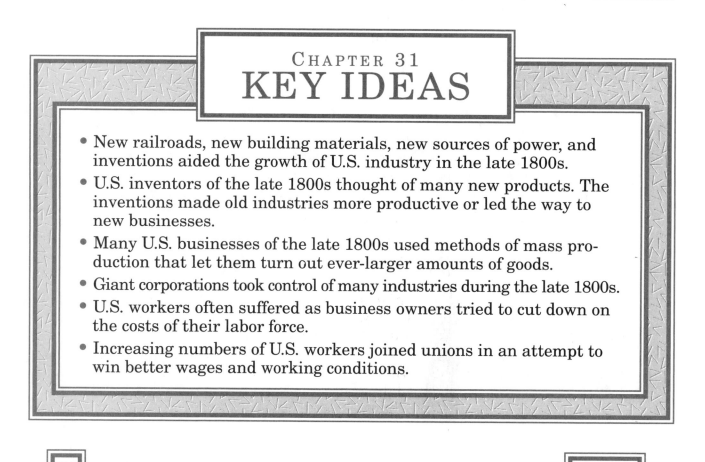

CHAPTER 31
KEY IDEAS

- New railroads, new building materials, new sources of power, and inventions aided the growth of U.S. industry in the late 1800s.
- U.S. inventors of the late 1800s thought of many new products. The inventions made old industries more productive or led the way to new businesses.
- Many U.S. businesses of the late 1800s used methods of mass production that let them turn out ever-larger amounts of goods.
- Giant corporations took control of many industries during the late 1800s.
- U.S. workers often suffered as business owners tried to cut down on the costs of their labor force.
- Increasing numbers of U.S. workers joined unions in an attempt to win better wages and working conditions.

REVIEWING CHAPTER 31

I. Reviewing Vocabulary
Match each word on the left with the correct definition on the right.

1. stock
2. monopoly
3. strike
4. corporation
5. mass production

a. a business owned by many people
b. tool used by unions to gain their demands
c. almost complete control of a good or service
d. turning out large amounts of something quickly and cheaply
e. a share in a business

II. Understanding the Chapter
1. How did railroads aid the growth of business in the United States?
2. Do you agree or disagree with the U.S. official of the late 1800s who said, "America has become known as the home of invention"? Explain.
3. Why were many new companies formed in the late 1800s?
4. Why did some people worry about the growth of monopolies in the late 1800s?
5. What hardships did workers in U.S. industries face in the late 1800s?

III. Building Skills: Identifying Point of View
Tell whether each of the statements below would most likely have been made by a factory owner or a factory worker.
1. I'm happy to see that so many new immigrants are arriving in the United States.
2. I'm voting for the candidate who supports an eight-hour workday.
3. If the lighting in that corner of the factory is kept low, there will be a yearly savings of $4,000.
4. I cannot support my family on my wages.

IV. Writing About History
1. **What Would You Have Done?** If you were an unskilled worker in a steel mill in 1878, would you go to a meeting to organize a union? Explain.
2. Write a magazine article explaining what you think was most important to the growth of business in the United States in the late 1800s: railroads, the steel industry, or new sources of power.

V. Working Together
1. Work with several of your classmates. In your groups, think of a new product or service that might be a success today. Write a description of your product to convince people to invest money in it. Then, create an advertisement for it.
2. **Past to Present** In the late 1800s and early 1900s, new inventions and discoveries changed the way people lived. With a group, discuss the changes that happened. Then think about inventions and discoveries that happened in the late 1900s. List five modern inventions and the changes they have made in people's lives.

IMMIGRANTS HELP BUILD THE UNITED STATES. (1865-1900)

How did immigration during the late 1800s affect the United States?

Crowded aboard a ship, immigrants make their way to the United States in 1890. Millions of immigrants made the trip in the last years of the 1800s.

Looking at Key Terms

- new immigrants • Chinese Exclusion Act

Looking at Key Words

- **pogrom:** an organized killing of an ethnic group, especially Jews
- **stereotype:** to develop a generalization or idea about a group that is probably not true
- **tenement:** a slum apartment building with many small apartments
- **assimilate:** to absorb someone into—or make someone part of—a culture or country

STUDY HINT

On a sheet of paper, make three columns. Label them Europe, Asia, and Latin America. Under each heading, list countries or places from which immigrants came during the 1860-1900 period.

A flood of immigrants poured into the United States in the late 1800s. Between 1860 and 1900, 13 million came from Europe, Asia, and other parts of the Americas. They hoped to work in the United States' growing industries. The immigrants believed the United States was a "promised land." They hoped their dreams would come true here.

1 Immigrants Arrive from Eastern and Southern Europe.

How were the new groups of immigrants different from those who came before?

The immigrants who came from Europe after about 1885 were unlike those who had come before. Earlier immigrants had arrived mainly from northern and western Europe. (See Chapter 22.) They came from places such as England, Ireland, Germany, and Scandinavia. Such people were called "old immigrants."

After 1885, more and more immigrants came from eastern and southern Europe. They came from such countries as Italy, Greece, Russia, and Poland. Such people were called **new immigrants.**

If you had stood on the dock as the "new" immigrants streamed off their ships, you would have heard many different languages. Some people spoke Italian or Greek. Jews from Poland and Russia spoke Yiddish. Still others spoke Croatian (cro-AY-shun) or Czech (CHECK) or Slovak (SLOW-vahk).

Why they came What caused the shift from old to new immigrants? Life was getting harder in eastern and southern Europe. Many people there wanted to go to the United States. Times were hard for small farmers in countries like Italy and Greece. Machines were taking over farm jobs. Rich people were buying up land and forcing small farmers to move.

Jews had their own reasons for seeking new homes. Five million Jews lived in Poland and Russia. All were under Russian rule. Russia's leaders stirred up hatred against the Jews. The rulers wanted people to blame the Jews—not the rulers—for Russia's problems. Mobs burned down Jewish homes. They killed Jewish men, women, and children. These organized killings, called **pogroms,** spread in the 1880s. Thousands and then millions of Jews fled to the United States.

Coming to the United States The first sight of the United States filled the immigrants with wonder. "Everybody was on deck," a 17-year-old girl remembered. "My sister and I stood pressed to each other, excited by the sight of the harbor. The Statue of Liberty suddenly emerged from the mist. Ah, there she was, the symbol of hope, of freedom, of opportunity."

More than five million European immigrants arrived in the United States from 1868 to 1882. Most new immigrants could not afford to buy land for farming. They settled in the cities of the East and Midwest.

Bad housing The immigrants often lived in large slum buildings, or **tenements**, that were divided into many small apartments. Two or more families often had to share a single room. Many tenements had no water except for a faucet in the yard. Rats lived in the rotting garbage that piled up outside. These conditions helped disease to spread quickly. An 1882 report stated that half the children born in Chicago died before they were five years old.

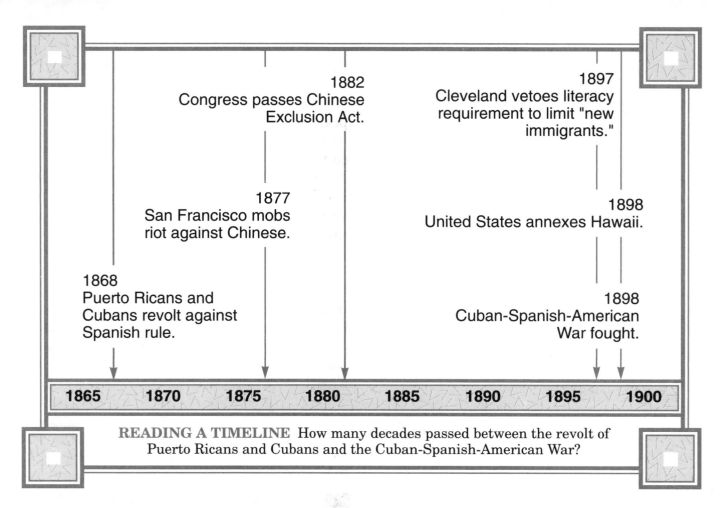

| 1868 Puerto Ricans and Cubans revolt against Spanish rule. | 1877 San Francisco mobs riot against Chinese. | 1882 Congress passes Chinese Exclusion Act. | 1897 Cleveland vetoes literacy requirement to limit "new immigrants." 1898 United States annexes Hawaii. 1898 Cuban-Spanish-American War fought. |

| 1865 | 1870 | 1875 | 1880 | 1885 | 1890 | 1895 | 1900 |

READING A TIMELINE How many decades passed between the revolt of Puerto Ricans and Cubans and the Cuban-Spanish-American War?

Immigrant neighborhoods Generally, each immigrant group lived in a neighborhood with people from their homeland. Despite the run-down housing, people in immigrant neighborhoods felt a sense of belonging. They gossiped about news from back home. They held religious services in the languages of their homeland.

Outside their own neighborhoods, the immigrants felt unwelcome. Many Americans resented the new immigrants. Most Americans—and most of the old immigrants—were Protestants. Many new immigrants were Roman Catholics or Jews. Some were Eastern Orthodox Christians. Many Americans did not trust the immigrants because of those religious differences. Also, many Americans **stereotyped** (STEHR-ee-ah-teypt) the immigrants as "dirty" and "ignorant." A stereotype is an idea people may have about a group that is not

necessarily true. Americans looked down on immigrants who did not know how to read or write.

Going to work Immigrants took the hardest, dirtiest jobs. Usually, they could not get better jobs. They worked long hours for low wages. Italians often dug ditches or helped put up buildings. Czechs and Poles worked in coal mines, steel mills, and meatpacking plants. Jews worked in clothing factories or sewed at home. The sweat of the immigrants helped to build strong American industries.

Becoming Americans Immigrants were eager to be **assimilated** into American society. To be assimilated into is to be absorbed into the culture or to adopt the customs of a new land. At school, children quickly learned English. They also learned new ways of acting and thinking. Often, they became ashamed of their parents' old-fashioned ways. Children wanted to fit in, to become "real Americans."

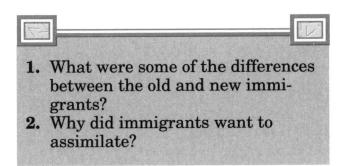

1. What were some of the differences between the old and new immigrants?
2. Why did immigrants want to assimilate?

2 Immigrants from Asia Settle in the West.

What problems did immigrants from Asia face?

Most of the immigrants from Europe arrived on the East Coast. On the West Coast, immigrants from a different part of the world arrived. They were from Asia—mainly China and Japan. Asians faced many of the same challenges as Europeans and other challenges as well.

Chinese women   As you read in Chapter 22, Chinese immigrants began arriving in California during the 1850s. Most of the Chinese in the United States were men. The few Chinese women worked in the family laundry or shop.

Mary Bong, who lived in Alaska Territory, was different. She and her husband dug for gold. They ran a dairy. They trapped wild animals. Later, Mary Bong became a salmon fisher. She rose at dawn, sailed out in her small boat, and fished all day. In the evenings, she came home and sold her catch.

Anti-Chinese feeling   Many Americans, especially laborers and factory workers, saw the Chinese as a threat. Like European newcomers, the Chinese had little choice of jobs. Employers paid them less than they paid native-born Americans. That made union members angry. "How can we compete against people who work for so little?" union members asked. Of course, the unions were partly to blame. They would not let most immigrants become union members.

Excluding the Chinese   Anti-Chinese feeling grew in the United States during the 1870s. Mobs attacked Chinese in many western towns and cities. The Chinese had few rights. They were not allowed to become citizens. They could not vote. Some laws were

Reading a Chart. Compare this chart with the one of earlier immigration on page 192. From which region has immigration grown at a fast pace?

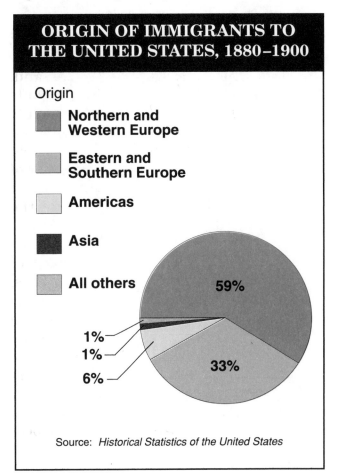

ORIGIN OF IMMIGRANTS TO THE UNITED STATES, 1880–1900

Origin

■ Northern and Western Europe

■ Eastern and Southern Europe

□ Americas

■ Asia

▨ All others

59%

1%
1%
6%

33%

Source: *Historical Statistics of the United States*

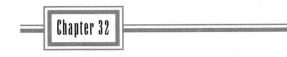

passed to protect the Chinese, but officials did little to enforce them.

Soon lawmakers began proposing laws to keep Chinese out of the United States. Congress passed such a law in 1882. It was called the **Chinese Exclusion Act.** Exclusion means keeping out. The act said that no Chinese worker could come to the United States for the next ten years. Another act made the exclusion last longer. Not until 1943 were Chinese again allowed to immigrate to the United States.

Arrival of the Japanese About the time that the Chinese were excluded, Japanese immigrants began to come to the United States. Japan was going through big changes. Its emperor wanted to make Japan a modern nation. Japan drafted young men into the army. It placed high taxes on land. Life became very hard for farm people. Many decided to leave Japan.

Thousands of Japanese took jobs on sugar plantations in Hawaii. The immigrants signed contracts to work in Hawaii for several years. At the time, Hawaii was an independent nation. In 1898, Hawaii became part of the United States. (You will read more about Hawaii in Chapter 35.) By then, 60,000 of Hawaii's 154,000 people were from Japan.

When their contracts ended, many Japanese moved from Hawaii to the West Coast. Most settled in California. Others came directly from Japan.

Because of their farm backgrounds, most Japanese immigrants became farm workers. Some Japanese bought farms of their own. Some started fruit orchards or tree nurseries. A few built up large businesses.

As the number of Japanese increased, they too aroused anger among some Americans. Feelings ran especially high in California. After 1900, efforts to cut back on Japanese immigration succeeded.

By the late 1800s, San Francisco's Chinatown was a bustling place. Here immigrants could find familiar foods and products.

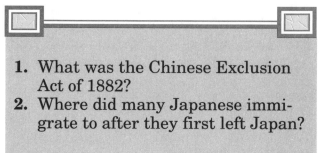

1. What was the Chinese Exclusion Act of 1882?
2. Where did many Japanese immigrate to after they first left Japan?

This 1892 picture shows Ybor City, Florida. It was built by the Cuban American Vicente Martínez for Cubans who worked in his cigar factory. Cubans came to Florida in great numbers during the fighting against Spain.

3 Immigrants from Latin America Find U.S. Homes.

What brought Latin American immigrants to the United States in the late 1800s?

Not all immigrants in the late 1800s came from Europe and Asia. Many came from lands just south of the United States in Latin America. Tens of thousands of Mexicans immigrated to the United States. Puerto Ricans and Cubans fleeing war and injustice came from the Caribbean.

Hard times in Mexico   In the late 1800s, a new land law allowed rich people in Mexico to gain large amounts of land. As a result, many Mexicans farmers had to go to work for the new owners.

Elias Garza was a Mexican who lost his land. "The owners gave us the seeds, the animals, and the land," Garza recalled. "But when the crop was in, there wasn't anything left for us, even if we had worked very hard. That was terrible. Those landowners were robbers." Like many of his neighbors, Garza moved to California.

A flow of immigrants from Mexico brought new people into the Spanish-speaking communities of the Southwest. Mexicans began to replace Chinese workers on railroads. Mexicans mined copper in Arizona. They picked cotton in Texas. They dug beets in Colorado. Later, Mexican workers moved north to work in the steel mills of Chicago. In California, Mexicans worked side by side with Japanese workers on large farms.

Puerto Ricans and Cubans   Many Puerto Ricans and Cubans came as refugees from war. Their homelands were Spanish colonies. In 1868, both Puerto Ricans and Cubans revolted against Spanish rule. The Spanish crushed those revolts. Then new uprisings broke out. Many Americans sided with the rebels. In 1898, the United States went to war against Spain. (See Chapter 35.) Puerto Rico came under U.S. rule, and Cuba became independent.

From the 1870s to 1898, thousands of Puerto Ricans and Cubans moved to the United States. Some were well educated and had professions. They settled in cities like New York, Philadelphia, and Boston. There they pursued their professions.

Others had neither education nor money. Many Puerto Ricans settled in New York. Some found work as cigar makers. Some even became owners of cigar factories. Poorer Cubans went to Florida. Many became cigar makers in places like Key West and Tampa.

Dreams of home   Most of the Mexican immigrants planned to return to Mexico. They came because even the worst jobs in the United States paid better than jobs in Mexico. Many Puerto Ricans and Cubans also planned to return to their homelands once independence from Spain was won. They collected money for the rebel cause back home. They plotted against Spain. After Spanish rule ended in 1898, many returned home. However, others stayed on in Florida or New York. They considered those places their new homes.

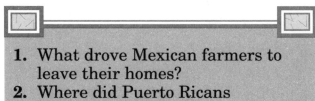

1. What drove Mexican farmers to leave their homes?
2. Where did Puerto Ricans and Cubans settle in the United States?

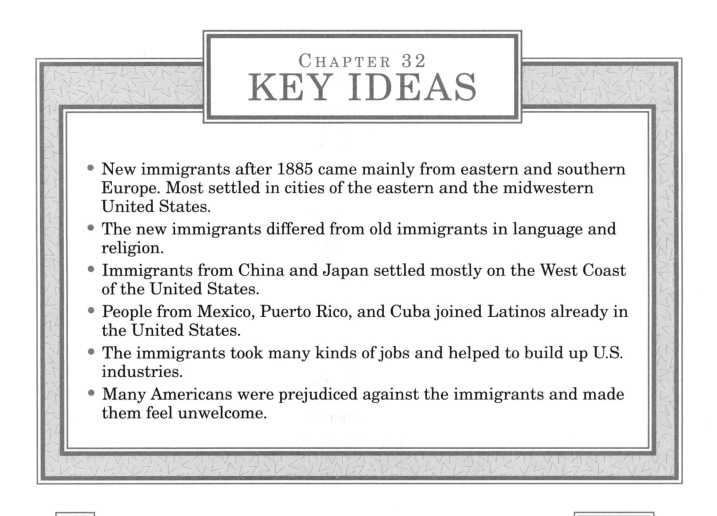

CHAPTER 32
KEY IDEAS

- New immigrants after 1885 came mainly from eastern and southern Europe. Most settled in cities of the eastern and the midwestern United States.
- The new immigrants differed from old immigrants in language and religion.
- Immigrants from China and Japan settled mostly on the West Coast of the United States.
- People from Mexico, Puerto Rico, and Cuba joined Latinos already in the United States.
- The immigrants took many kinds of jobs and helped to build up U.S. industries.
- Many Americans were prejudiced against the immigrants and made them feel unwelcome.

REVIEWING CHAPTER 32

I. Reviewing Vocabulary

Match each word on the left with the correct definition on the right.

1. assimilate   **a.** a massacre of a group of people, especially Jews
2. new immigrant   **b.** to absorb someone into a culture
3. tenement   **c.** a building with many small apartments
4. pogrom   **d.** a generalization about a group that is probably not true
5. stereotype   **e.** a person from eastern or southern Europe

II. Understanding the Chapter

1. Why did immigration from northern and western Europe decrease, while immigration from southern and eastern Europe increased in the late 1800s?
2. Why did immigrants tend to live in neighborhoods with other immigrants from their homelands?
3. What kinds of jobs did new immigrants take?
4. What conditions prevented Chinese immigrants from fighting for their rights?
5. From what countries did most Latino newcomers to the United States come? Why did they leave their homelands?

III. Building Skills: Compare and Contrast

1. Imagine that you are a Jewish immigrant in the 1890s. Write two sentences that compare your life in Europe with your life in the United States.
2. Reread the sections on immigrants from Europe and on immigrants from Asia. Make a list of experiences that immigrants in each group might have. Which experiences are similar? Which are different?

IV. Writing About History

1. Imagine that it is 1900 and you and your family have just immigrated to the United States. Write one or two diary entries describing your first days at an American school. What is new and strange? How do you feel about your new life?
2. **What Would You Have Done?** Suppose you are a member of Congress. You know that many voters in your district do not like immigrants. A bill proposes to cut back immigration. Will you vote for the bill? Why or why not?

V. Working Together

1. Work in a small group. Find out about immigrants who have settled in your community. Where were the first immigrants from? Where are the most recent immigrants from? What contributions have immigrants made to the community? Prepare a display of pictures and writings about "Immigrants in Our Community."
2. **Past to Present** Chinese and Japanese people were prevented from immigrating by U.S. laws. With a group, discuss why this happened. Also talk about why some groups today are not allowed into the United States.

THE UNITED STATES BECOMES A NATION OF CITIES. (1865-1900)

How did the growth of cities change life in the United States?

America's growing cities needed better means of transportation. This 1891 drawing shows New York City workers laying railroad tracks.

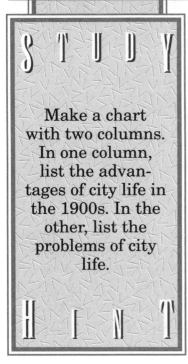
Looking at Key Terms

- heavy industry • skyscraper • cable car • trolley car
- reservoir • aqueduct • Hull House

Looking at Key Words

- **elevated:** a railroad that operates on tracks raised above the streets of a city
- **subway:** a railroad that operates in underground tunnels
- **epidemic:** a rapidly spreading outbreak of a disease

- **graft:** the dishonest use of a government position for personal profit
- **settlement house:** an organization intended to serve the needs of people in a poor neighborhood

The year was 1871. Chicago was the fastest-growing city in the United States. The city was less than 40 years old, but already nearly a half million people lived there. On October 8, Mrs. O'Leary went to the shed behind her house on the west side of Chicago. She was going to milk her cow. She carried a lantern, an old-fashioned light, with her. While she was milking the cow, the cow kicked over the lantern. The lantern set some hay on fire. Then, the shed itself began to burn.

Mrs. O'Leary and her cow may or may not have been real—no one knows for sure. But the fire that began that night was very real. It spread quickly. By the time the fire burned itself out it had destroyed most of Chicago.

1 Cities Grow in Number and Size.
What accounted for the rapid growth of cities?

The great fire of Chicago left the city in ruins. However, only two years later, the city was rebuilt. By 1890, 1 million people lived in Chicago. Nothing, it seemed, could stop its growth.

The growth of industry The years after the Civil War saw a huge growth in U.S. cities. In 1860, there were nine cities with a population of at least 100,000. By 1910, there were 50 cities that large. Philadelphia had a population of more than 1 million people and Chicago, a population of 2 million. New York had 5 million people. That made New York one of the largest cities in the world. (See the graph on page 280.)

Industry was the main reason for the growth of cities. Before the Civil War, Americans had moved from farms to cities to find work. They worked in clothing mills, ironworks, furniture factories, and slaughterhouses.

Industry grew even faster after the war. **Heavy industry**—the manufacture of such large items as trains and farm machines—became important. Heavy industry depended on steel. Therefore, the steel industry also developed. Pittsburgh, Pennsylvania, and Birmingham, Alabama, turned into major steel centers.

Chicago became the home of the meatpacking industry. Meat products were shipped from Chicago across the country in new refrigerated railroad cars. In New York City, thousands of small factories made clothes that were worn all over the nation.

There were other reasons for the growth of cities. Builders developed a way to use steel to make buildings. About the same time, a safe elevator was invented. These two inventions made it possible to build taller buildings than had even been dreamed of before. The new buildings were so high that people called them **skyscrapers.**

Transportation in the cities Improved transportation also helped cities grow. **Cable cars** were pulled through the streets by a moving cable, or thick steel rope. The cars grabbed onto the cable to move and let go of it to stop. Cable cars were built in many cities. Today, cable cars are a familiar sight in San Francisco.

Trolley cars were even more common. They drew power from electricity. The cars were connected to an electric wire that hung over the streets. Like cable cars, trolley cars ran along the streets on tracks.

Streetcars could carry many people. However, they were often slowed by other traffic in the streets. To escape this problem, some cities built **elevateds.** Elevateds are railroads that run on tracks raised above the street. An even greater improvement was to put the tracks in underground tunnels called **subways.** The first subway in the United States

opened in Boston in 1897. Elevateds and subways allowed people to move around cities quickly and at low cost.

City services Other improvements aided the growth of cities. A large city requires huge amounts of fresh water every day. Many cities could simply take water from a nearby river or lake. Cities such as New York were located miles from fresh water. These cities built **reservoirs,** or artificial lakes, to store water. They also built **aqueducts,** or canals and tunnels for carrying water.

Entertainment and culture For many people, life in the cities was pleasant and exciting. There were large department stores, such as John Wanamaker's in Philadelphia and Marshall Field's in Chicago. They offered clothes, furniture, and many other items for sale.

Elsewhere in the city, there were theaters and restaurants to suit every taste. Concert halls, opera houses, and museums brought the arts to new audiences. Many of the great buildings of today's cities were built at this time.

Such buildings include Symphony Hall in Boston, the New York Public Library, and the art museums of Boston, New York, Philadelphia, and Chicago.

The working people There also were many people who saw little of the cities' beauty and culture. These were the working people. Many lived in tenements. Others lived in small houses on the edges of the city.

Some of these people had moved to the cities from farms in the United States. Others were immigrants from Europe, Asia, and Latin America. Many lived in very bad conditions. They lived in unheated apartments without running water. Many had little to eat.

Many other working people had regular jobs. They lived comfortably, if not in luxury. There was food on the table and a fire in the stove. Sometimes, they were able to save money for the future.

People often lived in neighborhoods with others from the same part of the United States or the world. In these neighborhoods, social clubs and religious organizations brought people together.

Reading a Chart. Which was the second largest city in 1880? Which was the second largest city in 1900? Which city had the greatest percentage population increase between 1880 and 1900?

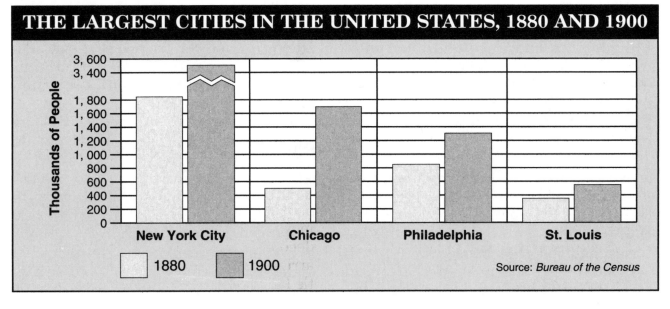

THE LARGEST CITIES IN THE UNITED STATES, 1880 AND 1900

Thousands of People

New York City   Chicago   Philadelphia   St. Louis

☐ 1880   ▦ 1900

Source: *Bureau of the Census*

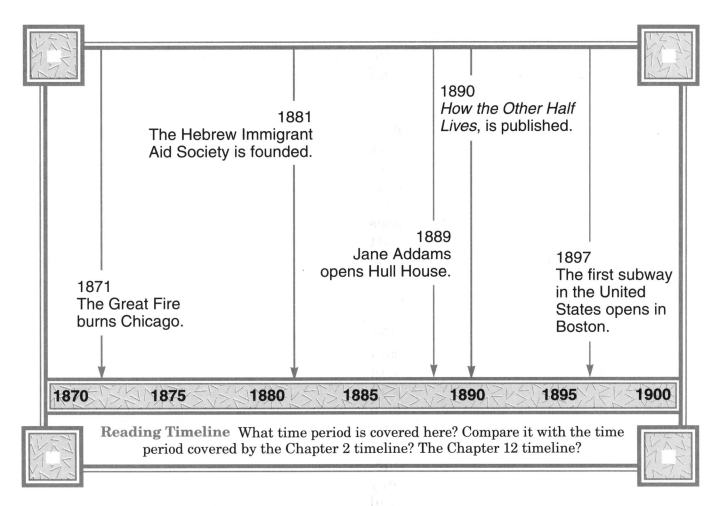

1881
The Hebrew Immigrant
Aid Society is founded.

1890
How the Other Half Lives, is published.

1889
Jane Addams
opens Hull House.

1897
The first subway
in the United
States opens in
Boston.

1871
The Great Fire
burns Chicago.

| 1870 | 1875 | 1880 | 1885 | 1890 | 1895 | 1900 |

Reading Timeline What time period is covered here? Compare it with the time period covered by the Chapter 2 timeline? The Chapter 12 timeline?

An Italian family in America The story of Alfredo and Malvina Maggia is like that of many city dwellers at this time. Alfredo left Italy in 1899 and sailed to the United States. At the time, he and Malvina were not yet married. When Alfredo found work, he would send for her.

In New York City, Alfredo contacted Malvina's brother Carlo. Carlo had moved there earlier. He had set up business as a carpenter in one of the city's Italian neighborhoods. Alfredo lived with Carlo's family and helped out in Carlo's carpentry shop. Soon, Alfredo learned enough English to find work as a waiter. When he had saved enough money, he sent for Malvina. They were married in 1906, and their son was born a year later.

Alfredo rose to an important job managing hotel restaurants. Their son went to college and became an executive in a major corporation. Alfredo and Malvina both lived until 1963, the year that their granddaughter graduated from college. Millions of American families have similar histories.

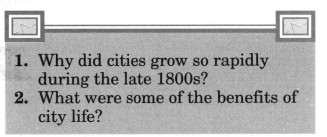

1. Why did cities grow so rapidly during the late 1800s?
2. What were some of the benefits of city life?

2 Cities Are Faced with Problems.
What challenges did people in cities have to face?

As cities grew, many of the people who moved to them had a hard time finding decent places to live. Usually, the new arrivals had little money. They had to settle for small, crowded apartments in tene-

ment buildings. The buildings were close together. There was little fresh air or light.

The spread of disease   City services often were not available. Many streets were unpaved. Sewers did not work. Garbage piled up in streets and alleys. Impure drinking water spread disease. From time to time, an **epidemic** (ehp-uh-DEHM-ihk) would strike these neighborhoods. An epidemic is a rapidly spreading outbreak of disease. In addition to these epidemics, there was a constant threat of tuberculosis (too-ber-kyuh-LOH-sihs). Tuberculosis is a disease mainly of the lungs that is spread by close contact with infected people. At that time, there was no known cure for the disease. Most victims lost strength and eventually died.

City and state governments gradually made the cities a bit safer. Garbage collection improved. Fire departments were set up. Governments built water supply and sewage removal systems. They paved streets. Public buildings and parks were constructed.

Dishonest politicians   Some city and state officials used the new projects to benefit themselves. Dishonest politicians stole public money. They gave friends and relatives jobs whether or not they were qualified. Using a government position for personal profit is called **graft.**

One of the most dishonest politicians was William M. Tweed, called "Boss" Tweed. Tweed held various offices in New York City and New York state from 1851 to 1871. The most famous example of his dishonesty was the "Tweed Courthouse." Boss Tweed built a new courthouse worth about $4 million. The

Reading a Cartoon. This cartoon is titled "Who stole the people's money?" What point is the cartoonist making? "Boss" Tweed is the heavy-set man at the left. How does the cartoonist make him look ridiculous?

WHO STOLE THE PEOPLE'S MONEY? — DO TELL. N.Y.TIMES.   'TWAS HIM.

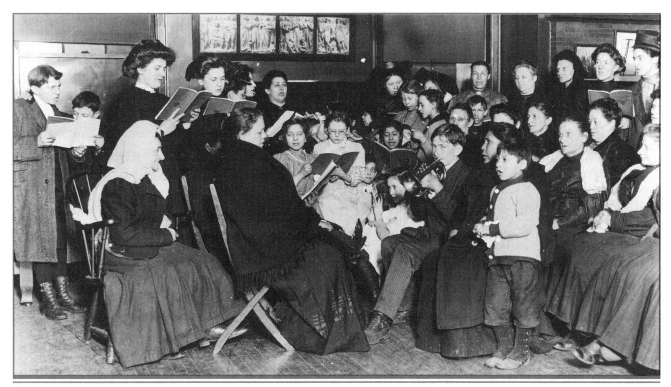

An 1896 photograph at Hull House in Chicago shows immigrant women and children singing American folk tunes. Settlement houses such as Hull House offered classes, clubs, and other services to the newcomers in the city.

taxpayers paid $12 million. The missing $8 million went entirely to Tweed and his friends.

A different kind of political "boss" appeared in some other cities. Boston's John Fitzgerald was one of them. Fitzgerald gained support from the poorer neighborhoods, mainly Irish American at that time. He built a strong "machine" of party workers. They saw to it that their supporters got the city services they needed. Fitzgerald and his machine were attacked as corrupt by the political leaders he had replaced. However, the voters kept him in office for many years.

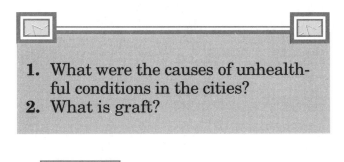

1. What were the causes of unhealthful conditions in the cities?
2. What is graft?

3 People Work to Improve Their Lives.

How did immigrants and others fight for better lives?

In the misery of the cities' worst slums, there were people working to make things better. Like many earlier reformers, some of these people dedicated their lives to helping others.

How the Other Half Lives   Jacob Riis (rees) was a New York City journalist. He wrote powerful reports on slum life. Riis's book, *How the Other Half Lives,* appeared in 1890. His descriptions of children living in filthy tenements shocked many middle-class readers.

Hull House   In Chicago, a young woman named Jane Addams took a bolder step. With a friend, she took over an old house in one of the city's poorest neighborhoods. In 1889, they opened it under the name of Hull House. She called it a **settlement house.** It was a place where she and others would settle in order to serve the people of the neighborhood.

Hull House offered kindergartens and a day-care nursery for working parents. Social evenings for the various immigrant groups in the neighborhood were also held—Germans attended on Friday, for example, and Italians on Saturday. Socials made it possible for new arrivals in the city to get to know one another.

Hull House grew and took over neighboring buildings. Its activities also grew. Soon they included classes on a wide variety of subjects. There were also meetings rooms for neighborhood organizations. Hull House even had a community theater. Most of the support for the settlement house came from women who were inspired by Jane Addams. They gave both time and money to help with her work.

Jane Addams wrote many books and articles about Hull House. Soon, its programs became widely known. Settlement houses sprang up in other Chicago neighborhoods and in many other cities.

Other organizations   Newcomers to the city were also forming their own organizations. Irish and Italian Catholics established social groups and church-supported schools. The Hebrew Immigrant Aid Society helped new Jewish arrivals find work and housing.

Many special newspapers were published for immigrant and other city groups. A number were written in the native languages of their readers. For example, New York City's *Jewish Daily Forward* was published in Yiddish. Other newspapers, like the *Chicago Defender,* served the city's African American community.

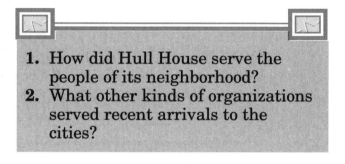

1. How did Hull House serve the people of its neighborhood?
2. What other kinds of organizations served recent arrivals to the cities?

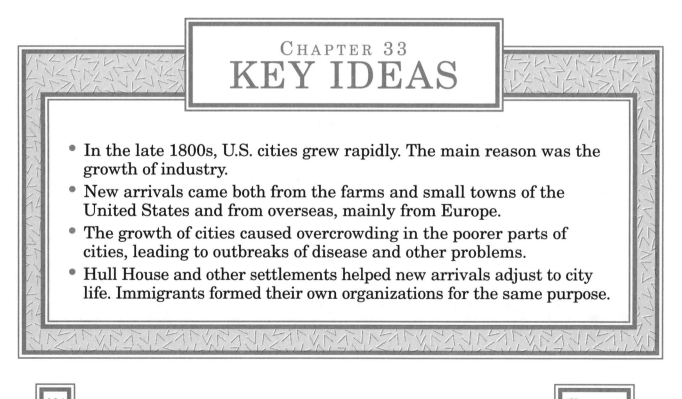

CHAPTER 33
KEY IDEAS

- In the late 1800s, U.S. cities grew rapidly. The main reason was the growth of industry.
- New arrivals came both from the farms and small towns of the United States and from overseas, mainly from Europe.
- The growth of cities caused overcrowding in the poorer parts of cities, leading to outbreaks of disease and other problems.
- Hull House and other settlements helped new arrivals adjust to city life. Immigrants formed their own organizations for the same purpose.

REVIEWING CHAPTER 33

I. Reviewing Vocabulary
Match each word on the left with the correct definition on the right.

1. settlement
2. subway
3. graft
4. epidemic
5. tenement

a. use of a government position for personal profit
b. an apartment building without an elevator
c. a widespread outbreak of a disease
d. a railroad in an underground tunnel
e. an organization providing services in a city neighborhood

II. Understanding the Chapter
1. How did the growth of heavy industry contribute to the growth of cities?
2. How did transportation in the cities improve during the early 1900s?
3. What entertainment and cultural benefits did people living in the city enjoy?
4. What kinds of hardships did new arrivals to the city often experience?
5. Who were Jacob Riis and Jane Addams? How did they improve life for the poor?

III. Building Skills
Study the bar graph on page 280. Next, use the data below to make a bar graph showing the growth of U.S. population in the 1800s. Then, answer the questions.

1800	5,308,483	1830	12,860,692	1860	31,443,321	1890	62,947,714
1810	7,239,881	1840	17,063,353	1870	38,558,371	1900	75,994,575
1820	9,638,453	1850	23,191,876	1880	50,155,783		

1. By how much did the U.S. population grow from 1800 to 1850? From 1850 to 1900?
2. Which ten-year span saw the greatest increase in population?

IV. Writing About History
1. Imagine that you are Alberto Maggia. You have been living in New York for about a year. Write a letter to Malvina, at home in Italy, telling of your experiences and your hopes for the future.
2. **What Would You Have Done?** If you had been a voter in Boston in the early 1900s, would you have voted for John Fitzgerald? Why?

V. Working Together
1. With a group, choose a large city in 1900. Create an advertising campaign to attract new residents, businesses, and tourists to your city.
2. **Past to Present** With a group, discuss how reformers in the late 1800s worked to improve the way people lived. Then, talk about groups today that are working to improve society. Choose one and write a sentence or two explaining its goals.

WOMEN GAIN NEW OPPORTUNITIES. (1865-1900)

What advances did women make in the late 1800s and early 1900s?

Students in a history class at Tuskegee Institute in Alabama, 1902. Tuskegee became a leading college for African Americans.

Looking at Key Terms

- suffragette • service jobs

Looking at Key Words

- **domestic:** someone who works as a maid, a cook, or a laundry worker

S T U D Y

After you read each section, take a minute or two, and write the facts you think are important. Check that your notes answer the section question.

H I N T

In the late 1800s, women were supposed to stay at home. Yet, many women wanted to use their energy and intelligence for good causes. Some women wanted to ban alcohol. Others tried to stop child labor. Still others wanted to work. Many fought for women's rights. Women joined together and brought about change.

1 Women Win New Rights.

How did women gain new rights?

In the 1800s, women had very few rights. They could not vote. They could not hold office. If they married, their husbands became the owners of their property. If women had jobs, the money they earned belonged to their fathers or their husbands. By law, husbands could hit their wives, as long as they did not seriously hurt them.

Once the Civil War was over, women began to demand rights for themselves. Former slaves could now vote. Women wanted the same right. The right to vote is called suffrage. Women who wanted the right to vote were called **suffragettes**.

A woman's "place" Being a suffragette required great courage. Many men were angered by the suffragettes. A woman's place was in the home, those men said. Early suffragettes such as Elizabeth Cady Stanton, Lucretia Mott, and Susan B. Anthony were often treated badly. Newspapers attacked them. Political cartoons made fun of them. Yet, the suffragettes fought on.

In 1869, women had their first political victory. Frontier life had made the women of Wyoming independent. They demanded the right to vote. The men agreed, but not because they believed in women's suffrage. They wanted to balance the state's population. Wyoming had 8,000 men and only 2,000 women. By allowing women to vote, lawmakers thought that they could attract more women to Wyoming.

The suffragettes did not stop with the Wyoming victory. They continued to press for the right to vote. As the years passed, more women from all parts of society joined the effort.

African American leaders African American women played an important role in the fight for the vote. The Rollins sisters of Charleston, Caroline Remond Putnam, and Mary Church Terrell fought for women's suffrage.

One remarkable African American suffragette was Mary Ann Shadd Cary. Cary was the first African American woman to become a lawyer. In 1870, she argued in court that women's suffrage was a legal right. This was her argument: (1) The 14th and 15th amendments gave all African American citizens the right to vote. (2) She paid her taxes and obeyed U.S. laws. She performed all the duties of a citizen. (3) Therefore, she was a citizen. She had the same rights as other citizens. One year later, Cary successfully registered to vote.

A little progress By the 1880s, women were making some gains. Several states now allowed married women to own property. Women could vote in four western states—Wyoming, Colorado, Idaho, and Utah. However, they still could not vote in national elections. Women's suffrage did not become the law in the United States until the early 1900s.

Educational opportunities During the late 1800s, women also made progress in education. The number of high schools in the United States grew. Dozens of new colleges and universities opened. More and more women went to college. Yet, educated women were not welcomed in many professions. In most states, it was against the law for a woman to be a doctor or a lawyer. As late as 1881, there were only 56 women lawyers in the United States. Most of them had to sue law schools to be admitted.

Improving the workplace   In 1888, Leonora Barry received an angry letter from a man in Pennsylvania. The writer called Barry a "Lady Tramp" because she was trying to bring working women into labor unions. Barry wanted to improve working conditions for women. She felt that labor unions were the best way to bring reform.

Barry and other brave women did much to help working women. They organized workers to fight for higher pay, shorter hours, and safer conditions for women in factories. However, women were not fully accepted in labor unions until the 1900s.

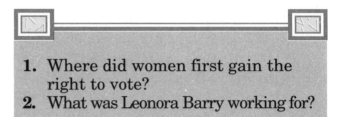

1. Where did women first gain the right to vote?
2. What was Leonora Barry working for?

This drawing shows women lining up to vote in the Wyoming territory. The Western states granted women the vote because they wanted to attract women to live there.

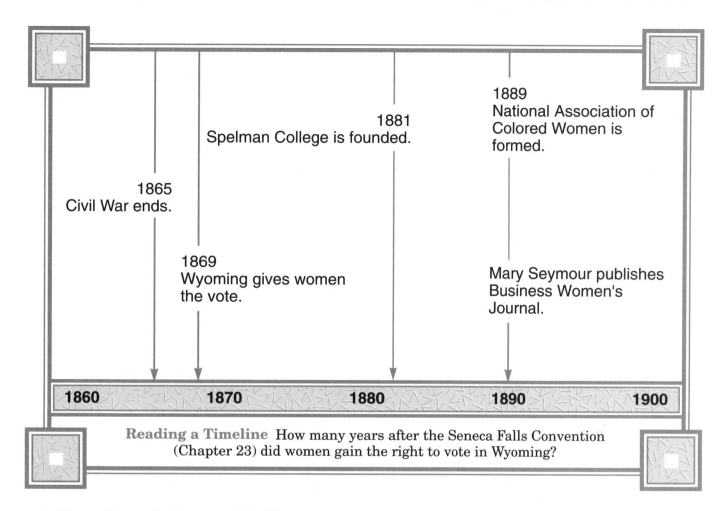

1865
Civil War ends.

1869
Wyoming gives women the vote.

1881
Spelman College is founded.

1889
National Association of Colored Women is formed.

Mary Seymour publishes Business Women's Journal.

| 1860 | 1870 | 1880 | 1890 | 1900 |

Reading a Timeline How many years after the Seneca Falls Convention (Chapter 23) did women gain the right to vote in Wyoming?

2 Women Enter the Business World.

What work did women do in businesses?

After the Civil War, new jobs were opened to women. Many were **service jobs.** These were jobs in which workers served or helped others. Women became office workers, sales clerks, and nurses.

By 1900, most jobs that were considered women's work were service jobs. A handful of brave women even managed to enter such professions as law and medicine.

An office job Office work attracted many young women in the late 1800s. It was clean work. It did not require great physical strength. Office work was also a new experience for women. Until the 1870s, only men had office jobs. Two inventions changed all that.

One invention was the typewriter. The first typists were men. Then women began to learn how to type. Many managers believed that women typed faster because their smaller fingers fit better on the keys. Women's pay was smaller, too. This made women typists a bargain for employers.

The second invention that brought women into the office was the telephone. The telephone was introduced in 1876. Soon, it was common in offices. The first telephone operators were men. Women quickly learned the skill. As with typing, a woman could do the same job as a man. However, employers could pay them less money. Employers rushed to hire women for the new jobs.

In 1890, 75,000 women held office jobs. By 1900, the number was over 500,000. Women had become a familiar sight in offices.

Women in Professions Clara Barton's work in hospitals during the

Angered by poor conditions in the garment industry, Chicago workers went out on strike in 1914. The workers, as you can see, were mostly women. They won their strike and went on to form a union that won other benefits.

Civil War showed that women could be nurses. After the Civil War, nursing became "women's work" partly because it paid too little for men. After two years of training, most nurses earned about $4 a week. Rules were very strict. Nurses had to live at the hospital. The hospital took room and board out of the nurses' pay. Women nurses usually lost their jobs if they married.

Most women who were interested in medicine became nurses. However, not all did. Elizabeth Blackwell had become the first woman doctor in the United States in 1849. (See Chapter 23.) Her sister Emily also became a doctor. The sisters founded a hospital for women in New York. Blackwell later built a women's medical school at the hospital. She opened the door for other women to enter the medical field. Still, some people claimed that medicine was no career for women.

Teaching Many educated women became teachers. By 1900, women teachers outnumbered men teachers three to one. In elementary schools, almost every teacher was a woman. Women teachers were paid about half as much money as men teachers. Principals and superintendents were almost always men.

Low pay was not the only problem that women teachers faced. Dozens of rules governed their actions. Teachers could not stay out late at night. They could not dye their hair, smoke, or wear bright colors. Most were not allowed to continue teaching if they married.

Businesses of their own Some women started their own businesses. Candace Thurber Wheeler of New York founded the Society of Decorative Art. The society encouraged women with artistic talent. It found markets for their work. Soon, there were similar societies all over the United States. Wheeler also helped found the successful Women's Exchange. The Exchange sold needlework, toys, and other products made by women.

Mary Seymour founded the first business school for women in 1879. She knew that women with typing and shorthand skills made welcome employees. By 1884, she ran four schools. She began publishing the *Business Woman's Journal* in 1889. Seymour used her business and writing talents to help many women's groups.

In the 1800s, new machines made it easier to farm larger plots of land. Farming and ranching became businesses. A number of women met the challenge of running these new businesses. One of the most successful women was rancher Henrietta King of Texas. Her husband died in 1885. He left her 500,000 acres (202,400 hectares) of ranch land. He also left a debt of half a million dollars. Within ten years, she paid off the debt. Then she began to buy more land. King doubled the size of the ranch. When she died, she left millions of dollars to her heirs.

African American businesses
African American women also created successful businesses. Maggie L. Walker became president of St. Luke Bank of Richmond, Virginia. In 1889, Madame C.J. Walker created a line of cosmetics for African American women. (See Chapter 29.) Madame Walker was the first African American woman to become a millionaire. She gave much of her wealth to charity.

---

1. What were the service jobs?
2. Name three successful business-women.

3 Discrimination Limits Opportunities for Women of Color.

What kinds of work were available for African American women?

By the 1890s, white women in the United States were making some progress in the workplace. Progress was much slower for African American women.

African American women were hired only for certain kinds of jobs. For example, most farm laborers and **domestics** were African American. Domestics worked as maids, cooks, and laundry workers. Even in these jobs, African American women faced discrimination. Given a choice, most employers would hire a white woman instead of an African American.

African American successes
Some African Americans women were able to overcome discrimination and prejudice. Several African American women managed plantations in the South. Mrs. Jane Brown and Mrs.

Maggie Walker (1867-1934) was a successful African American business woman. She ran the St. Luke Bank in Richmond, Virginia for many years.

Halsey leased land and a horse. The partners farmed the land for ten years. In that time, they earned enough to retire. Dr. Susan McKinney was the top graduate of the New York Medical School for Women and Children. She went on to be a leading doctor in the African American community. Sarah Garnet was the first African American principal of an integrated school in New York.

Many African American women thanked their college education for their success. Some attended African American schools such as Spelman College in Atlanta. Spelman opened in 1881. Its purpose was to educate African American women. Graduates of Spelman and other African American colleges usually became teachers in African American schools.

Women's clubs Many of these educated women were members of African American women's clubs. African American women wanted to change things. The clubs could help.

Josephine St. Pierre Ruffin organized the first national conference of African American clubwomen in 1895. The following year, Mary Church Terrell, Ruffin, and others formed the National Association of Colored Women (NACW). The NACW joined the clubs into a single unit.

The motto of the NACW was "Lifting As We Climb." It expressed the NACW's goal of helping others. Sixty-seven percent of NACW members were teachers. These women wanted to educate other African American women so that they could get better jobs. The NACW founded high schools and colleges. Clubwomen started day-care centers.

In the late 1800s, women of many backgrounds became involved in important reform movements. These women joined clubs like the NACW that were dedicated to public service. Reform and public service were becoming women's work.

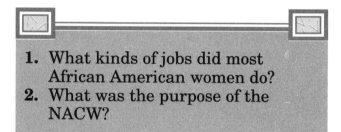

1. What kinds of jobs did most African American women do?
2. What was the purpose of the NACW?

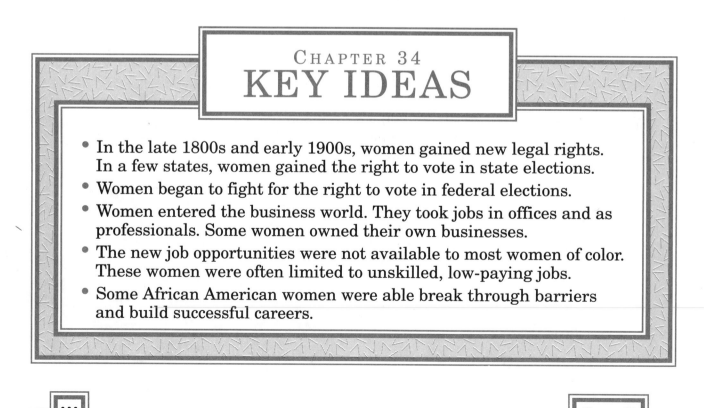

CHAPTER 34
KEY IDEAS

- In the late 1800s and early 1900s, women gained new legal rights. In a few states, women gained the right to vote in state elections.
- Women began to fight for the right to vote in federal elections.
- Women entered the business world. They took jobs in offices and as professionals. Some women owned their own businesses.
- The new job opportunities were not available to most women of color. These women were often limited to unskilled, low-paying jobs.
- Some African American women were able break through barriers and build successful careers.

REVIEWING CHAPTER 34

I. Reviewing Vocabulary

Match each word on the left with the correct definition on the right.

1. suffrage   **a.** jobs in which workers serve others
2. suffragette   **b.** the right to vote
3. domestic   **c.** African American women's college
4. service job   **d.** a job as a maid, a cook, or a laundry worker
5. Spelman   **e.** a woman who demanded the right to vote

II. Understanding the Chapter

1. Name three occupations open to women in the 1880s.
2. Why did women want to work in service jobs?
3. What two inventions gave women opportunities for office jobs?
4. What professions were open to educated women in the 1880s?
5. What did the NACW do to help African American women?

III. Building Skills: Reading a Time Line

Use the time line on page 289 to answer the questions below.

1. In what year was Spelman College founded?
2. Did Wyoming give women the vote before or after the Business Women's Journal started?
3. How many years passed between the end of the Civil War and the formation of the National Association of Colored Women?

IV. Writing About History

1. **What Would You Have Done?** If you had lived in Wyoming in the 1860s, would you have been in favor of women's suffrage? Explain.
2. Suppose that a woman from 1890 was suddenly transported through time to the present. Think of the questions she would ask about the 1990s and what answers you would give. Use the questions and answers to write a magazine interview.

V. Working Together

1. Choose several classmates. Work together to write a short scene about a woman applying for an office job in 1890. When the scene has been written, have members of your group act the scene in front of the class.
2. **Past to Present** The late 1800s was a period when many new job opportunities opened up for women. Discuss these jobs and jobs available to women now. How are women's jobs different today? Write two or three sentences that explain some of the differences.

THE UNITED STATES BECOMES A WORLD POWER. (1865-1900)

Why did the United States expand overseas in the late 1800s?

Queen Liliuokalani of Hawaii is shown in 1917, near the end of her life. 24 years earlier, she had fought to keep Hawaii free from American rule.

Looking at Key Terms

- sphere of influence • Open Door policy • Boxer Rebellion
- Platt Amendment

Looking at Key Words

- **imperialism:** the building of colonial empires

It was the first day of May in 1898. Ships of the U.S. Navy had arrived the night before in the Philippines. The Philippines Islands were a Spanish possession in the western Pacific. A Spanish fleet was anchored in Manila Bay, the most important harbor of the islands. As the Americans approached, Admiral George Dewey spoke to the ship's captain. "You may fire when ready, Gridley," the U.S. commander said.

Gridley's ship fired, and so did the other U.S. ships. The smoke cleared. The Americans saw that they had destroyed the entire Spanish fleet. Not one American had been killed.

The United States was now in a position to take over the Phillippines. Whether to do it was the question.

1 The United States Expands across the Pacific.

What led the United States to extend its influence in the Pacific?

In the late 1800s, **imperialism** became a very strong force among European nations. Imperialism means building empires. By the 1890s, a few European countries had taken over much of Asia and almost all of Africa.

There were several reasons for this interest in empires. The strongest ones were economic. Colonies were a source of raw materials. They were also places where manufactured goods could be sold. The urge to do good was also strong. Many Europeans felt a duty to bring European civilization to the rest of the world. A final reason was to protect places that a country already had. Europeans felt that controlling land around an important harbor or rich region helped to prevent attacks.

Building a U.S. empire The United States began to build an overseas empire just after the Civil War. In

1867, Secretary of State William H. Seward arranged for the United States to buy Alaska from Russia. The price was $7.2 million. Many Americans thought of Alaska as a huge, cold, almost empty land. They called the purchase "Seward's Folly." They were wrong. Alaska gradually became an important part of the U.S. economy. More important, the purchase gave the United States a long coastline along the northern part of the Pacific Ocean. Control of this coastline made it easier to protect U.S. merchant ships and fishing boats. Seward also took the first steps toward building a canal in Central America. He wanted to connect the Atlantic and Pacific oceans.

The United States also became interested in Hawaii. Through most of the 1800s, Hawaii was an independent kingdom in the Pacific. About 1820, a group of American missionaries arrived there. From that time on, American interest in Hawaii increased.

By the 1850s, Honolulu, Hawaii's main city, served the American whaling and merchant ships. Treaties granted special

Reading a Map. Which territories came under United States control as a result of the Cuban-Spanish American War of 1898?

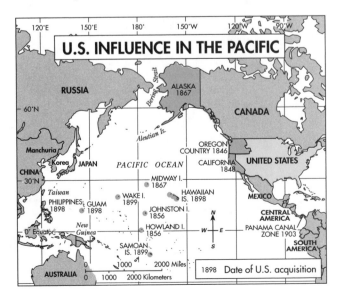

privileges to Americans in Hawaii. These treaties encouraged some Americans to build large—and very profitable—sugar-growing plantations. Hawaiians said of the missionaries, "They came to do good, and they did very well."

In 1891, a woman, Liliuokalani (LIL-ee-oo-oh-kah-lah-nee), inherited the Hawaiian throne. Liliuokalani was a Hawaiian patriot. She did not like the way her country was being Americanized. She began a program to reduce American influence. She wanted to restore the power of the royal family. These policies alarmed the Americans. They overthrew Queen Liliuokalani in 1893. Then the Americans set up a republic with themselves in charge.

A U.S. territory The new government wanted Hawaii to become a possession of the United States. President Grover Cleveland refused to accept it.

He believed rightly that the new government did not represent Hawaiians, only Americans.

In 1897, however, Cleveland was succeeded by William McKinley. The following year, the United States found itself at war with Spain. As a result of this war, the United States gained the Philippines. At about the same time, Japan surprised other nations with its powerful navy. A strong Pacific outpost suddenly seemed a good idea to Americans. On July 7, 1898, Hawaii became a possession of the United States.

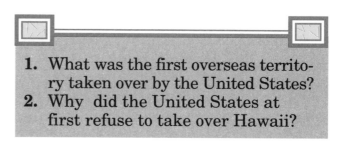

1. What was the first overseas territory taken over by the United States?
2. Why did the United States at first refuse to take over Hawaii?

U.S. troops scaling the wall of the Forbidden City in Beijing in 1900. U.S. troops were called in to help put down the Boxer Rebellion. This was an uprising of Chinese angry at the foreign control of their country.

III Building Skills: Making a Timeline

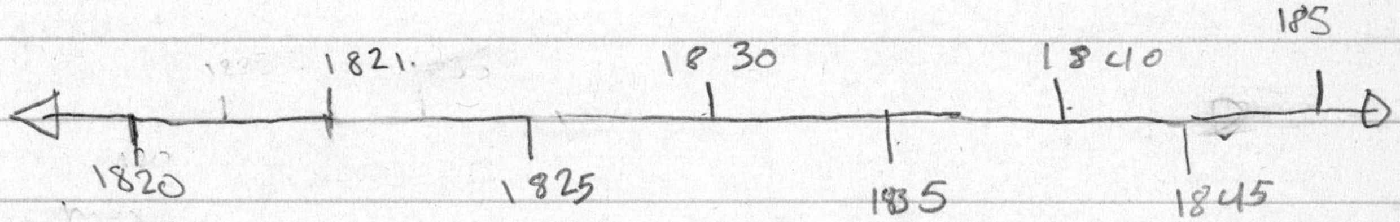

1820 -

1830 - mexican government outlaws u.s. imigration to Tx.

1835 - santa alma declares himself dictator of mexico

1840 -

1845 - congress annexes Texas

7:35 – 2:00
2:00 – 3:30
3:90 – 4:30

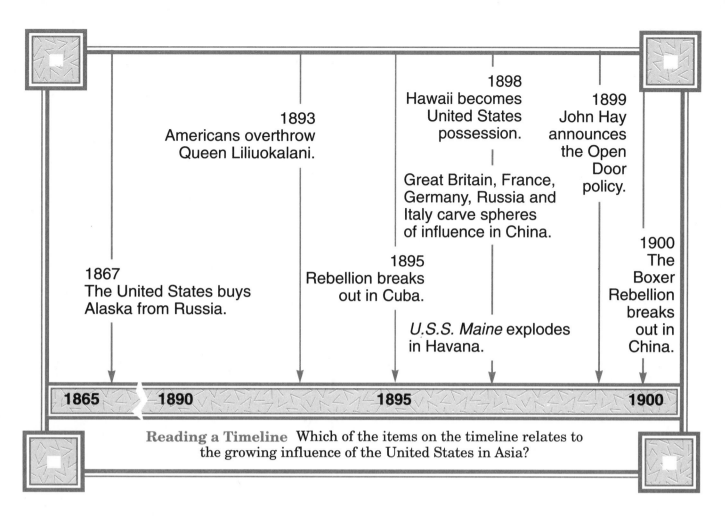

1893
Americans overthrow
Queen Liliuokalani.

1898
Hawaii becomes
United States
possession.

1899
John Hay
announces
the Open
Door
policy.

Great Britain, France,
Germany, Russia and
Italy carve spheres
of influence in China.

1867
The United States buys
Alaska from Russia.

1895
Rebellion breaks
out in Cuba.

1900
The
Boxer
Rebellion
breaks
out in
China.

U.S.S. Maine explodes
in Havana.

| 1865 | 1890 | 1895 | 1900 |

Reading a Timeline Which of the items on the timeline relates to the growing influence of the United States in Asia?

2 The United States "Opens the Door" to China.

How did the United States stop other nations from taking over China?

In the late 1800s, China was a huge nation with a weak government. Despite its weakness, it was an important trading partner for the United States, Europe, and Japan.

At this time, Japan was rapidly building its military strength. In 1894-1895, Japan went to war against China. Japan won easily. That showed just how strong it had become. It also showed how weak China was.

European countries feared that Japan might try to take all the China trade for itself. They hurried to set up **spheres of influence** in China. A sphere of influence is an area within one country that is controlled by another country. By 1898, Great Britain, France, Germany, Russia, and Italy had carved out spheres of influence in China

The Open Door policy For many years, the United States had insisted that in international trade it should have the same rights and privileges as every other country. These new spheres of influence seemed likely to harm American trading rights. Britain was also concerned.

In September 1899, U.S. Secretary of State John Hay announced a new U.S. policy. This policy was called the **Open Door policy.** The Open Door policy was strongly supported by the British government. The Open Door recognized the spheres of influence of the European powers in China. At the same time, it said, all nations had equal trading rights in China. This would mean that no nation had an unfair advantage. Only Russia of all the European powers rejected this principle.

The Boxer Rebellion Many Chinese were angered at seeing their country carved up by other countries. In 1900, a Chinese secret society formed. Its purpose was to drive "foreign devils" out of China. Europeans called the group boxers because its flag showed a closed fist. The Boxers moved into Beijing, the Chinese capital. There they took over a group of British government buildings. The Boxers took a number of hostages. An international army quickly formed to retake the buildings and release the hostages. The United States contributed 2,500 troops to this effort.

The **Boxer Rebellion** was soon put down. Some European countries, however, wanted to use the rebellion to gain greater control of China. They wanted even greater control over a weak China. The United States opposed this. The United States announced that the purpose of the international force was to keep China from being broken up. Another goal was to keep China open to trade with all countries. The United States used the Open Door policy to stop a small war from becoming a big one.

The United States could not really enforce the Open Door policy. It was nothing more than a set of statements about how the United States thought things should be. Yet for a time, it was quite effective in keeping China open.

1. What was the purpose of the Open Door policy?
2. What role did the United States play in the Boxer Rebellion?

3 The United States Fights for Spain's Empire.
What led to the Cuban-Spanish-American War?

At its nearest point, the island of Cuba is only 90 miles from Florida. Because it is so close, it is hardly surprising that Cuban history and U.S. history are linked.

After 1865, Cuba and Puerto Rico were Spain's only possessions in the Americas. In 1895, a rebellion broke out in Cuba. This uprising had an inspiring leader, José Martí (mar-TEE), who died early in the war. He became Cuba's national hero. Spain fought against Martí and the rebels harshly. Often, the Cuban people suffered cruel treatment.

The Cuban-Spanish-American War U.S. interest in this rebellion was strong. One reason was that Americans owned Cuban sugar and tobacco plantations. In addition, U.S. trade with Cuba had grown. The United States was also interested in building a canal in Central America. Islands near the canal became important for defense.

U.S. newspapers paid close attention to what was happening in Cuba. Newspapers reported every Spanish move against the Cuban people with great detail. To sell more newspapers, they made the Spanish policies seem even more cruel than they actually were. Sometimes, when there were no horrible stories to report, the newspapers would make them up. It was hardly surprising that the American people developed a strong dislike of Spain. Of course, they wished to aid the Cubans.

Remember the *Maine* In early 1898, President McKinley wanted to warn Spain. He sent the battleship U.S.S. *Maine* to Cuba on a visit. On

February 15, 1898, the *Maine* exploded in the harbor of Havana, Cuba's capital. Two hundred sixty American sailors died. U.S. newspapers took it for granted that the Spanish government had caused the explosion. They called for war against Spain. The U.S. government made a number of demands of the Spanish government. The Spanish government agreed to all of them. The United States declared war on Spain anyway.

The Cuban-Spanish-American War did not last long. U.S. troops invaded Cuba and defeated a Spanish army. Soon after, another U.S. force took over Puerto Rico with little resistance. Meanwhile, in Asia, Admiral Dewey had gained control of Manila Bay. He was ready to take over the Philippines.

In peace negotiations later that year, Spain agreed to give Cuba its freedom. The U.S. Army, however, remained in Cuba for four years, until 1902. During this time, it wiped out the mosquito that carries the deadly disease known as yellow fever. Even so, Cubans were glad when the occupation ended and the army went home.

The Platt Amendment Even then, the United States did not leave Cuba entirely. It insisted that Cuba include the **Platt Amendment** in its constitution. The Platt Amendment gave the United States the right to send troops into Cuba to "preserve order." That really meant to protect U.S. interests.

The United States also took over the governments of Puerto Rico, the

Reading a Map. From what U.S. port did the invasion army leave? Was the U.S. attack focused on the western or eastern part of Cuba? Give the approximate latitude and longitude of Guantánamo.

Philippines, and Guam. Guam is an island in the Pacific. The United States decided to keep control of Puerto Rico and Guam. There were two basic reasons. Each island was useful as a naval base. Also, the United States did not think that either island was ready for self-government. Neither had any experience in self-government. The United States felt that both economies were weak. The people of Puerto Rico and Guam had no choice but to accept U.S. control.

The Philippine question The issue of the Philippines was more complicated. Filipinos were fighting for independence from Spain before the U.S. Navy arrived. Many Americans believed strongly that the United States should turn the Philippines over to the Filipinos. Keeping the Philippines, they

said, went against everything the United States stood for.

Others said that any Filipino government would be so weak that the country would soon be taken over. The United States should stay to prevent that. They also argued that rule by the United States would benefit the Filipinos. In the end, the U.S. government decided to keep the Philippines. Even so, many Filipinos continued to demand their independence.

1. What was the role of newspapers in bringing on the Cuban-Spanish-American War?
2. Why did the United States take over the Philippines?

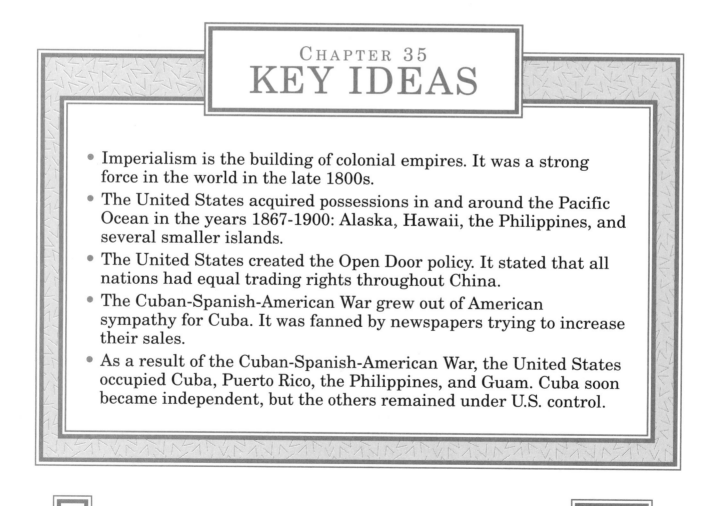

CHAPTER 35
KEY IDEAS

- Imperialism is the building of colonial empires. It was a strong force in the world in the late 1800s.
- The United States acquired possessions in and around the Pacific Ocean in the years 1867-1900: Alaska, Hawaii, the Philippines, and several smaller islands.
- The United States created the Open Door policy. It stated that all nations had equal trading rights throughout China.
- The Cuban-Spanish-American War grew out of American sympathy for Cuba. It was fanned by newspapers trying to increase their sales.
- As a result of the Cuban-Spanish-American War, the United States occupied Cuba, Puerto Rico, the Philippines, and Guam. Cuba soon became independent, but the others remained under U.S. control.

I. Reviewing Vocabulary

Match each word on the left with the correct definition on the right.

1. imperialism

2. sphere of influence

3. Open Door policy

4. Boxer Rebellion

5. Platt Amendment

a. U.S. plan to make sure that no country had an unfair advantage in China

b. the policy of building an empire by acquiring colonies

c. attacks on foreigners by a Chinese secret society

d. a provision in Cuba's constitution giving the United States the right to intervene in Cuba's affairs

e. an area within one country that is controlled by another country

II. Understanding the Chapter

1. What led European nations to follow a policy of imperialism?

2. Why did the United States fight the Cuban-Spanish-American War?

3. Why did the United States decide to take over Hawaii?

4. How did the U.S. use the Open Door policy keep China from being broken up?

5. What were the arguments for and against a U.S. takeover of the Philippines?

III. Building Skills: Reading a Map

Study the maps on page 295 and page 299. Then answer the following questions:

1. After 1898, what U.S. possession lay between California and the Philippines? Which is closet to California? To the Philippines?

2. What part of Alaska is closest to Japan? How far is it from Japan?

3. What U.S. state is closest to Cuba?

4. In the late 1800s, the United States hoped to build a canal across Central America in Nicaragua or Panama. Why would it be important to have friendly governments in Cuba and Puerto Rico?

IV. Writing About History

1. What Would You Have Done? If you had been in Hawaii in 1893, would you have sided with Queen Liliuokalani or with the group that overthrew her? Explain.

2. You have just read a newspaper report of the explosion of the U.S.S. *Maine.* Write a letter to the editor stating your view of what should be done about it.

V. Working Together

1. With five or six other students, organize a panel discussion. One person speaks for each of the following: Alaska, Hawaii, Cuba, Puerto Rico, the Philippines, and Guam. Discuss how the United States has behaved toward each of your regions.

2. Past to Present In 1900, an international army rescued hostages in China. What modern organization has sent international armies into countries to help people? With a group, decide when an international army has the right to go into a country.

THE AMERICAN PEOPLE FACE THE 20TH CENTURY. (1890-1900)

What was the nation like as it prepared to enter the 20th century?

Visitors look down on the 1893 Chicago world's fair. The fair showed how the United States had changed and grown since its founding.

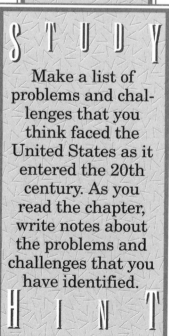

Looking at Key Terms

- Chicago World's Fair

Looking at Key Words

- **fiberglass:** strong material made from glass threads
- **calculator:** a machine that solves mathematical problems
- **network:** a system of roads that connect with one another
- **technology:** science used in practical ways
- **mural:** a picture painted on a wall

In 1893, the United States threw a huge party. Four hundred years earlier, Columbus had landed in the Americas. To mark that event, the nation hosted a world's fair. The fair would show how the nation had changed and grown since its beginnings. It would also give a glimpse into what changes many people thought the next 100 years would bring.

1 The Chicago World's Fair Gave Hints of Promises and Problems.

What glimpses of the nation's future did the Chicago World's Fair of 1893 and the city itself contain?

The city of Chicago put on the fair. Its official name was the World's Columbian Exposition. Most people called it the **Chicago World's Fair**.

Two cities   In May 1893, a crowd of 200,000 gathered at the fairgrounds on Lake Michigan. President Grover Cleveland gave a brief speech. In it, he called the fair the "time-keeper of Progress." Then he pressed an "electric button." Powerful electric motors hummed. Fountains shot water in the air. Flags unfurled from all the buildings. The crowd cheered. The fair had begun.

That summer, there were really two Chicagos. Both showed the progress, dreams, and problems of the nation. One Chicago was in the 200 buildings put up for the fair. The other was the everyday Chicago.

The White City   People called the fairgrounds the White City. The buildings there looked like huge palaces or temples. All were painted white. Thousands of new electric light bulbs were strung over them. Even at night, the fairgrounds glowed white.

The buildings lined broad roads and walkways. Electric passenger boats sailed through the White City on canals. A movable sidewalk carried 5,000 visitors at a time. Around the White City ran an elevated electric train, the nation's first.

Hopes and dreams   The White City showed what planners and business people hoped the nation would become. In its buildings, fairgoers could see the wonders of the modern world.

At the Chicago World's Fair, Americans saw the first zipper. There, they first saw **fiberglass** used. Fiberglass is strong material made from glass threads. Americans could hear their first long-distance telephone calls from Chicago to New York. In fair buildings, people cooked in electric kitchens and did sums on electric **calculators.** Calculators are machines that solve mathematics problems.

Many of the wonders that visitors first saw at the fair became common in later years. But the fair predicted few problems in the nation's future. The few troubles there were would be solved by science and industry.

The other city   The real Chicago was a very different place from the White City. Just 22 years earlier, a fire had burned the city to the ground. Its people rebuilt, however. By the time of the fair, the city had over a million people. Its railroad connections and its industry had made it the nation's second largest city.

The United States by the 1890s was becoming a nation of cities. Much of what visitors saw in everyday Chicago would soon become common in other cities. As one visitor from Europe wrote, "This American city, with all its problems and promise, is the future."

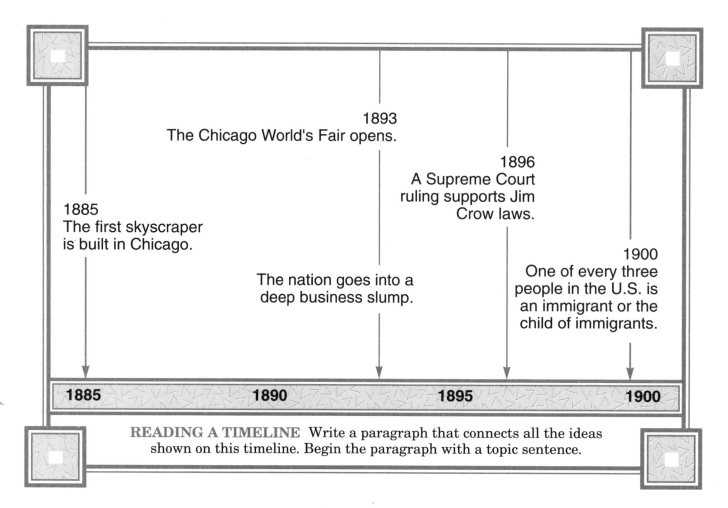

1893
The Chicago World's Fair opens.

1896
A Supreme Court ruling supports Jim Crow laws.

1885
The first skyscraper is built in Chicago.

The nation goes into a deep business slump.

1900
One of every three people in the U.S. is an immigrant or the child of immigrants.

| 1885 | 1890 | 1895 | 1900 |

READING A TIMELINE Write a paragraph that connects all the ideas shown on this timeline. Begin the paragraph with a topic sentence.

The city had a bustling business center, lit by electric lights. It had a **network,** or system, of streetcars and trains. It had clean, wealthy neighborhoods with broad streets, trees, and parks.

Chicago showed how science and **technology** could change cities. Technology is science used in practical ways. In Chicago, builders used steel beams to put up the nation's first skyscrapers. Engineers there reversed the flow of a river to help solve a sewage problem.

The city also showed that science and business could not solve all problems. Smokestacks poured soot and ash on the city. Factories and stockyards pumped out raw sewage. Poor neighborhoods had no parks and trees. People crowded in dirty tenements on streets crammed with garbage. Most earned barely enough to live in such places. Certainly, they did not earn enough to live someplace better.

End of a dream The fair closed at the end of October. By that time, a huge slump in business had spread across the nation. Businesses closed. Factories cut back production. Thousands of workers lost their jobs.

The fair buildings stood empty. People who had lost their homes began to move in. By winter, the cooking fires of the homeless blackened the white walls. That January, a fire burned many fair buildings to the ground. The problems of the present had for a time erased a vision of the future.

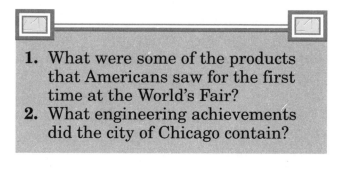

1. What were some of the products that Americans saw for the first time at the World's Fair?
2. What engineering achievements did the city of Chicago contain?

2 The United States in the 1890s Was a Nation of Many Cultures.

How did Chicago and its World's Fair reflect the many cultures that made up the nation?

The Chicago World's Fair said little about the problems facing the United States. It also ignored many of the different peoples who made up the nation.

African Americans at the fair The World's Fair was a "White" City in more ways than one. African Americans had been barred from jobs building the fair. Once the fair opened, they could not get even the lowest-paying, unskilled work.

African Americans were not really welcomed as visitors either. Chicago was a Northern city. But the fair had Jim Crow rules. African Americans could not eat in most of its restaurants. They could not use most of the public restrooms. The only place on the fairgrounds where they could use those facilities was in the building put up by Haiti.

Many African Americans protested. Frederick Douglass called the fair a white tomb. Antilynching fighter Ida B. Wells joined him in writing a booklet for foreign visitors. They called it "The Reason Why the Colored American Is Not in the World's Columbian Exposition."

Many people called the Chicago fair a model of the future. Its treatment of African Americans did, in fact, show the way that many African Americans would be treated well into the next century. Still, the protests of Douglass and Wells were also signs of the future. They showed that African Americans would not accept such treatment quietly.

Native Americans The fair paid little attention to the people Columbus met when he came to the Americas. Native Americans only had a place outside the main fairgrounds. There, a Lakota chief sat in a model of a Native American home.

Even while the fair was being held, Native Americans were losing more of their land. In 1893, more than 100,000 square miles (259,000 square kilometers) of prairie promised to Native Americans was opened to U.S. settlement. There was no sign of this at the fair.

Visitors to the fair would have no way to guess at the changes that lay ahead for Native Americans in the new century. They might not believe that Native Americans would continue fighting to hold onto their cultures. They probably could not see how Native Americans would win new rights as U.S. citizens.

Ida B. Wells, editor of a Memphis newspaper, was a fierce foe of lynching. She continued her fight, even when mobs destroyed her newspaper.

By 1893, almost all the Native Americans of the Plains had been pushed onto reservations. This 1893 photo shows leaders of the Lakota nation who have just been forced to move their people onto a reservation.

A place for women The male planners of the fair had given little thought to the role of women. However, women knew what a major part they had played in building the nation. Wives of the planners urged them to recognize women's roles. Women's rights fighter Susan B. Anthony joined them in their struggle.

In the end, there was a separate Women's Building in the White City. Sophie G. Hayden, a 21-year-old from Boston, designed it. Mary Cassat, one of the nation's most famous artists, painted **murals** for it. A mural is a picture painted on a wall. The building gave just a small hint of the increasing public roles that women would fill in the new century.

Many peoples The White City reflected few of the many other cultures that were a part of the nation. By the 1890s, the people of the United States came from more different backgrounds than did the people of any other nation on earth. Only the amusement park area called the Midway, outside the main grounds, noted these cultures. There, people could see models of German and Irish towns. They could rides camels through streets of an "Egyptian city." They could visit an "African village."

Many fair visitors from Chicago felt more at home on the Midway than in the White City. After all, four out of every ten people in the city had been born in other lands. The city had Polish, Irish, and German neighborhoods. Blocks of Italian homes were near blocks of Swedish dwellings.

The many cultures of Chicago again made it a model of the nation's future. In 1893, a new wave of immigration to the United States was building. By 1900, one of every three people in the nation would be an immigrant or a child of immigrants. Plus, immigration would grow more rapidly after that. In the next 14 years, over 14.5 million more immigrants would come to the United States.

This flood of immigrants would set off a great debate in the United States.

Many citizens feared "new" immigrants who came from southern and eastern Europe. They thought their backgrounds and customs were too different for them to adapt to U.S. ways. Some U.S. citizens believed that immigrants would take away jobs and drive down wages. Those Americans wanted to set strict limits on immigration.

Other citizens disagreed. They felt that immigrants had built the nation into what it was. New immigrants would only make it stronger and richer.

This debate would rage during the early years of the 20th century. It, too, was a glimpse of the future. In the closing years of the century, the debate would flare again. Only then, it would be about immigrants from Asia and Latin America.

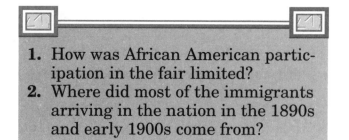

1. How was African American participation in the fair limited?
2. Where did most of the immigrants arriving in the nation in the 1890s and early 1900s come from?

3 Americans Held Ideas and Values in Common.

What factors helped make the varied peoples of the United States into one nation?

The United States at the end of the 1800s was clearly a varied place. Its people came from many different backgrounds and had many different interests.

Reading a Map. The U.S. in 1900 had 45 states and six territories. Name the six territories. Which two states entered the United States in the 1890s? Which three states entered after the Constitution, but before 1800?

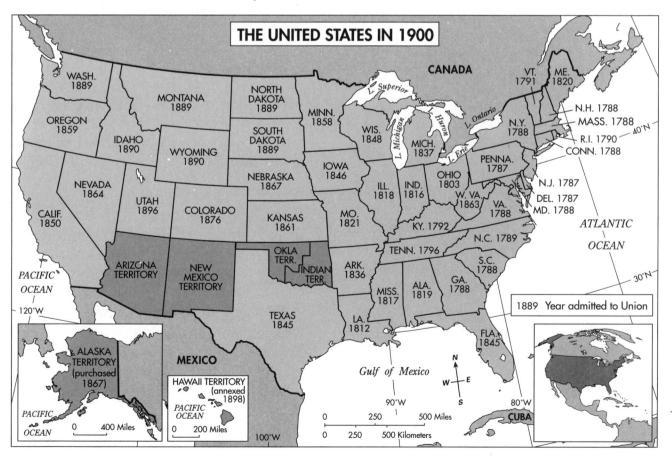

THE UNITED STATES IN 1900

CANADA

WASH. 1889
MONTANA 1889
NORTH DAKOTA 1889
MINN. 1858
VT. 1791
ME. 1820
OREGON 1859
IDAHO 1890
SOUTH DAKOTA 1889
WIS. 1848
MICH. 1837
N.H. 1788
MASS. 1788
N.Y. 1788
R.I. 1790
CONN. 1788
WYOMING 1890
IOWA 1846
PENNA. 1787
40°N
NEVADA 1864
UTAH 1896
NEBRASKA 1867
ILL. 1818
IND. 1816
OHIO 1803
W. VA. 1863
N.J. 1787
DEL. 1787
MD. 1788
CALIF. 1850
COLORADO 1876
KANSAS 1861
MO. 1821
KY. 1792
VA. 1788
ATLANTIC OCEAN
N.C. 1789
TENN. 1796
S.C. 1788
PACIFIC OCEAN
ARIZONA TERRITORY
NEW MEXICO TERRITORY
OKLA TERR.
INDIAN TERR.
ARK. 1836
ALA. 1819
GA. 1788
30°N
MISS. 1817
120°W
TEXAS 1845
LA. 1812
1889 Year admitted to Union
FLA. 1845
ALASKA TERRITORY (purchased 1867)
MEXICO
HAWAII TERRITORY (annexed 1898)
Gulf of Mexico
N
W E
S
PACIFIC OCEAN
PACIFIC OCEAN
0 400 Miles
0 200 Miles
100°W
90°W
0 250 500 Miles
0 250 500 Kilometers
80°W
CUBA

What helped pull people with so many differences together into one nation?

They shared a belief in the ideals of "life, liberty, and the pursuit of happiness." Americans had not always lived up to these ideals. Still, the Declaration of Independence and the U.S. Constitution gave Americans this dream.

Toward equality   The founders of the nation believed that people must have a say in their government. American women shared that belief. They would continue to fight into the 20th century for the vote that would give them their say.

African Americans shared the belief that "all men are created equal." They believed in the promise of the "equal protection of the laws." In the next century, they would use the nation's laws and courts to help them win that protection.

Immigrants to the United States had come from different cultures and political systems. Many would keep their cultures alive through foreign-language newspapers and clubs. Yet, they would come to understand and take part in the U.S. political system.

Many other U.S. citizens would look at the problems the nation faced as it entered a new century. There were Jim Crow laws, poverty, dangerous conditions in factories, and much more. But they would also look at the opening words to the Constitution, which said that the government should "establish justice, . . . promote the general welfare, and secure the blessings of liberty." As the 20th century opened, many Americans acted to ensure that those promises were carried out.

1. What right would women continue to struggle for in the 20th century?
2. How did many immigrants keep the cultures of their home countries alive in the United States?

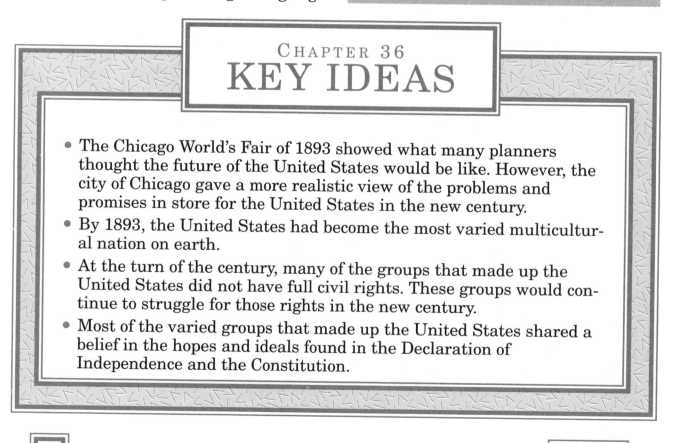

CHAPTER 36
KEY IDEAS

- The Chicago World's Fair of 1893 showed what many planners thought the future of the United States would be like. However, the city of Chicago gave a more realistic view of the problems and promises in store for the United States in the new century.

- By 1893, the United States had become the most varied multicultural nation on earth.

- At the turn of the century, many of the groups that made up the United States did not have full civil rights. These groups would continue to struggle for those rights in the new century.

- Most of the varied groups that made up the United States shared a belief in the hopes and ideals found in the Declaration of Independence and the Constitution.

REVIEWING CHAPTER 36

I. Reviewing Vocabulary

Match each word on the left with the correct definition on the right.

1. calculator   **a.** glass threads woven into textiles
2. fiberglass   **b.** science used in practical ways
3. network   **c.** a machine that solves mathematical problems
4. mural   **d.** a system of roads that connect with one another
5. technology   **e.** a picture painted on a wall

II. Understanding the Chapter

1. How did the future seen in the White City differ from that in everyday Chicago?
2. What problems did everyday Chicago suggest for the United States' future?
3. Why did Wells and Douglass write a booklet for visitors to the World's Fair?
4. How did Chicago reflect the different U.S. cultural groups in 1900?
5. What helped to unite the people of many different backgrounds and interests who made up the United States into one nation?

III. Building Skills: Predicting

Make a prediction about each of the facts listed below.

1. Fact: Immigration to the United States begins to increase sharply in the 1890s.
   Predict: How will U.S. citizens react?
2. Fact: The nation's first skyscrapers are built in Chicago.
   Predict: How will skyscrapers change U.S. cities?

IV. Writing About History

1. **What Would You Have Done?** Imagine that you are an African American who has visited the Chicago World's Fair in 1893. A friend writes to you and asks whether she should make a trip to the fair. Answer her in a letter.
2. Write a speech that Susan B. Anthony might have given to the planners of the World's Fair to convince them to include a Women's Building in the White City.

V. Working Together

1. Plan your own modern World's Fair. Form small groups of students. Will you present the future's problems, hopes, or both? Decide on five buildings or exhibits that your fair would contain. Consider dedicating some of your buildings to Native Americans, African Americans, Latinos, Asians, or other groups who were excluded from the 1893 fair. You can make drawings of the exhibits or write descriptions of them.
2. **Past to Present** In Chapter 36 you read about the promises and the problems in the United States as it entered the 20th century. With a group, discuss the promises and problems of the United States today. Make a list that shows what your group hopes the United States will become.

Glossary

abolition movement the campaign to abolish slavery (p. 203)

abolitionist someone who fought to end slavery (p. 203)

adapt to change to fit new surroundings (p. 9)

adobe bricks of clay sun dried (p. 19)

alliance a formal partnership between nations (p. 120)

ally a person or group who joins with others for a common purpose (p. 80)

amend to change or revise (p. 127)

annex to add into a nation (p. 178)

arsenal a place where weapons are stored (p. 217)

assassination murder of a public figure (p. 233)

assembly a group that makes laws (p. 68)

assimilate to absorb someone into or make someone part of a culture or country (p. 272)

bill a proposed law (p. 135)

blockade to shut off a nation's ports from trade (p. 225)

boardinghouse a house where room and meals can be purchased (p. 162)

border states slave states that remained loyal to the Union (p. 229)

boycott to refuse to buy, sell, or use goods from a person, company or country (p. 89)

cabinet a group of advisers that help the President (p. 145)

cadet a soldier-in-training (p. 179)

calculator a machine that solves mathematical problems (p. 303)

californios Spanish-speaking residents of California (p. 180)

canal waterway dug by people to connect two bodies of water (p. 170)

carpetbagger Northerner who moved to the South after the Civil War (p. 241)

cash crops crops raised for sale, rather than for a farmer's personal use (p. 63)

cattle drive method developed in the mid-1800s for taking cattle from ranches to railroads and finally to markets (p. 257)

civil rights rights given to all citizens by the Constitution (p. 249)

climate the average weather of a place over a period of years (p. 11)

colony a permanent settlement controlled by a more powerful country (p. 27)

compact an agreement (p. 53)

compass an instrument used for showing direction (p. 25)

compromise an agreement that gives each side part of what it wants (p. 128)

conquistador a Spanish soldier-explorer (p. 28)

consent to agree to something (p. 111)

constitution the basic laws under which a country operates (p. 127)

convention a meeting at which important decisions are made (p. 127)

convert to persuade a person to join a religion (p. 46)

corporation company that raises money by selling shares in the business (p. 265)

coureur de bois French fur trader (p. 78)

culture beliefs and ways of life of a people (p. 8)

debate a formal argument on opposing sides of a question (p. 106)

debt money people owe (p. 61)

debtors people who owe money (p. 61)

delegate a person who represents others (p. 105)

democracy a form of government in which citizens rule either directly or through representatives (p. 10)

diary a daily record of notes and information (p. 154)

discrimination treating a person differently because of cultural background, religion, or gender. (p. 182)

diverse different or varied (p. 8)

domestic someone who works as a maid, cook, or a laundry worker (p. 291)

draft law requiring people to serve in the military (p. 226)

drought a period of dry weather (p. 19)

duty a tax put on goods for sale (p. 93)

elevated a railroad that operates on tracks raised above the streets of a city (p. 279)

emancipate to free from slavery (p. 229)

embargo a government order preventing trade (p. 156)

environment the surroundings of people (p. 19)

epidemic a rapidly spreading outbreak of a disease (p. 282)

evict to force someone out of his or her home. (p. 187)

executive the branch of government, headed by the President, that carries out the laws (p. 136)

export a resource or product sent from one country to another (p. 43)

famine a time when there is not enough food to eat (p. 48)

federal system a system of government in which the national government shares power with states or regions (p. 129)

feminist a supporter of the women's rights movement (p. 195)

freedmen enslaved African American men, women, and children set free during and after the Civil War (p. 237)

frontier the edge of a country next to a wilderness (p. 169)

fugitive someone who runs away to escape the law; a runaway slave (p. 214)

geography the study of the earth and how people live on the earth (p. 10)

glacier a giant sheet of ice (p. 16)

graft the dishonest use of a government position for personal profit (p. 282)

habitant a small farmer in New France (p. 79)

homesteader person who got free government land on which to build a farm (p.255)

ideal an idea or goal that someone tries to live up to (p. 111)

immigration when someone moves from his or her homeland to live permanently in another country (p. 9) immigrant, (p. 187)

impeach to formally accuse a President or a high official of breaking the law (p. 239)

imperialism the building of colonial empires (p. 295)

import to bring goods into a country in order to sell them (p. 87)

impressment forced service, especially in a navy or other armed force (p. 155)

indentured servant a person who agreed to work for a set time without pay or transportation to a new land (p. 52)

irrigation a system of bringing water to crops through ditches (p. 98)

Jesuit a member of a special Catholic order (p. 77)

judicial the branch of government headed by the Supreme Court and involving the courts (p. 138)

legislative the branch of government that makes laws; Congress (p. 135)

lynch killing by mob action (p. 243)

majority more than half (p. 135)

mass production method of making large amounts of a product quickly and cheaply (p. 265)

massacre the cruel killing of a great number of people (p. 96)

midwife someone who helps with childbirth (p. 67)

migration a group of people moving from one place to another (p. 16)

militant aggressive; ready to take risks in support of a cause (p. 204)

militia a group of citizens who act as soldiers in an emergency (p. 98)

mission a community run by the Catholic church (p. 46)

monopoly a company with almost complete control of a good or service (p. 266)

multicultural many cultures (p. 8)

mural a picture painted on a wall (p. 306)

nationalism loyalty to or pride in one's country (p. 71)

navigator a person who can steer a ship accurately across the water (p. 25)

network a system of roads that connect with one another (p. 304)

neutral not taking sides (p. 148)

nomad a person who moves from place to place while searching for food (p. 17)

ordinance a law (p. 152)

overseer the person who watches over and directs the slaves' work (p. 164)

pamphlet a short booklet (p. 106)

peddler traveling salesperson (p. 190)

pilgrimage a trip to a religious shrine (p. 35)

plantations large farms where one crop is grown (p. 33)

pogrom an organized killing of an ethnic group, especially Jews (p. 271)

preamble an introduction (p. 110)

precedent an act or a decision that sets an example for later actions (p.144)

prejudice dislike of people who are different (p.181)

proclamation an official announcement (p. 229)

racism unjust treatment of a people by others who believe they are superior (p. 70)

ratify to approve (p. 127)

rebellion an armed resistance to a government (p. 101)

reform change, improvement (p. 195)

repeal to cancel (p. 90)

representative an official elected to act and speak for others (p. 88)

republic a country where people choose their own leaders (p.128)

reservation land set aside for Native Americans (p. 259)

retreat to withdraw from or escape a battle (p. 118)

rustler cattle thief (p. 257)

secede to leave or withdraw from (p. 221)

segregate to separate people by race (p. 248)

settlement house an organization intended to serve the needs of people in a poor neighborhood (p. 284)

sharecropper farmer who pays a part of his or her crops to a landowner as rent (p. 242)

slavery the system of owning people (p. 36)

slum a poor and overcrowded area of a city (p. 187)

smuggle to bring goods into a country illegally (p. 87)

sod top layer of earth made tough by

grass roots (p. 256)

spiritual religious song written and sung by enslaved African Americans (p. 63)

states' rights the idea that states have the right to decide certain issues without the involvement of the federal government (p. 220)

stereotype to develop a generalization or idea about a group that is not necessarily true (p. 272)

stock a share in a corporation (p. 265)

strike refusal to work until demands are met (p. 267)

subway a railroad that operates in underground tunnels (p. 279)

suffrage the right to vote (p.195)

synagogues Jewish places of worship (p. 59)

tariff a tax on goods (p. 146)

technology science used in practical ways (p. 304)

tejanos Spanish-speaking residents of Texas (p. 177)

tenement an apartment building with many small apartments (p. 271)

territory an area that is not yet a state (p. 152)

textile mill a factory where cloth is made (p. 161)

toleration allowing other people to practice their own beliefs and customs (p. 60)

traditions customs, practices, and ways of doing things that are handed down from one generation to another (p. 9)

treason to break the allegiance to one's country, including trying to overthrow the government (p. 110)

tribute payments that a powerful nation forces people it conquers to make (p. 22)

tyrant a cruel ruler who takes away the rights of the people (p. 106)

unconstitutional against or not permitted by the Constitution (p. 136)

vaquero Spanish word for cow hand (p. 257)

vassal a person protected by another stronger person in exchange for service (p. 38)

veto to refuse to sign (a bill passed by the legislature) (p. 136)

Index